Herds
of the
Tundra

▲ ▲ ▲

Smithsonian Series in Ethnographic Inquiry

William L. Merrill and Ivan Karp, Series Editors

Ethnography as fieldwork, analysis, and literary form is the distinguishing feature of modern anthropology. Guided by the assumption that anthropological theory and ethnography are inextricably linked, this series is devoted to exploring the ethnographic enterprise.

Herds
of the
Tundra

A Portrait of
Saami Reindeer
Pastoralism

▲▲▲

Robert Paine

Smithsonian Institution Press

Washington and London

Editor: Tom Ireland
Production Editor: Jack Kirshbaum
Designer: Janice Wheeler

Library of Congress Cataloging-in-Publication Data

Paine, Robert.
  Herds of the tundra : a portrait of Saami reindeer pastoralism
/ Robert Paine.
    p.   cm.
Includes bibliographical references and index.
ISBN 1-56098-271-3
    1. Saami (European people)—Domestic animals. 2. Saami
(European people)—Social life and customs. 3. Reindeer
herding—Norway—Kautokeino. 4. Transhumance—
Norway—Kautokeino. 5. Kautokeino (Norway)—Social life
and customs. I. Title.
DL442.L3P34 1994
306'.0899455—dc20   93-38390

British Library Cataloging-in-Publication data available

Manufactured in the United States of America
00 99 98 97 96 95 94   5 4 3 2 1

∞ The paper used in this publication meets the minimum
requirements of the American National Standard for Perma-
nence of Paper for Printed Library Materials Z39.48-1984.

Jacket illustrations: *(Front) Lavvo* and herd; *(Back)* A Saami pastoralist moves his herd onto late winter pastures. Photos taken
by the author.

For permission to reproduce any of the illustrations, please cor-
respond directly with the author. The Smithsonian Institution
Press does not retain reproduction rights for these illustrations
individually or maintain a file of addresses for photo sources.

FOR MICHAEL AND JESSICA

Contents

Acknowledgments

Sitting at my desk this late fall day in 1992, I try to comprehend that it was forty years ago when I first visited a Saami camp. It was a short visit, for I was thrown out! But more about that later. Here my duty and privilege is to thank some of the people without whom this enterprise would never have been started or, once started, would have been so much more difficult.

Franz Steiner at Oxford, Ethel John Lindgren-Utsi at Cambridge, and Örnulv Vorren at Tromsö were different guardian spirits for the aspiring graduate student and field ethnographer. Rist Anti in Karasjok and Lauri Keskitalo in Kautokeino vouched for me to the two men whose camps I eventually joined: Pers Nigga and Ellon Ailu. Up to Chapter 10, I believe this book is as much Ellon Ailu's as it is mine. As to Part Four, we have differences—but it is my earnest hope that the discussion of its issues makes some contribution to the future of Saami pastoralism.

And discussion has always been on the agenda with my Norwegian colleagues in Oslo, Bergen, and Tromsö. First, Harald Eidheim (I espied him fly-fishing on the tundra—it seemed it was he, not I, who was the Englishman!). But then, many others, including Vilhelm Aubert, Fredrik Barth, Ivar Björklund, Otto Blehr, Jan-Petter Blom, Terje Brantenberg, Ottar Brox, Nils Isak Eira, Georg Henriksen, Arne-Martin Klausen, Helge Kleivan, Per Mathiesen, Trond Thuen, Cato Wadel. I remember, too, sharing some of the fieldwork experience with Inger-Anna Paine née Gunnare of Jukkasjav'ri parish.

Forty years is a long reach in time! Persons in numbers beyond the possibility of naming begin to spring to mind, but I cannot forego mentioning Jean Briggs and George Story, whose intellectual companionship through the years at Memorial University of Newfoundland I especially value.

Several of the above read various chapters. I also thank Hugh Beach, Dag Elgvin, Anders Henriksen, and Bonnie McCay in this regard. My thanks, too, to Tony Schärer (many years back now) for efforts at collating my then unassorted field notes; to Olga Aune for the map of the spring migration (Fig. 6.3); to Odd Mathis Hætta for the biographical information on the principal players in Part Four; to Austin Rodgers for an abundance of skilled artwork; and, as so many times before, to Jeanette Gleeson for her discerning eye over my efforts at the computer.

The photographs from the time of the fieldwork were

taken either by me or Inger-Anna Paine (their appearance here owes much to the skills of the Smithsonian people). Other photographs appear by the courtesy and generosity of Ivar Björklund of Tromsö Museum, Anders Henriksen of Reindriftsadministrasjonen (the Reindeer Administration), and Björn Aarseth of Norsk Folkemuseum.

I have still to repay the generosity of Marc Gould, who spent much of one Newfoundland summer (admittedly it's a short season) sitting in our garden, copyediting some of my chapters. That and kindred tasks were continued by the Smithsonian Institution Press, and I wish to acknowledge my good fortune in having the indispensable support of the editorial team of Cheryl Anderson, Jack Kirshbaum, and Tom Ireland.

Through much of my time in Norway and for all of the later Kautokeino fieldwork, I was supported by a research fellowship of the Norwegian Social Sciences Research Council (Norges Almenvitenskapelige Forskningsråd): I was (and am) keenly conscious of my good fortune. Opportunities also came my way, at different times, to present the field material in lecture series at Stockholm, Tromsö, and Uppsala.

The writing began at a desk in the Scott Polar Research Institute, Cambridge, and was completed at home in St. John's. The SPRI was the right starting place, and, thanks very much to the unswerving personal support and understanding of Lisa—also an anthropologist, as it happens, though one of quite another cultural world—our home became the right place for the long haul.

St. John's, Newfoundland

Note on Spelling of Saami Words

To a Saami linguist, my spelling of Saami terms must seem like a bastardization—and so it is, yet there is an intention to it.

When I was doing field research and learning Saami, I would enter an approximate English phonetic transcription into my notebooks of all the words that interested me. Later, in the unrivaled Konrad Nielsen dictionary (three volumes, later extended to five), I found considerable discrepancies between my transcription and the dictionary entries. The Nielsen orthography, however, was most elaborate and seemed attuned to Norwegian phonetics (at the time that suited me because I was handling Norwegian, too). Thus, in this book, I have adopted a simplified Nielsen transcription pitched to English phonetics. There is, I suspect, some inconsistency to what I have done (I am far from being a linguist).

Today, the Nielsen orthography is being abandoned in many quarters and replaced with one that is more practical for Saami themselves. I considered having all the Saami words retranscribed in this new orthography but decided against it for two reasons: Besides promising a number of difficulties, it would artifically distance this book from the time, and the circumstances, in which it was written. Thus, writing in English, I stay with "Kautokeino" rather than changing to "Guov'dageai'dno," even though the latter—the Saami transcription of the name of the village and county—is now coming into use even among Norwegian-speakers in the north. It also features on recent editions of maps and road signs. However, such was not the case at the time of my fieldwork. Then, "Kautokeino" was known from one end of Norway to the other and in translation to English and other foreign languages. Likewise, I keep to the Norwegian rendering of "Masi."

English Phonetics of Saami Letters

č as in the *ch* of *which*
ð as in the *th* of *that*
ŋ' as in the *ng* of *anger*
ŋŋ as in the *ng* of *ring*
š as in the *sh* of *shop*
ŧ as in the *th* of *thread*
æ always a dipthong
' creates stop

Preface

16 OCTOBER

We find about sixty deer on Gævlemaras and take them with us for the rest of the day: little trouble except at the beginning. Wouldn't have managed, though, without a dog. Ellon Ailu let some of the animals approach us—investigate us—before releasing his dog. This way the animals weren't frightened. The dog then helped to "teach" (Ellon Ailu's word) the animals the direction we wished them to move. At first they went around in circles, but once we got the "nose" of the herd moving, the rest followed.

8 FEBRUARY

Daylight hours are short, although they are becoming longer. In twilight hours we collect wood. Lots of it. It's snug in the tent even though Ellon Ailu chides, "One shouldn't be too comfortable"—for then the herder becomes lazy and doesn't show his nose outside the tent. Today, though, we moved the tent (not the herd) to an area of new wood supply. It's especially important in the case of a relocated tent to bring the herd, when it rests, right up to it. Two reasons: familiarizes and tames the deer; the herd tramples the snow around the tent for us, making it much easier to move around. Of course our drinking (and cooking) water—melted snow—is now "urinated" by the animals, but nobody seems to mind.

12–15 MAY

Forty calves are born during the three days here. Calving is going well, but there is a problem. Dat'kuvarri is not a very suitable place: Each day some of the *čoavjek* (pregnant cows) manage to make their way down to the marsh along the Masi River, immediately to the north of us. Also, soon it will be imperative to take the herd across the river while the ice is still safe; but we can't move far at this stage of calving. If only we were on the other side of the river . . .

This book is about reindeer and their Saami (Lapp)[1] herders in the tundra landscape of northernmost Norway. Together, they move each year from the winter grazing grounds in the interior to summer pastures on coastal peninsulas and islands, and back again in the autumn. In all, they may cover five hundred kilometers—or less or more—on this annual round. There are scores of herds, thousands of animals, hundreds of pastoral families. I first accompanied a Saami camp on the autumn migration of 1951. Then in 1953 I was employed as a herdsboy for nine months, during which time I picked up a working knowledge of the North Saami language and some general understanding of camp culture and the behavior of reindeer. Engaged in other Saami research through the 1950s, I returned to these pastoralists for intensive ethnographic work for six months in 1961 and 1962, and have visited numerous times since.

I am an anthropologist. That is why I went north, and I offer this book as a contribution to the comparative study of pastoral societies. I hope it will interest other readerships too, despite its specialist subject matter, in the case of some, and exactly on account of that, in the case of others. On the one hand, there is the curiosity among urbanites about the nomadic pastoral life (and these nomads live on the fringe of Europe itself), added to which is the allure of the reindeer. On the other hand, there are the biologists, ethologists, and animal ecologists who have studied wild herds of reindeer or caribou. Of course there is the risk that the very detail these scientists are looking for disenchants the general reader—and I have kept the details in. But I have striven for readability, interweaving general accounts with extracts from my journal and expunging jargon.

Most of all, it is my hope that this book will find its way (in Norwegian translation, if not Saami) into the hands of Saami who have grown up since the early 1960s. Whereas in connection with the work of animal ecologists we are now probably at the stage in which controlled comparisons of the behavior of reindeer and caribou in wild and pastoral herds is possible and profitable, the situation of the young Saami is more one of a loss of knowledge of past practices.

Not long after the fieldwork, Saami reindeer pastoralism in Norway entered upon an epoch of accelerated change, technological and legislative changes most notably. Here are two examples (see Part Four for a fuller account). First, while I was in Kautokeino in 1961, a visiting salesman of snowmobiles left without a sale! People continued for a while yet with draft animals *(her'gi),* but within a few years snowmobiles were de rigueur. Second, for generations, the children of pastoralists—all of them, not just the boys or the eldest or youngest child—inherited a place, if they wanted one, in the family livelihood; but with the Reindeer Management Act of 1978, restrictions were enforced.

Hence the historical time of this account is important. Even though it was made by an outsider, this record may help Saami to recall the herd management of their parents' (or grandparents') generation. So it is especially important that I do not stray from how things were as I observed them at the time. Accordingly, through Parts One to Three, the present tense refers to the 1960s—as though without knowledge of what happened later. That is the subject of Part Four.[2]

Introduction

Kautokeino

Kautokeino is in Finnmark (Fig. I.1).[1] This northern-most province of Norway (and the largest, larger than Denmark) abuts Finland to the east and south, and for a short distance, Russia in the northeast. From the apical North Cape (seventy-one degrees north), a rugged, broken coastline stretches east—facing the Barents Sea—for two hundred kilometers, and south—facing the Atlantic Ocean—for another two hundred.

The county of Kautokeino, taking its name from the principal settlement, is a lichen-rich tundra land mass broken by rivers, notably the Kautokeino River, in the southwest corner of the interior of the province. To the east the tundra continues into the neighboring counties of Karasjok and Polmak, south and southeast into Finland, and west into the province of Tromsö. To the north is Alta County, where the Kautokeino River is called the Alta River, and the Atlantic Ocean.

Half of the thirty thousand Saami in Norway live in Finnmark, where they account for something under a quarter of the population.[2] There is a marked difference, however, between the coast and the interior (Kauto-keino, Karasjok, and Polmak) of the province in respect to the distribution of Saami and the expression of their culture (Fig. I.2). At one time the majority of Saami lived along the coast, but the inroads of "Norwegianiza-tion" have been so serious there that today, Saami-speakers constitute less than 10 percent of the coastal population. This ratio is reversed in the interior, where less than 10 percent of the population does *not* speak Saami.

The interior has a sedentary Saami population as well as the pastoral (reindeer) one. The latter move into the coastal region in the summer but have their principal dwellings near their winter pastures in the interior, where they also pay their taxes. In the county of Kautokeino there are over three hundred reindeer pastoral house-holds. The striking and unifying ecologic feature of the interior is the tundra and its abiding associations with Saami culture.[3]

At some 140 kilometers from the sea, the Kautokeino River passes through the village and county seat of Kau-tokeino: Over 80 percent of its two thousand people speak Saami as their mother tongue. They are reindeer breeders, farmers (combined with hunting and fishing), and employees in diverse administrative and service occu-

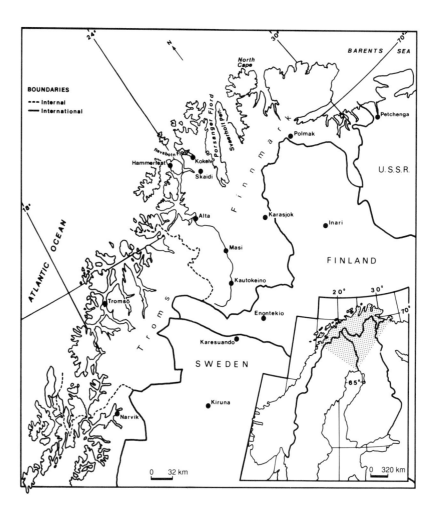

Figure I.1 Finnmark and its environs

Kautokeino village.

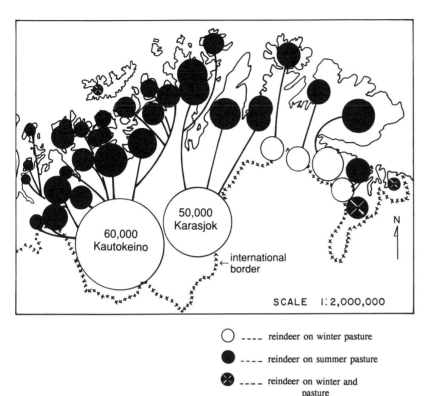

○ ---- reindeer on winter pasture

● ---- reindeer on summer pasture

⊗ ---- reindeer on winter and
        pasture

Figure I.2 The scale of reindeer pastoralism in Finnmark, 1961–1962. Adapted from Ö. Vorren 1962

pations. Among the few monolingual Norwegian-speakers are NATO personnel. Downstream and a little less than halfway to the coast—but still inside the county of Kautokeino—the river runs through Masi, whose population of four hundred is, with few exceptions, Saami.

Downstream of Masi, the watercourse takes on its name as the Alta River, marking topographic, ecologic, and cultural changes. The open tundra, with its vast bed of lichen, providing winter pasture for the sixty thousand or so reindeer of Kautokeino County, is replaced by wooded escarpments through which the river winds and rushes, and then by meadowland and pine forest along both banks. Here the Saami nowadays live as a very small minority among the Norwegian and Finnish immigrants who began arriving two centuries ago. The primary occupations are farming (in a conspicuously more favorable ecology than that found upstream), slate quarrying, and salmon fishing in various combinations. The river reaches the sea at the small town of Alta: an urban environment, a regional center, a focus of growth. In earlier times, even this lower reach of the river was exclusively Saami, with reindeer pastoralists, and hunters before them, camping and moving across the terrain.[4]

The Writing

I wrote this book around the herd as the indispensable first step toward understanding a pastoral society. The chapters take us through the pastoral year, beginning with the summer—when animals are growing—and concluding with the appearance of a new generation of calves in the spring. And it is written from the perspective of a particular pastoral reindeer range known as Gow'dojottelit, or Middle Range, of Kautokeino. Its distinctive features will be noted as we come to them, and comparisons drawn with the other reindeer ranges of Kautokeino.

Still more specifically, the book is an account put together from my following Ellon Ailu, at different times, through the pastoral year of 1961–62. He and some of

Ellon Ailu.

his camp companions at various seasons are the principal personae dramatis of the chapters that follow (Fig. I.3). They feature particularly in the extracts from my journal, and I cite from it as the surest way available of imparting the contexts of the accidents and the contingency plans and disagreements that belong to reindeer pastoralism. I hope the journal also suggests how the enthralling challenge of the fieldwork was finding coherence in the countless pieces of data, and how part of its reward was the extent to which the project was shared with Ellon Ailu and others.

More than that, I like to think I was their Boswell. But how far do I succeed? Indeed, how possible is it to succeed? I wish to report what the pastoralists do, but my understanding of that may be different from theirs. Like us all, Saami *codify* their knowledge. As well, codification orders perception. It enables these pastoralists to communicate with each other expeditiously but exactly, rather than loosely, and provides parameters for conduct as well as criteria for decisions. Their codification is itself the

cardinal *cultural* resource that they share, to the exclusion of even other Saami-speakers who are not pastoralists. Each pastoral season, for example, is codified. Yet the code is by no means always explicit, so the outside observer often depends on inference for its understanding. A chancy business.

One way I try to reduce this element of chance is through attention to context. Of course, facts do not arrange themselves. Nevertheless, their arrangement was, to a significant extent, delivered to me. The Saami themselves see the pastoral year as a cycle, as framework-giving. A great deal must have passed me by, and sometimes I was thrown back onto my own interpretations, but still, much that went into my notebooks followed from what I was told I should perceive.

Learning

I would like to give an account of my learning process as an ethnographer with these people. Alas! Any systematic account eludes me, as I think it would have at the time, too, and perhaps that suggests the nature of the process—osmosis? Certainly much reached me through the degree to which and manner in which our every day revolved around the herds.

My personal experiences of this situation swung abruptly to and fro between chaos and order. Chaos—*cherchez le rein*—was my immediate subjective readings of days and nights spent retrieving animals, perhaps only to lose them again, as would so often happen in the shortening days of autumn. Then, order was camp life. Gradually, I became more discerning, putting happenings into (more or less) appropriate context. I became aware, too, of differences between seasons. Compared with autumn, spring is order, not chaos. As we moved off the tundra, slowly making our way to the coast with the cows and their calves, exhausted as we might be, our first concern at the end of each day was where the animals would settle for the night—*gardez le rein;* only after that did we make our camp.

So there were two strains at least—and a tension between them—to my learning process. Observing Saami observing animals, listening to what they told me about the animals, and recording as nearly as possible in their words what they told me—that on the one hand. And on

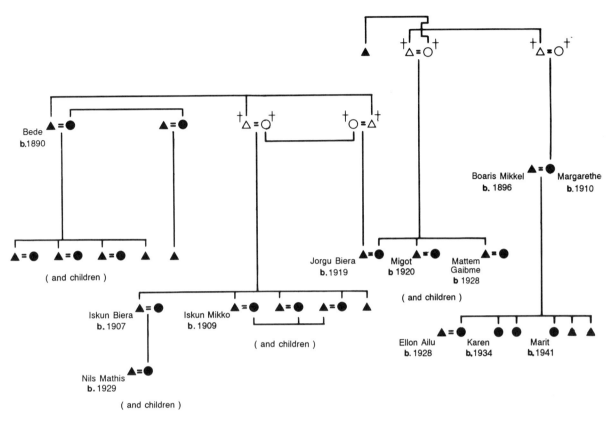

Figure I.3 Principal personae dramatis

the other, my subjective register of it all. Although in my journal, by and large, I left out that register, I still recall it today.

In the camps, I was helped by the way Saami would listen to each other. A herder, say, would come into the tent and recount, in detail, what had been happening with the herd. He would be heard through to the end even though it might seem we already knew it all from others. It was important to get *his* account. Any discrepancies between accounts would then be weighed. What a helpful procedure for the ethnographer struggling with the language and living by "accounts"!

Also important was that my fieldwork with the pastoralists was not all in one place or all at one time but with three different groups and separated by years. So I had several entries into the field, and in the intervening time, there were the years living in the north (when not in Finnmark or neighboring Finland and Sweden, most often with Saami, I was at the Department of Saami

Ethnography of the Tromsö Museum). All in all, a usefully prolonged and varied learning experience.

Entering the Field

The journal entries, I say, are not so much accounts of what I saw as of what I was directed to see. However, one has to understand such directions. That they are given at all likely presupposes an element of mutuality of purpose or at least of trust; I think I eventually won this, although, as we will see, I certainly got off to an inauspicious start.

1951

Within a few days of stepping off the trawler that had taken me from Grimsby to Tromsö in North Norway,[5] I pitched my small tent on the edge of a Saami camp at Skaidi. It was July. The camp was in sight of the main road (Riksvei 50), and there was a state guest house a quarter of a mile away. Tourists abounded. Not a sensible choice—I was just another tourist. But instead of staying at the guest house, I put up that tent and hung around, and (truer to the tourist role) took photographs, particularly of the children. After a day, I walked away. My intention was to go off into the hills to find the Skaidi herd. There were only old men, women, and children at the camp. I thought I understood that the men and youth were away calf marking, but I was far from clear where, which is not surprising: I understood no Saami and next to no Norwegian! I hitched a lift down the road to the village of Olderfjord in Porsanger Fjord, where I had the name of someone whom I was told would be able to help me.

"Saami Rasmussen" (as he was known to Norwegians) was used to the likes of me. *He'd* take me to a reindeer camp—in a few days. He was from the fjord but had lived in Oslo for some years. He knew the Saami nomads were "interesting" to us foreigners, and, clearly, we were interesting to him. Perhaps he saw himself as a kind of ambassador. At any rate, my dependence on him grew apace once my initial request had been put. In other circumstances the drinking and the fishing, but mostly drinking, would have been beguiling. But I had something more in mind. We "conversed" with bits and pieces of English, Norwegian, and Saami. At least I was learning my first Saami phrases. A word that kept cropping up was *verdi:* He and the "headman" *(oaive-olbmai)* of the camp were verdi, Rasmussen said. That is, they were partners in a relationship of reciprocal services and goods between a nomad and a sedentary.[6] Was I to be fitted into this web of reciprocity?

This camp was some distance off a dirt road: no tourists. But as before, the only people in the camp were women and children and an old man who apparently wasn't Rasmussen's verdi. The other men were away in the terrain, calf-marking. A prolonged discussion ensued between Rasmussen and some of the women. Meanwhile I ingratiated myself with the young children with some success, for I arrived stocked with licorice all-sorts. There was acrimony in the raised voices. The women obviously objected to Rasmussen's plan of leaving me with them. But that is exactly what he did!

I was sitting just inside one of the tents with a clutch of children around me. One of the women picked up my rucksack (with rolled-up tent) and took it outside. I followed. So did the children and the dogs. A few yards off was a small stream, and I decided to pitch my tent on its far side, at least for the night, and then, who knows, I might find my way to the men. That was not to be. Turf sods were lobbed over the stream. There was no future here. The only reason there could be for staying was to save face, which I tried for a while. Then I saw the better of it, packed up, and left.

It was a beautiful northern "night" of daylight as I walked the twenty kilometers down to the coast. My mood, though, was anything but sublime. I had to acknowledge I had made some poor judgment calls, and that for the time being, at any rate, there would be no nomad camp. The gravel road led to Revsbotn Fjord and the Saami village of Kokelv. Summoning all nerve that was left in me and trying to ignore the staring faces behind the windows of every house I passed by, I walked into the village shop and asked where Anders Utstie, the schoolmaster, lived. I managed to mispronounce "Utstie," which is a rather uncommon Norwegian name, mixing it with "Utsi," a common Saami name. Standing there in the village shop, I was a source of amusement, not a threat. Anders, an immigrant from the south, lived with his Saami in-laws, and they took me in.

My reaching Kokelv was not entirely accidental. Örnulv Vorren of Tromsö Museum had suggested it would be a useful place to study, and he had given me Anders's name. Yet it was, for me, a fall-back plan. As it turned out, I spent about eighteen months of the 1950s in the villages and hamlets of Revsbotn Fjord and wrote two books about them.[7] The fjord became one of my homes between periods with reindeer pastoralists and visits to my supervisors at Oxford (I had graduate degrees to take).

Though Kokelv was a Saami village, visitors were spoken to in Norwegian, and accordingly, that's what I learned. Only when I returned in 1958 did some people speak Saami with me. I participated in the seasonal rounds of work (from summer hay-making to winter fishing) and sometimes put myself on the local labor market (at slightly below the current rates), enough to be self-supporting. Yet that first summer I was restless: I wanted to accompany a pastoral group on their autumn migration into the interior.

By chance, I met Nils Mathis up in the hills behind Hammerfest, a town on the island of Kvalöy, a couple of hours by local steamer from the village. He found me looking through my binoculars at reindeer. He was friendly, unmarried, and a few years younger than me. We chatted in Norwegian (to the best of my ability, it was now early September) about who we were. He was *ræŋ'ga* (herdsboy) to one of the owners of the herd I had been watching. We walked back to the town, where he introduced me to his Hammerfest verdi, with whom he was staying while taking driving lessons. On the morrow he was going by bus to his camp—actually a couple of timber cabins—at the other end of the island. I could come along with him, if I liked, and talk with them there about the possibility of my involvement in the autumn migration.

This time things were more on an even keel. Nils Mathis was really sponsoring me. I could more or less say what I wanted to say (though in Norwegian) for the occasion. There seem to be two concerns: Would I be a physical burden? Could I pay my way? I provided assurances on both accounts. A deal was struck, and I headed back to Hammerfest, where I knew I could secure a temporary job on a construction site.[8] The rest of the month was spent feeding a cement mixer, interspersed with visits to the camp.

I joined them in the first days of October. Animals had to be rounded up and herded to a southern promontory of the island where the sound, between island and mainland, was the narrowest, though the current was correspondingly strong. These were the kind of days that I had been wanting: working the terrain *as a herder;* sleeping out in the open around a fire; enjoying camp camaraderie. I even felt marginally useful (which I probably was not). However, it was all a good deal more strenuous than I had anticipated, and my feet, now clad only in moccasins, were tenderized from the scree-strewn terrain. It was cold at nights, as well, after the fire died. Some animals (perhaps a couple of hundred) eluded us in the broken, alpine terrain of the island. But between 8 and 10 October about two thousand animals swam the

Summer cabin on Kvalöy.

sound—following "leader" animals wearing bells, themselves led by a herder holding a rein and sitting in a rowboat.

Later, there were other dramas: the week-long separation of the large herd into smaller ones for the winter; moving our caravan of baggage-laden, reindeer-pulled sleds over (or through) rivers not yet properly frozen; and my first experiences of herding at night. We were three weeks in the tundra landscape of Sæinos (northwest of Alta), and I filled a notebook. But leafing through it now, I'm glad to see that I acknowledged I had little *understanding* of what was going on around me. Certainly I began to get a sense of the temper of camp life with its shifting tempo, and I recorded *who* was undertaking *what* and *when,* but the *whys* often remain clouded, and I am sure some of the *whats* really eluded me. It was an adventure for sure, but the ethnography did not amount to much. The key to the level of understanding I wanted was, naturally, a bilingual competence. That meant time, and time had run out. I had left Oxford for a "summer's field work," and when we came off the tundra to the farmstead of a Finnish-speaking (but trilingual) verdi outside Alta we were already into November. It was a wrenching decision, but I had to leave—for the time being.

1953

I had come to the tundra village of Karasjok to learn Saami. I lodged with Rist Anti. He was one of my teachers, and he taught me a lot, although there *was* a difficulty with his oral tuition. He was invariably chewing a plug of tobacco as he spoke, and, much to the merriment of some of the children of the village, my pronunciation was, parrot-wise, distorted accordingly![9] One afternoon in January, Rist Anti had a visit from Pers Nigga, a verdi. I was in the kitchen when he entered. The drift of the conversation was that his herdsboy had left to take up a contract with the Danish government in Greenland. To my astonishment, Rist Anti suggested that he try me as a replacement! I don't know whether Pers Nigga himself had that in mind when he entered, but we quickly came to an agreement: I'd work for him in return for board and clothes and a spot of pocket money (cigarettes and beer). I was with him until October.

Not too much went into my notebooks, mostly language notes, but by the end of those months I was bursting with confidence. I had made it! The Saami language was still a struggle, but that is what they spoke to me for the most part. I was told I used the "grammar" of a child, but they liked my pronunciation (thanks to Rist Anti, after all), and the range of my vocabulary repeatedly surprised them. But then, I kept close to the world of reindeer, and of kinship, as one might expect of an anthropologist. I began to unravel some of the whats and whys that had been out of my reach. My tasks were menial, but that didn't bother me as long as they kept me in contact with people, and they were varied.

By this time, I was pretty familiar with the Finnmark scene as a whole. Having first accompanied a Kautokeino group, the time I was now spending with a Karasjok group—our summer pastures were out on Spiertanjar'ga (Svaerholt)—gave me some basis for comparing these two centers of North Saami reindeer pastoralism. Karasjok herd management, I realized, was overly "extensive," with only periodic contact between herder and herd. This meant long spells of little management interspersed with short, hectic ones. With the slackened control, knowledge of the herd—the hallmark of pastoralism—seemed to be in serious decline. But Kautokeino herd management had not come to the same pass, and I knew that I should get myself back there. Before that could happen, though, I had to complete my research in Revsbotn Fjord. And in the interval, I married Inger-

Ellon Ailu and author.

Anna Gunnare. Her father had been a reindeer owner in the Swedish Saami District of Talma with summer pastures in Troms Province, Norway, bordering on Finnmark.

1961–62

Lauri Keskitalo, whom I had known for some time, a local savant and one-time reindeer herder, one-time mayor of Kautokeino, and, at this time, a Saami handicrafts teacher and consultant, introduced us to Ellon Ailu. Inger-Anna and I accompanied Ellon Ailu and his wife, Karen, on the spring migration.[10] We paid for our keep and helped out as needed; it was understood that we were there because I was going to write an account of herd management. During the summer Ellon Ailu and

Karen visited Tromsö, where he and I went carefully over my notes. I returned alone in the autumn and the winter to Ellon Ailu, visiting other camps, too. Not employed by Ellon Ailu, I was free to move around, placing myself in strategic places at the right times.

Ellon Ailu and I hit it off well. He understood what I was about, and I don't think I embarrassed him too much. Sometimes we would be alone in the terrain for several days, and Ellon Ailu (whose Norwegian was better than my Saami) would switch to Norwegian when I didn't understand in Saami. But when other Saami were around, it was strictly "Saami only" between us, and I would fetch the water for our coffee kettle.

1979–1989

I have paid visits to the north since concluding that field sojourn with Ellon Ailu. Of particular relevance are two applied research field trips: one in 1981 to prepare an expert witness brief for the Norwegian Supreme Court concerning a hydroelectric project on the Kautokeino River, the other in 1987 and 1988 to assess the effects on Saami reindeer pastoralism in Norway of radioactive fallout from the explosion at Chernobyl.[11] Besides Kautokeino, these research tasks took me to Karasjok, Masi, Alta, Tromsö, Snåsa, Röros, and Oslo. In these places I met several of the principal actors of Part Four of this book, as well as Ellon Ailu and others from earlier years. Ellon Ailu is still an active herder-owner. He has also taken a leading role in the professional affairs of the pastoral community, particularly as president, over a number of years, of the Kautokeino branch of the national association of Saami reindeer owners.

Much has changed for better and for worse, and now—thirty years after first meeting Ellon Ailu—I try, in Part Four, to give an account of the changes. The task is quite different from that of the rest of the book. There, I draw my field notes into sensible sequences; here, I must find my way through a morass of documents. Whereas I was not aware of bias in compiling my field notes (which is not to say that I claim for them the elusive commodity of objectivity), here, the issues covered are highly contentious and controversial, and I *am* conscious of a gut empathy with one side.

That empathy is grounded in my field experiences during the 1960s, and there is the danger of romantic entrapment—as though the contemporary issues pitch "the" Saami together against the interfering world outside. Such was arguably the case in the 1960s, but today, the pastoralists themselves are not of one mind about the changes.

So my difficulties have to do with more than the documents. Once again, my position is quite different from Ellon Ailu's. He, living with the changes through these years, remains contemporaneous. His herd management today takes precedence over what he taught me in 1962, but that year was my only experience: 1962 is *the* pastoral story. What I now *read* rearranges in part, subverts in part, leaves untouched in part, that which I earlier *knew.* That much said, I elect, again, to take the role of chronicler, even as I am aware that a chronicler necessarily interprets; and I strive to be evenhanded and, especially, to bring in a broad range of Saami opinions. In the final analysis, though, Part Four offers a point of view—about which Ellon Ailu, for one, has some reservations.

Part One
Saami Reindeer Pastoralism, 1962

▲ ▲ ▲

Tell them that we don't just *wander.*

A REINDEER OWNER

1.
The Pastoral
Logic

While Saami reindeer pastoralism is historically recent (three to four hundred years), the link between Saami culture and the reindeer is ancient. It was one of the first animals to inhabit the land after the retreat of the ice, nine to ten thousand years ago. When the Saami came into Fenno-Scandia, the reindeer, from the first, was an important source of food and clothing. Beyond that, it featured in the cosmology of the Saami.

Summarized diachronically, at the time of the earliest records (one thousand years ago), all Saami groups hunted wild reindeer and probably kept some "tamed" reindeer as decoy and transport animals. By the time of the early Middle Ages most Saami groups combined hunting with some degree of reindeer pastoralism. Over the last three hundred years reindeer pastoralism has become the specialized occupation of selected Saami groups, with a wide register of reciprocal relations between them and settled groups on the tundra or along the coast.[1]

It is noteworthy that the transition from hunting to pastoralism was undertaken with the *same* animal, and reindeer pastoralism, across the northern reaches of the Old World, is probably unique in this respect.[2] This meant that much of the hunters' experience, skills, and technology was transferred and adapted to the emerging pastoralism. Its emergence, furthermore, happened without an intervening and biologically significant phase of taming-and-breeding of the animal. Equally noteworthy from the comparative perspective is that this pastoralism is based on one species—the reindeer, and not on a combination of animals, as is more often the case with other pastoralists (combinations from among sheep, goats, cattle, horses, camels, yaks, llamas, etc.). Important, too, for this pastoralism is that the reindeer and the wolf have existed through the millennia in a prey-predator relationship. Even as man extinguishes the wolf (and by 1960 that had virtually happened in Finnmark), wolf-oriented behavior persists, in several ways, among reindeer (see Appendix 1), and the pastoralist draws advantage from it.[3]

Of course there are continual changes in the practice of the pastoralism itself. Perhaps the most significant change historically (and with accelerated speed in the twentieth century) has been away from milk production in combination with the slaughter of animals for meat (in some areas to the south of Finnmark, milk production had been the more important element) to meat production alone. Milking and milk processing, unlike the slaughter for meat, meant a heavy daily routine of work for the pastoralist, so the herds were likely to be correspondingly smaller, with a greater proportion of females. Meat production has been characterized by underproduction, and this is something that will be discussed in the later chapters of this book.[4]

Reindeer are wealth for the pastoralist. We do well to note at the outset how this form of wealth ordinarily reproduces itself steadily and has a market value, but it is easily lost, or stolen, in the terrain and may be decimated through natural catastrophes (explained later) or, less dramatically, otherwise harmed by poor herd management.

The seasonal movement of herds between pastures is influenced both by the animals' biology and physiology and by ecologic factors that the pastoralists take into account. For example, the annual spring migration off the tundra and towards the coast responds to, among other things, the animals' need for protein (grasses) and the pastoralists' wish to save the lichen beds on the tundra for the winter.

The diet of the reindeer is at all times limited to a few plant species. However, there are significant seasonal differences of choice. While there is snow cover (November–May), reindeer ordinarily exist on lichen, principally *Cladonia rangiferina,* which they reach by digging through the snow with their forefeet. As soon as the spring thaw begins, they search for a few species of soft and juicy grasses. Throughout the summer, they prefer a selective grass diet. In the autumn they are most interested in mushrooms and toadstools.[5]

The migrations, then, are not undertaken to escape or even reduce the climactic or ecologic differences of the seasons; this is not possible in the subarctic.[6] Instead, a schedule of movement is devised so that the animals draw most advantage from the markedly different conditions of each season.[7]

The herder learns the behavior patterns of his animals, but that is only half the story. The behavior of a herd is itself influenced by decisions taken by the herder. Thus it would not be true to say that the herder follows his herd or that a herd will follow its herder wherever (and whenever) he may wish. Both parties follow a common schedule or routine. It is true that this has been worked out by the herder, but the only feasible schedules are those tak-

ing account of the animals' needs, the herd learns the schedule and adapts to it, and this means that it becomes very difficult to make changes in it. We can very well say that some of the constraints the pastoralist places upon his animals also come to constrain his own behavior. Of course changes *are* made in migration routes, calving places, rutting places, and so on, but they always entail risk, uncertainty, and extra work.

Reindeer are individually owned and inherited, by women and children[8] as well as men, but herded collectively by perhaps several families, combining to make one work unit. This herding unit, whatever its size, is known as a *sii'da,* and individual families are likely to group and regroup in different sii'da formations in the course of the pastoral year as the owners find optimal. The smallest sii'da are likely to be in the spring, perhaps two or three closely related families or even one family alone, and the largest in the summer. Women, especially the unmarried, may well join men in the herding.

These are fundamental arrangements, and they need emphasizing. Behind the obvious facts that the principal source of property and wealth is on the move, and in order to retain possession its owners must be on the move as well, there are these considerations: The *pasture* of a herd must be frequently changed in both quality and size—failure to do so could be catastrophic; the size of the *herds* must also be varied in the course of a year as the quality of a pasture is affected by the number of deer on it; and since the size of the herding unit should be kept in rough correspondence to that of the herd, there is a concomitant shuffling and regrouping of reindeer *owners* as herding partners. Thus, the absolute value of each of the three factors of production—pasture, herd, and owner—will vary, but their relative value to each other should remain in balance.

Note should also be taken of how, in this reindeer pastoralism, ownership of animals and control over them are separate matters. The reindeer is long-legged and can move fast over varied terrain (in most circumstances outpacing and outdistancing a dog); and in certain seasons of the year, it is its nature to roam widely while grazing. Nevertheless, castrated animals are trained to pull sleds, cows are sometimes milked, and herders do use dogs, lassos, bells, and corrals; but their control of the herd depends fundamentally on their knowledge of grazing patterns at different seasons and in various kinds of terrain and weather.[9]

In short, reindeer herding is most exacting, not only physically but also in respect of the demands it makes on insights into herd behavior. From time to time the herder will be expected to locate a herd that is not in sight, even to predict its movements and to bring it under control. Yet there are too many factors over which little or no control can be exercised for herding to be a thoroughly exact task. Carefully laid plans are brought to nought by bad weather, the intrusion of another herd, or any one of a number of disturbances in the terrain (people, dogs, vehicles, machines). A situation that is seemingly under control can deteriorate in minutes or less.

So, running through this reindeer pastoralism, there is the contrast between learned behavior patterns and repetitive cycles and routines and their frequent, if only temporary, disruption. Thus an imperative of the work organization is that whoever is on the scene must *act* on behalf of the group. It is, then, a work organization in which authority is distributed pragmatically and much dependence placed on the exercise of discretion. There is probably no better way of coping with the difficulties that face reindeer herders.

Two other features are worth stressing. First, the animals and the herds into which they are constituted are separable (herding units) and, ultimately, divisible.[10] Second, the herder wishes to work *with* the herd even as he strives to exert his will over its movements, and the freedom to separate and to recombine herds is crucial to this end.

The world knows the Saami reindeer herder as a "nomad." Some distinctions are necessary, though. First, it is important to add, *pastoral* nomad. This brings together two factors: livestock rearing and spatial movement (there are nomads who are not pastoralists and pastoralists who are not nomads). But the "bringing together" has to be specified.

There are different patterns of movement. Are the herders and their animals in continuous association—do they move together? Or is it rather a case of successive points of intersection through the year? And what of the duration of the movement: Are the animals continuously

on the move, or is it really more a matter of moving between seasonal pastures? And what of the herders?

Broadly speaking, since World War II there has been less "continuous" movement among the Saami pastoralists themselves than earlier, and this emerging seasonality of movement is worth denoting with its own term: transhumant pastoralism or, simply, transhumance.[11] At the same time, though, we note that the herds' patterns of movement have changed little. Herding has become more "extensive" (as the literature calls it) at certain seasons, with the animals unattended or not all members of a pastoralist family present at all the seasonal camps.

In respect to livestock rearing, the fundamental question is whether the herd is an intrinsic value for a pastoralist or a market commodity. Certainly, and unsurprisingly, the market factor has increasing importance. However, it is the qualifying factors which are of interest. All whom I knew held to both values: intrinsic and market. Few, however, balanced the two in the same way. To understand the issues, however, we must have some knowledge of how a pastoral herd, as capital, is highly differentiated on account of the animals' sex, age, fecundity, docility, weight, color, and other factors. The values given them within the domain of "subsistence" economy and its associated culture may well differ from those given within the domain of the market economy and its culture (e.g., "lean" meat valued by the non-Saami market, "fat" by the Saami consumer). Not only that, but each season may present the pastoralist with options that bestow benefit in one value and cost in another.[12]

But whichever way these values flow, pastoralism implies radical control over herds of animals. The pastoral intervention in the life cycles of animals, for instance, makes it meaningless to speak any longer of the natural longevity and death of those animals; indeed, the pastoral enterprise is based on the ability to preempt the natural death of the animals. The sexuality of some of the animals is no more safe from pastoral intervention (e.g., castration). Thus, the sex and age composition of a herd is, ideally, an artifice of the pastoralist, who, at the same time, allocates different "tasks" to his animals (more on this in the next chapter).[13]

I mentioned cultural codification in the Introduction. Much of the code (its core, really) is constructed around the herd. More than a matter of taxonomic distinctions, it includes those decisions each owner makes concerning the allocation of his or her animals; especially regarding their slaughter. The different allocations also tell us much about how the Saami pastoral code is beset by change and, most difficult of all, by the imperative of handling, somehow, what appear to be incommensurable values.

One may tend to think of nomads as free at least from the restrictions of territorial boundaries. I doubt whether this is true of any nomads; it certainly would be a serious misrepresentation of pastoral nomadism. However, the nature of the pastoral boundaries and the manner in which they operate need to be understood. A farmer's fields and a pastoralist's reindeer range refer largely to different logics of territoriality.[14] The pastoral logic follows from constraints we have already discussed, especially the

variations in pasture and herd sizes with concomitant regroupings of herding partners. (Of course, they are at once constraints and moves of optimal opportunity.) A reindeer range is not an exclusive territory: The pastoralists have rights of occupancy and use, and people other than the pastoralists are likely to have their usufruct there as well. So it is Crown land that is not individually owned and cannot be sold.[15]

The state and the pastoralists do not necessarily see eye to eye on these matters. The state presses for greater regulation of the pastures, whereas the pastoralists are either indifferent (perhaps disregarding the regulations) or refuse to agree. For instance, entry into the winter pastures should not happen before a set date in the autumn, and all herds should have left these same pastures by a certain date in the spring. On the whole, the herds are moved within this timetable. This happens not out of pressure to

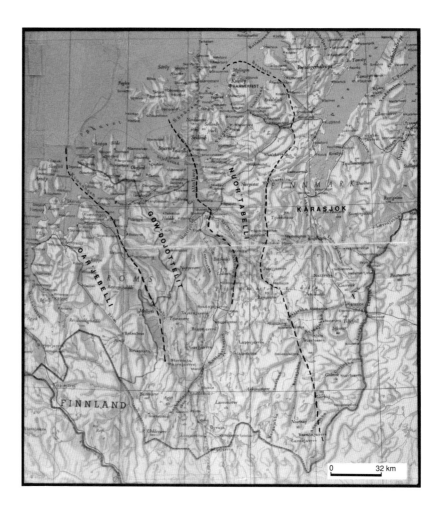

Figure 1.1 Kautokeino reindeer ranges

conform with regulations, but because the timetable is sensible and (usually) ecologically feasible.[16] The far-flung summer pastures (all in all, about seven thousand square kilometers) include the outfield to scores of settled coastal communities of varying combinations of ethnicity: Norwegian, Saami, Finnish. So the state requires the pastoralists to be registered with a legally designated "reindeer district" (thirty for all of Finnmark, about a dozen of which pertain to Kautokeino). Again, this amounts to little more than a non-Saami and administrative recognition (albeit in a simplified version) of the pastoralists' own summer groupings—and it is the latter of which notice is taken in this book. The state would have liked to assign specific winter pastures to each pastoralist. Here they meet a blank refusal from the pastoralists who argue that in the winter, at any rate, all must have an 'exit clause' from the pasture they customarily occupy. Were it otherwise, local changes in snow and ice conditions (remembering that reindeer dig through the snow cover to reach the lichen beds) could well be catastrophic. Whereas there is a network of fences (added to each year) crisscrossing summer and autumn pastures, in the winter pastures, significantly, there are none.[17]

The pastoralists, then, are extremely wary of undue restriction to the movement of their herds.[18] Yet some restriction is necessary: It is fundamental but voluntary, arising out of the pastoralists' own appreciation of the nature of their work. The key is a herder's need for intimate knowledge of terrain, and knowledge, too, of how animals seasonally use a terrain. The inclusive area of Kautokeino pastures is too large and varied in this regard for any one person to master. Accordingly, there are three pastoral ranges: West, or Oar'jebelli; East, or Nuor'tabelli; and Middle, or Gow'dojottelit, on which my account is based (Fig. 1.1). This is not a legislated arrangement; in fact, it is not even officially recognized. Yet for each pastoral family their particular range constitutes the primary territorial and social unit in which they live and move. It is also where most of them are born and stay after marriage.[19] This speaks not only to a strong pattern of territoriality but also to one of partnerships based on kinship and affinity (a herder has most or even all of his siblings and cousins with him on the same pastoral range, as well as a large number of in-laws).[20] Thus the range is, to an impressive extent, an inclusive social network. Successive generations belong to it, ensuring its social reproduction.

At the same time, Oar'jebelli, Nuor'tabelli, and Gow'dojottelit are animal ranges: Cows return to their calving places of previous years, yearlings return to the place of their birth, and bulls make for favored rutting places—all within the same reindeer range. Naturally, animals do stray from a range (especially in the autumn, as we will see), and people do leave their natal range, sometimes taking a herd with them, but the pastoral range is really not threatened, either in precept or practice.[21]

On Oar'jebelli, in 1961–62, there were around fifty families, sixty on Nuor'tabelli, and seventy on Gow'dojottelit. As for numbers of animals, estimates vary considerably (I discuss the matter in Chapter 8); my working figure, however, is approximately twenty thousand on each of the three ranges. Gow'dojottelit, though, is more crowded with animals, as well as having more families. Herds, on average, are smaller on Gow'dojottelit, but there are more of them. As will be shown, much of the explanation has to do with the character of the terrain.

In sum, the reindeer pastoralist operates with an ecologic "model" of territory, not a geographic one. Pastoral ranges are superimposed on the "natural" (prepastoral) cycle of movement of the animals between seasonal habitats. And, a matter of some importance, this ecologic model is socially maintained by the pastoralists.

A coda is necessary: The ecologic model is under threat. In Part Four, pastoral and nonpastoral voices will be heard on the matter of ecologic viability and responsibility, and the nonpastoral drown out the pastoral. Indeed, Saami reindeer pastoralism is, in the 1990s, charged by some as ecologically *ir*responsible, promoting a tragedy of the commons situation on the tundra. But here I would like to cite the annual report of the Reindeer Administration in Finnmark at the beginning of the 1960s: "1961: pastures for reindeer are reduced year by year. Large conifer areas are protected, hydroelectric schemes spoil large areas. Cabins are being erected in good pasture lands without any control; the pastoralists are not consulted. All this is damaging to reindeer pastoralism and should be controlled."[22] The message was repeated in 1962.[23]

2.
Herding
and
Husbandry

With pastoralism comes herd management, and the distinction between herding and husbandry. The pastoralists themselves see their work as all of one piece, simply as a way of life. Certainly both herding and husbandry mean constant and accurate observation of the herd, so that the knowledge and experience acquired in the one domain is valuable also in the other. I make the distinction to draw attention to some important differences in the tasks that befall a pastoralist, and beyond that, to indicate the two kinds of relationships that each reindeer owner has with his animals, and with his fellow pastoralists.

Initial Scenarios

Imagine that one winter's day two reindeer owners are watching a herd as it grazes. They scan all the animals many times through their binoculars, checking (by several methods) that all the animals are present, noting the direction in which the herd is moving, and considering together when the herd should be moved to other pastures. Account is taken of wind, temperature, and snow conditions; where the herd has pastured in the preceding weeks; and the risk of mixing with other herds in the

vicinity. These men are two of several owners whose animals are together in one herd for the winter; they work together as *herders*. The two men return to their camp and discuss herding tactics with the remainder of their fellows, their partners for the season.

Later in the day, when the herd is at rest, one of the men returns, this time wandering slowly among the animals, perhaps with his lasso poised for throwing. He is now only interested in the animals bearing the earmarks of his wife, himself, their unmarried children, and perhaps a few other dependents. These are the animals of his family herd, and his concern is with their physical condition (particularly their weights), whether any yearlings still remain unmarked, which bulls he should castrate, whether his few cows that failed to calve last spring show signs of pregnancy this year, and so on. The man is joined by his wife, and together they continue the inspection of their family herd capital, occasionally conferring with each other, sometimes making a decision. A daughter is getting married at Easter, and for that occasion the family needs new white reindeer moccasins, and one of the younger children a new white reindeer overcoat (of several calf skins). The couple are also consider-

Table 2.1 Pastoral Herd Structure

Age	Castrated (meat and work)	Male (luovas herd)	Female (njiŋŋalas herd)
First twelve months		miessi	miessi
Twelve to sixteen months		čærbmak	čærbmak
Autumn second year		varek	vuonjal
Autumn third year	gaskek	vuobis	aldo
Autumn fourth year	meat (gaskek); work (her'gi)	godduhas	aldo
Autumn fifth year	her'gi	goassohas	aldo
Autumn sixth year	her'gi	mar'kan	boaris aldo
Autumn seventh year	her'gi	nammalappen	boaris aldo

ing the dowry (drawn from the family herd) they will be giving their daughter. These are some of the considerations of *husbandry*.

Herding is the day-to-day work with a herd. It concerns the relationship between herd and pasture as directed to the welfare of the animals and, if necessary, to the exclusion of the comfort of the herders themselves. Husbandry, on the other hand, has to do with the herd as the harvestable resource of its owners. While the tasks of herding, then, are those of the control and nurture of animals in the terrain, husbandry is the efforts of the owners in connection with the growth of capital and the formation of profit. The problems of herding are those of economy of labor, and they may usually be solved by owners in conjunction with each other; those of husbandry concern the allocation of capital, and here each family herd is usually wholly responsible unto itself.

In sum, successful herd management, embodying both husbandry and herding, rests upon diversified pastoral knowledge and skills. In the sections that follow I look at how these are attained and applied.

Composition of a Pastoral Herd

A basic framework for the organization of pastoral knowledge is the system by which a Saami divides a herd[1] into different categories of animals (Table 2.1 and Fig. 2.1). The pastoralist is interested in his herd primarily as breeding stock, and for this reason its composition

will be different from that of a herd in the wild. There are six basic components to a pastoral herd, as seen with a husbander's eye: the calves and yearlings together (without sexual designation), junior cows, senior cows, junior bulls, senior bulls, and castrates.

Beyond the distinction of sex, those of age and status are important as indicators of individual animals' allotted contributions to pastoral production. This is particularly true with male animals, always a minority in a pastoral herd. As few as ten to fifteen bulls may serve one hundred cows. Other male animals will be kept for their meat and others as draft animals, and still others will have been slaughtered in their first year for their skins—sickly animals, for example (see tables in Appendix 1). Ideally, one should not have to slaughter female animals; however, the husbander will eliminate those of low fecundity, those that do not nurture their calves satisfactorily, and even those that are inclined to stray away from the herd with their calves.

It is on the basis of their age that bulls are distinguished, one from another, up to their seventh year, though the senior bulls may be referred to by the collective term, *sarves*. These distinctions are especially important at the time of the rut. Castrates, however, are called *gaskek* (from the verb "to bite"—as I will explain), and those that have been trained as work animals are *her'gi*. When wishing to refer to bulls and castrates together, the term is *luovas*.

After her second year a cow is known as *aldo* until she

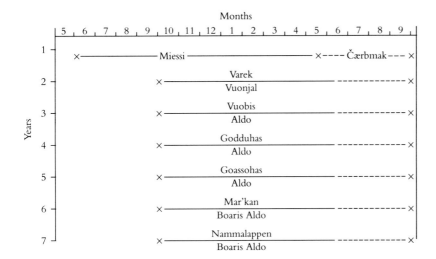

Figure 2.1 Age-classes of reindeer. Terms for male animals are given above the lines; for females, below

reaches (if allowed) her sixth year, when she becomes *boaris aldo,* or "an old cow." Here the pastoralists' principal concern is whether the teeth of a boaris aldo are still in such shape as to allow her to browse efficiently enough—for this is of consequence to her calf. (Mothers ordinarily have milk in their udders right up to the autumn, but calves can survive without milk after midsummer.) Before calving, the female herd as a whole is known as *čoawjek,* or pregnant; after calving simply as *njiŋŋalas,* female. After calving, there arise fine distinctions concerning reproductive failure or postnatal mishap. The term *rodno* in its strict usage refers to a cow that did not calve in a particular year; but its colloquial use is of a much wider range, inasmuch as any female of over two *without* a calf may be referred to as a rodno. The circumstances by which a cow became calfless vary, and it is knowledge of the circumstances that permits rational decisions (or controlled, as opposed to speculative or even random ones) regarding which cows to slaughter, and when to do so. It is appropriate to hold over discussion of this elaborate knowledge and its codification until Chapter 6, "Spring Calves."

The nonage or juvenile animals are those under sixteen months: *miessi* (calves) for the first twelve, after their birth in May–June, and *čærbmak* (yearlings) for the last four, up to the time of the second rut after their birth. (Accordingly, Fig. 2.1 shows this first "year" as one of sixteen months.) Saami pastoralists are very conscious that this is the period in the life of the animal when the odds are greatest against its survival. Seasonal fluctuations in weight and physical condition afflict all reindeer, but none more than the calves and yearlings. Perhaps for this reason, these young animals are not designated by sex. Certainly, as pastoral capital, they are regarded as quite uncertain. One cannot really "count them," Saami told me, until they become two-year-olds: *varek* (male) or *vuonjal* (female). The possibility that some vuonjal will conceive and bear calves is a matter of anticipation each year. Those that do are known as *vuonjal-aldo.* But vuonjal that do not calve are not known as rodno. Sometimes there are *miessi-aldo:* a female that calves in her second spring (when she would normally become čærbmak.) Varek like to run in the rut, though they will be chased away as long as the senior bulls have the energy.

The Kautokeino pastoralists accept that they cannot control the paternity of their animals, given the intermingling. This does not appear to be a vexatious issue among most of them (though some owners with the larger herds complain that they are, in effect, providing stud animals for others). Of course, they are (like all pastoralists at all times) extremely interested in the annual reproduction of their herd, but their actual intervention is limited. Sometimes a bull that is overspent at the rut, but still holding at bay younger and more virile bulls, will be deprived of its dominant status by the sawing off of its antlers. Careful accounts are kept of cows' pregnancies and post-pregnancies, and those with the poorer case histories are likely to be slaughtered. In talking about the

Left foreground, young male without antlers, having shed them in the autumn; right foreground, white calf; background: cows.

genetic strain of their animals, the key term is *nalli,* progeny in the female line.[2]

The naming system, then, that Saami pastoralists use for their reindeer serves as more than a mnemonic: The names impart relevant information about the animals' life cycles and the husbandry decisions that have to be made. The names help to show how they think about their animals and how the value they place upon them can change with changes in the animals' life cycle, some of which arise out of the pastoralists' own interventions.

Two Systems of Recognition

Aside from body build and color, an animal's antlers aid the pastoralist in individual identification (Fig. 2.2). Sex and age-class are generally determinable, even at a dis-

tance, by this method, though varek and vuonjal antlers may well be confused. More significantly, the pattern of the spread of antlers is likely to be sufficiently constant from year to year for the skilled herder to be able to make individual identification; behind the skill lies discerning observation and retentive memory. Identification of individual cows on this basis is, however, more difficult than with male animals.

Bulls lose their antlers after the rut (castrates some time later), cows not until after they have calved in the spring (rodno some time earlier). Growth of new antlers happens during the summer and is completed just before the rut—signaling new age-classes. Herders, watching the growth of antlers through the summer, anticipate the changes in status; for instance they may refer to a bull in its second year as *vuobis-čarve-dakkat*—literally,

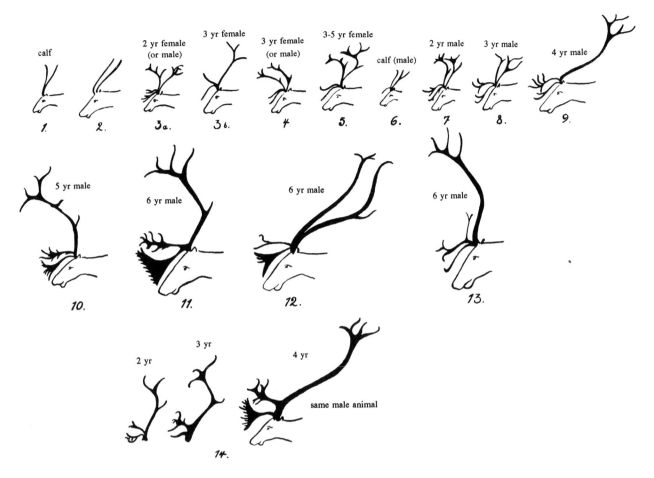

Figure 2.2 Age and sex recognition by antlers. From original drawings by Mikkel H. Buljo of Kautokeino (Nielsen and Nesheim 1956:98)

"making the antlers of a three-year-old male."

More important still, though, is individual identification in respect to *ownership* of an animal. This happens through an elaborate system of earmarking with "words," or *sadjek*—that is, notches—cut in the ears of the animal (Fig. 2.3). Every individual—man, woman, child—has a registered combination of "words": This is his or her ownership mark, and it is normally given in early childhood.[3] Thus in any family there will be a number of earmarks; in a camp, many more. In composing earmarks for their children, parents will elaborate upon the basic compositions of their own marks—the parents themselves having different marks, often of sharply divergent composition; or a child may be given the mark of a now deceased relative. While there appear to be no prescribed patterns of allocation among the children, everyone in

the family, and perhaps beyond it, will be familiar with the relation of one mark to another or the history of a particular mark that comes to the family.

In Kautokeino in 1964 there were approximately 1,400 registered earmarks,[4] and possible combinations of sadjek were many times that number. The Reindeer Administration tended to see the outcome as confusion.[5] All reindeer owners with whom I spoke about the matter disagreed strongly. As one of them, Nils Isak Eira, put it, "I can see that so many reindeer marks can confuse the Reindeer Administration, but that is absolutely not the case for us reindeer owners. . . . The more reindeer marks there are in use, the easier it is to identify the individual animals." By "identifying," Nils Isak Eira means more than merely recognizing: It is "to know an animal's history and all the relevant data about that animal." He

Making antlers. *Luovas* at Baddjeluobbaljav'ri.

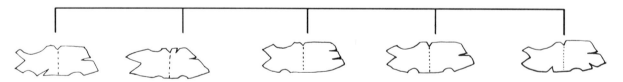

Figure 2.3 Reindeer earmarks of five siblings. Adapted from Solem 1933

dwells on the attention given to the composition of earmarks: relatedness of composition within a family and
distinctiveness vis-à-vis other families' marks. He stresses
the important challenge of "knowing" *(dowdat)* as many
earmarks as possible and how that knowing "gives status
and demonstrates your proficiency."

Of course no owner will know (or need know) all of
the 1,400 marks. The marks one needs to know are those
of owners in one's own and neighboring seasonal camps.

This is still a large number, but it is feasible knowledge.

Nils Isak moves the importance of reindeer marks beyond even the matter of ownership, noting how earmarks
are of considerable cognitive importance. Possession of an
earmark helps assure a child's commitment to this livelihood. Nor must the aesthetics of reindeer earmarking be
ignored. Some compositions are ugly *(fastes)*, others
handsome *(čabbat)*, and clues are dropped in this way
about the personality of owners.

Castration

As part of the process of allocating animals to different ends, castration is noteworthy for the calls of judgment and planning it presents the husbander. "Castration" is, by intention, not even always of the same physical effect.

It is appropriate to begin with the reasons for castrating a reindeer. Stock breeding (fattening for the market) is but one reason of several, and in the 1960s it was still not the most important. Senior bulls—some, or as many as possible—from the previous year are castrated in an effort to reduce aggressive (and wasteful, from the husbander's point of view) competition between bulls at the rut. Among *goassohas* (five-year-olds) that take part in a rut, some are always likely to succumb to fatal exhaustion; and besides, protracted competition between bulls prejudices the desired synchrony of the rut. I was very early taught that participation by the largest possible number of bulls is no formula for a "successful" rut; quite the contrary.

Animals of selected age-classes and other specific physical attributes may be castrated with a view to their slaughter later in the year, more likely for domestic consumption (besides meat, skins for clothing) than for sale, or a combination of the two. Then there are those castrated for training the following winter as draft animals or "leaders," without which the long biannual migrations would not be possible. Finally, as long as castration is performed so as not to sap the animal's strength, there is the benefit of having animals, at all seasons, that are less prone to stray: Castrates increase herd centricity.

The husbander (often in consultation with his wife) makes the specific decisions in respect to age-classes. Varek (two-year-olds) are not castrated, not even in anticipation of slaughter later in the year, for two reasons: one, they have strong body growth and will quickly recover the weight they lose during the rut as junior competitors; two, a husbander adopts a wait-and-see policy towards his varek: What promise of strength is there in the individual animal? What will be the husbander's priorities of allocation next year?

In allowing, say, half of his *vuobis* (three-year-olds) to enter the rut, the husbander is thinking ahead. Some of these he hopes will run also in next year's rut. Of those

he castrates, he has two things in mind: tender and fat meat (smoked and dried, it is a staple ration in the spring camps) or strong young males that can be trained as draft animals.

Many husbanders view *godduhas* (four-year-olds) as the ideal age-class for the rut. But they prefer to train younger animals for draft work, so if godduhas are needed for that work, the time for castration is early in the summer; later, castration is more likely to be for meat.

As I suggested, in a bull herd of several age-classes, the presence of many five-year-olds at the rut is not usually seen as an advantage, so many husbanders who can afford to do so castrate them principally for the market. However, those with small herds or with the rut taking place away from other herds (or a husbander who has miscalculated his allocations) may not have enough three- and four-year-olds to allow them to remove their five-year-olds from the rut.

Traditionally, castration has been performed by biting (*gaskek*) and then squeezing the glands. There is no incision, nor any risk of infection; however, it probably causes the animal much pain. It is this gaskek method rather than any other that allows for gradations of emasculation. How sharp the bite? How hard the squeeze? But cold temperatures cause a hardening of the glands, and to attempt gaskek then—impracticable as it would be—could seriously endanger the health of the animal. Instead, an incision into the scrotum is made and the glands removed; even so, there is the danger of infection. Commonly, then, castration has been performed in the summer using the gaskek method. This was still true in 1961–62, although after 1957, in Norway, the traditional methods were illegal: All castration was to be done with specially designed tongs.

There are those who regularly use the tongs but make one cut instead of the recommended two; Ellon Ailu is one of these. He makes two cuts only when he has to castrate an animal just before the rut. But many more have tried the tongs and reverted to gaskek. Tongs leave the animals weak, they say. That may matter little if the animal is to be slaughtered, but it can be a serious drawback in the case of draft animals.

The noun, *gaskek,* besides being the collective for all the castrates of a herd, is also the term for an individual castrate through its first winter. Thereafter the animal is a *nammoaive* or "velvet head [antlers]." Whereas bulls shed the velvet of their antlers in preparation for the rut and soon after the rut loose the antlers themselves, leaving them *nul'po,* or antlerless, through the winter, castrates retain velveted antlers through the rut and perhaps well into winter. Just *when* a castrate loses its antlers varies a great deal and is principally determined by the "strength" of its castration and when it was done. An animal castrated well before the hormone growth that presages the rut is likely to lose its antlers a few days later; otherwise, the "weaker" the castration, the longer antlers are retained through the winter.

An animal that is "lightly" castrated in order that it may be a strong draft animal is known as *čalloher'gi* (*čallo,* to rub off). Like a bull—which it still is, in small part—it attempts to rub off its velvet. Some may even partake in the rut, but then these are no longer čalloher'gi but *rakki-her'gi* (*rakki,* rut). The longer one waits in the summer to castrate an animal, the greater the likelihood of a čallo- or rakki-her'gi. The unpredictable, aggressive behavior of rakki-her'gi can be dangerous; and should they copulate, weak progeny (it is said) can be expected. Such troublesome castrates (at the rut) are likely dealt with in the same way as a senior bull one wishes to keep out of the rut—their antlers are sawn off.

For the various reasons that have been noted, castration should be done in the summer, along with calf-marking. However, herds are free-ranging, or *væitalis,* to such an extent that castration is undertaken whenever the chance presents itself from late spring up to the rut itself—and still there will be animals that elude the husbanders. The point that I want to conclude on, however, is how "castration" of an animal gives its owner options rather than foreclosing them all. If the animal proved difficult to train for work, it will be slaughtered for consumption, the market, or both; *or* it will be left to run in the male herd, tamer and heavier than the bulls, until the owner chooses to "consume" it.

Herd Control

There are other husbandry tasks besides those I have been describing, and they will feature in the seasonal

chapters, which follow. But I think that two general points have been illustrated: It falls to the husbander to make allocations of his herd; but for the appropriate implementation of his decisions, much is likely to depend on his and his companions' work as herders in the terrain.[6] So I now look at the principal means of efficient herding.

Herders are always running into difficulties. When herds get mixed, they "repair" the system: Herds are separated. So herding in reindeer pastoralism is a continual process of retrieving or reestablishing control. Because there is limited predictability and no sense of absolute control, "fault" abounds. No work is done according to a blueprint. Everyone is involved—alone, with a partner, or in a group of herders—in the struggle to keep things going. These conditions foster not blame but responsibility, tempered with a great deal of pragmatism. When things go wrong, the discussion is about how to correct the situation, and it is usually accepted that there is no one "correct" solution, but several possible ones. "Good" solutions are based on intimate experience and knowledge of herds in the terrain and may well involve the cooperation (if necessarily loosely synchronized) of a few herders. Thus, in a most marked fashion, problem situations become learning situations, ensuring the reproduction of the Saami herding culture. There will be more to say about this, but for the moment, let us look at various herding aids and devices and how they are used.

SIMPLE TECHNOLOGY

First, there is the personal equipment of a herder: binoculars (all seasons); skis (winters); and the constant companion and worker: his dog. These extend his range of surveillance, his mobility, his stamina. His lasso, carried slung over one shoulder and under the other, extends his reach when working at close quarters with the herd—corral work, typically.

Then there are devices to help bring, and keep, the animals near him at different seasons: smudge fires and salt licks (summers) and even his own urine (winters and springs). Two others call for special discussion: fences (especially summers and autumns) and bells (all seasons).

Reindeer fences, primitive and flimsy in construction

though they may have been, predate reindeer pastoralism,[7] and the post–World War II years have seen their construction on a scale representing a considerable capital investment. It draws government assistance for the cost of materials and for some of the logistical expenses. The reindeer owners themselves, however, must supply the labor (usually their own) to erect the fences and maintain them. All this is in marked contrast to the simplicity and negligible cost of the other herding aids and devices. The fences are different on another account as well: They can be a source of dissension among herders. For in the case of the same fence, the benefit (increased herd control) may fall to one camp while the disadvantage (reduced mobility, adversely affecting herd control) falls to another—all depending on which side of the fence one's herd is. This kind of situation occurs typically in the autumn, before and after the rut; in the spring, most fences are likely to be deep in snow—with snow "bridges" over them—and thus inoperative.

Because fences are used to increase herd control at the expense of the animals' mobility (and it may well be that the reduced mobility factor operates selectively, as just suggested), questions are continually posed about the possible effects on the animals. The answers depend very much on how the fences are used by the herders. Fences can be "open" for short or indefinite durations. Herders of a camp may have the *right* to open and close a fence, but there may be unwelcome social costs in terms of relations with other camps.

All of these herding aids operate from, as it were, "outside" the herd, but there is one exception. Reindeer bells are placed "within" the herd. The bells are hung around the necks of selected animals, but they are also "within" the herd in a more significant way: The bells cause particular animals to group together more consistently than they would otherwise. Thus the bells can provide herders with up-to-date information about the whereabouts of the herd as a whole or, and this is particularly important, the likely whereabouts of animals that have strayed from the herd.

In overview, these various aids comprise a support system appropriate to the nature of the work facing herders. Even the presence of fences does not of itself tell a herder what to do. He has to decide. This kind of relationship

with technology is consonant with conditions of poor predictability. Nor do any of the aids call upon technically specialist knowledge for their use. They are available to all, so their use becomes a matter of judgment and responsibility. Accordingly, there are periods of self-imposed restrictions: Early in the autumn lassos and dogs may be used, but not during the rut. In the spring, the bulls and cows are usually separated, and, again, lassos or dogs are not used when attending the cows and their calves.

BELLS

More needs to be said about reindeer bells and how they provide herders with information about animals in the terrain. It is especially in autumn, the season of restless and scattered herds, that a herder draws upon his knowledge of bells. A bell tells him not simply the location of some of his animals; more than that, if he recognizes the timbre of the bell—and remembers the animal he attached it to and knows the animal's habits—then he can approximate how many, and even which, animals are following the bell (or more strictly, following the animal bearing the bell). This is particularly helpful while herding at night, one of the more exacting autumn tasks. "What bells were missing?" is often the question that greets the herder returning to camp at dawn. On the basis of that information other herders will go into the terrain with a good chance of finding the animals that strayed.

Bells are used not only for finding animals, they are also a valuable means of herding. Thus when the task at hand is that of leading a herd from one grazing area to another or across a frozen lake or along a spring migration route, bells are likely to be placed on "lead" animals. Moving herds through fog-bound terrain may only be possible through the use of leader bells. The leaders may be animals who are usually found in the vanguard of a herd of their own accord; or others, notably her'gi, who are hand-led by a herder.

The bells vary in size and weight (from a tea-bell to a cowbell), and herders refer to them in terms of their sounds. Thus *čuojal* has a clear, high timbre that can be heard across relatively great distances, whereas *roappe* (or *čuojatæbme*) produces a low, cracked sound that does not carry as far.

The use of bells faces a herder with a series of decisions. How many bells? Which bell on which animal? The utility of such a decision once made can be undone by changes in the terrain and the weather, and in the location of a herd in relation to others. What is a good strategy while moving between pastures in daylight may (if continued) exacerbate problems while herding at night. Not surprisingly, then, there seems to be no consensus, even among herders of the same camp, as to the most efficient use of bells. Migot (see Fig. I.3) places čuojal bells on animals that are prone to keep in the front of a herd on the move, and roappe on animals that usually take up the rear. This arrangement, he says, enables him to locate quickly at dawn the boundaries of a herd that was unattended at night. Ellon Ailu, on the other hand, ordinarily prefers to put his bells on animals that keep well inside a herd. In his opinion it is unwise for a "leader" or a "straggler" to wear bells, except in controlled situations. Their bells would draw other animals away from the main herd, creating an unpromising situation for the dawn herder, whose job is to account for the whole herd. Even when moving with the herd under optimal conditions, Migot uses čuojal bells among the animals in the vanguard, arguing that it is wisest to recognize that part of the herd will surge ahead anyway, and their bells help one to reestablish contact. Ellon Ailu, for his part, says that this will simply mean more animals than otherwise leave the main herd in this fashion.

Opinions differ, too, with regard to the number of bells that is most advantageous. Some herders, more than others, make the point that herds become unduly dispersed through the use of too many bells, but there is no consensus on what constitutes too many. Certainly, when a herder is so bewildered by the variety of timbres that they no longer convey information to him, it is clear he is misusing bells.

Disagreements on these matters are not easily resolved, nor is it strictly necessary that they are, as long as herding partners understand each others' calculations and, of course, know which bells have been placed where. However, given the changing composition of herds and their accidental mixings with each other, especially during the

autumn, this prerequisite is not readily obtained.

In full winter conditions, relative to other seasons, the animals cluster. They pasture more intensively (digging through snow) over smaller areas, and their owners, as long as their animals are, in fact, pasturing well, are usually pleased not to have to move them. On this account, then, bells are not so important a component of herd management at this time of year. However, several winter camps may have pastures close to each other, even to the extent of overlapping, and herders of the different camps use bells to help keep their separate herds apart. The bells are meant to draw the animals of each herd together; sometimes, however, the bells of one herd attract animals from another herd. This is most likely where neighboring winter herds shared the same wide summer pastures: A bell that was followed in the summer can now draw an animal away from its rightful herd (from the owner's point of view).

Another distinctive feature of winter is the use of the *gil'ka*—a bell with a high tinkle. They are placed on animals that have recently joined a herd (through purchase or as a gift). Not only do they carry the "strange" earmarks of their previous owners, but they are likely to be restless. Such an animal will carry a gil'ka while it "gets to know" where it now belongs. Should it find its way back to its earlier herd (say in the spring), the tinkle of this bell will announce its presence. Ellon Ailu regards the gil'ka as an abomination: "They are not proper bells, they are difficult to hear and quite bewildering if there are too many." But then, he is less dependent on bells than most. Whereas Migot, for example, preferably listens to bells and then conjectures as to the whereabouts of animals, it seems Ellon Ailu's preference is to walk, run, or ski to find where they are.

In spring and summer there is less use for bells than in the other seasons. During the spring migration it is common practice for the herder to be in front of the herd leading by hand a bell-her'gi. Difficult terrain is negotiated in this fashion. There will likely also be bells among the animals at the rear of the herd on spring migration, lest they begin to stray or fall too far behind. Many fewer bells are used in the summer. One reason is that the animals are left to themselves until the August roundup. Also, during the summer molt the leather thong or strap

Her'gi in harness.

from which the bell hangs can cut deep sores into an animal's neck. A bell can also be dangerous on other accounts at this season out on the coast, as I explain in the next chapter. Even so, circumstances sometimes warrant the use of bells in the summer, provided the choice of the animal is carefully and knowledgeably weighed. Some animals tend to hide away in the landscape, perhaps evading the August roundup: A bell may help herders to find them. Inexperienced animals are lost each year through falls off precipitous cliff paths, and even older animals are known to be foolhardy in this respect, so some herders attach bells to cows (with calves and yearlings in their following) known not to venture off the safe paths.

It is noteworthy that bells have an important place in reindeer herd management even though hearing is not the animal's most dependable sense. That is their sense of smell (Appendix 1). They even use smell to confirm what they hear. Animals that faintly hear a bell against

the wind will veer downwind, and by this means they not only hear the bell better but are able to smell what they have come to associate with a bell: other reindeer, and possibly people and their dogs.

RECIPROCAL LEARNING

A process of reciprocal learning occurs between animals and herder. In the everyday round, this is especially evident during a herd's rest periods, or *liv-ai'ge,* of which there are four in the course of every twenty-four hours. The duration of each varies from between two hours to as little as half an hour when the ground is wet or the herd hungry on account of poor pasture. Whenever possible, the herd is brought to rest in the close vicinity of the camp, thus ensuring a regular consociation of herd and people. The element of routine is important. The children of the camp learn to behave quietly and observe the deer (and discipline is required of the camp dogs, too). The animals, it is believed, come to associate the noises and smells of a camp with security. At all events, animals of a herd handled in this way show no alarm when persons walk among them. Thus it is especially during rest periods that owners (in their role of husbander now) replenish their knowledge of the animals, inspecting them leisurely at close quarters.

The process of reciprocal learning does not depend upon all animals of a herd being equally involved. Followers are less involved than leaders. But the herders do not leave the matter there. The animals they select for work (sled-pulling and packing) learn the most about the human element, which is always there somewhere at the edge of the pastoral herd. They especially become familiar with camp sounds, smells, and movements, and their calm behavior may reassure the herd. Herders are likely to place leader-bells on them when moving a herd from one place to another. These work animals (castrates) appear to have high status among the other animals, probably because they retain their antlers longer than the bulls and because of their close association with the herders. These, then, are the *tamed* animals of a pastoral herd.[8] As bells provide herders with intelligences from within the herd, so these tamed animals are brought into the camp domain, where they learn and, in turn, "teach" the herd.

But out in the terrain and for the herd as a whole, it is usually a matter of the degree to which the animals are controlled rather than of their tameness. Of course, increased control can lead to increased tameness of a herd—but *that*, paradoxically, can put difficulties in the way of the herders. It is a pastoral case of "familiarity breeds contempt": over-tame animals are, for instance, unafraid of the herders' dogs and stand their ground; they become sluggish and unresponsive. "They're too tame,"[9] the herders say of their animals by the end of a spring camp. That means more work for the herders. Yet by the end of a summer in which the animals were left to roam, they are "too wild" *(hil'bat)*. One wants the herd leaders to respond readily to the signals of herders and their dogs, and a degree of nervousness and alertness among the herd as a whole helps.

Herders, for their part, learn to monitor herd signals and build up that detailed knowledge of leader-follower relations in their herds: which animals follow immediately behind a leader, or behind particular leaders; which take up the rear; and which are inclined to wander. Herders' awareness, *on a herd basis,* of individual animals and their idiosyncrasies almost certainly exceeds that of the animals themselves.

TALENT

With so much depending on the herders' levels of expertise, it is not surprising they themselves talk about this in terms of talent *(fitmat, særra,* or *haga),* disposition *(luondo),* and, of course, knowledge *(dietto).* Whereas the word for "disposition" and the word for "knowledge" are not restricted to contexts of reindeer management, the three words designating "talent" are. (Outside the reindeer context, men and women may be referred to as simply "competent" or "clever," *čæp'pe).* Furthermore, each of these words has its own connotations and domains. Fitmat is talked about as though it is innate or intuitive talent (depending on the context). Exceptional understanding of reindeer behavior is fitmat, so is exceptional memory of reindeer earmarks. Both men and women can be fitmat. There is a word, too, for the person who finds it difficult to recognize animals—*dii'hme.* To be *særra* or *haga* indicates a more instrumental and learned skill: for example, to be able to "read," at unusually long

distances, the small cuts that constitute an earmark, and to throw a lasso well. Also, these two terms are sex specific. Only men are særra, and only women are haga.

Nevertheless, it is not enough for a herder to be "talented" should he (or she) also be lazy or dishonest; in such a case he will still be regarded as a liability by other herders. What should be remembered here is that the difficulties of herding mean that each herder is presented with many opportunities to render his fellows favors or disfavors. So when herders talk approvingly among themselves of the luondo of one of their number, they are usually referring especially to his agreeableness and his readiness to do his share of the work. For a good herder is also a reasonable person to work with; if he is not, then it will be said that he "spoils" whatever herding talents he has. A person who is proud, in the sense of arrogant *(čæw'lai),* does just that. Knowledge, then, owes as much to disposition as it does to talent, and it is likely to be the energetic person with a comprehensive social network who accumulates the kind of knowledge that counts in reindeer management.

I have often been asked what place "luck" has in Saami accounts of relative success in reindeer pastoralism, and I think the answer is, very little. They tend to attribute this kind of good fortune to a person's ability, talent, and hard work. On the other hand, the tendency is to explain a person's failing fortune as bad luck. Perhaps connected with this is the keen sense of how the natural circumstances of pastoralism vary from place to place, and that on the temporal plane things may change precipitately. Thus, while he may see his camp-mates as fitmat or dii'hme, a Saami pastoralist is reluctant to say that people in other camps are doing things in a wrong way—even though he says of himself that he is doing things the right way. In short, he is simply doing things the way he knows best; each works within the limits of his own experience.

The Pastoral Factor

To change perspective: Reindeer may well be better off in the wild. Pastoralism is a system of impositions. Reversion to the wild state is a constant possibility: "a pull like that of a rubber band, as soon as the herder loosens his grip."[10] The important point is that control is imposed through working *with* the herd, as far as is possible. Were it otherwise, reindeer pastoralism would not be possible.

The mobility and nomadism of reindeer would have been insuperable obstacles to pastoralism had it not been for other imprinted elements of their animal behavior. (These are spelled out in some detail in Appendix 1.) The predictability of their cycle of seasonal pastures, their synchrony in breeding, and the critically important bunching response to predators help to make collaboration possible. Herders have good reasons for encouraging synchrony at calving and know that this depends on the rut taking place in natural conditions. Relinquishing their tactical control over the animals at that season makes good ecological sense. This all means that pastoral reindeer "live, from the biological point of view, more like wild than domestic animals."[11]

Still, much about reindeer pastoralism is far from collaborative in this sense. We may wonder how it is that the enforced separations of animals into the herds of different owners does not destroy reindeer social organization, leaving individual animals disoriented. For these separations cut across the seasonal segregations of wild reindeer on the basis of sex and age. And does not precipitate removal of animals, by slaughtering, affect the social organization of the herds?

In part, that kind of social organization is not present to destroy. A reindeer herd does not depend for its maintenance upon the animals' individual awareness of each other.[12] Dominance hierarchies are decided on the basis of physiological criteria. Animals replace each other readily in the herds. As long as there are enough experienced animals to assume (noncompetitive) leadership, losses of individuals by slaughter or herd-splitting are probably not disruptive of herd life. Pastoral herds are usually smaller but more stable in composition than wild ones, where "frequent splitting and coalescing of groups and herds throughout the year" is stressed as characteristic;[13] and the grouping together in "matriarchal bloodlines"[14] may be even stronger in pastoral than in wild herds. Further, it would be wrong to stress exclusively the disruptive implications of pastoralism on a herd: Pastoralism also engenders routine.

But herders do, sometimes, inflict physiological damage on their herds. It may arise through ecological miscalculation, too narrow ecologic parameters of possible action, or overexposure of the animals to stressful roundups and corral work. Or all of these. Inevitably, pastoralism fetters animals. Wild reindeer may be healthier and heavier on account of their being free to exploit fully their naturally selected, open-range foraging behavior.[15] For example, Alaskan caribou choose their own winter pastures and so can avoid ranges with snow deeper than sixty centimeters, but, says one report from reindeer pastoralism in Scandinavia, "Our reindeer are forced to dig in 70 to 80 cms. snow depths."[16] Moreover, the weaker individuals—which in a pastoral herd may be protected (though this varies)—are eliminated through natural predation. In sharp contrast, pastoralists' herds tend to ecologic overcrowding, and the price can be undernutrition and disease. Even the protection against carnivorous predators that pastoralists are able to give their animals has its price. On the testimony of older Kautokeino herders, protection by close herding may itself raise the level of physiological stress among the reindeer and their susceptibility to infectious diseases. On the other hand, should the wolf be eliminated (as has been virtually the case on the Kautokeino tundra since the 1950s), there tends to arise an oscillation in the herding pattern between open-range seasons and periods of repeated roundups and corral work. Current research by biologists at the University of Tromsö confirms this also places the animals under noticeable stress.[17]

However, the principal point for us is that reindeer pastoralism rests upon the successful deciphering of herd behavior by the herders. Thus the experience of a leader animal is not only the "common property" of other animals[18] but, in a pastoral herd, of the herders as well. As already suggested, there are elements of reciprocal learning here. Animals learn about their herders' order of things, as well as herders about their animals'. Herders often talk about how their animals "learn." It is essentially a reactive ability. The animal reacts to some of its experiences or to its sensory interpretations of these experiences. The reactions of leaders are reproduced by the followers. Indeed, a herd is held together by "followership" (rather than "leadership"—a perilously anthropomorphic term). Herders point out how what was learned by one generation will likely be passed on to the next. This rudiment of memory paradoxically presents herd management with a considerable difficulty whenever there is a change in plan. For supposing there is to be a change in migration routes or seasonal pastures, how are the herders going to "unlearn" the experience of the older animals, among which are the herd "leaders"? On the other hand, this memory allows reindeer to habituate themselves to less attractive conditions, which the pastoralists select for them.

Such questions as these—about herders' knowledge of herds, and herd "acceptance" of herders—are what much of the chapters that follow are about.

Part Two
Seasons,
1962

▲ ▲ ▲

God so made the Saami that they could find their way about the tundra.
If it weren't so, they would have perished long ago.

A compass only shows you north and south, it can't tell you the lie of the land
or where to lead the herd.

REINDEER OWNERS

3.
Summer Growth

Gæsse: June–September

Most summer pastures of the Kautokeino herds are out on peninsulas—the *njar'ga* herds (Fig. 3.2). A few are on offshore islands to which the animals swim—the *suolo* herds. Some others are inland, out of sight of the coast—the *nanne* herds, and some of these are on the high terrain around the tree line—the *or'da* herds. This chapter centers on the njar'ga type of herd management characteristic of Gow'dojottelit. Differences between njar'ga and nanne management are taken into account in a separate section.

Most Gow'dojottelit herds reach their summer pastures in June, *after calving*. The exceptions are a couple of nanne herds, and the suolo herds that make the swim over to the islands before calving, arriving in late April. Already by the beginning of September, the pastoral summer has passed by, and herders are preparing to move or are already on the move to autumn pastures. Yet it is this brief northern summer of constant daylight that is the important season of growth and bodybuilding for the animals. The protein-rich diet of grasses and fiberless foliage is easily digestible, and its mineral content gives

quick nutrition, so by the end of summer there may be several centimeters of fat on the backs of the animals.

The summers are particularly crucial for the calves and yearlings. The most rapid growth in the life of a reindeer takes place in the first sixteen months of its life—and that growth is almost wholly confined to the two summers within this period. In the intervening winter, the young animal often has a hard time maintaining its body weight. The view generally held was that an animal is hardly worth slaughtering for its meat (its hide is another matter) until it reaches the end of this rapid growth period. Of course the size, weight, and health of yearlings vary. Not least among many factors is the quality of the summer pastures. Calves are even more variable in their weight than yearlings, so that some are only half the weight of others in September. After the rate of growth slows down, at the end of the second summer, differences begin to appear between the sizes of the males and females. Whereas females usually reach their peak weights in their third year, the larger males gain weight more slowly and are probably at their heaviest in the fourth and fifth years.

For the calves and yearlings, the nutritional value of

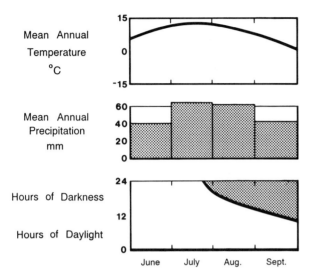

Mean Annual
Temperature
°C

Mean Annual
Precipitation
mm

Hours of Darkness

Hours of Daylight

Figure 3.1 Climate: June–September. From Hansen 1960

summer pastures is an important determinant of the chances of survival through the first winters of their lives; for the sexually mature animals, it is a determinant of their virility or fecundity at the rut in October. The pastoralists are acutely aware of these *predetermining* consequences of the summer season. A poor winter, I was taught, can be quickly compensated by a good summer, but animals may well have trouble surviving through the winter if the summer pastures have not been optimal. Pastoralists are quick to compare the sizes of animals from different summer pastures; they relate winter mortality rates to conditions of summer pasture; and it is these conditions that are invoked—more than any other single factor—in the discussions of calving percentages.

Yet for all that, the summer is a slack season for the

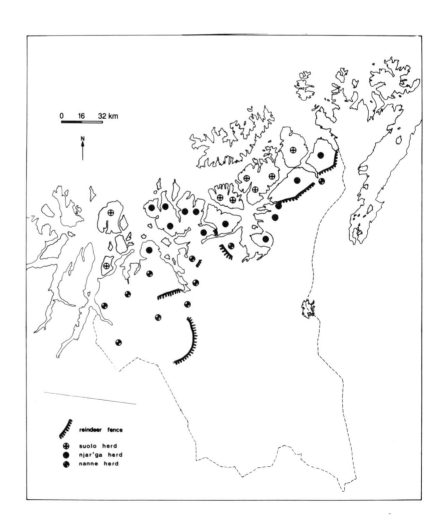

Figure 3.2 Summer herds: *Njar'ga, suolo,*
and *nanne*

pastoralist. Until toward the close of the summer, herding is minimal or absent. Instead, the animals are left to themselves to best explore the varied diet of the summer ranges. The pastoralist reasons that beyond bringing them to a good grazing range, there is little he can do to forward the nurturance of his animals at this time of year. Indeed, optimal nurturance in the summer correlates closely with free-range movement (væitalis). Furthermore, the herds are larger (and so fewer) than at any other season.

The pastoralist does not lose much knowledge of value about his herd by this arrangement, in contrast to other times of the year. Really the only protection his herd needs at this time of year is against the occasional cliff falls of overventuresome and inexperienced animals and, altogether a more serious matter, predation by the nonpastoral population of coastal districts. But there is little that can be effectively done about these things.

Summer ranges vary in quality, of course, but there are many factors to the variation, discouraging pastoralists from absolute judgments. The element of pastoral uncertainty is heightened by local changes in natural conditions (especially temperature) from one year to the next. The changes themselves are not predictable, only their consequences; both, changes and consequences, are frequently commented upon: "Yes, there can be many rodno [calfless cows], . . . but the number varies with the year. This year was bad because we had such a hot summer the year before, but we have hopes for next year because this summer was cooler."

Njar'ga Herds

Summer pastures along a broken coastline of peninsula, inlet, isthmus, and offshore island are largely demarcated topographically. The miles of fences stretched across the terrain *completes* the effect of enclosed ranges. From the time these pastures were first taken into use, however, short stretches of fencing, crude enough in construction, were erected across gaps in natural boundaries: between shore and lake, or shore and glacier, or over hill and valley. In other words, summer was a season of large herds and lax herding, relative to other seasons, long before the state-subsidized fences were built. Today, though, the

herds are still larger, and summer herding has been reduced still more.

Gow'dojottelit especially provides striking instances of this kind of topography and of the use of short fences to "complete" naturally enclosed summer ranges. Consider the seven pastures and herds (I–VII) in Fig. 3.3. Clearly, movement onto the peninsulas in July and off them in September has to be synchronized, although it is done informally. What is less obvious, perhaps, is how each of these pastures contains ecologic alternatives necessary for a herd during the summer: access to the shoreline for salt, to low-lying pastures for early vegetation, and to mountain pastures for cool in the heat of the summer and relief from insects (respite may even be sought on the glaciers). This means there are likely to be patterns—both by the month and by the day—in the wanderings of animals between locations within a specific pasture.

The luovas, or male herds, arrive some weeks before the cows and their calves, the separation having been undertaken before calving, and they are taken to the farthest reaches of the summer pastures. In the course of the summer they will mix with the cows and calves. However, in two cases, the male herd is kept separated: primarily as a means of efficient pasture use in the case of herd II, and as a precaution against poachers in the case of V. These arrangements bring more work with them, but they also improve owners' knowledge and control over the male herd.

At one place on the migration out to the summer pastures, the male herds of I–IV swim across a fjord, but the females with calves, coming afterwards, take the long way around the head of the fjord; on the return migration, all animals swim the fjord. Noteworthy, too, is the use made of shorelines in moving herds around this terrain. (A bonus of shoreline is, of course, its salt deposits.)

The ideal summer is cool, wet, and windy. Northern winds are cool, and they draw the animals down to the coast and shorelines again. On windless days in midsummer, or days with southerly winds, the deer move up to higher ground and tend to bunch there. Reindeer coats offer little insulation against heat. Moreover, at this time of year the animals are in molt—or just coming out of it—so their coats also offer little protection against insect bites either.

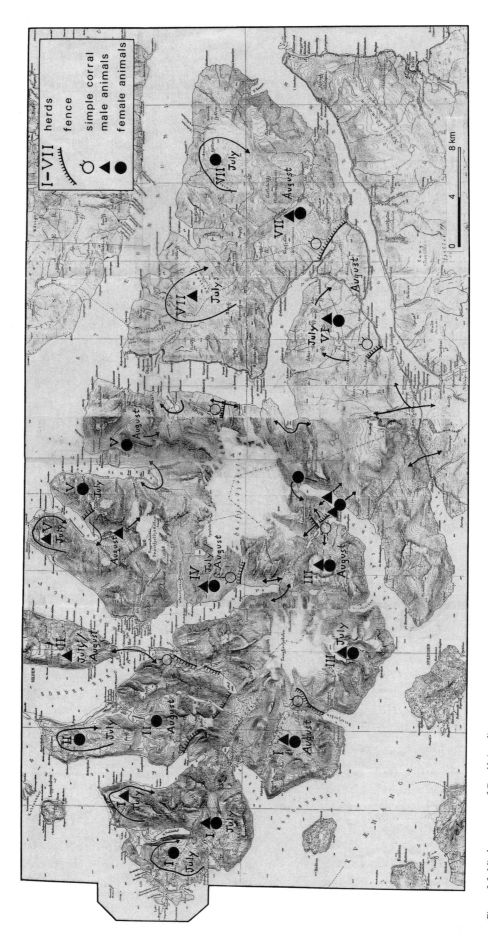

Figure 3.3 Njar'ga pastures of Gow'dojottelit

In this rugged terrain, encompassing glacier and sea cliff, some animals will always be lost. Mothers and their calves tend to scatter. Younger cows may venture out onto precarious cliff paths, where dislodged stones can result in one or several animals falling to their death. Older cows are less foolhardy. The risk with her'gi lies in their relative tameness: They wander off alone, un-alarmed at the poacher's approach. Bells may be attached to elder cows, but it is unwise to do so with her'gi: Their heavier bell and collar may get entangled in the summer's undergrowth, and a bell, too, can alert the poacher.

Owners want to earmark as many of their calves as possible in good time before leaving the summer ranges. For this purpose there are permanent marking corrals at strategic places, but in most areas these roundups, in late July or early August, are only partially completed: The animals are likely to be too widely scattered over varied terrain. However, some marking will be done and—very important—a few animals will be slaughtered for their hides for clothing and, secondarily, for fresh meat.

As was mentioned, reindeer begin to shed their heavy winter coats during the spring and early summer, pre-senting a rather ragged appearance until the new hair be-gins to grow in July and August (adult males tend to molt first). That is the best time to take the hides, for there will be a short and even coat of new hair (and calves have shed their "nursery" coat of reddish-brown). Later, the hair lengthens, and the hide is not so useful; by winter, it will be ruined by the mass of gorm flies lodged under the skin. The gorm fly larvae are from the summer pastures. The flies breathe through tiny holes bored through the reindeer skin. They leave their host in the spring through the same holes, to pupate on the ground and repeat the cycle.

Calf hides are the most highly prized for clothing, especially winter overcoats, and among them the white most of all. So some white, or *gabba,* calves are taken re-gardless of whether they are male or female. A compen-satory belief among pastoralists is that white calves are more delicate and attract the flying insects, so their ex-pected longevity is, in any case, less than others'. How-ever, other owners make a point of not slaughtering their white calves, taking pride, instead, in having mature gabba animals running in their herds. Reluctant to take a calf from an experienced mother, owners also look for

injured calves or those that seem prone to stray, and cer-tainly, any who have "lost" their mothers. Such decisions bear witness to husbandry knowledge: knowledge that can only be pieced together by frequent visits to the herd through the year. The hides of yearlings are especially suited for workaday clothes but less for ceremonial occa-sions, where sartorial effect is important.

It is not practical to preserve much meat in the sum-mer, so whatever is slaughtered will be consumed more or less straight away. In addition to some calves and a yearling or two, a cow that is without a calf may be slaughtered—and any other animal whose injury preju-dices its survival. At summer camps there may well be a chance to sell joints of meat to local people and visitors, but few owners really want to slaughter at this time of year, beyond domestic needs.

Important supplements to the pastoral diet are fish (fresh or salt-water) and wild berries. An important sup-plement to the cash earnings of households is roadside sales of Saami handicrafts: tourist trade principally. Men and women fish and collect berries and make and sell handicrafts, but only women engage in the back-break-ing work of cutting sedgegrass in mosquito-infested marshes. After considerable manual preparation, the sedgegrass *(suoi'dne)* is used to line moccasins (in place of a sock, over which it has several advantages). The loca-tion of summer camps—as opposed to the herders' tent *(lavvo)*—takes into account access to these supplementary pursuits rather than to the herd, which is free-ranging.

It is in September that the herders put the greater ef-fort (many days and nights) into rounding up the animals from the summer pastures. Parts of herds will have al-ready started collecting by fences that now serve to pre-vent any mass movement off the summer pastures before the herders themselves are ready. Cows with calves are usually among the first to arrive at the fences, and with them there will always be some yearlings and rodno. Likely among the last to come will be mature males—both bulls and castrates, especially the latter; for they have roamed the freest and farthest during the summer. Some of them never turn up.

The areas in front of the fences become seriously over-grazed, and quickly so at that. This means that each day an animal spends "waiting" there, it loses some of the condition it built up over the summer. Owners worry over deleterious effects on the October rut, on the strength of animals through a hard winter, and on calving next spring. The situation of the lactating cows is particularly critical. They suffer a loss of weight, and because the timing of usterus is influenced by weight, cows come into usterus later with succeeding pregnancies.[1] This means later calving, and these mothers have least opportunity to draw benefit from the summer diet. As a consequence, the cows of more pregnancies are lighter and less fat in August and September than cows of fewer pregnancies. Even so, good autumn pasture before, during, and after the rut should allow these cows to put on fat and weight again.

With the bulls, however, the reverse sequence is more likely. Coming to the fences late, they will have heavy body weight (lean meat) thanks to their unencumbered summer grazing on a protein diet, but they will lose weight dramatically during the rut. Because males have more growing to do than females, a young male may be heavier at the end of a summer than a female of the same age, but it will also be leaner.[2] Fat meat is favored by Saami, lean by the Norwegian market. The fattest animals will be cows without calves and females entering sexual maturity at the end of their second summer.

Here, then, we have the rudiments of a prescription for slaughtering choices. Indeed, already in August, when at the marking corrals (where they also castrate some adult males), owners start planning their slaughtering options for even as far ahead as the coming winter. Castrates may be sold on-the-hoof just before leaving the summer pastures (counted as autumn slaughter); or sold after the rut at the large sorting corrals near a road, also on-the-hoof; or they may be allowed to fatten on the fungi and lichens of autumn and early winter, and be butchered December and January for domestic consumption—with or without the sale of joints. Even then, in January, the option to sell the castrates on-the-hoof is still viable. Finally, an owner may decide that he will, after all, save some of those castrates as working animals.

On the female, or njiŋŋalas side of the herd, options present themselves especially regarding rodno: whether to give a barren animal or one that lost its calf another "chance," or to slaughter her. On account of the fatness of her body meat, she is unlikely to be sold on-the-hoof

and will be butchered for domestic consumption. Most of all, though, attention is always centered upon each current batch of vuonjal: They should be sexually mature, say the Saami, but how many, and which, will conceive this autumn?

Or'da as an Alternative to Njar'ga

Owners are quick to point out how animals, particularly the younger ones, from different summer pastures compare. Most interesting are the points of contrast—which I heard so often—between njar'ga (peninsula) herds and the or'da herd (the nanne herd that does not come down to the coast at all and spends much of the summer around, or above, the treeline).

Or'da calves are the larger and heavier—"almost as big as their mothers"—and the calving percentage is higher. "We had seven miessi-čoawjek this year," boasted Danel Anti, the Nestor of the or'da camp; and it is acknowledged by njar'ga owners that on the or'da there are fewer rodno, most years if not always. These differences are attributed in part to the late summer conditions of the or'da animals. Instead of gathering and waiting behind a fence, they are free-ranging within an area abutting the autumn grounds. Animals that would move on into the autumn pastures already are not stopped by a fence but are turned back by herders, or they "escape" and are retrieved later. This means early grazing of autumn vegetation—mushrooms and other fungi in particular—in advance of the njar'ga herds, which will pass through some of this terrain a few weeks later. Another factor is that the or'da animals enter the rut undisturbed by repeated corral separations, unlike the njar'ga herds (more on this in the next chapter). Or'da pastoralism also enjoys a logistical advantage over njar'ga: the or'da herd has shorter migrations, which is a factor of special significance for calves and yearlings.

Not all factors, though, favor the or'da. Calves are heavier and the calving percentage higher, but losses are greater. Animals on the or'da suffer most from gorm fly and nosefly larvae, some calves and yearlings becoming so debilitated that they succumb to a hard winter. It is the or'da animals, too, that are likely to suffer the most from flying insects. Without breezes coming in from the sea, there is little relief. In desperation, animals may stampede over the terrain, trampling vegetation underfoot. Much of the terrain is stony, and broken legs are not uncommon. Or, they bunch on snow patches in the high terrain, and bunched, the animals are the most susceptible to disease.[3]

Left alone in these conditions, animals would disperse far and wide, something that or'da pastoralism—without fences—cannot afford. So in contrast to late summer, when the harassment from insects has abated, a continual herding watch is maintained through June and often into July. Njar'ga men certainly exaggerate the burden of summer herding that thus befalls the or'da group, but I read the exaggerations as compensation for the better weights and higher fecundity of or'da pastoralism.

Njar'ga men live in family camps during the summer; not so the or'da men. Most of their women and the younger children and old people remain behind in the lower-lying plain to the south (spring and autumn pastures), where they fish the lakes with nets. Thus the or'da men and women are, at their separate locations, in a world virtually empty of non-Saami. Not so the njar'ga people. They engage in the summer tourist trade; they have guest relationships (verdi) with families in the coastal villages. Exceptionally, these are Norwegian-speakers; more likely they are Finnish- and, of course, Saami-speakers. There is a wide range of reciprocal exchange in kind between the pastoral and farming/fishing verdi.[4]

Historically, there have always been a few or'da herds among the Kautokeino pastoralists. After World War II, or'da pastoralism had a more "traditional" look about it than njar'ga pastoralism, principally on account of their smaller herds, which were kept under watch through the summer. But by the early 1960s much had changed. Overcrowding of other summer pastures made the or'da attractive as an alternative and, concomitantly, or'da pastoralism became more free ranging—but still without fences. There was much talk in the early 1960s about the long fences that were to be thrown across the or'da. Predictably, a typical njar'ga comment was: "They don't

have [many] rodno now, but just wait when they get their fence!"

Why—the question presents itself—intrude fences into reindeer pastoralism, then? The answer is always the same: to increase control over expanding herds and reduce the toil of herders through the summer. But "control" through the use of fences is a different kind of control from herding. A njar'ga man says, "In late summer one side of the fence is like a flowerbed, and the other is quite torn up and trampled by the animals." It is this situation that Danel Anti left behind when he decided to build up a herd on the or'da.

29 AUGUST

Animals are collecting in ever increasing number behind the fence that closes off Joakkonjar'ga [area VII in Fig. 3.3]. Migot explains that in this cool weather the deer come down to the fence of their own accord. One doesn't have to spend days on a roundup, he says; that pleases him. Moreover, "It's no good pushing them back, for one would be working against their nature: They wish to draw inland." But this doesn't mean that as the animals come to the fence they are let through. Far from it. Some are likely to be here—also "against their nature"—for two or three weeks; and, take note, these are the weeks the *or'da* animals are enjoying the early autumnal vegetation.

But the men are not idle. The "lazy" summer months are now over. Rather, the fence is the principal place where calf-marking and castration of bulls is carried out. There is a corral by the fence [as there is in most cases—see Fig. 3.3]. A few persons, Ellon Ailu for one, deplore this situation as it has developed over the last few years. He thinks (though I doubt that he ever says as much directly to Migot) one *should* "push them back"—it would be healthier for the animals (there is still much pasture). And one *should* have organized roundups to ensure that as few animals as possible are left behind for the winter (perhaps to die: a poacher's prey or starving on account of ice conditions). Too many are being left behind, Ellon Ailu insists.

Meanwhile no move can be reasonably made off the peninsula until other herds who would otherwise be in our path have begun on their migration.

The herd of several thousand deer was passed through the fence on 15 September, a week behind herd VI. Herds I to V left later in a sequence of their own.

4.
Autumn
Commotion

Čak'ča: September–October

As summer closes, the days become shorter, the weather harsh. Animals move up an age-class (except calves). The rut approaches, and movement of all herds and camps is *luksa,* or "in," towards the winter pastures. In other contexts luksa is the compass direction south, but in the autumn herds move luksa irrespective of actual compass directions—just as in the spring they move *davas,* or "out."

The bases of grasses and sedge plants that remain green longest, and fungi—especially mushrooms—are searched out as the herds move across the autumnal landscape. If not hindered, animals will range widely, most of all the mature males (bulls and castrates). Calves are becoming fairly independent, feeding on their own even though they still take milk from their mothers. They can manage alone now without their mothers, but even during the rut, when they are not getting any milk, they still try to run with their mothers. Herders, though, are well aware of the chances of calves becoming "lost" at this time of herd mobility. It can happen when the deer scatter in search of mushrooms, especially under cover of darkness or in mist and rain, and towards the end of the rut when

older bulls, through fatigue, lose control of their harems, and the younger males begin to pursue the cows. It happens especially in the confusion around the large separation corrals (near the perimeter of the winter pastures) when animals are passed through the corrals not once but several times.

The construction of these large-as-possible corrals (described below) has to be considered in conjunction with the crowding of animals behind summer fences, followed by a rush of thousands onto the autumn lands—all within a few weeks. Inevitably, there is some loss of control over herds and loss of knowledge as to the whereabouts of animals. The purpose of the corrals is to restore control and reconstitute the herds. But the costs are high in wear-and-tear on animals and herders. So in strongest contrast to summer, autumn is a season of exertion. More significantly, it is the one time of the year when these pastoralists sometimes end up not working "with" the herd, thereby adding to toil and strife.

I will try to depict the situation in some detail. It is one that is truer of most njar'ga herds—Joakkonjar'ga included, notwithstanding their deliberate delay in letting the animals through the fence—than it is of the nanne,

43

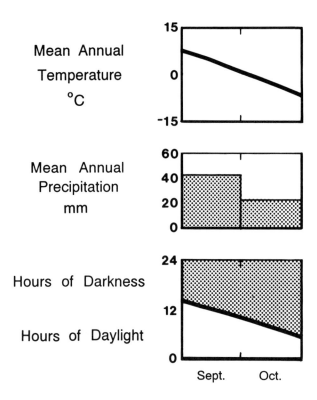

Mean Annual
Temperature
°C

Mean Annual
Precipitation
mm

Hours of Darkness

Hours of Daylight

Figure 4.1 Climate: September–October. From Hansen 1960

Herders used to guide their animals to "traditional" rutting places, and, it is said, the animals "knew" these places. Families would encamp there. Herders watched the rut and avoided disturbing the animals. Today, the destination, after letting the animals through the fences, is another separation corral: a destination that herders have in mind, but not their animals. Herding on the way there begins to take on the character of "heading them off at the pass."

The animals are in rut on the way to the corrals, while they are passed through them (which can take a couple of days), and after the corrals, too. The trauma can be considerable for a thousand or so animals milling around within an enclosed space, without food, and with herders bodily handling them. There is the same anxious talk about the possible effects on the animals as at the summer fences.

Often, then, the owner of a njar'ga herd can expect to leave the separation corrals with a good fraction of his animals missing (temporarily, he hopes), and it may well be December before he has them all together. By the same token, the herd he takes into the winter pastures will include a number of animals that are not his—*vierro boccu* (strays). Nevertheless, the autumn slaughter takes place at this time.

Buyers come to the corrals. It is convenient for owners to sell some animals here, and it is a time of year when cash is needed for domestic reprovisioning. But the drawbacks are also prominent in the minds of the owners: rupture in their herd knowledge at this time and temporary loss of condition of the animals around the corrals. Of course, decisions pertaining to on-the-hoof sales need not be very selective: some castrates, and also some varek (males entering their second year), for they are especially likely to lose weight during the winter. Each owner will have some of these animals in the herd that has gone through the corrals. Among the varek, though, he would like to select the smaller and lighter and those that are inclined to wander, but it is precisely that degree of selection which is often not possible at this time of year. Based on his observations of his animals through the seasons, an owner will, more likely than not, have *individual* animals in mind for butchering for domestic consumption. But he may not find them at this

whose herders manage, on the whole, to keep them out of the way as njar'ga animals pass by on their way to the corrals. Yet all but the youngest herders remember when smaller herds, and a larger number of them, would separately leave the summer pastures, under control, and disperse themselves across the expanse of the autumn pastures in preparation for the rut.

Dispersal of animals at this time of year makes good ecologic sense and benefits herds and herders alike. It is the *crowding* of animals and the *mixing* of herds of separate owners, followed by their forcible *separation,* that runs contrary both to the welfare of the animals and to the interests of their owners. But that earlier herd management, now a thing of the past for all but a few, meant day-and-night herding through the autumn. Even if herders were prepared (and could agree) to continue with this, their best efforts would be largely undone in the situation created by the summer fences.

Thus in the majority of cases, the rut *(rag-ai'ge)* is no longer a distinct interval or period of the pastoral cycle.

time. Rodno (calfless cows) are always candidates for do-mestic consumption: they have "failed," and they are fat; he knows that he has some, but he cannot find them. In-stead, he may take a vuojnal (female entering her second year) or two, especially the delicate-looking among them.

Thus the autumn slaughter takes on the character of a culling of the herd, and the selection anticipates, to some degree, probabilities of the "natural" decrease of particu-lar animals during a hard winter.

Luksa!

As noted in the previous chapter, the Joakkonjar'ga herd of several thousand animals was let through the fence on 15 September. Aside from the possibility of mixing with other herds, there was concern over the weather that might be encountered along the way. Besides cutting down herders' visibility, rain induces restlessness, and fog listlessness in the animals. Either way this makes for prob-lems. But the weather was a bit better than expected for the time of year, and most important, the herders count-ed themselves lucky in having a wind to work with that was regularly from the same direction. (Other things be-ing equal, reindeer move against the wind.) It was an easterly, too, which suited well—coming off the tundra, as it did, towards which the herds were heading in a southeasterly direction.

With a herd this size, the risk of dispersion from herd-ing at night is too great. So one depended upon the wind to keep the animals together through the night. Even if the deer had moved by morning, the herders felt they knew (on account of wind direction) where to go to find them. During the day, the herd had a tendency to scatter, but with a party of nine herders, each of whom knew how deer graze and move over the terrain and, as well, intimately knew the terrain itself, the situation was manageable. If there was a pattern to the dispersion, cows with their calves kept to the higher ground, while the males sought the rich vegetation of the valleys, or *vuobme.*

Naturally, it is not always so easy, and there were diffi-cult days. Not for nothing is this season also known as *hil'bat ai'ge*—the time when animals are least tame. Be-hind them is a free-range summer, and in front of them is

the rut. Each day brings fresh grasses, sedges, and fungi, and likely enough, abrupt changes in the weather. Herders codified the autumn landscape: *varri,* or hilly, open terrain (in the cool temperatures of autumn), was associated with *logjes,* or "tame" animals; vuobme with unmanageable ones. Indeed, the cows were kept on the higher ground because if they first get a taste of the rich vegetation in a valley, it is difficult to keep them moving as a herd. The mature males, on the other hand, were al-lowed to enjoy the valley because it would overtax the herders to prevent them. Besides, it is in the vegetation of the valley that the animals—many of whom were to be the studs in the rut—add weight and strength. Some her'gi might be left behind in this way, but one could de-pend on the bulls moving inland for the rut. There is a hazard, though: Some bulls may well wander off with those from other herds that have been attracted to the same valley.

For the same reason, it is only if there are no other an-imals in the vicinity that the herd will be brought for the night to the richer vegetation of a vuobme. More usually, on autumn migration one collects the herd as best as one can in the afternoon—dusk falls early—and releases it on a long, dry hillside with a wind blowing down its slope.

This procedure of letting the herd move at its own pace during the day while keeping watch over its various sections, collecting it towards the end of a day, and leav-ing it unherded through the night is known as being *væitallitit* (as opposed to the open-range, unherded, or wholly væitalis condition associated with summer). The absence of snow makes herding more difficult, not easier. On the one hand, the animals' sense of smell is height-ened, triggering their search for a diet of variety; on the other hand, they leave no tracks behind for a herder to follow. (I never failed to wonder, though, at the clues an experienced herder could decipher.) Hence the special dependence, at this season, on bells; and before the rut commences, dogs are used.

Physically, it is the season of most discomfort for herders. It is cold but also wet, meaning that one cannot change into the winter leggings and moccasins of rein-deer hair (summer skin leggings and moccasins are with-out hair). Herding parties do have a lavvo (the herders' tent, as opposed to the *goatte,* the roomier family tent);

Lavvo.

nevertheless, there will be nights spent without shelter. There are sufficient rations, and there is usually wood for the fire.

The rut began after the herd had traversed the or'da. Meanwhile, Danel Anti's herd (XI in Figure 4.2), no longer on the or'da but still in the general vicinity, was being kept under close watch to prevent mixing with the njar'ga and some nanne herds that were passing through the same terrain.

The multiple corral at Luossavarri was in sight on 24 September, but the herd could not be taken to it because

there was already a reindeer separation taking place. While they waited, herders had a hard time keeping the animals together on the hills to the south of the corral.

Separation Corrals

The two multiple-pen separation corrals through which most Gow'dojottelit animals are passed lie within a few kilometers of each other along the Alta-Kautokeino road at Stuoroaive and Luossavarri. In my journal entries I refer to them as Corral One and Corral Two, respectively. For convenience of schematic presentation in Figure 4.2, these two corrals are drawn as one. A good distance to the southwest there is another multiple-pen separation corral, situated along the migration routes of Oar'jebelli herds, also shown in Figure 4.2. Corrals One and Two, at any rate, were first used in the autumn of 1958.[1] Although the Reindeer Administration designed them and supervised their erection, herders were not instructed how to adapt to their use. By 1961, most herders had become habituated to the corrals, and there had arisen an understanding that all herds were required to pass through them. Some owners, however, spurned this understanding with impunity, and the Administration failed to enforce what was generally understood to be its directives in this matter.

Structure of a *goatte.*

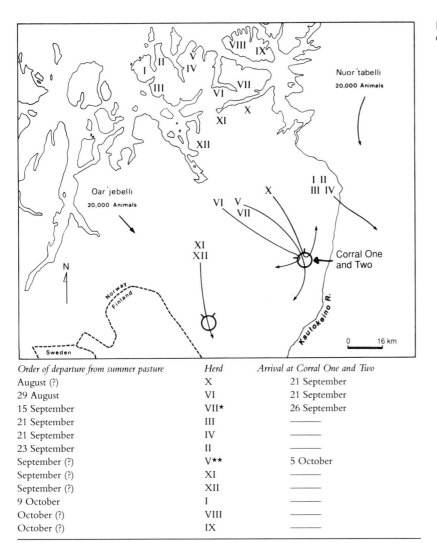

Figure 4.2 Autumn movement on Gow'dojottelit

Order of departure from summer pasture	Herd	Arrival at Corral One and Two
August (?)	X	21 September
29 August	VI	21 September
15 September	VII★	26 September
21 September	III	———
21 September	IV	———
23 September	II	———
September (?)	V★★	5 October
September (?)	XI	———
September (?)	XII	———
9 October	I	———
October (?)	VIII	———
October (?)	IX	———

? = date uncertain

  VII★ = the Joakkonjar'ga summer herd; in six visits to the corrals between 26 September and 20 October, it divides into three herds: VII[1], Iskun Biera with Jorgun Biera; VII[2], Iskun Mikko and Iskun Iskun; VII[3], Migot and his brother, Boaris Mikkel, and son-in-law Ellon Ailu (see Fig. I.3)

  V★★ = the male herd only of the VII[3] group

Following the sketch of Figure 4.3, the principle of the corral is simple enough. A herd is driven into the entrance (sær've-gar'de)—formed by two long arms, or vuorbmanak[2]—which is then closed behind them. Usually it is a matter of several hundred deer at a time (and a couple thousand during a full day). Next, some of these animals are let into the corral proper, which I call the stockade. For the first years, its sides were simply wire fencing, but it soon proved necessary to reinforce them with planking. Not only did this make the stockade stronger against the crush of animals, but by cutting off vision it also quieted the animals somewhat. Here the work of separating them takes place.

As far as ownership is concerned the animals that come into the stockade are a mixed herd (sær've-ællo). Now they are separated into the herds of owners who will be in partnership (combined herd, same camp) for the coming season. In the sides of the stockade are gates leading to six pens for the separated herds. Animals are dragged into the pens. At first, men used their lassos for

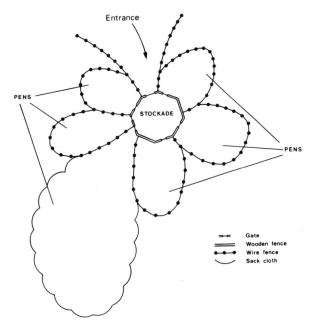

Figure 4.3 Multiple-pen separation corral

this task, but there was not enough space and too much commotion. So lassos were cut shorter. But by 1961 it was also common practice, inside the stockade, to seize an animal bodily and, with help, push, pull, and bundle it into its owner's pen.

Of course, separation itself, *rat'ket* (a key concept, about which there will be much to say in the next chapter), is nothing new; but there is an innovation of considerable significance in the way it is being done at these corrals. All the different owners or partnerships who have animals in the mixed herd separate them, at the same time, from the owner (or partnership) who has the most. His animals, left in the stockade each time, are the *vuoðða* (another key term: in the distribution of family capital, for instance, the vuoðða are the animals left with the parents after married children have been given their portions by anticipatory inheritance). Before bringing more animals into the stockade, the vuoðða itself will be put into one of the larger pens.

By this arrangement, those who have the vuoðða— who have the most animals at the corral—have the *least* hard, physical work to do. They place themselves near

A multiple-pen separation corral from the pen behind the stockade The Alta-Kautokeino road is in the background.

the gates to the different pens, watching to see that none of their animals are inadvertently (or otherwise) taken out of the vuoððo.

Stuoraoaive and Luossavarri are near the road to make it easier for buyers to draw up to the corrals with their large transport vehicles, as well as for owners from other herds to visit the corrals (an important factor). There is stream water in the vicinity—in the entrance area for the animals, and by the roadside for herders, their families (there may be a herders' tent or two), and the butchers. However, lack of water and pasture inside the corral itself is a matter of concern to all, especially when animals are left overnight in the pens.

As can be seen from the photographs, the "walls" of a pen may be sackcloth. Ordinarily, the animals do not test a pen for its strength; rather, they circle around and around (counterclockwise) or lie down (during their rest periods) away from the sides of their pen. However, if suddenly frightened—by the headlights of a passing vehicle at night, for instance—they may, in trying to jump over the sackcloth, knock it down. But the advantage of sackcloth is the considerable one of portability. Herders

carry sackcloth with them so that, without much bother, they can put together a simple pen when away from the corrals.

There are, then, two spatially separated activities at this season: autumn herding and pasturing, and the separation at the corrals. Accordingly, on 20 September I reach the corrals ahead of Ellon Ailu and the Joakkonjar'ga herd. I begin by renting a cabin (at Bingis) along the road between the two corrals. The cabins are being used as an overnight stop by herders, too, so I am well placed to glean information on what is happening with different herds. I traveled there by bus from the coast, bringing my typewriter, a couple of cases of beer, and a bicycle. Later, I will rejoin Ellon Ailu's camp in the vicinity of the Luossavarri corral.

20 SEPTEMBER

Some *nanne* herders [of herd X] also on the bus. We all get off at Corral One, where a large *nanne* herd has just been brought into the *sær've-gar'de*—waiting. Separation will not begin before

Anticlockwise movement inside the
stockade.

A bell-*her'gi,* and in the background, the
sackcloth wall of a pen.

Lassoing a *goassohas* for slaughter.

tomorrow. Men busy marking calves: using lassos to catch them.

I go to get myself fixed up with a place in the cabins.

21 SEPTEMBER

Cycle to Corral Two. No herd there—just a solitary *goatte*. It is Iskun Biera's wife and younger children: She expects the Joakkonjar'ga herd [VII] in about a week.[3]

Hitch a ride on a lorry back to Corral One, where separation is now in progress: primarily a *nanne* affair [X as *vuoððo*]; Bede [VI] has a pen, he is also taking whatever animals there are there from Spalca [XII]: affinal link between owners. In all, over two thousand animals. An old man of the *njar'ga* herds, Jovna Tommes [III], is here, and a young fellow from one of the *nanne* herds is pulling a few deer for him—they are also put in the care of Bede. "Pulling" *(gæs'sit):* one usually grasps a hind-leg, it kicks like a pneumatic drill. Iskun Iskun and some other Joakkonjar'ga men are now here (they came by bus today). They don't have a pen: they're looking for unmarked animals.

Each group has its own *lavvo* alongside the corral. The separated animals will be taken away tomorrow to join their herders' herds. I'm told that *nanne* animals are getting used to the routine with summer fences and autumn corrals, and so are not coming to the summer fences as early as they used to. True? Laggot [X] opened part of their fence on 8 September. Bede [VI] passed through that terrain earlier and without event. Each of these *nanne* groups and Bede have their herds under watch in selected places across the autumnal tundra; but all fear that there will be mixings later on, especially when the Joakkonjar'ga herd approaches. There was a separation here already last week, when the majority of animals were *sarves,* unlike now.

Girls of Laggot [X] are active as autumn herders.

22 SEPTEMBER

During the night, animals from several pens escaped. They were frightened, some say, by the headlights of a passing lorry, and others say by a dog. In their panic they knocked over the sackcloth and escaped. They are now kilometers to the south, and it will certainly take a day or two to bring them back—and by that time their numbers are likely to have been swollen with *vierro boccu* from other herds.

24 SEPTEMBER

It is Sunday. It has taken this long to round up the animals that escaped. They are now close to Corral Two and will be brought there tomorrow. I bicycle to Corral Two. Lots of herders and tents. Overnight in the tent of one of Joakkonjar'ga group.

25 SEPTEMBER

A long day at Corral Two. Pulling animals into pens. Bede [VI] was *vuoððo.* Finished at dusk. Bede's animals taken, under close watch, to join the remainder of his herd some kilometers to the southwest. As the *nanne* herds are farther away (to the north

At the corral: watching, listening, telling.

and northwest), their animals will remain in the pens (it is hoped) overnight.

It was peaceful and good-humored work at the corral. Some fifty animals, from different owners, were sold on-the-hoof to a Kautokeino buyer, who came with his lorry. As the rut is not yet far advanced, there is still time to sell (and so remove from the rut) a number of *goassohas*. The news is that Ellon Ailu and company with the Joakkonjar'ga herd are waiting on Dat'ku-varri to come down to the corral.

26 SEPTEMBER

No mishaps last night; and early this morning, while the *nanne* animals are still in the pens, the Joakkonjar'ga herd [VII] is brought into the corral. This allows the *nanne* herders to re-trieve strays before they leave.

As a pen becomes filled, the animals are let out and kept un-der watch in their separate herds, a kilometer or so away from the corral. There are enough people around (including chil-dren) to be able to do this. In the afternoon, the *nanne* groups leave with their animals.

There was a continual stream of visitors to the corral today—women and children as well as men—inspecting our animals and noting which of theirs are here (even if they can't take them away at the moment). Among them was Unni Issat [II], another Nestor among *njar'ga* owners. He'd come by 'bus, and he had his leg pulled mildly about his "driving" from the coast (punning on the verb *vuojat:* to drive a herd of animals). But he

was treated with respect and friendliness—he didn't even have to produce his own dried meat and coffee; and there was more joking: "Had he found any of his animals?" "Four or five." Then Ellon Ailu's wife, Karen, asks with deliberate innuendo: "a dark *aldo?*" No, Issat hadn't noticed such a one.

Work at the corral comes in starts and stops, and in the inter-vals information is being exchanged all the while. Nothing much about the migration itself—that seems to be routine: but specific questions and comments like "Lost any *her'gi* this year?" or, "I'm looking for a such-and-such calf." I suspect that these are also "routine" in a way, but are, nevertheless, necessary probes for herding information.

Some people are voicing strong dissatisfaction with the way in which the animals are handled in the corrals: Mothers be-come separated from their calves; there is no water (and, of course, no pasture); and animals shouldn't be left in crowded pens overnight. Some fear that these conditions will mean more *rodno;* others doubt that, saying that poor summer grazing is more responsible; yet others believe that putting animals through the corrals so close to the rut, and even during it, will mean not more *rodno* but more *gæssek*—calves born towards the beginning of the summer.

27 SEPTEMBER

Rain and mist last night, and we lost a number of bells—so it is unlikely that we will be able to bring the herd back to the corral before tomorrow, or this evening at the earliest.

Now the news is that Unni Issat's herd [II] is crossing the Kautokeino River these days and that Jovna Tommes's [III] is already across—without either of them coming through the corrals. So I'm filling in time this rainy day (while others are out herding) enquiring around the tents as to what people feel about those herds going straight to the autumn pastures (pastures which will be used later by others here).

No news of our male herd [V]; Migot is leading it.

28 SEPTEMBER

The Joakkonjar'ga herd [VII] is still out of sight. Ellon Ailu spends the day around his tent at the corral—he says it is the turn of others to get the herd back here. I think he sees part of the difficulty as too many herders (though they are all needed at some juncture) with too little coordination.

29 SEPTEMBER

Still rain and mist, and still there are bells missing: But what has been rounded up of the Joakkonjar'ga herd [VII] is being brought to the corral. Later in the day: trouble as the herd approaches the corral—undisciplined dogs. Eventually we get the animals inside the *vuorbmanak,* just before dusk. Will start on the separation in the morning.

Meanwhile, the male herd of Migot and Mattem Gaibme, Boaris Mikkel, and Ellon Ailu has arrived [V].[4] It is not brought to the corral but is being pastured a little to the southwest, where it is hoped that it may act as a lure to the missing bells that have thus far foiled all our efforts.

30 SEPTEMBER

Iskun Biera [VII[1]] is *vuoððo.* Other pens: Iskun Mikko and Iskun Iskun [VII[2]]; Migot and Mattem Gaibme, Boaris Mikkel, and Ellon Ailu [VII[3]]; and Bede [VI], who also "pulls" what-

ever animals there are from Spalca [XII]; and Danel Anti [XI]. Must be over two thousand animals in all—nevertheless, we are finished as dusk falls.

But then, most of our effort is undone: Iskun Biera lets out his herd and drives them into the wind—it seems they are safely away. Twenty minutes later the combined Migot and Mattem Gaibme–Boaris Mikkel and Ellon Ailu herd is released; then through the enveloping darkness we hear shouts and dogs barking—the two herds are mixed. Curses and curses. Despondency. At least the male herd [V] wasn't involved in this mess (they're still under watch).

1 OCTOBER

Sunday at Ellon Ailu's tent. Some of the now mixed-again Joakkonjar'ga herd crossed the Kautokeino River in the night—two of the Boaris Mikkel children sent to fetch them back (a rather vain gesture?). Other children sent to watch over the male herd. Otherwise a day of rest—defiantly so.

2 OCTOBER

Visitors! Two men from the Laggot *nanne* herd [X] who are upset that our male herd [V] wasn't brought into the corral on Saturday—they say they are sure they have animals in that herd and have been waiting for several days. One of them says that he actually tried to ring the reindeer police on Saturday but couldn't get through. Ellon Ailu, before he married, had been a herding partner of one of the two men and managed to soothe the visitors. He explained that the *luovas* had been kept away from the corral so as not to add to the pressure of an already large separation on Saturday. "We're not trying to hide animals," he assures them. "How could we . . . in this present flux?"

Afterwards, Ellon Ailu and I leave to visit Bede's camp—half an hour's walk. Ellon Ailu timed it so that we arrived when the animals were at rest. The women were milking. Ellon Ailu wanders carefully through the herd, making a close inspection. He spots a yearling with a Nuor'tabelli earmark. He knows its owner. He lassos the animal and hairmarks it: owner's initials on the left flank and his own (as finder) on the right flank. He does all this without saying anything to the Bede people; tells me that the hairmarks will help ensure the animal is not "lost" (i.e., stolen, perhaps slaughtered, though it is unlikely that Bede's people would do that). We wander over and chat with some of the Bede men—Bede's sons. Friendly. One of them sees a calf (with its mother) that he has been looking for: It is without earmarks but is hairmarked [owner's and finder's, as above]. He cuts his earmarks. This mother and calf were brought back to the camp just the other day.

Hairmarking a yearling.

We return to our camp before dark. The Boaris Mikkel children are back empty-handed from the east side of the river, and Iskun Biera and Migot have not gone across. This sets a problematic situation: There are animals on both sides of the river, and, in both cases, the herds are mixed. Ellon Ailu is anxious lest more animals cross—mixed and unherded. He would like to take all that are on this [west] side back to Corral One. On the other hand, perhaps we should wait until we hear from Migot or Iskun Biera about the situation on the east side of the river. He says that what he most of all wants to avoid is being on the east side for the next month or so with a large herd that is both mixed and has lots of *vierro boccu*. For that means a constant stream of visitors looking for their animals at the same time as one has to undertake separations. It becomes well nigh impossible in such conditions to establish and maintain a herding routine of one's own: something that he values highly.

When we went to sleep, nothing had been decided as to what we will do tomorrow.

Delay

In fact, we do not cross the river for another two weeks even though there is good pasture waiting for us, ahead of others, on the other side. There are several reasons for this delay. First, there is Ellon Ailu's point that the first priority must be to round up the animals that are dispersed on both sides of the river and bring them to Corral Two for separation into several autumn, perhaps winter, herds of manageable sizes.

Another reason is, "Nobody wants to leave the corrals until all the herds have been passed through them." Aside from animals of other age-classes that have become separated from their owners, of particular account here are the unmarked calves that are brought to the corrals; and many of these have become separated from their mothers—they are *ædnihis miessi*—placing their ownership in doubt. A special twist to this is that a disproportionate "share" of these calves is likely to remain in the vuoððo at each separation (and earmarked, or possibly hairmarked, accordingly)—unless, that is, other owners are present to reclaim their animals and acquire their share of ædnihis miessi.

Finally, to cross the river puts one out of reach of those buyers who come to the corrals with their mobile slaughter equipment (or who simply pile animals, alive, onboard a truck). Later in the year, when on the winter pastures, owners will move deer across the tundra to Kautokeino or Karasjok for on-the-hoof sales. But autumn sales are, as I have stressed, necessary too.

3 OCTOBER

Discussion continues. Suddenly, Ellon Ailu and I are off to Corral One on the chance that the *or'da* herd of Danel Anti [XI] has been brought there. I also have a feeling that Ellon Ailu had had enough of all this talk about what should and should not be done—and this is the escape.

We hitch a ride with a meat-buyer from Kautokeino who is hoping to do business in Corral One. There is no herd there, but a group of men waiting for it, including some Laggot *nanne* [X]—they think that the *or'da* herd is being kept up in the hills and "out of trouble" by its veteran herders. Ellon Ailu reckons that they—the *or'da* people—will have their hands full keeping their herd together and marking their own calves, so they'll have little time for illicit marking of others'. Nevertheless, he seems worried: "It's important to be at the corral when a herd like this arrives; indeed, it's best to see the herd before it's brought into the corral. We've learned that in the last years: avoids trouble at the corral." There's talk about some of us going up into the hills to the herd. I'm all for it. But not Ellon Ailu, who gets a lift back to camp with the buyer, who is returning to Kautokeino. I decide to stay to see what develops; nothing does. As he was leaving, the buyer asked one of the *nanne* men to be sure to ring him when the *or'da* herd does finally make the corral. The man agrees but was quite obviously worried lest that would be taken as binding him and others to sell. The buyer tries to assure him that it wouldn't.

4 OCTOBER

No sign of the herd. Men who arrived here from Corral Two say that a large part of the Joakkonjar'ga herd that was still on this side of the river, from the failed separation of 30 September, has now managed to cross the river. Ellon Ailu and two of Boaris Mikkel's daughters and also Iskun Biera himself have gone after them. They are not expected to return for some days.

5 OCTOBER

Yesterday's news confirmed by Migot who has turned up here [Corral One]. The animals escaped crossed the river at about the time he and Iskun Biera were on their way back, empty-handed, from the east side. The animals that are still on this side of the river are being put through Corral Two: Iskun Biera's animals [VII¹] are *vuoððo*. Migot left his brother at that separa-

tion [VII³ and VI] because he had heard that the *or'da* herd had come to the corral here. Iskun Mikko's and Iskun Iskun's joint herd [VII²] is still intact and on this side of the river.

Meanwhile I have decided to give up waiting here for the *or'da* herd. I'll visit Bede's camp tomorrow—Ellon Ailu often talks about Bede's herd management as "proper" (meaning, besides probity, traditional?).

6–8 OCTOBER

At Bede's camp over the weekend. Much talk (and, for me, instruction) about the considerations different owners have concerning the selection of animals for slaughter. I also begin to realize how important to many Saami are their views about reindeer meat and its proper treatment, and their objection to some current Norwegian-imposed practices [see Chapter 10].

9 OCTOBER

To Corral Two. Separation in progress between that part of Iskun Biera's herd that *is* separated [see 5 October] and the Iskun Mikko-Iskun Iskun herd; they mixed in the fog last night. Iskun Biera's new herdsboy "pulling" for him as Iskun Biera himself is on the other side of the river. Several of us "pulling" Migot and Mattem Gaibme, Boaris Mikkel, and Ellon Ailu [VII³].

A meat-buyer from Kautokeino doing cash business at the corral.

The separation completed in afternoon. I hitch a lorry up to the Bingis cabins, where I learn that Ellon Ailu had rung me on Saturday [7 October] from a house on the east side of the river: He was about to swim a herd back across the river, and I was to come at once!

10 OCTOBER

Rang the house from which Ellon Ailu had called me: was told that the herd is still over there, and Ellon Ailu is out in the terrain somewhere. Doesn't sound good. While I was deliberating what to do, a Norwegian-speaking meat-buyer from Alta stops at the cabins. He is new to the business of buying direct from the Saami and says that he has arranged to purchase tomorrow over one hundred animals from Laggot *nanne* [X]. He sets up his mobile slaughterhouse. I decide to stay for this, and will afterwards find my way back to Corral One and to Ellon Ailu's camp nearby.

11 OCTOBER

Fog with rain last night, and it continues that way today: naturally, no animals. Meat-buyer doesn't appreciate the difficulties

The Eggan Anti family moving to autumn camp.

(doesn't seem to have knowledge of them) but rather assumes that all herds are under watch and hence under control all the time! But he has a problem—his five slaughterers that he has brought with him from Alta are under contract at their own risk, not on a *per diem* basis.

I helped Eggan Anti and family [XI] to get ready for their move to their autumn camp in the hills to the southwest, where they will also fish, with nets, in Soadnjajav'ri. I'd have liked to join them, but I have to meet up with Ellon Ailu. Eggan Anti intends to visit the Oar'jebelli multiple corral as soon as his family is settled in their camp. His herd [with Danel Anti, XI] has not yet come to the corrals here. He rented a tractor (300 kroner) for the cross-country move.

In late afternoon I persuade the meat-buyer to drive me down to Corral Two. Surprise! Animals—but by no means all—*were* brought back from across the river, and the separation between Iskun Biera [VII²] and Migot and Mattem Gaibme–Boaris Mikkel and Ellon Ailu [VII³/V], and some other pens, is in full swing.

Hurriedly, I introduce the meat-buyer to Ellon Ailu. He is noncommittal—the buyer should come around to our camp this evening. The separation is completed without a hitch. The two herds under close watch and well apart.

Boaris Mikkel, this evening, is persuaded to slaughter tomorrow for the Alta meat-buyer, who will pay 4.60 kroner per kilogram. Afterwards, though, he remembers that he had promised to sell to another man—a well-known Kautokeino buyer who speaks Saami. Apparently, *he'd* only offered 4.50 per kilogram, but Boaris Mikkel believes that he could now get 4.60 from him. The discussion late into the evening on this matter didn't run in the Alta buyer's favor: Earlier in the day he had said to me he was offering 4.85.

12 OCTOBER

Rain. Nonetheless, Ellon Ailu and I hitch up to Corral One to be there should the *nanne* herd arrive. But they didn't turn up that day either. Ellon Ailu told the Alta buyer the deal with his father-in-law was not possible because the herd had dispersed.

Back at camp later in the day. The Kautokeino meat-buyer would have taken thirty animals from Boaris Mikkel, but (genuinely in this instance) foul weather brought this to nought. Ended up with Boaris Mikkel selling three lame *her'gi* whose combined weight was no more than one hundred and thirty kilograms. There is good rapport with this buyer, who gives cash on the spot without the meat first having to go through the official control, and this weighs heavily in his favor. He is driving a lorry-load of meat to Oslo this month.

Tomorrow we move camp to Hemmugiedde [on the west bank of the Kautokeino River], where Boaris Mikkel has a house, and Ellon Ailu says that we'll take the herd over the river at the first opportunity. In the dark and a drizzling rain, we lasso a number of *her'gi* (the herd is nearby) and tether them ready for tomorrow's move.

13 OCTOBER

Last night a whole lot of animals crossed the river again. This was not intended. Migot and Iskun Biera, once again, are going

The Mattem Gaibme family at camp,
12 October.

Boaris Mikkel's wife and younger children on
the move, 13 October.

after them. To find them: not to bring them back, I think. The
rest of us proceed with our move down to Hemmugiedde.

It is imperative that we take as many animals as possible with
us when we cross over the river. So tomorrow some of us are
going back to Bede's camp to collect our *vierro boccu* there—
Ellon Ailu made a note of them on our last visit. Because of
Bede's reputation for honesty, specifically in reindeer matters,

more than his share of *vierro boccu* are "pulled" into his pens at
separations for safekeeping.

Then, says Ellon Ailu, we'll cross the river with the herd, set
up a *lavvo,* and begin helping Migot and Iskun Biera to collect
the dispersed animals. Separation into autumn herds (using
sackcloth pens) will follow. These are the plans, at any rate.
They raise, not for the first time over these weeks, the question

of whether or not the Migot and Mattem Gaibme–Boaris Mikkel and Ellon Ailu unit stays together or splits into two: Boaris Mikkel and Ellon Ailu (father-in-law and son-in-law) as one, and Migot and Mattem Gaibme (brothers) as the other. Very delicate matter. There were similar discussions in the spring. Nothing is decided now, of course, nor was that the intention. My guess is that discussions will continue well into the autumn—the issue then becoming the arrangement of winter partners. Doubtless, Migot and Mattem Gaibme and their families are talking about it, too.

14 OCTOBER

All the men at Bede's camp are away when we arrive—some with their herd, others at the Oar'jebelli corral. Chat with Bede's wife in her tent while waiting for the herd to be brought to the camp for its rest period. We learn (or perhaps I was the only one who didn't know this) that Bede is going to stay on this side of the river for a while yet.

To work. Choose a dry place a little apart from the herd and to the lee of it; cut some birch branches for sticks and string our sacking around them: a simple pen. Boil coffee over our own fire by the pen while waiting for the Bede people to finish milking—Marit [one of the Boaris Mikkel unmarried daughters who accompanies us] thought this was shameful—*hæppat*. I'm not sure whether it was *our* behavior or, just possibly, the Bede people's behavior—not offering us coffee—that Marit found shameful. And I didn't ask!

Lasso the animals and then haul them over to the pen; no large animals among them. Marit looks after the pen. Three of us handle the animals [Ellon Ailu, Mattem Gaibme, and I]. While this is going on, Ellon Ailu marks a calf for one of the Boaris Mikkel boys and Mattem Gaibme one for his nephew— neither are *ædnihis miessi*: wholly legitimate markings, as far as I can tell. Boaris Mikkel himself appears with the main herd (good timing), bringing it close to the pen and windward of it. We open the pen and the animals, about fifty of them, rush into the herd. Presto! The operation went so smoothly that it seemed simple—actually, with the bells from the Bede herd well within earshot it was tricky: nicely executed. We herd very carefully on the way back to Hemmugiedde.

Much talk this evening about slaughtering now for domestic meat that would be consumed in the spring (salted and dried); and there's talk too about *her'gi* (already yesterday we used them for the move here). Which ones are still missing? Which *spailek* (castrated but not tamed) should one begin to train?

Ellon Ailu (perhaps because he has detected my bewilderment from time to time) explains that this year the animals were more wild *(hil'bat)* than usual. But is that true? The winds are constantly changing, he says (but they weren't last month); the

Milking at Bede's early autumn camp.

lichen beds are becoming trampled; the fog and the wet have added to our difficulties. The animals "know" there are wide marshes and lichen beds on the other side of the river. He also mentions the humiliation he feels when, at this time of year, herders from other camps come to collect their animals and "there are no animals at your camp—you don't even know where your own are."

The herd is going to be left unattended tonight. I am astonished but assured it won't move—not away from the river bank, for the terrain was overgrazed, and not across the river, for there was good pasture around the house. So, tomorrow *we* swim the animals across instead of trying (as we have been) to bring them back.

15 OCTOBER

Anticlimax (for me). The women say we *shouldn't* swim the herd over before Migot has returned with the other part. The animals are all around the house and in the meadow (they didn't wander). The women seem to like it that way. They plan to milk. One of the boys sent out to hinder a large part of the

A family caravan traversing wet terrain, 13 October.

herd which looked as though they were about to swim across. The discussion drags on. Suddenly (and finally, as it turns out), Ellon Ailu gets up from the kitchen table and tells us *he* is going to take the herd across and that his father-in-law (Boaris Mikkel) agrees to help him.

Action! Word sent over to Mattem Gaibme's house. The women do some quick milking.

Ellon Ailu leads *(laidestit)*—with a *her'gi*—the animals down to the water's edge, where Boaris Mikkel is waiting in a rowing boat. The herd begins to follow. Women and children shoo on stragglers. Watching us from a hilltop overlooking the river is the solitary figure of Bede. He gives no sign; nor we. It is almost dusk by the time all the animals are over on the far side. There, Boaris Mikkel slaughters an *ædnihis miessi*—which Ellon Ailu points out to him—and also a *vuonjal*. Some *her'gi* are secured, ready for tomorrow. We all row back in the dark.

Tomorrow we *have* to leave?

The Rut

On the way from the coast, bulls battle. Afterwards, the corral work "hides" the rut, so it is not until we are across the river that I am much aware of it again—but by that time it is near its end.

There are two recognizable phases. The rut begins with the senior bulls pitting their strength against each other. The vanquished are driven away, for the time being, and the victors are left, for a while, with a harem to service.[5] The herders, besides keeping the animals moving toward the destination they have chosen—for example, the corrals—take care to prevent younger bulls, her'gi, and calves that are momentarily separated from their mothers from wandering off on their own. Junior

The rut: above, rivalry; bottom, exhaustion.

bulls sometimes join the company of her'gi around the edges of the herd, away from the harems.

Before the fence-and-corral complex stamped its character on autumn herding, the rut was that season, above all others, when herders reacted in response to the signals passed between the animals. This was even true, to a remarkable extent, in respect to the composition of "a herd." The following account, from a man in his sixties, is really a recollection from a few years back:

Sarves fight until they find out which of them is the strongest. That animal we call the *aidna-valdo*—"the king," if you will. He keeps "his" herd together; so we speak of *sarves guoðohit čora*: "a small flock herded by a bull." He also keeps the fighting down, for the other bulls are fearful of him and keep away. His *čora* [small collection of reindeer] is *čokki:* "tightly herded"—and that's how we liked it to be during the rut. . . . But eventually the aidna-valdo tires, he loses control, and then his harem is likely to stray—go to a vuobme with their calves—or disperse—chased by several younger bulls. So we have to *guoðohit* [herd] too.

Today, the aidna-valdo is not so prominent. For one thing, there are so many senior bulls that evade castration that few can maintain dominance for very long. This is a reminder that the prominence of the aidna-valdo was, to a degree, an artifice of pastoral strategy. Second, most herds that I observed were being moved across the terrain during the first and dominant phase of the rut—and moved very much on the herders' timetable. Only a few of them spend time in a traditional rutting place *(raggat saggje)*—and by traditional, I also mean places that the bulls and cows "know."

The second and concluding phase of the rut, called *gip'poragad,* or *gip'porag-ai'ge,* is when the vuobis and varek take over. Cows are in usterus for forty-eight-hour periods until coitus results in conception. There are always some cows who are in usterus to the end of the rut, even though they mated earlier with senior bulls. Hence *gipragat,* the activity of gip'poragad. The junior bulls seem to have no firm order of dominance among themselves. This means that the cows are not "herded" but, instead, are likely to receive competing attention from several younger males. A graphic feature of gip'poragad is evasion by cows of this "mobbing," as they are chased

through the herd—calves, even, may try to mount their mothers. Gip'poragad is responsible for late calving, independent of the other factors I have already mentioned, and the progeny from unions with junior bulls are, I am informed, likely to be smaller.[6]

On coming out of usterus, a cow returns to its calf. Although a cow may well let her calf stay with her while she is in usterus, her milk supply will have dried up during usterus. It is now resumed.

The day after the herd had been swum over the Kautokeino River, I accompanied Ellon Ailu into the terrain on its east side. We had one her'gi as a pack animal, carrying our food and a canvas sheet for an improvised lavvo, and some blankets. Ellon Ailu had several things in mind: He wanted to find out where the animals that had been swum across the evening before were heading; if possible, to contact Migot, who would probably be in the terrain around Nappulsaiva; to assess the conditions of the pastures; and to consider where to locate a camp for the next month or two.

My original notes are densely packed with topographic detail, but I offer these edited extracts as an example of how I learned a little more about how these pastoralists move over the terrain and make sense of a situation that would, for others, have quickly reduced itself to a "blindman's bluff" (Fig. 4.4).

16 OCTOBER

We find about sixty deer on Gævlemaras and take them with us for the rest of the day: little trouble except at the beginning. Wouldn't have managed, though, without a dog. Ellon Ailu let some of the animals approach us—investigate us—before releasing his dog. This way the animals weren't frightened. The dog then helped to "teach" (Ellon Ailu's word) the animals the direction we wished them to move. At first they went around in circles, but once we got the "nose" of the herd moving, the rest followed.

Sixty animals is not a herd *(ællo)* but a *čora:* a small flock. Ellon Ailu explains that we will use this *čora* as a possible lure to help us find the herd, or rather the "edge" *(roawda)* of the herd. What we are doing is *čorastad'det.* At dusk, we leave the animals north of Vuordnasjav'ri, and Ellon Ailu expects we'll find them in the morning in the *vuobme* around Gallovarri. We spend the night in a turf cot at the north end of Vuordnasjav'ri.

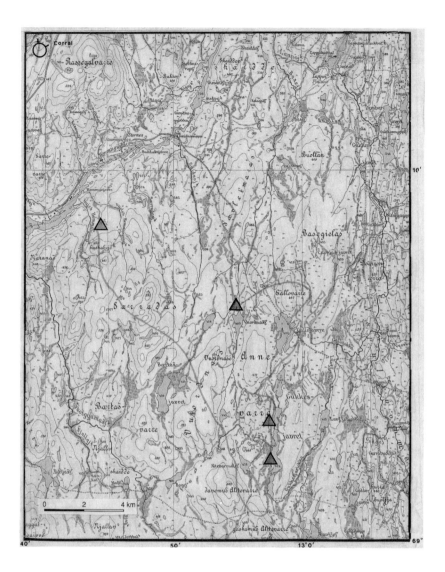

Figure 4.4 Journal map: 16–19 October

17 OCTOBER

Out at around 6 a.m. There had been an east wind during the night. The *čora* grazing in a *vuobme* northwest of Gallovarri has now become a small herd of two hundred. A south wind now. We move *doares biegga*—that is, to the side of the wind—in an easterly direction in the hope of locating an edge of the herd which may be somewhere between Nappulvuobme and Gukkesjav'ri; Ellon Ailu surmises that Migot may be on the far side of Nappulvuobme and working that edge westwards.

While there is a strong tendency among reindeer to move against the wind (moving into smell), there are occasions when the herder will want to move deer *doares biegga*—as we are doing—or even *with* the wind *(biegga mielde)* in order to reduce the risk of animals traveling so fast that contact is lost.

We walk to the top of Gallovarri; Ellon Ailu walks or moves

at a half-run from one hilltop to the next—impressing upon me that *that* is the way to look for animals *(varadat)*. Never use a dog, he says, when the deer are not in sight—for example, one might *suppose* that there are deer on the other side of a hill, but one can't *know* what's there or what situation may arise unless one can see. Indeed, one should be able to see the circumference of a herd before releasing a dog.

But today the visibility is poor, with overcast skies and drizzling rain: We see nothing. Boiled coffee, ate smoked meat. Moved around Gallovarri to within three kilometers of Nappulsaiva. Nothing. So we turn south along the east side of Gallojav'ri, herding, with the dog, all the time.

There are occasional *gip'poragad* dramas all day long: a cow perhaps followed by its calf, chased by half a dozen *vuobis* and *varek*, dashing through the herd. Ellon Ailu calls this group a *sarak-čora*. We have few *sarves* with us. The *her'gi* keep very much to themselves, often in the front of the herd.

An hour or so before dusk we are between Gallojav'ri and Gukkesjav'ri. Visibility still poor. Deciding what to do, Ellon Ailu draws me into consultation, as he has done before. I still find this remarkable but realize that it is "natural" behavior between herders *(sii'da guoibme)*—they always talk things over amongst themselves. I also believe, though, that some of the discussions among the family, in which an issue is turned over and over and over again, drives Ellon Ailu to distraction.

We now assume that there are no animals this side of Nappulsaiva. The poor visibility handicapped us, but we have several bells in the herd—including *her'gi* bells—and these would have attracted animals to us. Possibly, we agree, Migot has taken a herd west over to Særradas (between where we are at present and Hemmugiedde). Our decision is that we should make our way back there with the animals we have. Possibly tomorrow. We leave the herd on the southeast slope of Annevarri. It will move off the hill in the night, says Ellon Ailu, probably making for a nearby *vuobme.* Our night quarters is a turf cot alongside Gukkesjav'ri.

In the night I hear both a *her'gi* bell and an *aldo* bell, and a number of animals passing the cot in a southerly direction. I'm too tired, I don't wake Ellon Ailu, it doesn't seem necessary.

18 OCTOBER

Up at 5 a.m. We soon find the animals—much where Ellon Ailu predicted. We round them up (their number seems to be nearer three hundred now) and move them, using the dog all the while, to Gaskemus Altevarri, where they have a rest period. There are half a dozen *her'gi* bells missing. They are only followed at this time of year by other *her'gi* and *spailek,* but it is still serious enough. Ellon Ailu is slightly apprehensive lest these animals wander into Unni Issat's herd, which—going on the experience of previous years—will be somewhere to the south of us. So we have to fetch them—means taking the whole herd with us.

When we return to Gaskemus Altevarri we find Mattem Gaibme and Marit Kemi there. Coffee and meat. Talk. They left Hemmugiedde yesterday and were able to reckon roughly where we would be on account of the movement of the small flocks they saw, and later they heard *her'gi* bells. Together we will herd the animals back to the other side of Særradas. It is agreed that this means night-herding on the way there. Apparently the people left at Hemmugiedde are waiting word that "the herd" (!) is on the Særradas heights—then they will make camp there.

There is still only poor visibility, and much of the day is gone. A slight wind from the south means we have to move *with* the wind. The animals are reluctant at first, but we manage all right with so many of us and the dogs. We release the herd

for the night at a *vuobme,* perhaps a kilometer across, between lakes (Gukkesjav'ri and Altevarrejav'ri). I'm surprised at the choice. Ellon Ailu explains that it is suitable with a small herd such as we have, but we would be unable to hold a larger one there, we would have had to take it to a dry and open place such as Annevarri (a few kilometers on).

Ellon Ailu and I take the first night watch. It becomes a night of instruction for me:

"Only *daža* [non-Saami] suppose that reindeer rest at night and do not move. They move as much at night as during the day—especially if they hadn't pastured well during the day. They have 'night-sight' and can move as quickly as during the day: *Sarves* even continue the rut at night."

"At this time of year they have rest periods at dusk, in the middle of the night, and just before dawn. We usually herd in two watches between these rest periods, though sometimes we may herd only up to around midnight: *værkeguoðohit.* When we do that it is important to be out again before dawn breaks."

"During a rest period of the animals, one should remain in the lee of the herd so that one can hear the bells of any restless animals that may start moving off, probably into the wind. Then one has to run around the herd to stop them. Mustn't use a dog."

"If one has to move a herd at night, try to do so *with* the wind and in one direction. This minimizes the risk of dispersal. Should one have to change direction, find the 'nose' of the herd. That may not be at all easy at night, but not to do so will likely mean that different parts of the herd are left moving in separate directions."

"Reindeer are blinded by torchlight, and if the light is shone directly on them they may run straight at it—this can be dangerous, especially during the rut."

"One should bring the animals back to camp for the dawn rest period, and it is as well to return by the same route as was used on the way out, the previous evening. This way there is a chance to collect any animals that might have been left behind during the night, and stray animals, too, that may have been attracted by the spoor of the herd. Mothers and calves that have become separated are likely to wait for each other in this way."

Ellon Ailu stressed how more harm than good can be caused by inexperienced herders at night. This possibly explains some of the accidents of the past weeks and perhaps was a reason for *not* night-herding at times. We turn in around midnight. We don't wake Mattem Gaibme and Marit—*værkeguoðohit* after all.

19 OCTOBER

Ellon Ailu wakes us—he had visited the herd again at dawn. A *čora* without bells slipped away in the night. Mattem Gaibme and Marit go to bring it back—all the way to Gaskemus Altevarri.

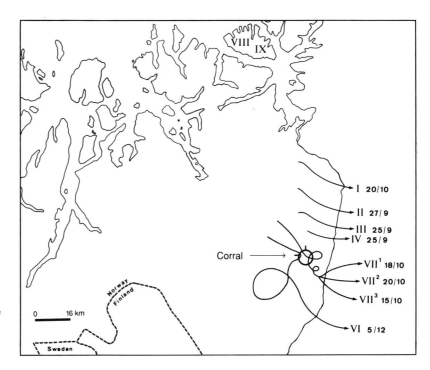

Figure 4.5 The njar'ga herds' crossing of the Kautokeino River. Herds VIII and IX move to the mainland in late autumn but do not cross the river

There is little wind, and the day turns out to be uneventful. Reach Særradas in the late afternoon. I leave the others there and reach Hemmugiedde one hour after dusk to report on what has been happening. Two of the Boaris Mikkel boys will go up to Særradas tomorrow.

Failure to Adapt? Adaptation?

"Things are so different now," says Bede:

We used to hold our herds closely herded, so we *all* had our own animals around us in the autumn camps. Of course, people were always visiting each others' camps to see which animals had strayed into which herd. . . . Sure, we would have to make a separation, but that would be between herds that had been together during the summer, and it would happen at a time and place chosen by both parties, either before or just after the rut.

Before those extra miles of fence were in place and before the multiple corrals were put up, the rut happened in specific places, and it was a notable time of close observation of one's animals—hence of important husbandry knowledge, too. Bede, and others, regret the changes that have overtaken them in this regard. Of the various shortcomings, perhaps the most grievous is the failure of what was intended by the multiple-pen corrals: a shortening of the time spent on separations. Similarly, the summer fences have led to less, not more, control over the herds.

Half of the njar'ga owners do not take their animals through the corrals: I, II, III, and IV (Fig. 4.5). (However, as noted in the journal, some old men from these herds are at the corrals, observing, and having some strays hairmarked for them.) One of these herds, Anti Biera's (I), is large, probably larger than Iskun Biera's (VII[1]), and perhaps the largest on Gow'dojottelit. When he crosses the Kautokeino River on 20 October, it is rumored that he has up to two thousand *strays* with him. I am surprised by the acceptance of these evasions of the corrals by those who *did* take their animals through. The explanation is: There were already too many animals in the vicinity of the corrals; these four herds (I, II, III, and IV) are the last to leave the summer pastures (it therefore follows that the strays they bring with them are the animals that got left behind from the herds that had moved earlier [e.g., V, VI, and VII]); and these animals will be retrieved later at separations on the autumn-winter grounds. Anxiety over nonappearance at the corrals, as we saw in the journal, is directed at the *or'da* herds. This is principally on account of strays (e.g., from VI and VII) ending up in Oar'jebelli herds. Even in this case, though, actual criticism is muted, and I think this is attributable in part to the respect for owners who still manage to keep their herds tightly herded through the rut.

Likewise, other herders approve of Bede and his family because their herd *is* passed through the corrals *and* held together. (Bede leaves the summer pastures in advance of all the other *njar'ga* herds.) Visits to Bede's camp gives me glimpses, I suppose, of pastoralism of a yesteryear: The animals pasture within boundaries set, more or less, by the herders who have a *lavvo* near at hand. During the rest periods, or some of them, the animals are brought to the camp. As one of the sons says, "These two streams [passing through the camp area] are a boundary which even children can understand, and everyone in camp knows that the animals must be kept between them." Earlier generations had used the same place. The women milk regularly. I am told that Unni Issat and Jovna Tommes (II and III), too, have "traditional" autumn camps and regulated pasturing and herding—but on the other side of the river. Anti Biera, by contrast, leaves the summer pastures long after the others, keeping his herd on the move through the rut. He "moves and pastures and reassembles, moves and pastures and reassembles—all the way to his autumnal pastures on the other side of the river," says Migot. While an arduous routine—and an innovative one as well—for the herders, it is one to which the animals adapt easily, especially the cows, although there is a higher than usual risk of losing bulls along the way.

Concerning the situation in which herders found themselves at the corrals, there are sentiments of regret and frustration and impotence. The summer fences and corrals in combination are an example of a constraint put upon a herd by herders turning into a constraint placed on the herders themselves. One of the milder verdicts

was, "A lot of work has to be repeated, perhaps several times." One consequence often voiced is that "it is useless to herd early in the autumn because herds become mixed later anyway" (this makes Anti Biera's routine all the more interesting). Perhaps the same point can be usefully put in terms of an emerging discrepancy between *size* and *scale*. The fenced-in herds, and the corrals to which they are to proceed, are enormous compared to all that was previous, and the scale of authority structure among the pastoralists appears quite inadequate in this situation.

Already in these first years of the use of corrals, pastoralists have different perceptions of the corrals. I think, for all, they are a new meeting place that they value despite the deplorable aspects. More significantly, I noticed a generational difference. For the young men, unlike their elders, work at the corrals has an ambience of *tournament*. Beyond the simple opportunities that corral work offers to demonstrate physical prowess, there is the competitiveness centered on the acquisition of unmarked calves that are without their mothers. The competition is over who can mark the most to themselves. I remember vividly, at the end of a frenetic day at the corrals, the sharp dressing-down that Margarethe, the wife of Boaris Mikkel, gave a teenage son of hers who, the moment before, had been impressing (successfully) his younger sister with an account of his prowess in marking to himself an unmarked ædnihis miessi. Margarethe was shocked, and very anxious: "What if that calf *found* its mother and the mother belonged to so-and-so—and the calf now carries your mark?" Sometimes, a "motherless" calf would be intentionally separated from its mother while both were at the corral. Obviously, to mark such a calf to oneself was particularly dangerous or foolish; so it would be hair-marked, the message being, "I, whose initials this calf now carries, found it without a mother and without any marks of ownership, and if it remains motherless, I claim it." Calves claimed in this way were then pushed into the pen of this de facto owner.

5.
The Dark
and
the Peace

Dal've: October–April

As October passes into November, autumn *(čak'ča)* changes into winter *(dal've),* but there is no sudden metamorphosis. Rather, both seasons are present for a while, and one hears the phrase *čak'ča-dal've.* Stretching beyond this intermediate period and into January is the period of winter that the Saami know as *skabma-ai'ge* (or *skabma-dal've),* the time of darkness. Not only are the days now the shortest in the year, from around the end of November to the middle of January the sun is below the horizon— but also, snowfall is heaviest.

The short daylight hours notwithstanding, much activity is pushed into this first part of winter. The principal business is reconstituting herds from the autumn and then, during the last days of December, separating into the smaller camps and herds of the later and longer period of winter. So there will be men, and some women, away on a round of visits to other herds, and every camp receives its visitors. There will be many deer separations, all handled without recourse to the big corrals.

We no longer sleep out on the open ground but within the shelter of a tent; the winter clothing of reindeer hair is donned; her'gi are no longer used as pack animals but now pull sleds. Dominance within the herd passes from the post-rut, and now antlerless, bulls to the cows who retain their antlers until after calving.[1] Then there are the shifts in the herders' technical conversations. Early in October, these were peppered with topographical references incorporating *biew'la,* the term for "bare of snow," but as November approaches, one begins to hear the extensive vocabulary for snow *(muotta).* With snow cover the animals *ruw'galit,* that is, leave the herd one behind the other, in single file. As long as the terrain was bare of snow they were more likely to *bieð'ganit,* that is, leave bunched together or in a broad phalanx.

Of the wealth of snow-related terms, I learned to use only a few, but I heard dozens. Not only does snow put new dimensions on the physical landscape, it affects relations between the animals, between them and their herders, and, in consequence, between the pastoralists themselves. Snow cover carries evidence of recent and prevailing wind and weather conditions. It is "read" for clues to the movement of a herd or the whereabouts of animals that have strayed. Snow surface is a factor controlling the mobility of animals and men and, particularly

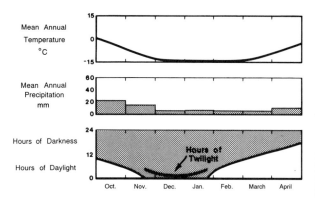

Figure 5.1 Climate: October–April. From Hansen 1960

serious, of their relative mobility one to the other. Perhaps most important of all, reindeer have to dig through snow to reach the lichen beds, so the condition and depth of snow affects, quite directly and at all times, the physical well-being of the animals. Of course, the precise significance of snow changes, crucially, as the landscape changes topographically and calendrically.

In this early period of winter, then, the pace of things has not slackened much from autumn. But by January, or before, that changes, too. The landscape is under a thick blanket of snow, and the temperature stays well below freezing: Winter literally envelops the pastoralists and their animals. The area over which a herd pastures shrinks as the animals spend more time, and burn more energy, digging through to their food supply. They stay closer together. Likewise with the herders: Now in their smaller winter camps with, at last, their own animals, the Saami know the months of deep winter (January to March) as *rafes-ai'ge,* time of peace.

The peace may be threatened, however. There is always the possibility of a diminishing food supply or one that the animals cannot reach at all. There have been years of catastrophe. This in strong contrast to the summer and autumn, when animals wander freely, savoring the variety of grasses and fungi. Otherwise, though, and ordinarily, the daily problems of herding during deep winter are minimal. So, time is given to essential undertakings beyond the routines of herding, undertakings of very different kinds.

For one, owners take stock of their herds. Small num-

Winter reindeer clothing—overcoat, gloves, leggings, moccasins.

bers of animals—up to a couple of hundred, say, among several owners—will be herded across the tundra to be sold on-the-hoof in Kautokeino, perhaps in Karasjok. And it is especially now that families butcher and prepare meat for domestic consumption through the spring and summer. Since autumn, families have mostly been eating meat boiled fresh or smoked. Those with poorer economies may have sold some of the better joints and delicacies (marrow bones, tongues, and the like). The blood is never wasted, but cooked in a gruel for the dogs. The meat now being prepared for the spring, however, is salted, hung, and dried. This is *giðða-nieste,* the staple that herders will have with them in their rucksacks. Because it is dried, it is especially important that this meat is taken from a fat animal. Indeed, some owners make a point of taking a young female. Others, who could afford to butcher a young female but perhaps take a young bull instead, will be ridiculed behind their backs.

In stark contrast to the toil of the "dark" winter, now is the time for social visiting and courtship. By April we are in *giðða-dal've,* the spring of the winter, and as many who are able leave their camps and herds to spend a few days in the church villages of Kautokeino or Masi for weddings and baptisms (usually at Easter);[2] drinking; and *joiking,* a Saami balladry. Then there are the preparations for the spring migration. Families who shared herd and camp through the winter may each be going to their own spring camp. If so, their animals must be separated. Soon afterwards, in the case of many family herds, bulls will be separated from the cows.

The Dark: November–December

As far as Bede was concerned, the departure of herds to the east side of the river vacated pasture for his own herd. For in line with traditional practice, Bede intended spending all of October and November on the west side. However, there was muted criticism from other voices: Ellon Ailu and some others crossed over as early as they did to draw advantage from the broad acres of fresh pasturage. Further, I was told, there would be less need to herd over there, and in crossing the river, owners effectively withdrew their labor from the corrals, even though there would certainly be a number of their animals passing through them. It was against the strong element of truth in these suggestions that I tried during that late autumn and early winter to understand what Ellon Ailu and his companions were about.

Ellon Ailu acknowledged the "charges," if we're to call them that, and responded. Certainly, there is an advantage in being early (on a pasture), but that is in the nature of pastoralism as he understood it, and I think all the Kautokeino pastoralists would agree. The question is, rather, what damage is done to others in forwarding one's own interests? There is a strong quid pro quo strain running through this culture, and Ellon Ailu has a keen sense of what constitutes "trespassing," both morally and prag-

matically. He had no intent to trespass on the rights of others, nor did he believe he was doing so.

This brings us to the issue of herding, or its absence. There would be trespass if the animals ruined a pasture—made it *doldi* by trampling or repeated cropping—that was going to be later used by others. The more extensive the pasturing, the less depletion or damage would incur. In short, it was in the interests of those whose herds were to follow that Ellon Ailu practiced open-range pasturing. At the same time, his animals would benefit, too. But, as I will explain, it did, paradoxically, tax the herders. However, that "cost" was one they thought worth paying.

Between herders on either side of the river there was, in fact, an interdependence, an indirect, even unintentional, cooperation. For it was not simply at the corrals that strays swelled herd numbers, they were also crossing the river all the time. By November there were over one thousand among the still unseparated Joakkonjar'ga animals on the east side of the river. This amounts to a not inconsiderable burden for the herders, from whose presence the others, still on the west side, were likely to derive benefit.

Through November, as anticipated, and December as well, Ellon Ailu and his parents-in-law had two family tents on Særradas. Within handy reach of Hemmugiedde and a commanding view out over the terrain, its dry, open, sloping spaces also lent themselves to the recurring tasks of husbandry.

Ideally, the deer were to be left to pasture lightly over a wide area. (Incidentally, an additional advantage in this for the herders who would follow was that the mushrooms and other fungi would be effectively culled so that their animals would have less cause to disperse.) However, there was constant apprehension lest the southeasterly winds—the same that accompanied the animals from the coast—would attract them further and further south, even to the boundary with Finland, where they would be stopped by a reindeer fence. Indeed, some flocks did go that far and had to be retrieved much later in the winter. And from other directions, other herds were moving into the terrain. So some constraints had to be put upon the movement of the Joakkonjar'ga herd, not least so that the factor of *incoming* strays did not get wholly out of control.

Every effort was made (without a fence) to keep the

herd within an area of approximately ten square kilometers to the south of Hemmugiedde and west of Nappulsaiva. Paying scrupulous attention to changing wind directions to draw every advantage from them, the idea, by no means always fulfilled, was to have the animals move over the wide pastures in large circuits fanning out from the camp (Fig. 5.2). Most times, by this arrangement, the animals pastured against the wind (or alongside the wind: doares biegga); but if the wind did not change for some days and the animals continued to move in that same direction, it became necessary to turn them around and herd *with* the wind to complete the circuit.

Although changes in wind could often be worked by the herders to their advantage, other vagaries in the weather could not. There were still days of thaw and of rain interspersed between days of frost and snow. Besides making animals restless (sodden resting places), such weather raised the herders' apprehension, for it is in these conditions that ice forms over the lichen beds.

The ideal situation is when snow falls quickly, layer upon layer, without periods of thaw and in the absence of much wind, leaving dry and light snow. In these circumstances, there can be successive pasturing of the same terrain, but to do that in conditions of wet snow that subsequently freezes is likely to ruin the pasture, scouring it with snow crusts. Conditions can change dramatically from one year to the next. It is left to the herder to adapt.

In the first few days of snow, or more correctly, the first centimeters, the deer are little affected. The smells of the landscape are not entirely shut off by the thin snow cover. In all probability, though, the herder finds himself less mobile than he would wish, with insufficient snow for easy traction of skis and sleds. Rain or thaw compounds his situation: slush. However, one advantage of snow is that the animals leave more easily discernible trails in it. But this is not always the case. Wind or fresh snowfalls can speedily obliterate all traces—all surface traces, I should say. A herder will sometimes get down on his knees to carefully brush aside new, powdery snow to reveal a spoor. And the spoor will be "read." Another advantage of snow cover is that it becomes much easier to lead (laidestit) reindeer across the terrain: using a her'gi and bell, one person (the *laidestæggje*) may well be able to

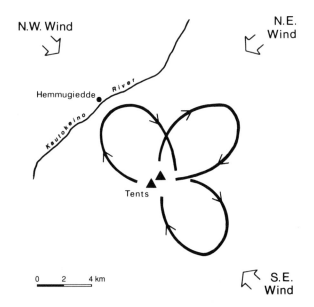

Figure 5.2 *Skabma ai'ge* circuit

manage, where several would be required without snow cover.

Besides close-up visual clues such as trails in the snow, herders in the darkened landscape are particularly dependent on *sound* clues as to the whereabouts of their animals, and on one sound in particular: the plaintive calling of calves *(ruw'ga)* as they follow their mothers, especially when they slip away from the herd. Quite indispensable at this season is, of course, the herder's knowledge of both the terrain and the way reindeer are likely to use it. So often a herder *knows* where animals that he cannot see but can hear are going. Returning out of the darkness into the herders' tent, he'll drop the comment, "Boccu ruw'galit jæg'ge-raige/joga-raige/jav'ri-raige/mielde" ("the animals are going to the marsh/river/wood/ lake")—and they may wander for miles along a river course if not stopped.

Ordinarily, the deer will pasture slowly into the wind, feeding in craters they dig with their forefeet in the snow. Ordinarily, as I have said, when they move away it is in single file (economy of effort?). Only the coldest of weather with strong winds will cause them to bunch together for shelter, and then, if they have to move, it may be *with* the wind. As the snow depth increases so animals

Cratering.

spend more time "cratering" through it, one observes the advantage her antlers bestow on the cow over the bull—she uses them to possess such craters as she wishes.

As long as they can reach the buried lichens, the animals now wander less; likewise, herding circuits are shorter. The animals' pasturing becomes more intensive. All the while, darkness is stealing what had been daylight hours. If an indifferent matter for reindeer (I think it is), for the pastoralist it means fewer hours for many of their herding and husbandry tasks.

The retrieval of animals and separation of herds are recurring tasks through November and December (fortunately, snow cover makes it all easier). Retrieval is a different matter from separation. There are various time-honored methods, depending on the number of deer involved. Several dozen or so animals can be handled using a portable pen of sackcloth (see journal entry for 14 October and photographs). The animals are pulled into the pen; in winter, their forefeet loosely tied together, they may be dragged—that is, slid—over the snow to the

pen. It is also considerably easier in winter to control the animals after their release from the pen, even if one's own herd is not nearby for them to join.

Small parties of two or three persons will travel with her'gi and sleds—loaded with provisions, tent, and their portable pen—collecting animals from a number of different herds. As the days go by, they expect to have more and more animals with them before finally returning to their own herd and camp. The process whereby more animals are added each day is simple enough, but it does call for exact timing.

Just before the pen is opened, one of the party sets off with his bell-her'gi (he will either be on skis and pulled along by the her'gi or, more often, he will drive the her'gi from a sled). The her'gi must move fast and into the wind. Others follow behind, using their dogs to bring back into the flock any animals that may try to double back or take off in some direction of their own (Fig. 5.3). Speed is so important during the first moments after release because of the counter-attraction of the scent from

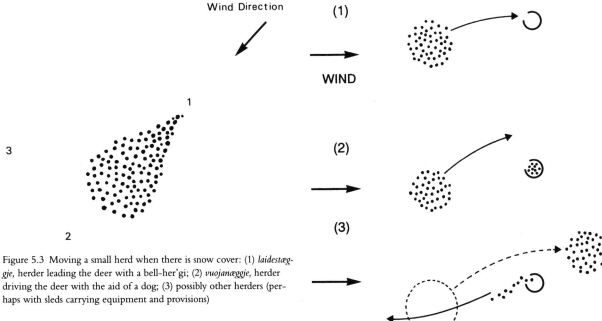

Figure 5.3 Moving a small herd when there is snow cover: (1) *laidestæg-gje,* herder leading the deer with a bell-her'gi; (2) *vuojanæggje,* herder driving the deer with the aid of a dog; (3) possibly other herders (perhaps with sleds carrying equipment and provisions)

Figure 5.4 Extraction of deer from a herd in winter: (1) animals transferred from herd to small, sackcloth pen; (2) herd moved to leeward of pen as soon as extraction is completed; (3) animals in pen freed into the wind, led away by herder with a bell-her'gi

the hosts' herd. To help matters, the herd is moved to the lee of the pen before it is opened (Fig. 5.4).

My journal entries for these months record sii'da members journeying to Nuor'tabelli and Oar'jebelli, as well as to neighboring herds. There was always someone away, perhaps for as long as a week. All the while our own herd—gradually being reconstituted—was under watch, and visitors *(guos'sek),* looking for their own animals, were received.

At various places over the winter pastures, there are also stationary pens (wooden constructions primarily), just as there are pens in the summer and autumn grounds for calf-marking, principally. One finds these carefully placed in the terrain where control over herds will be optimal: in the winter, say, on an isthmus in a chain of frozen lakes and, perhaps, at a place equally convenient for several camps (Fig. 5.5).

When it is a matter of retrieving just a couple or so animals from a herd, the pen can be dispensed with. Instead, one simply lassos the animals and binds their legs. After the host herd has been moved away, the bound animals are released, either joining the visitors' flock or fastened behind one of their sleds. This method is an occasional feature of all seasons.

I use the phrases "hosts' herd" and "visitors' flock" to depict the cultural context in which all these operations occur. (As noted, those who come to take animals are known as guos'sek.) The concern is with strays, and as that affects all herds and camps, there is mutuality. More important than that, however, herders are retrieving their property. So there are courtesies—drinking coffee together—and there is work cooperation. The hosts bring their herd close to the visitors' pen, they move to leeward on completion of the operation, and there is no obstruction. The visitors walk freely among the hosts' herd (the animals will be at rest), lassoing and removing individual animals. The hosts may watch closely to see that none of their own animals (most unlikely) or others, belonging to their kin or network of partners in neighboring camps, are removed. Sometimes a work party traveling from one herd to another will be made up of persons from different camps.

There will be delays that add days to the journey. Perhaps those who are visited do not, at that moment, have their herd together, and the visitors' work party may join

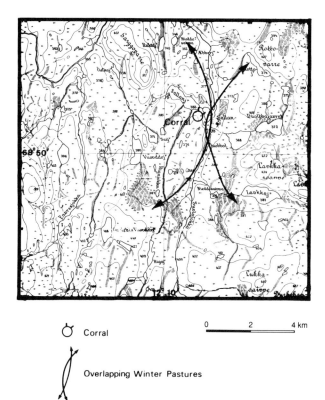

○ Corral

Overlapping Winter Pastures

Figure 5.5 Placing of a small winter corral

0   2   4 km

in the work. And always, there is the weather. These are contexts in which fellowship is as likely to be extended as any hostility (host and visiting herders may share the same tent), and inevitably, there will be a flow of information.

Thus far I have been describing *extraction* of animals from a herd, not the *separation* of herds. We saw how, in the autumn, large corrals, a recent innovation in Kautokeino, are used for separation (and the traditional pen is incorporated as a component). However, the traditional method of separating herds *without* any corral is still in use, particularly at the beginning and end of winter. Laborious and slow though it may be, by this process the animals are spared the deprivations of the procedure at the corrals. Also, parties to the separation work more interdependently than ever is the case at the large corrals. However, whereas the corrals allow for the separation of a mixed herd into several parts, this traditional mode separates a herd into two parts only. Where there are several

parties involved, several separations are necessary.

There are two phases to the operation (Fig. 5.6). In Phase 1, the party with the fewer animals in the mixed herd *(sær've-ællo)* begin. Working from the perimeter of the herd, they push and prod and "shoo" their own animals into the center of the herd. After a while they beckon the other party to come and take away their animals that are there along the herd perimeter. This process is continued until the balance in the number of animals remaining in the mixed herd turns in favor of the first party. The roles are now reversed. The first party rests, the other clears the perimeter of *its* animals.

Phase 2 begins when the size of what remains of the mixed herd is about the same as that of the smaller of the two separated herds *(čiel'ga-ællo)*. Animals belonging to neither of the two parties—that is, vierro boccu—will still be in the mixed herd, and they may constitute a good proportion of it. So the two parties who are separating their deer from each other now separately begin coaxing their own animals to opposite ends of what is left of the mixed herd and over to one or the other of the separated herds. Sometimes, the last few animals will be lassoed, tied, and dragged to its owner's herd. At this stage, each party helps the work of the other, even as each posts "sentries" to stop any of their animals going into the others' herd (as with sentries in front of the pens in corral separations). Eventually, there are only the vierro boccu. These may be left behind in the terrain as an unwelcome burden. Or they may join either or both of the separated herds (unmarked calves are likely to be taken along).

As is the case in the corral separations, the party with fewer animals in the mixed herd does more work—considerably more if the difference in the number of animals is marked. However, here neither party is vuoððo, and whoever has the larger herd does not necessarily draw any advantage concerning vierro boccu.

The work is such that there will be much shouting and cussing, but all are aware how essential it is that the animals are not unduly frightened, for then the herders' control can slip away. In particular, the use of dogs in the work must be most circumspect. Such is not always the case, of course, and much work must be redone.

In all its aspects, the work is easier with snow cover for

Phase 1
al'go-rat'ke

sær've-ællo

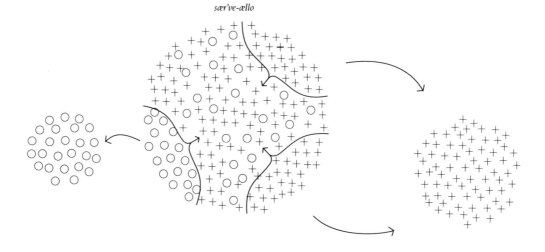

Phase 2
čuol'de-rat'ke

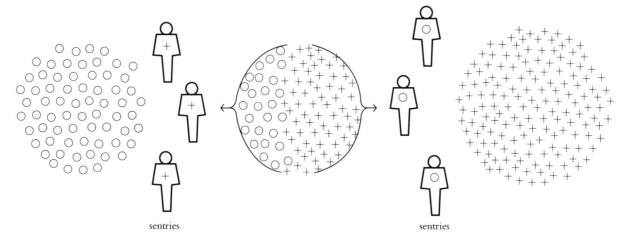

sentries

sentries

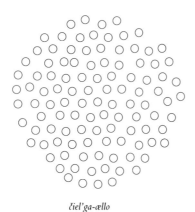

čiel'ga-ællo

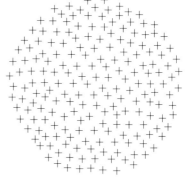

čiel'ga-ællo

Figure 5.6 Separation without corral.

Moving onto late winter pastures with a bell-*her'gi* on rein behind the sled.

reasons that are, by now, familiar. One chooses an open, flat, dry, and roomy site. A place that is already known to the deer is also an advantage. And one prays for a day without wind and the distracting scent of other deer or vegetation that it might bring. Careful consideration, along much the same lines, has to be given, as well, to the places where one takes the separated herds. The frozen surface of lakes and rivers is often favored.

It is not at all unusual for these separations to take several days.[3]

The Peace: January–April

Usually by early January the now divided herds of the Joakkonjar'ga summer group are in the southeastern corner of the Kautokeino winter range. To the east lies Karasjok winter pasture (without a fence marking the boundary), while all along the southern perimeter is the border with Finland and a reindeer fence. It is a low, undulating area, in contrast to the mountains of the coast. My dominant winter impression is that of wide expanses of birch and willow scrub, a monotonous landscape, broken occasionally by rounded hills. In the summer, there are myriad lakes, streams, and bogs whose waters drain into the northward-flowing tributaries of the Kautokeino

River or the Karasjok River. The summer heat can be excessive, with swarms of flies and mosquitoes; over much of the landscape is a thick carpet of lichen. But now, in January, the snow flattens the landscape still more, so that there are few natural boundaries between the many herds spread across its hundreds of square kilometers. The rich vegetation of the marshes, of the kind to which the reindeer were drawn throughout the autumn and even early winter, are buried under deep snow. The animals now feed exclusively on the lichen beds wherever accessible. In exceptional winters, when the reindeer cannot reach the lichen, they will have to browse, as best they can, on what standing vegetation there is: dwarf birch and hanging moss especially.

Whereas summer herds are large aggregations on physically separated pastures, on this winter terrain herds are smaller (so there are more of them), and pastures constitute an *overlapping* quilt (compare Figs. 3.2 and 5.7). The absence of physical obstacles means that animals could wander of their own accord from one end to another of the total Kautokeino winter range. That herds, by and large, stay put on "their" pastures is attributable, first and foremost, to the natural attraction each pasture holds for the animals. In years of hunger, however, animals will want to wander. The total pattern amounts to a fairly eq-

Feeding on lichen beds.

uitable spatial distribution of herds across the total area. True, there is a tendency towards overcrowding in areas closest to Kautokeino and a corresponding under-utilization of pastures farthest away from the village. But taken as a whole, the characteristic condition is one of separated herds pasturing separately without commotion, often in near proximity to each other.

Of course this would not happen, let alone be sustained, without the intervention of herders. But that, in turn, would be worth little without up-to-date knowledge of local changes in climatic conditions: temperatures, wind force, depths of snow. To complete this necessary knowledge, the herder needs a case-history of how the snow fell during the preceding months or weeks. All may augur well, or the indications may be such that he devises possible alternative pasturing strategies with his fellows. So, as in summer, one is safest where pasture is ecologically varied *(suoitce)*, even on a micro scale. Thus Boaris Mikkel stressed the importance of being able to

move locally between vuobme and open tundra (Fig. 5.8). In the vuobme, snow is less likely to become tightly packed than it is on the windswept tundra; however, it often becomes too deep, especially for the younger deer. It is then that one might take the herd to pasture on the open tundra, but the viability of that move will depend on several natural factors, one of which is that the sun of late winter may "bake" a snow crust on the exposed slopes. Perhaps by that time, though, the depth of snow in the vuobme will be reduced anyway.

In short, one looks to trace a viable path between changing alternatives. These also affect the balance of mobility between deer, dog, and herder. In the vuobme, the deer are at an advantage, so much so that they are "not afraid" of the herders' dogs; whereas out on the open tundra, reindeer are more likely than dogs or herders on skis to break through the snow crust, losing mobility and speed. Inasmuch as the deer are herded, they are deprived of a measure of their freedom to ex-

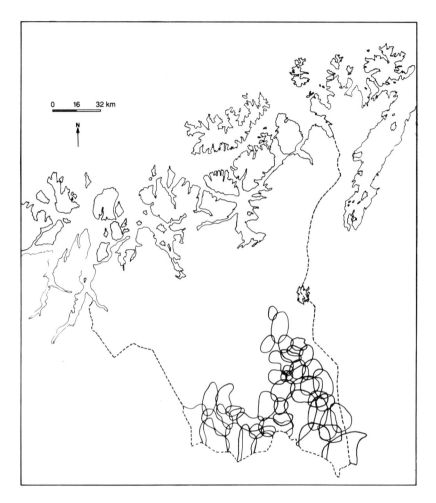

Figure 5.7 Winter pastures

plore and find pasture, and it is left to the herder to compensate for this constraint he has imposed. Using his ski staff he will, when necessary, test the depth of snow, the strength of a crust. Exceptionally, he may dig some craters, and when access to lichen is impossible, he will cut foliage and pull down hanging moss for his animals.

I now draw from my journal two days on the winter pasture of Boaris Mikkel with Ellon Ailu, his son-in-law, whose joint herd is a separate unit for this period of the winter. Between these two entries, the activity pattern has changed slightly but significantly.

8 FEBRUARY

The third day at the *lavvo*, and I think our last [others will take our place]. We are northwest of the cabin on the far side of the *vuobme* and the lakes. That is, somewhat further to the north-west than ordinarily, as a signal to Iskun Biera. If we hadn't moved, reasons Ellon Ailu, then Iskun Biera's herd would encroach. The safe supposition is that Iskun Biera doesn't wish to mix herds, therefore he will see that his animals don't encroach. I enquired about the wind. What wind there is, is from the south. But Ellon Ailu reminds me that at this time of year it is not much of a factor. In those first days of snow cover, before Christmas, one wouldn't be able to hold one's own against a herd moving into the wind; but that's no longer the case.

However, Ellon Ailu also tells me of an incident two winters ago when Unni Issat's herd [II in Fig. 4.2] had come too close. Despite Ellon Ailu's protestations, Unni Issat did not move away, and the two herds mixed at night—a week's work to get them separated again. I'm not sure what this means. Did Unni Issat *want* to mix herds? (Ellon Ailu shrugs.) And can one, then, be sure about what Iskun Biera is up to? (Another shrug.)

At any rate, our routine [Ellon Ailu; Boaris Mikkel's daughter, Marit; and I] has been to ski around the herd—Marit start-

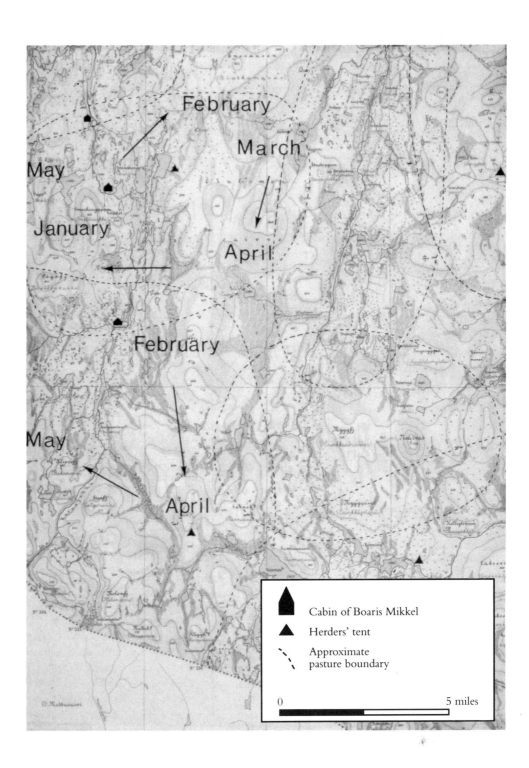

Figure 5.8 Winter
pastures of Boaris
Mikkel and
neighboring herds

Lavvo and herd.

ing off in one direction, Ellon Ailu and I in another. More ac-curately, it is not around the animals themselves but around the areas of trampled snow *(fieskes)*. This tells us where the animals have been during the night. So we are looking for trails of any that may have wandered off (the key phrase is *algus fieskes manat,* "to move outside the trampled pasture") and of others that may have wandered in.

However, stable temperatures and easy access to lichen beds have meant that only a few have strayed down to the *vuobme* immediately to our west—we use the dogs to bring them back.

The herd is pasturing peacefully. Nevertheless, Ellon Ailu (perhaps more because I am writing things down than on ac-count of Iskun Biera) insists on the need, even in these present circumstances, of always completing the herding circuit twice: to double-check. We bring the herd to the *lavvo* for its middle-of-the-day *liv-ai'ge.* This is the convenient time and place to slaughter and butcher a carcass, and to make fast any *her'gi* that one thinks will be needed (perhaps by the people back at the cabin). If the snow is deep and loose, one may make the circuit by *her'gi*-pulled sled, and we did this when moving the herd from one location to another. One experienced herder alone can just about manage these tasks in the quiet of winter, but he must have a dog to help him. Most likely, he alone will not "lead" but "drive" a herd from behind, with his dog taking care of the sides of the herd.

Daylight hours are short, although they are becoming longer. In twilight hours we collect wood. Lots of it. It's snug in the *lavvo* even though Ellon Ailu chides, "One shouldn't be too comfortable," for then the herder becomes lazy and doesn't show his nose outside the tent. Today, though, we moved the *lavvo* (not the herd) to an area of new wood supply. It's especially important in the case of a relocated *lavvo* to bring the herd, at one of its rest periods, right up to it, as we did. Two reasons: familiarizes and tames the deer; the herd tramples the snow around the *lavvo* for us, making it much easier to move around. Of course our drinking (and cooking) water—melted snow—is now "urinated" by the animals, but nobody seems to mind.

Ellon Ailu talks about pasturing for the rest of the winter. Quite straightforward. He hopes to keep along the slopes of the hill formation just to our southeast through March and April. He will be somewhat concerned about mixing with the Nuor'tabelli animals to the east—especially if there is either an east or west wind. Some of the deer *always* wander around there, attracted by the *vuobme* and *joga-rai'ge* (river course) of Bavtajokka. But he seems confident about it. Then in May, or just prior to leaving the winter pastures, the plan is, he says, to pasture back close to where they began in the New Year: near the cabin for convenience, and there won't be too much snow in that lower ground by that time.

At rest around the winter pasture cabin.

I also learn the nice point that another reason (aside from the possibility of mixing herds) for not wanting another herd even temporarily on the pasture that we are using is the difficulty it makes for reading trails. After a snowfall it becomes extremely difficult to distinguish old and new trails: "Are they from our own deer or theirs?" This consideration encourages some herders to pasture, first of all, around the perimeter of an area. That is exactly what Iskun Biera did in the middle of the 1950s, when Boaris Mikkel first came to this area. Iskun Biera was here before Boaris Mikkel.

23 MARCH

At the cabin at Buolčajav'ri. I've returned from a visit among Oar'jebelli herds, where there is more snow and less wind, primarily on account of the undulating and wooded terrain. So the snow is deep right through to the spring. This means one can't pasture the same place twice, as one does here. Indeed, animals succumb more easily to exhaustion, ending perhaps in starvation, especially the calves and yearlings. Not uncommon for Oar'jebelli herders to cut foliage and pull down hanging moss. On the other hand, the danger of icing (wind and sun induced) is far greater over here. I started telling Ellon Ailu my "discoveries"—as though he didn't already know!

Here our herding situation has become more relaxed. The youngsters (Boaris Mikkel's children) do most of the herding. They would like to use the *lavvo,* away from adult supervision, but this is discouraged. Instead, they are sent off each day to bring back the herd to the cabin here, in time for the midday rest. The youngsters are questioned closely about where they find the herd, and about trails—particularly whether there

were signs of neighboring herds having pastured near ours.

Actually, attention now seems to be less focused on herding and more on the selection of animals for on-the-hoof sales to Karasjok and for domestic slaughter here. Some joints are being smoked in a *lavvo*—summer rations. And on *her'gi* training; each of the teenage children has their own *her'gi* and so are able (with parental permission or acquiescence at any rate) to make unaccompanied trips to visit boy- and girlfriends in other camps.

Training a her'gi essentially means taming it, and there are two aspects to this. First, the animal is familiarized with people and their dogs at close quarters, so that, losing much of its fear of people, it becomes docile and compliant enough to handle. Second, the animal is taught some basic commands. The code is extremely simple. Among the first things it is taught is to associate the presence of people with its left side: Her'gi are approached from the left.[4] Then it must be taught to respond to two commands: Turn left! Turn right! These are communicated through tugs on the one rein, which, secured around its head, hangs on the left side of the animal and is held, when it is being driven, by the person in the sled; or, when the animal is part of a her'gi-and-sled caravan, the rein is secured to the back of the sled in front of the animal.

One trains spailek to become her'gi beginning, sometimes, the winter following the animal's autumn castra-

A *spailek* being trained as a draft animal.

tion or, more commonly, after waiting a year. By waiting, one is able to observe the behavior of the spailek in the herd. Many spailek will be rejected for training, on various grounds, and sold for meat.

Training begins by loosely tying a spailek to a tree near the camp—"familiarization," a component of which is getting used to restricted movement. Next, it will be brought into the company of experienced her'gi, the more docile among them. Tied to the sled that the her'gi is pulling, the spailek has no choice but to follow. Only after some experience of that will it be attached to a sled in a caravan with experienced her'gi both in front of and behind it. Favorite occasions for this part of the training program are the caravans that take heavily loaded sleds of meat to distant Kautokeino or Karasjok. If all goes well, this training is seen as an assurance that the animal can be used on the spring migration to the calving grounds. The animal is now a her'gi, but much effort has still to be put into training it to understand and obey a driver's signals with the rein.

Indicative of the cultural importance of her'gi, there is a rich vocabulary concerning them. In part, the vocabulary elaborates on their behavior traits. Of particular im-

portance, I think, it also distinguishes a ranking among her'gi based on how an animal responds to the driving signals. The most prized her'gi responds to a "right turn," as well as to the simpler "left turn," through tugs on the single rein that is always on the left side of the animal. But many—otherwise prized for their strong work capacity—need to have the rein flicked over their spread of antlers and down onto their right side before executing a right turn. (Nor is it all that easy to make that flick of the rein without getting it entangled with the antlers.) This part of the training activity actually begins with two reins, one on each side of the animal, and some her'gi (or some trainers) never manage to get beyond that stage. Even experienced her'gi may be put onto two reins for a short period at the beginning of winter, after months out of harness. Those who remain least tame will be used only, if possible, in sled caravans. But a herder will want to have a few her'gi that he can depend on when working with the herd. Among these few, some may be better suited to help him lead (with bell), others to help him drive from behind the herd.

Among limitations on how many her'gi a family may have are the size of their herd and the energy given to

Her'gi dievva: a tethering place.

training the animals.[5] But everybody from teenagers up wishes to have their own driving animal, and the larger family likely needs more animals in the baggage caravans. The length and difficulty of migration routes and the distance of winter pastures from one of the villages are also determining factors.

Small Herds

I had supposed all would agree that small herds are the most suitable for winter pastures. After all, it seems to be an ecologically sound proposition: The larger the herd, the more likely it is that the animals trample the snow into a hard compacted mass, whereas the smaller the herd, the more efficient the grazing in terms of area. This can be restated in terms of reduced risk. It is easier to find alternative pasture for smaller herds, and there is also likely to be less need to do so. But there was no such consensus. Aside from not being at all clear about how small is "small," I was failing to take into account differing dispositions and circumstances of individuals. Thus Jorgu Biera, a small owner *and a loner,* speaks in favor of small herds but not in ecologic terms. Boaris Mikkel, on

the other hand, says he would prefer to combine herds rather than spend so much time avoiding a neighboring herd. But until Ellon Ailu became his son-in-law (in 1958), Boaris Mikkel had only his wife and children to help him. For Iskun Biera, with six or more times the number of animals Jorgu Biera has, the question had a ridiculous slant to it: His herd *is* large. Does that mean he should divide it in the winter? Clearly not. What he needs are more herders, and therefore he and one of his brothers stay together for the winters, making a combined herd that is still larger. Another argument I heard was that a "large" herd is more easily found in the terrain.

Interestingly, the older people relate the issue back to the pre-World War II winters, when there were wolves, and they did not necessarily agree either. Some argue that "large" herds were too easily dispersed by wolves, making it easier for them to pick off individual animals, but others say it was only with large herds that one had a sufficient number of herders to protect deer from these predators.

In practice, at any rate, winter herds are, and probably always have been, smaller than summer herds.[6] And all agree that in really bad winters, the best (or only) chance lies in dispersal, that is, in "smaller" herds.

The tripartite division into reindeer ranges loses much of its force on the winter pastures, but it is important to understand why. True, there is an absence of natural boundaries across the Kautokeino winter range; however, there *are* ecologic differences—for example, the one between Oar'jebelli and Gow'dojottelit (journal, 23 March). There can also be sudden changes in snow surface conditions on the *same* pasture, which engage the critical attention of every herder and account for the weak, nonexclusive notion of usufruct. Certainly, particular herds become associated with particular pastures over the years, although the pattern, essentially one of partnerships, is always changing. Nonetheless, each owner has right of access, when in need, to alternative pastures. It has to be this way, they say. An owner who intended to return in April to the area where his herd pastured in January, but finds that a change of a degree or two of temperature has taken away that pasturing option, must go elsewhere. This may mean another man's pasture, yet any notion of trespass is in abeyance at such times. Such crises may not be localized to a single herd. Deep snow on the Oar'jebelli edge of the winter pastures or icing on their Nuor'tabelli edge may lead to a mass exodus—east or west. Such has happened, and the acknowledgment is, always, that owners may take their animals to wherever they have a chance of saving them.

This is not to say there is never distrust—"Was his situation such that he *really* had to encroach on our pasture?"—or never plain ill-will. There is. It belongs to the politics of this reindeer pastoralism, with its fine-graded weightings of opportunism versus reasonableness, competitiveness versus partnership.[7]

The notion of trespass has become aggravated by the erection of family cabins out on the winter pastures. Boaris Mikkel, who also has a house in Hemmugiedde, built his cabin at Buolčajav'ri in 1958, two years after first coming to that winter pasture and the year his eldest daughter married Ellon Ailu. Among the factors in his choice of site were river water that never froze over, a supply of wood fuel, and an ideal *her'gi dievva:* the place near to camp where one pastures, perhaps while tethered, the draft animals. The her'gi dievva should be windblown enough for the snow not to be deep and sheltered enough for it to be powdered, and it should have ample lichen. Boaris Mikkel is upset when others who reach the winter pastures before him bring their animals in the vicinity of the cabin. This is *baha,* "bad," but not, interestingly enough, *hæppat,* "shameful." What does he do about it? He probably pays back in like currency, he says. However, he does not rupture all future relations between himself and the offender by reporting the incident to the Reindeer Administration or the sheriff. The Administration, as far as I could make out, would like more "regulation" concerning winter pastures; "allocation" is a key term with them. But they are ineffectual. On the other hand, individual owners have brought complaints to the Kautokeino branch of the national association of Saami reindeer owners. The association declines to take a stand, seeing it as a "matter of conscience" for the individual pastoralist. Jorgu Biera probably voiced the core sentiment of many (appropriately dressed in metaphor and ambiguity) when he said to me, "Each man respects another's her'gi dievva."

6.
Spring Calves

Giðða: April–June

As at the end of summer all herds and camps moved "in" (luksa) towards the winter pastures, so now, in the spring, all movement is "out," or *davas*.

The new vegetation draws animals *davelli* (outward). Grasses are sought in place of the winter fare of lichens, for example. For njar'ga herds at least, davas is probably associated with a desire for salt, which the coastal vegetation supplies. If these factors weigh most with the males, for the cows (herders tell me) it is the return to their calving places (or places of birth), before anything else, that moves them davelli. But this means that their davas will be rather different from that of the male animals. Herders take this into account should they separate the males and cows into two herds, and, as we will see, the male herd is always placed on the outer side of the cows. For the herders, the movement is also part of the essential rotation of feeding grounds. It saves the delicate lichen beds—soon to be without a protective snow cover—from being overtrampled. The move off the tundra also spares the animals the worst of the mosquito plague.

The final destination of the spring migration is the summer pastures. Some herds reach these pastures before calving. However, many others move first to the calving grounds, in much the same areas where the rut took place (Fig. 6.2). All the njar'ga groups of Gow'dojottelit make spring camps for several weeks in the vicinity of their calving grounds, and only after that do they begin on the last and longer leg of the migration to the summer pastures. During all this time the animals are kept under close watch.

Even though owners have been able to acquire a sound knowledge of their herds during the last months of winter, and the animals have been relatively undisturbed, there is a pervasive feeling of uncertainty about the approaching calving season. In talking about what the spring may bring, herders look back over the seasons of the year that is coming to an end: "Last summer was too hot," or "The animals stood too long behind the fence," are typical reflections on which rest their forebodings.

How these adverse conditions may have affected the vuonjal will be uppermost in their minds. An animal may show no signs of being with calf until the moment of birth is near, and this is especially true of the younger cows. Some say a cow that is not going to calve may shed its antlers before calving time, instead of ten days after-wards; not all herders agree, however. (I was also told that if the herd is in poor condition after a hard winter, there is more chance of antlers falling early; and that since the separation corrals have been in use a greater number of cows lose their antlers before calving.) The numbers of two-year-olds that calf can vary appreciably from year to year. Nor do herders express much confidence in the ability of vuonjal to nurse and nurture their calves—the highest percentage of lost calves is among first-time mothers, I am told.

But attention will also be paid to how the calves of *older* cows fare: Are their mothers able to graze efficiently enough to provide their offspring with enough milk? Owners have a delicate balance of considerations to take into account here. It is not before the end of summer that a calf can be expected to survive without its mother, and foster parentage is usually not an option. If the calf is

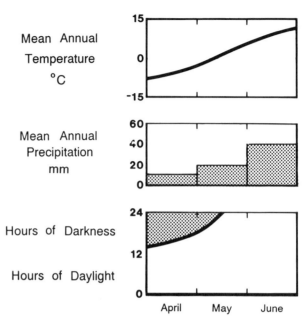

Figure 6.1 Climate: April–June. From Hansen 1960

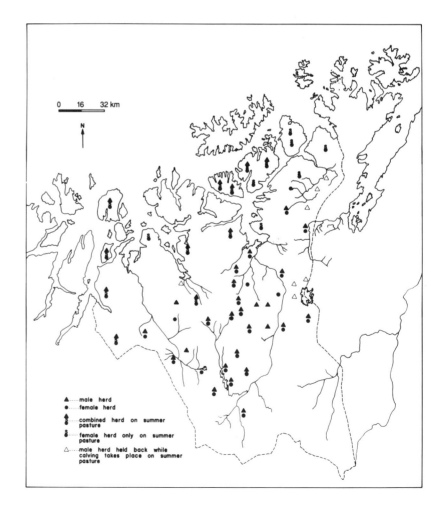

Figure 6.2 Spring herds

not getting the nourishment it needs, one option is to kill both cow and calf. But few will do that. The older cow, let us suppose, may have had difficulty browsing on summer grasses last year because its teeth were too ground down, but it managed much better when it was able to return to a lichen and fungi diet in the autumn: It even put on some weight. And its calf (of last year) did survive its first summer. So the mother was allowed to live; she came into usterus, and now she has a calf again.

All the njar'ga groups, before setting out for the calving grounds, separate male animals from cows. There are several reasons. For one, the bulls and castrates (especially the former), unless held back, will range widely in search of fresh vegetation that the spring thaw is uncovering. It is quite usual for the departure of the male herd from the winter pasture to be delayed until calving is well advanced at the spring camp. The concern of the cows, on the other hand, is to find sheltered places to drop their calves, and they have to be herded carefully to prevent them from scattering and "hiding" in the landscape. Another reason for the separation is that although a cow that is pregnant or has a newborn calf tolerates other females, she will be nervous and restless in the presence of male animals.

The date on which the first calf is dropped and the period that elapses until the last calf is born are likely to vary from herd to herd, and even from one year to another within the same herd. Among several factors, the most important is the duration of the rut in the previous autumn and the conditions prevailing in the herd at that time. While it is usual for calving to be concentrated in the first half of May, some calves may well be born before the herd of pregnant cows sets out for the spring camp and even while the cows are still in the same herd as the males. These early calves, and their mothers, will be left behind (perhaps near a settlement where the reindeer owners have kinsfolk), or they will follow later with the male herd. More calves are likely to be born on the way to the spring camp, perhaps a journey of two days; these will be taken along on sleds, their mothers following.

Herders usually have a particular location in mind for the calving ground. It is also common for a group to return to the same location each year. Whether they occupy it in any particular year, however, depends on a couple of factors. First, the convention of usufruct with respect to calving grounds is left broadly interpreted, and the principle of "first there" is also accepted. Second, the number of calves already born en route may cause the herders to abandon their original plans. So they may have to settle for a calving ground which is, in their opinion, less than ideal. Its selection may be forced upon them in a situation of decreasing options as calving progresses. Yet the consequences of this are usually not too serious. The terrain is, by and large, suitable, and herders have an intimate knowledge of it.

10–11 MAY, RIEBANVARRI

On the edge of the winter grazing grounds, our camp overlooks the Kautokeino River, and across it are the calving grounds. The separation into čoavjek and luovas herds has been completed. Yearlings are allowed to join either.

The move from the winter pastures was later than usual this year, and three days were spent encamped on the way here. It has been a winter of such heavy snowfalls that it is as well to delay arrival at the calving ground as long as possible. But some thirty calves have already been born, and we cannot delay any longer. The calves (and their mothers) are to be left with the male herd, and we are about to set off with the čoavjek for Dat'kuvarri, some 30 kilometers to the northwest.

This will be the first year that the herd of Migot and Mattem Gaibme and the herd of Boaris Mikkel and Ellon Ailu are together in the spring. There is a disagreement between them over which of several possible calving grounds we will go to, and, more immediately, which route we will take to get into the calving ground area on the other side of the Kautokeino River. Migot (speaking on behalf of his brother as well) wishes to follow their customary gæi'dno—reindeer trail—that is circuitous between the hills. Ellon Ailu (speaking for his father-in-law as well; the old man was not present) wishes to go directly over the hills, as is *their* custom.

Ellon Ailu more or less concedes to Migot. Karen, Ellon Ailu's wife, is furious. But then Migot concedes. The one argument was that keeping off the hills is not only a longer route, but because there is so much snow this year the *raide* [caravan] will be in difficulty. The reply was that the weather is cold enough to ensure a good surface in the valleys and, besides, there is too much snow everywhere. Karen insisted that the weather could change—perhaps a warm spell tomorrow, who knows? Then the valleys can be treacherous (slush and water); on the hillsides, the herd, going before the caravan, will plough a gæi'dno for the caravan.

It was not decided, as far as I could tell, where we would make our spring camp. We are a party of six.

Nursery *(Aldo Manus)*

Herders usually choose a calving place on a long and gentle southern slope whose optimal exposure to the sun should ensure an early melting of its snow cover. The slope should drain well in the thaw, and it should be rich in lichen. In such a habitat the pregnant cows, and mothers with their calves, will have less reason to roam. Since newborn calves sleep much of the time, with their mothers grazing or dozing nearby, it is important that the ground be relatively dry: On wet ground reindeer become restless. And the open ground of such a site (over which herders keep constant watch) helps to give protection from predators.

However, some herders actually choose a calving ground with a vuobme nearby. Their reasoning is as follows: The open slopes are exposed to snow or rain or cold winds from the interior (one hopes for warm winds from the coast); when such conditions arise, cows may search for the relative shelter of a vuobme and its offerings of a variety of shrub and grass vegetation. By anticipating this eventuality and letting their animals pasture, under watch, in the nearby vuobme, these herders feel they exercise control through responding to the needs of their cows. Others, though, regard the dangers of this course of action too great to risk.

In the hours before her delivery, a cow will try to withdraw from the herd, and, as though trying to alleviate her labor pains, her movements may become unusually contorted. On observing such symptoms, the herder moves the animal (but without using either lasso or dog) into the *aldo manus* (nursery) of the calving ground. It is here that she gives birth and nurses her newborn for the first few days. The nursery is likely to be sited on the lower edge of the southern slope for greater protection from the wind. In the case of a difficult delivery, a herder becomes midwife. At birth the mother licks the calf all over, thus ensuring, among other things, that it will be able to urinate. The calf can suckle immediately and within twenty-four hours is able to follow its mother around the nursery.

As calving progresses, all those cows who have yet to deliver are herded down to the nursery, while those whose calves are already strong enough are taken back up the slope, probably into the vicinity of the camp. For a while at least, provided there is sufficient lichen for the herd, the cows that have calved successfully exhibit no urge to move davelli.

Essential to this calving process is the factor of protection, even of comfort, which herders provide. What has to be stressed is that they have taken this responsibility from the animals. We know from the behavior on calving grounds where herders are *not* present that the cows do not calve in such close proximity; rather, each seeks her own niche, and each has to secure her own protection and comfort (and her calf's). Some cows will be drawn to a vuobme, others to a hillside, depending on what they "learned" as calves. But in the situation that I am describing, there will be a herders' tent sufficiently far up the hillside of the calving ground that there is an unobstructed view in all directions. The herders' presence, then, eliminates losses of newborn calves to predators; except, that is, in a vuobme, where the undergrowth helps a predator to make an undetected approach and, at the same time, may impede the flight of a calf. Nonetheless, a reindeer cow can be spirited in her defense of her calf; and until she sheds her antlers some ten days after giving birth, she possesses a formidable weapon. But—to emphasize the point again—she has no enemies (except for the occasional undisciplined or excited dog) on the herded calving ground.

In the crowded nursery, a cow uses her antlers, through a sideways movement of the head inclined towards the ground, to sweep a personal space for herself and her newborn. The movement of herders through the nursery is of no apparent concern. Indeed, the animals themselves are inclined to crowd around the tents and baggage sleds (as soon as the calves are able to leave the nursery), licking the tarpaulins for traces of salt. But here there is a real danger of the cows and their calves becoming "too tame" at the spring camp, so that, once the migration resumes, there are difficulties (particularly because one should not use the dogs to help herd cows and their calves) in getting the animals to heed signals and urgings.

By being in attendance at spring camps, herders gain valuable knowledge of their animals at this critical phase in their life cycle. Most valuable of all perhaps, one is

Licking the tarpaulin for its salt taste. Note the mutual unconcern of deer and (disciplined) dog.

able to distinguish between the different categories of rodno: cows that may be sterile (a three-year-old or more that still has to calve: *stainak,* or *sæiva-rodno*); cows that failed to calve this time but have done so in earlier years (rodno); and cows that lost their calves this spring *(čoavčes)*. With this knowledge, decisions regarding which cows to slaughter will be better informed.

As an example of the importance of knowing *how* a cow lost its calf, consider the category čoavčes (or *šadda-rodno,* became calfless). Some cows will lose their calves through no fault of their own; but others may have refused to suckle their offspring (younger cows) or may have had too little milk (older cows); and a cow that is prone to wander with its calf away from the main herd is likely to become a čoavčes. The calf may survive but be "lost" to another herd.

If a cow rejects her newborn in favor of her yearling,

she will be known as a *suoppa-rodno.* This is particularly likely to happen when the mother-yearling relationship is not severed before the mother drops her calf (a critical indication is the prolongation of the nursing relationship until the rut in the fall and its resumption afterwards). If the yearling cannot be separated from its mother it will be slaughtered in the hope that the mother then will begin to nurse her calf. However, should the same behavior repeat itself the following year, it is likely that the cow (now called a *sæiva-suoppa-rodno*) will also be slaughtered.

Female yearlings, particularly, are prone to resist severing the bond with their mothers. There is also a likelihood that cows who calved as two-year-olds will, in the following year, reject their new calf in favor of their first-born. Thus a situation can arise in which a cow and her two-year-old daughter, both of whom calved but (for whatever reason) are now without their respective calves, keep together. The two animals will be referred to as *sparro-rodno (or rotsun),* calfless cows who are "linked."

However, a cow followed by its yearling but not its calf, need not be a suoppa-rodno at all. The yearling may have rejoined its mother after the calf died in circumstances for which the mother is blameless. Where such is the case, the cow is known as *čærbmak-ædne.* One also occasionally sees a mother followed both by its calf (which it is nursing) and its yearling, and even by the yearling's calf. This indicates that a mother-yearling relationship can exist without necessarily interfering with the mother-calf relationship. The terms for such a grouping of animals is *ædne-čuovvo-ragge:* literally, a mother followed by a line of animals. If this mother is not prone to wandering away from the herd, a bell will be placed on her and the group left intact.

In summary, knowledge of the female herd as a whole is most important. Spring is the crucial season in this respect, and particular note is taken of the behavior of the younger cows at this time. The percentage of two-year-olds that calve is regarded as a significant index of the well-being of the herd. Occasionally, yearlings will calve *(čærbmak-aldo).* The inexperience of these younger cows may lead them into difficulties, and herders should be at hand to observe and help. By the time a cow has calved for the second time, it has a biography on the basis of which its owner is able to predict her behavior in various situations.

12–15 MAY, DAT'KUVARRI

6 a.m. [12 May] Boaris Mikkel leads the *čoawjek-ællo* [pregnant female herd] over the hills—he is *laidestæggje,* and his wife, Margarethe, *vuojetæggje* (driving the herd from behind). Two of their children and Migot accompany them. 8 a.m. Boaris Mikkel and Margarethe have returned. They simply started the herd on its way—over the hills. They will remain in Hemmugiedde. Ellon Ailu, Marit, and I set out with the caravan. The *luovas-ællo* [male herd] is left pasturing, under watch, on Riebanvarri. *Čoawjek-ællo* moves at a leisurely pace. Fortunately no calves born en route. On our way we saw the Bede *ællo* (not yet separated) and Iskun Biera's *čoawjek-ællo.* We reach Dat'kuvarri and put up a *lavvo* after dark.

Forty calves are born during the three days here. Calving is going well, but there is a problem. Dat'kuvarri is not a very suitable place. Each day some of the *čoawjek* manage to make

their way down to the marsh along the Masi River, immediately to the north of us. Also, soon it will be imperative to take the herd across the river while the ice is still safe; but we can't move far at this stage of calving. If only we were on the other side of the river.

Raggi-oai'vi (the name denotes a rutting place) is where we would like to be. Boaris Mikkel and Ellon Ailu were there for calving last year. It is a dry hillside. Plenty of room. No river or marshes. Migot and Mattem Gaibme know it, too, and like it. However, it may be too far (some twenty kilometers), now that calving is starting in earnest.

We decide to cross the river at all events (Fig. 6.3).

15–22 MAY, MAZEVARRI

We dared venture no further than to Mazevarri, and the six kilometers (in a northwesterly direction) took us as many hours: slush and newborn calves. We were a long procession and separated by hours: first the *čoawjek,* then the *raide,* and last of all—moving slowly—the *aldo manus.* Note: There are now two cow herds, in effect. The *čoawjek* that still have to calve. The *aldo* that have.

The nursery is on the southern slope of the hill. Most of it is free of snow. Calving is proceeding well.

What has been a problem is the lack of a good view over the neighboring terrain, especially due west and to the northeast, where there are other herds—including Iskun Biera and Anti Biera's—within a few kilometers of us. (There would have been a similar problem at Raggi-oai'vi.) So we moved our tents over to the northern brow of the hill in the hope of correcting our situation, but the *čoawjek* are now drawn farther away from the nursery (where they should be before they calve). It is agreed that we should move again, but it is difficult to do so at this late stage of calving. An overcrowded nursery—which looked so large (to me!) when we came here a week ago—finally forces the decision on us.

23–31 MAY, SOADNJAJAV'RI

This move (no more than three kilometers) suits the change in our situation. Here we have a better view of the terrain. Most of the cows now have calves, and those who were born first are already quite active. The nursery is now on the northern slope of Mazevarri, but it is dry. The herds to the east are a little closer to us now, but it is mainly open ground, and we are also partially separated from each other by the southern end of the lake [Soadnjajav'ri].

Two of our small group return to Riebanvarri to help with the *luovas* and the baggage caravan (for us all, for the remainder of the migration). When the main party joins us we will all

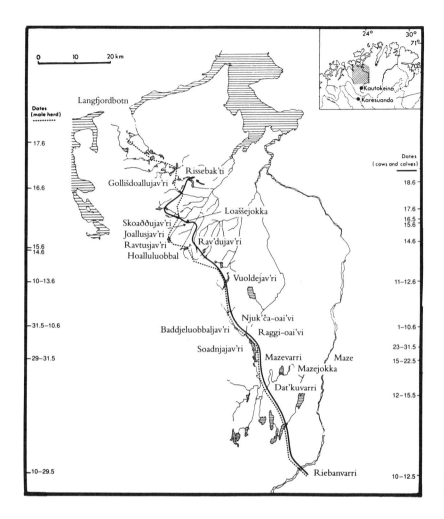

Figure 6.3 Spring migration routes. Map by Olga Aune

move on to Baddjeluobbaljav'ri. The yearlings that are with us are increasingly restless. I am told that they will quiet down when the *luovas* arrives. Fishing through the ice.

The *luovas* has arrived (29 May) and is pastured on the hill immediately *davelli*. Suddenly, there are so many people here: four families. And there are too many dogs in the camp now. Those that have been working with the *luovas* are badly disciplined, and one calf was killed. We also temporarily lost control of the *luovas* when the children who were looking after it tried to herd it (with dogs) in a fog.

It is still undecided when we will move on: a number of different opinions. It is likely, though, that the *luovas* will leave tomorrow, the cows and calves following in their own time. The baggage caravan remains packed, and the families are using *lavvo*.

Spring Camps

The migration to the coast cannot begin in earnest until a few weeks after calving. There may be several short moves, always davelli, to new pastures, but the calves must be allowed time to gain strength before the long journey. This period is known as *gidda-gæsse,* the spring of summer, and it is the time of the spring camp proper. The few herders who watched over the calving are now joined by their families, who bring with them the male herd. The simple herding tent is replaced by the more comfortable and spacious family tent, and proximity to a good fishing lake is taken into account when choosing the camp site.

Herding routines now encompass the male and female

At Soadnjajav'ri. The up-turned sleds serve as food racks for reindeer products: dried meat and, for the dogs, blood in bladder containers.

Alarm! Note the camouflage of the calf, and the bell-*čoawjek* in the background.

Trespass! Look carefully; there are two calves.

herds. Although they are still kept separated, herders are able to move from the one herd to the other. The male herd is taken on relatively wide pasturing circuits and brought back each day to a position that is "in front of" (davas) the cows and their calves. This way the cows are left undisturbed (for it is most unlikely that any of the males would wander "back" towards the winter pastures). Moreover, any cows that manage to wander (in the general direction of the spring migration) are likely to be observed by the herders who are with the male herd. Were the arrangement the other way around and the cows pastured "in front of" the males, the encroachment of the males into the cow herd would always be a likelihood, and should any of the cows wander, there would be less chance of finding them.

This arrangement is less effective, however, in controlling the movements of the yearlings and, to a lesser extent, the various categories of rodno. The latter may wish to break away from the cow herd with its calves, and they may not be at ease in the male herd. There are likely to be rodno with each of the two herds, and the herders will be concerned that they do not stray from either. The behavior of the yearlings is still more unpredictable. Some wish to stay with their mothers, and others may readily join the male herd. But either way, many of them will become stragglers when the migration is resumed, either because they are disregarded by their mothers or because they are unable to keep up with the male herd. Meanwhile, at the spring camp, yearlings are more restless than the male herd. They tear away from groups of browsing animals, and herders have to use their dogs to bring them back. In their inexperience, they are also accident-prone. And gorm fly larvae add to their troubles. It is little wonder, then, that owners are resigned to relatively severe losses among this age-class. Yearlings, they say, are "stupid" *(jallas)*, and they are "tired" *(vaiban)*. (As already noted, they remain undesignated by sex until the end of the summer, their second one.)

The landscape steadily changes character at the spring camp. After 21 May the sun does not dip below the horizon. Despite brief snowstorms, and even in those years when overcast skies withhold the sun for many hours, the snow retreats almost daily, and the spring vegetation begins to grow apace. These changes mean that the decision to move out to the coastal summer pastures must soon be taken. But in deciding *when* to begin the move to the summer pastures, opposing considerations have somehow to be balanced. The longer one waits, the stronger the calves will be. But the longer one waits, the more difficult the journey for the calves on account of the thaw and spring floods (for rivers have to be negotiated). The situation with the male herd is quite different. The animals are strong enough for a forced march (though some of the yearlings will fall behind), and for much of the way, the route may be above the tree line and so away from the problem of thaw. There may be little pasture or shelter, but the journey can be completed within three or four days. The cows and calves can take three weeks on theirs.

Usually in the first days of June, preparations will be made to move, before it is decided exactly when to move. Rain or cold winds from the interior can delay departure (even on migration, herds tend to veer into the wind). Another cause of delay can be the movements of other herds in the vicinity. But the prospect of exhausting good pasture in the spring camp area brings urgency to the move. Typically, a period of warm winds from the coast, winds that will draw the animals forward (and which may defy all efforts to keep the male herd pastured in the vicinity of the spring camp), will end such a period of indecision.

31 MAY–10 JUNE, BADDJELUOBBALJAV'RI

Both herds left Soadnjajav'ri on the thirty-first, the *luovas* traveling over the frozen lakes and arriving within a few hours. They are now pastured on the south side of Njuk'ča-oai'vi (there is another *luovas* on its north side) and are brought down to the camp every twenty-four hours. There are always some herders with them, usually two children. The cows and their calves were moved slowly along the gentle slopes along the east side of

Soadnjajav'ri, arriving in their new pasture on 1 June. The pasture is in a *vuobme* relatively free of snow, on the south side of the Njuk'ča-oai'vi massif. It is a couple of kilometers to the east of our camp. We have a *lavvo* out there and take turns keeping watch. There are still some *čoawjek*. We have some *vierro boccu* in both herds.

One of the dogs has killed a yearling, and at earlier camps dogs took two calves; maybe there were other instances too. Each family slaughters: Ellon Ailu a *rodno;* Migot (to share with his brother) a sick *varek;* and on Boaris Mikkel's instructions, one of his daughters (not one of the teenage sons) kills and butchers a yearling.

Our camp is on the southern edge of the lake. Instead of *lavvo,* we now have four family tents. We can expect to be here a week, time enough for the calves to gain strength. Everybody spending much of their spare time fishing through the ice. The talk is principally about who will go with which herd when we move, and about what we suppose other camps' plans are. Halcyon days! Ellon Ailu and I away for three days (on skis) on a visit to the village of Masi, thirty kilometers to the east.

10–13 JUNE, VUOLDEJAV'RI

This camp is on the edge of the mountains we have to cross. *Luovas* arrived here on the tenth, the cows and calves on the following day. The baggage caravan remains packed, and we all use but two *lavvo.*

We left Baddjeluobbaljav'ri the day after we were visited by herdsmen from the camp to our west (Spalca). They were about to start on the move to the coast, and, inspecting our *luovas,* they retrieved some of their own animals. Today (11 June) Ellon Ailu and I visited the *luovas* of Danel Anti's camp *(or'da)* to our northeast and retrieved some of our animals, and also picked up more information about the present locations and movements of other herds. On the basis of what we learned, we apparently move on tomorrow.

No longer is there a *čoawjek-ællo,* simply an *aldo manus.* Calving is completed (though there will probably be some *gæssek*); so the cow herd is one big nursery.

Migration to the Coast with Male Herds

On leaving the spring camps, the male herds reach the coast in a matter of a few days, following an alpine route (not manageable for the nursery) on account of its snow cover and traveling by night (which is now light) for the sake of lower temperatures.[1] Along with this herd goes the baggage train together with most members from the spring camps (certainly any children and old people). Because the sleds will be fully loaded, it is important that they are drawn over firm and, preferably, frozen snow—an "iron surface" *(ruov'dicuono)*. A dozen or more her'gi each pull one or two sleds.

13 JUNE

Luovas herd and a baggage caravan of twenty-nine sleds leave Vuoldejav'ri. A party of nine. One *lavvo*. The route is to be along high contours. The baggage caravan is to lead the herd, and must keep to snow- or ice-covered terrain. Adults (men and women) work with the caravan, while the strenuous herding work is left to three youths.

14 JUNE

Already at Hoalluluobbal early in the morning. Made camp and slept during the day.

15 JUNE

Poor progress last night on account of wet snow. Camped for the day at Ravtusjav'ri. Fishing. A sled mended. Left before midnight.

16 JUNE

Hard snow surface last night and made good progress. Reached Gollišdoallujav'ri early this morning. The pattern that has evolved is for the baggage caravan to move ahead of the herd, sometimes waiting for it to catch up. In the vanguard of the herd (and often alongside the caravan) are the few cows that are with us. The *luovas* animals themselves tend to fan out over the terrain; yearlings usually in the rear. The young herders are rebuked for using their dogs on this stony terrain to keep the *luovas* animals together.

17 JUNE

Despite slushy snow conditions, the caravan set a hard pace through the night, and by the morning the coast at Langfjord-botn was in sight. Rested for five hours before descending to the fjord.

18 JUNE

The herd taken out to the summer pasture by two herdsmen. Remainder make camp near Langfjordbotn to await the cows and calves [a week's wait].

Migration to the Coast with Cows and Calves

It is left to a few herders (men and women) to undertake the longer and more difficult journey with the cows and calves. Their meager supplies, including a herding tent, are packed on the backs of trusted draft animals *(logjes-her'gi)* because the route renders the use of sleds impractical at this time of year. Whatever route is chosen, calves will need much rest and physical help from the herders, especially when traversing rivers and ravines. All the while they (and their mothers) need to graze, and if for no other reason than that, the high-altitude routes along which the (fast-moving) male herds are taken are not practicable. There would always be the risk of not enough pasture easily available (the terrain may be stony; where there is pasture, it may be under ice crusts). Herders speak loosely of expecting to reach summer pastures near Midsummer Night, 23 June.

The cow herd—now known simply as njiŋŋalas—moves slowly and is allowed to stop more or less as it wants. Except when crossing a frozen lake (see journal that follows) and on a few other occasions, the herd is not led. It finds its own pace and its own way along the route chosen for it. Yet the herding can be arduous. As soon as cows begin to wander off on their own, they must be brought back into the main herd, and others that begin to lag behind must be chivied on (if dogs are used in this work, it must be with great caution).

While moving, herders place themselves on the sides of the herd and at its rear. Two should be able to manage if necessary. Each looks after one side of the herd and alternates with the other in the rear position. In this way, the rear and one or another side of the herd are always patrolled. The danger of dispersal is particularly likely after one of the rest periods, for should the herders doze off while the herd is resting, they may awake to find some of the animals gone. Herders are very alert to the sound of animals' bells after a period of silence: Reindeer often shake themselves after resting, before rising to their feet.

A cow that finds its calf has been left behind will turn around and run back with neck and head outstretched, calling her calf with that characteristic ruw'ga, plaintive

Marit as *raidulaš,* June 14.

and deep-throated, noted in the chapter on winter pasturing. The herder at the rear of the herd lets her pass. The calf, too, calls all the while. Some time later the mother may rejoin the herd with her calf. I am told that when they become separated from each other, a mother and calf return to the place where they were last together, or where the herd had its last rest period. They may wait there for each other for up to twenty-four hours.

A calf that is without its mother may be allowed by another cow to suckle—a circumstance that probably saves the lives of many calves. Indeed, it is not uncommon to see two calves (not twins, which are very rare) suckling one cow, but few cows will take a foster calf permanently, whether in place of their own or besides their own (cf. previous description of mother-yearling relationships).

Just as calves are born before the calving grounds are reached, so there are always likely to be some born on this last phase of the migration. These summer calves (gæssek) will almost certainly have to be left behind. Sometimes one comes across them again—probably in the company of their mothers—in the autumn. A percentage loss of newborn calves is always to be expected. One hears the saying, "Until it lives to hear the cuckoo [i.e., until it reaches the coast], a calf is uncertain."

Whether it is more advantageous to be behind or in front of another herd is a particularly pressing question when traveling with the nursery. However, there is no uniform answer. In general, those who are behind have to take care to hold their animals back, and those in front can be reasonably sure that most of their stragglers will be herded by those behind and thus still reach a summer pasture—if not the owners'. On the other hand, animals that are behind can sometimes draw advantage from following the already-trampled snow or the smell of the herd in front, and herders may draw advantage from learning about problems those in front of them are experiencing as they traverse the terrain. But much depends on the local, variable natural conditions and, ultimately, on *who* is in front or behind.

14 JUNE, RAV'DUJAV'RI

With the nursery. We left Vuoldejav'ri on the twelfth, a party of four: Ellon Ailu, Mattem Gaibme, Marit, and I. Marit is *raidulaš*, that is, in charge of our two pack animals, moving the *lavvo*, and making our temporary camps. Up to this point we have made steady progress along a route a couple of kilometers to the north of that taken by the *luovas*. But tonight we ran into problems at this lake.

The Rav'du River had to be crossed, and the lake (itself part of the river complex) seemed the best place to do so. Although there was already water on its ice surface, it was strong enough to bear the weight of our herd. The river itself was far more treacherous. The ice-bridge onto the lake, however, was already broken into many sections of only a few yards breadth. The animals were reluctant to venture out on the ice, and we had to force them, Ellon Ailu leading with a *her'gi,* Mattem Gaibme and I chivying and shouting from behind.

A number of calves slid into the water between the cracks in the ice-bridge, and the ice around the bridge broke in places under the weight of some of the cows. None of the animals drowned. Some managed to get onto the safe ice of the lake itself, others scrambled back onto land. Cows that became separated from their calves began running back and forth across the ice-bridge, more fell into the water; and in the pandemonium a mother and its calf, a pregnant cow, and a yearling ran off to the east (with a following wind). In the end, it took over an hour to get the herd across this small lake.

15 JUNE, JOALLUSJAV'RI

With the herd across at about 4 a.m., we are in the *lavvo*, pitched on the east side of the lake. Although there is some danger that the herd will wander, we assume it will stay close to the west bank of the river (as long as the wind stays in the east). The fog that has descended also makes herding rather impractical. We have not slept and eaten properly since leaving Vuoldejav'ri—we are making up for it.

I write this at midnight, prior to our moving on; we are perhaps three kilometers west of Rav'dujav'ri. The herd *did*

scatter—as we found out late this morning when we were awakened by the *lavvo* blowing down in the wind. The fog had cleared, and there were no animals in sight. It rained in the night, and this probably made the animals restless. Leaving Marit to move the *lavvo* to where we are now, we set out northeast, scanning the terrain between the Rav'du and Joallus rivers. Although the wind had veered from west to south, it was not until we reached the edge of a broad *vuobme* that we caught up with the herd. Ellon Ailu remarked that the change in wind direction had helped, all the same, to hold the deer back. Without a south wind they might have continued still further, in which case they would have scattered more widely while passing through the *vuobme* and crossing its various marshes and streams. There was no difficulty in collecting the animals together, and we let them rest a while before beginning to herd them west, over the Joallus River and toward where Marit was moving the *lavvo*. As we watched the herd it became plain that a number of animals were missing. We sighted them on the far side of the gorge—which we had supposed to be impassable at this time of year by cows with their calves—further down the Joallus River.

It was not until early this evening that we had all the herd collected at the *lavvo*. Ellon Ailu went over the gorge, while Mattem Gaibme and I took the main herd across the Joallus River at a safer spot upstream. The southerly wind helped.

When we came upon the herd on the edge of the *vuobme,* we noticed that the animals that had fled from the crossing of Rav'dujav'ri were now back with the herd. Presumably they had crossed over the Rav'du River downstream. Ellon Ailu had predicted as much at the time, and for this reason he had not sent his dog after them. The animals, he said, would be drawn back by the scent of the herd. However, had there not been a westerly wind at the time we might not have seen those animals again.

17 JUNE, VADDEJAV'RI

We reached Loaššejokka by 6 a.m. yesterday and saw the *lavvo* already pitched [by Marit] on the far side of the river. The weather was warm with bright skies, and the animals moved very slowly, wanting to graze the new grass along our route. We rested the herd for several hours before crossing the river at about 10 a.m. One calf drowned, and a *čora* broke away on the other side but were brought back by Marit. Two newborn calves were carried across the river.

We let the herd make its own way up the mountain pass and to the lake—Skoað ðujav'ri—while we boiled coffee at the *lavvo* and ate a clutch of wild duck eggs. Up at Skoað ðujav'ri (wrapped in cold mists) we were almost in serious trouble again—trying to herd unwilling animals across bad ice and in a direction they did not wish to go. The breeze off the snow-covered mountains, across which our route lay, brought no smell, whereas in the lee of the mountains, but quite off our route, there was the early vegetation of a *vuobme*. We eventually got them across but still lost control of them on the far side of the lake, with the result that we had to spend many hours collecting the herd together again: difficult work in this high terrain with mists.

Have only had snatches of sleep since Joallusjav'ri; nevertheless we are moving on, after this rest period, towards Rissebak'ti. That means negotiating the *rašša*: a stony massif. There are two possible routes—over the top *(baggjel-rašša-jottet),* or the circuitous route by way of mountain passes *(vuole-rašša-jottet).*

Apparently *baggjel-rašša is* feasible even with a nursery, and it is the route Bede sometimes takes—but only in good weather, and it looks as though we are in for mists and rain. (Ellon Ailu has been across it but without a herd.) Certainly Mattem Gaibme has no enthusiasm for that alternative. So we are going *vuole-rašša.* Even so, it will be difficult terrain, and we are now repairing our moccasins with thick leather patches.

We are leaving behind six of the smallest calves with their mothers, including a *gabba* of Migot's. A calf drowned while crossing Galmijokka. Another, deserted by its mother, we kill and dine off the boiled meat. Ellon Ailu says that the *luovas* will already be at the coast, and we'll be there in three days.

7.
Patterns and Process

In concluding this account of the pastoral year—a record from within Gow'dojottelit, for the most part—I begin with a closer look at *herd knowledge* and compare situations on Gow'dojottelit with those on the Oar'jebelli and Nuor'tabelli ranges. Next, I consider differences in the *social relationships* of herding and husbandry. Finally, I propose a *model* of herd management followed by an account of the *checks and balances* that belong to the model as dictated by the logic of Saami pastoral partnerships. These are all things to be borne in mind when discussing pastoral production in the chapters that follow.

Herd Knowledge

It is possible to compare three annual cycles of herd knowledge across the Kautokeino reindeer ranges (Fig. 7.1). Their on-the-ground distribution is approximately thus:

A: most njar'ga herds, characteristic of Gow'dojottelit;
A/B: a few nanne herds;
B: all suolo herds, most nanne herds, and a few njar'ga herds, characteristic of Oar'jebelli and Nuor'tabelli.

The principal differences in herd knowledge appear to rise from the following circumstances:

A and A/B: calving grounds on spring pastures with herders in attendance; B: calving grounds out on summer pastures without herders in attendance.
A: critical crowding behind fences and around autumn corrals; A/B and B: avoidance of critical crowding at fences and corrals.

To begin by comparing alternatives A and B, in both cases there is a gap in the cycle of herd knowledge, but it occurs at different times of the year. In the case of B, it begins when the animals are let loose on the summer pastures, before calving, and it is late summer before herders can begin to reassemble herd knowledge. They retain serviceable herd knowledge through the autumn. But for A, the autumn is the period of lost knowledge, perhaps not reassembled before December–January.

The herders of Gow'dojottelit (A), who reaped the knowledge gained from being close to the animals during calving, liked to tell me that it is *the* most valuable herd knowledge one can have. At the same time, they ap-

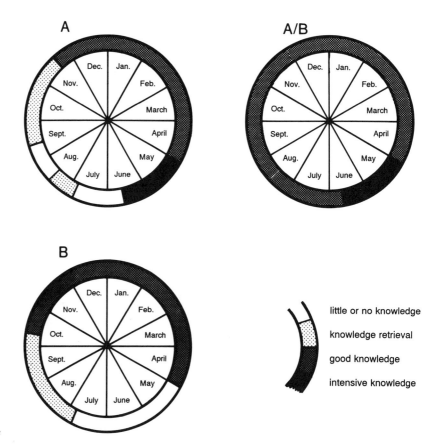

Figure 7.1 Annual cycles of herd knowledge

peared envious of the appreciably lighter work load of herders on the other ranges. But there really was no choice. The peninsulas of Gow'dojottelit can only be reached through a narrow isthmus (see Fig. 3.3). Were the herds to attempt to pass through it, all in the last week or few days before calving, they would almost certainly become mixed with each other, with little chance of the herders being able to do much about it. Furthermore, these summer pastures, with much stony and high-altitude ground (snow-covered into June), are barely sufficient for the short summer. On this account, too, it would be unwise to bring the herds out there to calve.

Those who pursue the spring option (B) argue that to require calves a few weeks old to move on to the distant summer pastures from spring calving grounds overtaxes their strength. They also say that once the herds have reached their summer pastures (before calving), it is wiser to let the animals roam freely. This is for a combination

of reasons: the cows, immediately before and after calving, need to be undisturbed, and, say these herders, their own presence would be disturbing; on arrival at the summer pastures, adult male and female animals are likely to choose different terrain, so the cows are (naturally) undisturbed on that account as well; whereas the calving grounds on the spring pastures are rich in lichen and have early green vegetation, this is not so on summer pastures in May–June, and it is best to let the animals roam free to find their nourishment.

There is, however, one notable difference between Oar'jebelli and Nuor'tabelli in their practice of option B. In a significant number of Nuor'tabelli cases (but only one on Oar'jebelli), only the cows are taken straight from winter to summer pastures, where they will calve, and the male herd (having been separated) is held back under watch.

Of course, there is little choice available to those

Table 7.1 The Status of Spring Herds

	Oar'jebelli	Gow'dojottelit	Nuor'tabelli	Total
Combined herd only on summer pasture	5	4	2	11
Female herd only on summer pasture	1	0	6	7
Male herd held back while calving takes place on summber pasture	1	0	6	7
Separated herds (x2) during calving on spring pastures	10 (5x2)	30 (15x2)	12 (6x2)	52
Total herds	17	34	26	77

herders who swim their animals out to summer pastures on islands (the suolo herds). The young calves could not manage the swim (though by the autumn most of them are able to swim back to the mainland in the company of their parents); and after the swim is over, the imperative of leaving the animals in peace gains force.

Table 7.1 is a numerical summary of the distribution of spring herds across the three ranges—whether on spring or summer pastures. The separated male and female herds on the spring pastures during calving are usually sufficiently close to each other (for at least a part of the spring—see spring journal, Chapter 6) so that both can be herded from the one camp.[1] These camps are accordingly more familial in composition than others, and on Gow'dojottelit especially, on account of their number there, two or even several camps may well be in sight of each other. Although there are more herds on Gow'dojottelit than either of the other two ranges, there are not more animals, simply smaller herds (on average).

Moving ahead now to the end of the summer, the herd knowledge difference between options A and B is reversed. Chapters 3 and 4 described how the plight (in this respect) of the Gow'dojottelit herders begins around the summer fences and is compounded by the place that separation corrals have in the autumnal routine. The topography and the density of animals on the terrain have much to do with it. There is little space to maneuver, nor does any owner much wish to delay the exit of

his herd from the summer pastures (which would be one way of improving the situation), so there is crowding in space and time.

This is in strong contrast to what had been happening since the middle of the summer with the nanne and njar'ga herds of option B. In their case, the terrain allows for easy movement from summer to autumn pastures (no narrow isthmuses causing bottlenecks in deer movements). Indeed, the animals are not stopped when they begin wandering south even in July. In the case of Oar'jebelli (information from Nuor'tabelli is less certain), it is generally late August when they reach a fence—the first of two—that temporally halts them. Here marking and castration are carried out, and the reconstitution of herd knowledge begins. The animals are then let through this fence and left to pasture loosely, attended or unattended, until the rut is concluded. Some mixing of herds will have occurred, but not on the scale of the njar'ga herds of Gow'dojottelit. All the while the animals are working their way farther south, until they are halted by a second fence about where the autumn pastures are left behind. The reconstitution of herd knowledge continues. About the end of October, animals are let through this second fence and then herded into separation corrals. At this point, most of the owners have reconstituted their herd knowledge.

It is among the nanne herders of the A/B grouping that herd knowledge is the most complete. Calving takes place on spring pastures, and the move to summer pastures is a relatively short one. To hinder the scattering of their animals, perhaps in several directions (as their sense of smell and need for protection from flying insects dictate), some watch will be kept over the herd even through the summer. The herding watch continues through the autumn, this time to hinder mixing with other herds, principally njar'ga herds. So there is virtually no break in either the cycle of herd knowledge or the cycle of work.

The benefits and costs that likely accrue to these annual cycles—measured in terms of estimated calving percentages, losses and weights of animals of different age-classes, and what I suppose I know about the aspirations of the herders—will be assessed in some detail in Chapter 9. I have spoken of "options" to suggest how the herders and owners are themselves aware of different patterns and combinations thereof (there are more than I have described). Very often an owner speaks of the conditions and arrangements of another as though it offers a practical alternative to his, even when, clearly, he knows he will not or cannot change. But each year there *are* those who change, perhaps by arranging a move to other pastures—possibly to another range. As the chapters that follow suggest, there may also be a cumulative change in the character of Saami herd management as a whole.

Herding and Husbandry as Social Relationships

As suggested in Chapter 2, each side of the herding-husbandry distinction embodies its own kind of social relationship. Now, as we approach the important and complex matter of pastoral production, and having in mind what we have learned about the annual cycle, it is appropriate to elaborate.

Decisions in herding are shared by those owners whose animals are in the same herd. They are short-term decisions; herding tactics are not planned beyond the duration of a season or a migration, and only rarely for as long as that. They are often ad hoc decisions in response to unforeseen and unpredictable contingencies. Moreover, a wrong or inopportune decision in herding is usually reversible; at least its damage is only temporary.

On the whole, it is otherwise with husbandry deci-

sions. First, each is selective, with the long-term in view. Many, moreover, are irreversible (to castrate, to slaughter), but not without leaving options as to subsequent courses of action.[2] Were it otherwise, the penalties attached to mistaken decisions would be altogether too high.

Second, the decisions of husbandry are not shared. They are those of the married man, and possibly his wife, for each family herd. In other words, married men do not interact as husbanders, and unmarried children are expected to execute the orders of their parents and not make husbandry decisions themselves. However, as the head of a family herd, a man is more senior custodian than owner. The family lives off its herd and derives its earnings from it. At the same time, the herd is also a capital asset that is redistributed in the next generation. (Each year the parent-husbander should select and earmark animals for each of his children, daughters as well as sons, and they will receive the animals bearing their mark when they marry.) For all these reasons, the decisions of a husbander are, or should be, based on long-term planning. While a good memory is important in herding, the consequences of a good or poor memory are greatest in husbandry.

The husbandry relationship, then, is exclusive to one family herd and is the relationship between generations. Adult status is obtained when a person is permitted to deny his parent the right to castrate or slaughter an animal bearing his (or her) own mark. That is not ordinarily achieved before marriage. The husbander is called *ised,* the only term of superordination in the culture. By contrast, the behavior between the men of several family herds (each of them a husbander) who are brought together in a herding relationship is largely between equals, regardless of differences in wealth, age, and domestic status.

A good part of the reason for this is that reindeer herding generates what may be termed discretional authority.[3] Circumstances force a decision on a member of the herding unit at a particular time and place. This person then acts in the light of his personal experience and group training, his action having consequences for all other members of the group. A group must sanction this kind of decision-making when it is unable to control which of its members may be faced with the necessity. It may well be that, when a fog descends, or when the herd becomes mixed with another, it is the young and relatively inexperienced who are with the herd, and it is their responses to the untoward events that count. There is unlikely to be time for them to refer the decision to their elders. Yet herding decisions are not undertaken haphazardly. Even in full knowledge that "decisions" made around campfires may be upset by unpredictable turns of events, herding tactics are discussed ad nauseam. When herders return to camp they are questioned in great detail about what actually happened. The camp conversations prepare herders for decisions in moments of crisis, as well as helping to evaluate and disseminate information.

In fact, it is the younger and unmarried men and women, without domestic responsibilities, who usually have the heavier herding duties. This is a striking aspect of the allocation of work while on migration. On the spring migration, for example, the most valuable section of the herd, the pregnant cows and, subsequently, their newborn calves, may be herded and moved by young men and women, some of whom are no more than apprentices in herding skills, while the married men are with the baggage and family caravans that move with the bull herd.

It is necessary to note, though, that while its labors may fall more on the young(er) than on the old(er), herding does afford esteem. Further, while herding is not by itself enough to ensure attainment of wealth, it is a prerequisite. And qualifying the point of the previous paragraph, wealthy owners continue to live near the herd, sharing the rough tent life with only the simplest of comforts, and to take some share of the duties of herding. There is a very good reason for this: No one can expect to retain a large herd (or have a herd grow year by year) unless he is somewhere on the scene himself. The herds of the old and physically inactive diminish rapidly. Their calves are marked by younger men, perhaps those they employ, or even their own sons.

Herders may work alone for days, but more often in partnerships. These are likely to change in accord with the seasonal regrouping of herds. There are also occasions when herders of different camps must work together: to separate herds that have become mixed, to retrieve ani-

mals that have wandered a distance. On account, then, of the context in which they happen, herding decisions are made on the basis of an assumption of equality among the owners. This also makes sense in terms of the roles of herder and husbander: Both fall to an owner. In herding, he is one of several partners (guoibme), but with reference to his family herd, he is boss (ised)—no matter how many (or few) animals there are.

In short, a man's reputation among his fellows does not slavishly follow herd size. Several factors intervene. One (to be explored in Chapter 9) is herd composition, beyond the matter of its size. Another flows from recognizing how, at any given time, herd size is bound up with the maturation of the family, for which the husbander is the senior custodian. One wants to know: Are the children still with the family herd? Or have they left, each taking a number of animals with them? It is also conceded that even the most diligent husbander may suffer severe diminution of a family herd through a variety of natural catastrophes. So it is with good reason that these pastoralists are forever asking themselves: "How long has so-and-so been rich?" and "How long will he stay rich?"

A Model of Herd Management

Although the model of herd management hinted in Chapter 1 may not be achieved very often by reindeer owners, all strive towards it.[4] It takes the form of the following proposition: *A prerequisite of viable herd management is the possession of three assets in commensurate proportions: herd, partners, and pasture*—in other words, the three factors of pastoral production.

Failure to achieve such commensurability leads to difficulties: a large herd is likely to suffer continuous depletions if there are insufficient partners for its management. Partners who would otherwise wish to remain together may have to separate if pasture is insufficient for their combined herd, and large and excellent pastures will be lost by those who have but a small herd to others, who have a large herd.

On this basis, the ideal proportions of herd management may be depicted as those of an equilateral triangle (Fig. 7.2). Whether or not this model is attained, by referring to it while studying conditions, we may be better

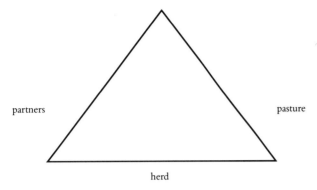

Figure 7.2 Model 1: Herd management of commensurate proportions

Men own the animals, but the animals, by their habits, hold an important key to the social organization of the pastoralists.[5] What I said in the Preface about an impressive logistical accomplishment (the annual Kautokeino round over hundreds of kilometers with thousands of animals in scores of herds and hundreds of pastoral families) has now been heavily underscored in the seasonal accounts. In this context, then, we may think of our equilateral triangle as a structure of *order* and distortions to it as signs of a descent into *chaos*. Compare, for example, the two periods of winter or spring with autumn.

Partnerships: Checks and Balances

In offering an explanation wrapped in a tidy framework, our model also raises many questions. Above all, how does this model *work?* In particular, how are *partnerships* sustained? Changed? Protected from abuse? And when it occurs, how is abuse handled? The seasonal chapters offer a number of clues; however, they are left embedded in and separated by particular contexts. This is not entirely satisfying, and I now attempt to present a synoptic answer.[6]

Saami pastoral society is acephalous, that is, without an authority that reaches to all of the constituent units. This must be our starting point, and the importance of partnerships follows in large part from it. The common building blocks for herding partnerships are brother/sis-

able to grasp the kind of arrangements pastoralists hope to have, or must have, if they are to continue as pastoralists.

We know from previous chapters that there are seasonal variations in optimal herd size and concomitant changes and shuffling of herds, partners, and pastures. Accordingly, the equilateral triangle of our model will change in scale at each season, and the number of herds on each of the ranges will change (Fig. 7.3).

The model also serves to remind us of a couple of other basic matters. First, that pastoralism is a particular *intersection* of two populations, better still, two societies: animal and human. Each is as much in and of the equilateral triangle as the other. The intersection is doubly made:

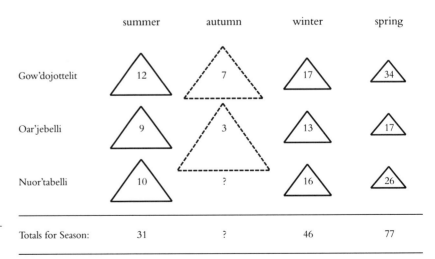

Figure 7.3 Seasonal changes in scale of Model 1 (number of herds). Broken lines indicate uncertainty; question mark indicates insufficient information

	summer	autumn	winter	spring
Gow'dojottelit	12	7	17	34
Oar'jebelli	9	3	13	17
Nuor'tabelli	10	?	16	26
Totals for Season:	31	?	46	77

ter, brother/sister-in-law, and cousin. This is well illustrated by the groupings of people we have encountered. As set forth in the figure of the principal personae dramatis (see Fig. I.3), there are these three groupings, or sii'da: the Bede group, formed around the marriages of two sisters and the children of these marriages; the Iskun group, formed around a sibling group of which Iskun Biera is the oldest member, together with a cousin, Jorgun Biera, and children of their marriages; and a group formed around the two brothers, Migot and Mattem Gaibme, and their cousin, Margarethe, who is married to Boaris Mikkel, and their children—including Ellon Ailu as son-in-law of Margarethe and Boaris Mikkel. As we know, these three may split into smaller units in winter and spring, or in the summer they may coalesce (except for the Bede group).

In the case of any such sibling group, not all the siblings are necessarily in the same unit, and this has interesting implications. It means that other combinations, at other seasons or in other years, are available—whether or not they are ever actualized. And this, in turn, suggests that relations between partners, even should they be close kin, are contractual. Thus there can be no assumption that because partners are commonly close kin, relations will be harmonious or endure over time. The conditions of the informal contract between such partners matters more than their mutual kinship. Each herder-owner is concerned with protecting his own interests, including the considerable autonomy he (or she) expects to enjoy in the management of his own affairs. Thus, even a father who wishes to have his sons with him cannot bind them; all he can do is to make it attractive enough for them that some or all of them will wish to stay, as partners.

Usually, the rationale behind a particular partnership can be understood in terms of our model. Thus, a common reason for partnerships between married siblings is that each tries to claim usufruct to pasture used by his (her) parent. The most likely way of achieving this is through cooperation with one's siblings, thus muting the rivalry between them. Partnerships between rich and poor owners can also bestow mutual benefit in respect to the logic of our model. The rich owner may have pastures of suitable size and quality for his herd, but few or no adult children. Partners with small herds can thus pro-

vide him with the herding personnel he needs without unnecessarily straining the pastures they use together. Alternatively, an owner may have a large herd and first-grade pastures, yet his herd still may not be large enough in proportion to the size of the pastures. If such a situation is not corrected, other owners can be expected to encroach, progressively reducing both the value of the pastures and the control the original owner has over his herd. To prevent this happening, he tries to select—and entice—partners whose presence will fill the pastures without substantially increasing the actual number of animals. The enticements are better pastures than could otherwise be expected by an owner with few animals, and pastures now well protected through this alliance. Furthermore, the small owner(s) need not keep many stud animals of his own—those of the larger owner suffice. He is thus able to slaughter a greater proportion of bulls, thereby saving his precious cows. (Elements of these partnership strategies will be evident in the discussion of different herd compositions in Chapter 9.)

Ideally, a herding relationship is one of high mutual dependence and trust. Differences in wealth need not detract from this ideal. On the other hand, differences in the size of the seasonal unit do diminish it: Partnerships are worth the most on spring pastures and the least on summer pastures. An altogether more subtle consideration is the effect *changes* in partnerships have on the matter of trust in this culture of high competitiveness. For a seasonal partner is also, at other seasons, the partner of others. More serious still, an ex-partner may become the partner of one's serious rivals in another herding unit.

What we see beginning to emerge is a diffuse system of checks and balances of a highly situational kind. If the principle of contract—in association with notions of satisfaction and multiple quid pro quos—is the more everyday expression of the system, other sanctions become evident as soon as relations become strained.

The availability of rat'ket, the separation of herds, is one such sanction. It is available to all (though, as we saw in Chapter 5, the costs are not the same for all herder-owners). This means that where relations reach a critical low point, separation may take place, even in the middle of a season, on the peremptory insistence of one or several members of the unit.

More likely, though, is a recourse to ridicule: a potent sanction in a culture where personal reputation is a matter of supreme importance and where many hours are spent in camp circles with those who are competitors (for reputation) as well as partners. However, the effectiveness of ridicule as a sanction is heavily circumscribed. For one thing, it must be of a light and subtle touch, or relations will deteriorate further. Besides, herding units may find themselves carrying someone who does less than his (her) share of work, as the price of having others as worthy partners. But because this kind of person helps his partners less than he might, they do less for him than for each other.

Respecting sanctions between herding units, it is in the nature of their relationship to disturb, from time to time, each other's herd management, whether deliberately or by accident. Even when this happens by accident, failure to signify displeasure and to issue a warning is to invite its recurrence. Usually there are no alternative courses of action other than encroaching upon the pastures or taking the animals of the other unit. Both can be serious matters. Moreover, their exercise must be finely regulated: A distinction is always made between acts that are intended and understood as warning signals and those intended and understood as acts of vindictiveness or aggrandizement. From this arise two problems in particular. One is the communication of a warning signal so that it will be clearly understood as such. The other is the delivery of the sanction so that it affects only those for whom it is intended, whether a particular individual or a particular group. At some seasons, and in some years more than others, many encroachments on pastures are made out of ecologic constraint, usually provoking but minimal responses. In other instances, however, encroachments are part of a deliberate policy of expansion by one unit at the expense of others, and this can lead to escalation.

Owners see a world of difference between the illicit marking of an ædnihis miessi (Chapter 4) and, say, the slaughter of such a valuable animal as an adult cow or a her'gi belonging to another. In their discussions of the meaning of such acts, herder-owners note whether or not the parties responsible have arranged matters so that their identity and their reasons become known. The line drawn between "thief" and "policeman" in such cases is clear in principle if not always in practice.[7]

Part Three
Cultures
of Possession
and
Production,
1962

I was rich, our corral was full. And my wife was as round as myself.

NILS NILSSON SKUM, REINDEER OWNER AND ARTIST
(CAPTION TO ONE OF HIS PAINTINGS)

There are too many animals.

HAVARD MOVINKEL, REINDEER AGRONOMIST

8.
Value Shift

Kautokeino, 1962. There are still many who see the world the way Nils Nilsson Skum did, whether or not their corral is actually full.[1] "Culture" is closely tied to the *possession* of as many animals as possible, and, seemingly, this value in the herders' lives is not in contention with other values. I say seemingly, because allocations still have to be made, and the owner of a full corral, with his wife, can feel pulled in several directions. For instance, more animals in *their* corral probably means fewer in their married childrens', yet an equal part of the persistent value system is the redistribution of the family herd among the children. *Possessive individualism* is passed from generation to generation.[2]

Other problems of allocation will come to light. But "way of life" itself is uniformly simple (by our material standards), and (at the moment) unproblematic. Few own houses, fewer own cars, all move with their herds; at different times of the year they live in tents or cabins or houses. Even so, it will be noticed whether or not a family gives itself plenty of meat to eat, and whether the better joints are sold or consumed. And do they have warm clothes, and new clothes, too, for special occasions?[3] In these and other ways, families continually scrutinize each

other, and some, failing the moral test, will be reputed as *hanes,* miserly, or *čuorbe,* incompetent.

However, there are those (currently a minority) who put a new twist to this pastoral possessive individualism. They enjoy a cash income beyond that necessary for subsistence needs; and in a radical departure of value, instead of a full corral (or besides that), some are interested in a bank account. To this end, male reindeer, other than a few stud animals, are marketed at a young age and not kept to fill the corral. This emergent interest in possessions beyond the herd seems to signify a shift from pastoral possession to pastoral *production*. Not surprisingly, these people find support for their aims from the small circle of functionaries, Saami as well as non-Saami, engaged in the everyday administration of reindeer pastoralism or in researching and planning its future.

The present chapter, then, provides some of the background for understanding the beginnings of a likely shift in pastoral values. I trace the change from a traditional marketplace to Kautokeino's cooperative slaughterhouse, and interrelatedly, movement between intensive and extensive herd management.[4] Some Saami perceive these changes as threatening their pastoral raison d'etre.

A caravan on its way to the Bossekop market. Photo from the Wilse collection, Norsk Folkemuseum.

Bossekop Market

Each December and March, for centuries, pastoralists had journeyed to Bossekop, a coastal village at the mouth of the Alta (Kautokeino) River, with caravans of reindeer-drawn sleds loaded down with meat and skins. The journey to the coast could take a week, and after a week or so at the market itself, the caravans would make their way back across the tundra carrying a variety of goods and provisions. Some families would make the expedition in both December and March, probably including visits to relatives and other camps en route.

Boaris Mikkel, born in 1896 and now Ellon Ailu's father-in-law, used to trade at Bossekop—first with the merchants who gathered there, many of them Finnish-speakers, then with the peasants who had come in from their coastal settlements, mostly Saami- or Finnish-speakers. Of course there were Norwegians, but it was pre-dominantly a Saami and Finnish concourse, and bilingualism in those two languages was nothing unusual. Norwegian was really the third language, and this was even truer of the religious meetings held during the market days.

Earlier, trading had been done without money. Boaris Mikkel, in his account to me, speaks of the "exchanges" he made with the merchants and peasants, usually done in cash by that time, but the cash values of the goods exchanged were often "balanced." The pastoralists, at any rate, preferred this way because it gave them more freedom to trade with different merchants. With some merchants and some peasants, however, there would be a verdi relationship, and in those cases no cash would likely pass hands (see Introduction). Basically, the pastoralists traded joints of meat for the different goods offered by the merchants and peasants. The better joints were traded with the merchants. He recalls:

We'd prepare for the market towards the end of November. . . . I might exchange two flanks and two shoulders for flour, sugar, coffee, margarine—and, of course, there was the free glass of schnapps [jogastat] that the merchant offered before we began. . . . Then we'd trade with the peasants [mærralaččat]. They brought ptarmigan and mutton and wool to the market, and gloves, shirts, blankets, and cloths that they had made; also oil for our moccasins, and fish liver, and fish too. We might exchange meat and fish weight for weight, but they had to give more weight of fish. The meat we traded with the peasants was usually breasts, throats, perhaps some legs and backs. And we sold them skins—to the merchants too. . . . But there would always be some parts of each animal that we butchered for the market that would be kept for our own use. We liked to keep the ribs, they are good dry provisions to have when out herding

Ready to trade. Photo from the Wilse collection, Norsk Folkemuseum.

[nieste-biergo], and the marrow bones, too, for their fat. We'd use the blood. And we were always careful that we had enough sinew for ourselves—peasants would want to buy those from us too.[5]

When Boaris Mikkel was a young man, market caravans were focal undertakings of the pastoralists' winter. Although the Bossekop market was by far the most important trading outlet for the Kautokeino pastoralists, their caravans fanned out across the tundra and to Karasjok in the northeast, Enontekio (in Finland) in the south, and Karesuanto (on the Finnish-Swedish border) in the southwest. Here it is proper to speak of trading relations: Even with the advent of cash, there was a strong personalized element to the exchanges between vendor and buyer (and, of course, these roles would be interchanged). Also important is that the pastoralists were able to spread the butchering and sale of their animals through the winter, so there was a synchrony between this side of pastoral production and herding routines and the domestic consumption of meat.

The Bossekop Model

The Bossekop market did not survive World War II, but it is widely recalled as a kind of model of how one should trade (even by some of those too young to have experienced it). After the market closed, Boaris Mikkel would do business with the several merchants who were in Kautokeino by that time, others in Karasjok, and (with improved road conditions) yet others who came up onto the tundra from Alta and Bossekop itself. Some of these merchants were Saami, and of those who were not, most spoke some Saami. They all paid cash. Some would give credit. Most important of all, Boaris Mikkel did not let himself be tied to one buyer or to the sale of whole carcasses only.

But today (1962), the cooperative slaughterhouse in Kautokeino wants a monopoly of sales and whole carcasses—the aggravation this ferments among many of the reindeer owners is behind the argument that will be reported in Chapter 10. Meanwhile, Boaris Mikkel prefers to do business with private merchants. Last year Ellon Ailu and he took a small herd to Karasjok. He said he got a better price in Karasjok (than at the Cooperative), but that is only part of the story. He stayed on the merchant's premises; he himself (with Ellon Ailu) slaughtered the animals and butchered the carcasses, saving what he wanted; he bought provisions. In short, there was a *verdi* ambience, appropriate when trading reindeer meat.

Private merchants, or the more trusted of their assistants, also visit winter camps. They wish to buy animals on-the-hoof (probably employing some herders to help take them back to Kautokeino). Usually, cash is paid on the spot; but not being able to weigh the animals, the price becomes a matter of much discussion. A median weight for the animals—or several such weights, one for the immature, say, another for young bulls, another for the fully grown—will have to be agreed upon, as well as the kroner-per-kilogram price, and the one calculation influences the other. Merchants tell me this is a risky business for them, but it *is* an effective way of "getting the animals off the tundra."

This transaction is *ællemin vuovdet*—"living sale," or on-the-hoof, as I term it. But private merchants also remain interested in buying the better joints of meat, or *gaupe-biergo,* à la the Bossekop market. Usually, gaupe-biergo amounts to two-thirds of the value of the animal. The other third is kept for domestic consumption—*nieste-biergo*—and some animals are slaughtered entirely for domestic consumption.

To summarize, then, animals are disposed of in three different ways: on-the-hoof (ællemin vuovdet), for cash only; joints (gaupe-biergo and nieste-biergo), for cash, and some meat for domestic consumption; domestic (nieste-boccu), all for domestic consumption. In the course of a year a family will use all three of these, or perhaps just two of them: domestic and joints or domestic and on-the-hoof. Now, before looking at the allocations made by families between these alternatives (Chapter 9), we must consider the intrusion of the cooperative option as an alternative to the Bossekop model.

The Cooperative Option

Whereas the Bossekop model is founded on diverse utilization of the reindeer—in other words, intensive husbandry—the cooperative option maximizes sales on-the-hoof twice or three times a year. Intensive husbandry necessarily meant intensive herding, pretty much for the whole year, but the cooperative option is associated with extensive (or lax) herding for much of the year. However, we must be careful about how these factors are connected.

Certainly, there is an increasing need for cash—for

consumer goods, for taxes—and that emphasizes the "market" component of a family's herd; and certainly, increasingly "extensive" herding is also a contemporary (post-World War II) phenomenon. But extensive herding is *not* necessarily seen by the pastoralists as the optimal market strategy. Many, in fact, hold to the contrary proposition, associating effective market production with the surveillance and control of herds. Rather, the key variable in this whole matter is *work commitment* among the pastoralists. As noted earlier, there is always a work commitment with intensive herding but extensification means alternating periods of more and less work, or even of none: This kind of routine is now widely regarded as more congenial.

Periodic on-the-hoof sales to the Cooperative, then, may seem to fit well with this emergent work pattern, just as it also seems to take care of the need for cash. But this is not true for all. There is the owner whose desire to continue with intensive herding is thwarted through its extensification by others on the same range. His animals, too, are swept into the væitalis herd. Then there are those who support extensive herding (for the reason given) yet whose weak economy does not permit many on-the-hoof sales. For all—large and small owners alike—the extensification of herding makes it difficult to *select* animals for slaughter: One may simply not have the requisite herd knowledge, or not at the time it is needed. This situation is grievous to all who still embrace this traditional value, and it is particularly hard on the small owner who may, despite all, have to end up slaughtering some of his cows.[6]

However, there are situations in which extensive herding does not give rise to such prejudicial disjunctions in the relation between herding and husbandry. Much depends on *when,* in the ecologic cycle, herd knowledge is lacking, and *when,* in the production cycle, it is needed. This brings us back to the observations in the previous chapter.

Herd knowledge in the spring, characteristic of Gow'dojottelit herds, is consonant with the Bossekop model of production, which builds on detailed husbandry knowledge. But where production is based on the slaughter of young animals (one-year- and two-year-olds, especially males), the Oar'jebelli tendency, the loss of this knowledge in the spring is not prejudicial. What matters is the greater control of Oar'jebelli herds—certainly compared with Gow'dojottelit herds—in the autumn. The Cooperative encourages autumn (over winter) slaughter as the optimal time to put reindeer meat on the market. But, as we will see, even Oar'jebelli owners resist this. On Gow'dojottelit, at that time of year, loss of herd control, and hence knowledge, is inimicable to planned decisions concerning slaughter, whether it be the Bossekop model or the cooperative option.

Concerning pastoral control over the breeding of the animals, there are compelling reasons for *not* attempting to increase the little control there is. Collective herding means that animals of different owners run together, itself a disincentive for selective breeding. Unless all owners practice selective breeding, the few who do are likely to find their selected stud animals expending their energy on cows of other owners, and conversely, some of their own cows will be serviced by inferior stud animals of other owners. Also, for pastoralists who believe their individual security rests with the *number* of their animals, breeding for quality is a secondary matter. In fact, some take things to the other extreme, maximizing herd size even when this may prejudice potential market yields, for crowding and overgrazing commonly lead to decreases in animals' weights and deterioration of their health.

A fundamental point in the central theme of this chapter needs stressing: What I have been describing in neutral terms as changes in markets and management touches a pastoral nerve. Much of the Saami pastoralists' sense of self is fortified through their control over their animals, *including their disposal.* This goes beyond which animals to slaughter and when, important as these matters are, to consideration of the manner in which the slaughtering is done and by whom. As Saami who will speak in Chapter 10 make so clear, the cooperative option turns these matters into issues as never before.

How Many Animals?

How many animals do these pastoralists *really* own? The world over, nomadic pastoralists are reputed to "fix" their animal numbers when they cannot withhold them altogether. The Kautokeino Saami are no exception. But if pastoral numbers are fictions, what stories do they tell?

Annually, each owner is obliged to provide the tax authorities and the Reindeer Administration with figures of herd size. The figures to the Administration address a number of matters besides overall herd size, such as fertility rates and losses to predators. The tax authorities, however, are only interested in herd size, that is, estimated capital. Instead of direct taxation, a system of percentage taxation is used. So what matters is the number of animals one owns, not the number slaughtered for income. Twenty percent of the herd is exempted from tax. The remainder is taxed at set rates,[7] irrespective of herd size (i.e., capital wealth).

The richer owners are happy with this method, but the poorer owners find it unfair, and, significantly, the county officials complain that it generates too little tax money. There should be a shifting percentage scale, says the smaller owner. County officials would prefer direct taxation, calculated on the numbers of animals slaughtered. But the skeptic asks, how could one possibly control the slaughter returns? Indeed. But with the present system, what control is there over estimated herd size? One positive feature of the present system from the Administration's point of view is that, if anything, it encourages people to slaughter more (reducing their taxable income accordingly); direct taxation would reverse this effect.

At all events, the 1959 tax lists for Kautokeino are revealing. The pastoralists totaled 41.6 percent of the taxpayers. They also accounted for 64 percent of declared and taxable capital in the county and 30.5 percent of total income, but only 19.2 percent of the total tax revenue.[8] This suggests not simply that the pastoralists' tax returns were too small (even though this is surely true), but that the richer owners were taxed too little.[9]

Then there is the issue of the relation of the one set of figures to the other. Two widely held assumptions are that the figures submitted to the tax authorities are lower than those sent into the Administration, and that neither of these authorities is privy to the other's figures. The second of these assumptions might strike one as naïve;[10] the first is almost certainly correct. However, it is the factors behind the figures to the Reindeer Administration that are especially intriguing.

For one thing, there is a background of countervailing sentiments. Pride is taken in herd size—inordinate pride, one may say, but it must be veiled. One will hear only a rich owner saying he has less than he has. A young man, though, lives for the day when he has an expanding herd. (That is likely to come about—if it does—at much the same time as he has to "give" portions of the herd to his children so that they may start their family herds.) What one says of *others'* herd size depends very much on context, with interpersonal and what can best be called pasture-strategic factors mixed in. But when I mention what some owner has told me is his herd size, I am usually told that the figure is too low. That is no surprise. It must also be stressed that herd size is little talked about but *constantly observed.*

Yet the figures an owner give to the Reindeer Administration are a part of his validation of pasture needs (how strong a part, I hesitate to say). For both he who wishes to move to a better summer pasture and he who wishes to stay where he is and ward off others have cause to put in an inflated return to the Administration. My belief, then, is that the figures submitted to the Reindeer Administration are as high as individual owners dare go. Al-most certainly higher than the figures to the tax authorities, they are still appreciably low. How low?

There is no one answer to that. It depends not only on the individual owner but whom one asks to comment. For instance, two persons give me their considered estimates of the herd size of twenty-three Gow'dojottelit owners. The one reckons that the figures submitted to the Administration amount to no more than 52 percent of "real" herd size; the other put it at 62 percent. Both individuals have first-hand knowledge, over many years, of the Gow'dojottelit people and their herds. He who gave the 52-percent figure works in the sheriff's office, where the hiding of animals is a matter of official concern. We can well suppose a factor of professional skepticism in his estimates. It is worth noting that his estimates vary remarkably little for the individual herds: from 51 percent to 54 percent. The other informant (they are both Saami-speakers) has had more varied and perhaps more personal contacts with the Gow'dojottelit people, and his estimates of the figures from the individual herds reach from 59 percent up to 78 percent of "real" herd size.

9.
Composing Herds

While government authorities and their experts worry over total numbers and "overgrazing," an abiding concern of the pastoralists themselves is herd composition. Herds of the same size may be variously composed, and in this chapter I look at some patterns of distribution of animals between the six principal components of a herd—calves and yearlings, junior cows, senior cows, junior bulls, senior bulls, and castrates. The stories these figures tell are those of the *proportionate* value of each component to all of the others. Few things interest the pastoralist more, and they loved talking to me about it. Especially, they enjoyed puzzles of the "well, if x what of y?" kind.

So I began to construct herd budgets (as I called them) cooperatively with those men, and a few women, I knew best and who had a fair sense of what I was about. (The battery of numerical tables this produced are collected in Appendix 2, denoted here as Tables A.1 through A.12.) A budget would be pieced together through several sessions—and there were false starts. I never asked a person to construct his own herd budget (nor did I attempt a budget for Ellon Ailu's herd, he being my more constant companion and helper). Rather, I would ask owners and

herders, both from Or'da and *not* from Or'da, say, to consider specific points concerning "an Or'da herd of 500 deer before calving." The "x" and "y" included considerations of how the specific ecology of Or'da, and ownership of 500 animals rather than 200 or 1,000, affected herd composition and management decisions. "I'm trying to get an idea," I would say, "of the kind of calculations you/they make in Or'da, and I'm wondering about this . . ." Sometimes respondents had particular owners in mind rather than any generalizable notion of "Or'da" herd management, and this became a matter of discussion. My rule of thumb became not to incorporate much about personal herd management circumstances and strategies unless I heard the same things from independent sources or had reliable enough first-hand observations myself.

At any rate, I badgered my helpers for explanations of whatever figures they came up with, and I learned a great deal from the small disagreements between my helpers—perhaps two or three of them together, wherever we happened to be. I was seldom rebuffed. (Iskun Biera, though, cared little for this intrusive exercise.) The budgets pose more questions than I can answer (though others may see answers where I do not); but they have also led me to questions of which I would not otherwise have had much awareness. The whole process was broadly generative for me, bringing me closer to the compositional logic of herd structure and the variables from herd to herd.

Of seven budgeted herds, five are from the Gow'dojottelit range, of which three are from Joakkonjar'ga (Table A.1). The latter are herds of identified owners about whose husbandry I had strong first-hand knowledge: Iskun Biera, Iskun Mikko, and Jorgu Biera. Here, especially, I tried to take account of owners' personality, lifestyle, and family situation in explaining marked differences in herd size: 1,000, 400, and 200 animals before calving, respectively. The other two Gow'dojottelit herds are from Or'da, where I had limited first-hand experience. Here, beyond difference in herd size again (500 and 200), we are led into a comparison of nanne and njar'ga conditions. Finally, there is the opportunity for interrange comparisons and contrasts between Gow'dojottelit herds and two on Oar'jebelli (herd sizes 1,000 and 500, with variations on the njar'ga and nanne adaptations).[1]

To recapitulate: The herd sizes from before calving are those with which we begin; increments, losses, and slaughter over the next twelve months are then fed into the simulated budgets of the herds.

There are three crucial proportions in the makeup of a pastoral herd: cows to calves, cows to males, and bulls to castrates. That between cows and calves is the one most open to "natural"-come-ecologic factors and the least controlled by the pastoralist. Or rather, his control is reactive (the option of eliminating cows that, for some reason or another, fail to give birth or fail to nurture their calves successfully). By contrast, the proportions of males to cows and of bulls to castrates are, of course, in the hands of the pastoralist. Most important of all is the relation between these three proportions and absolute numbers. Here, sight must not be lost of the fact that the proportions and even the absolute numbers are outcomes of constraints or opportunities. These may be ecologic, economic, or aesthetic, and they vary from owner to owner. But before proceeding to those differences, it is important to notice how the basic proportions of *all* herds change in the course of the cycle of an ordinary pastoral year.

It is helpful to envisage the cycle as one that continually moves between reproduction and production, where "production" amounts to the animals taken out of the herd for slaughter (Fig. 9.1). The autumn rut is an important pivotal point in the cycle. There are more bulls before the rut than after, when a number are castrated for work as draft animals or for slaughter later in the autumn or winter. However, the ideal picture of bulls = reproduction, and castrates = production does not hold. For several reasons we will come to, there are still more bulls slaughtered than castrates. Then in the spring, last year's calves become yearlings, making way for a new crop of calves, whose numbers, every owner hopes, will more than make up for the depletion of stock through the previous year. Should yearlings be included in the breeding population? As the lesser distortion, I have excluded them, even though, at that second rut in their lives, they become varek and vuonjal, respectively.

For the task before us, this all means that the herd is a moving target. With the change in status, in the autumn, from yearling to young male and female, the bull and cow herds are swelled significantly. Some animals counted before the rut as "bulls" must be counted again, after the rut, as "castrates" (and the pre- and post-rut totals kept separate). Therefore our summaries of herd composition, losses, and gains refer specifically to certain points in the pastoral year: before calving; pre-rut, during the rut, and post-rut; and after winter slaughter.

Preliminary Overview of the Seven Herds

Perhaps the first thing to note is that there is little variance between the herds in either percentage increments from calves or percentage losses of animals—the differences are in the slaughter percentages. It is the same with the various components of a herd: cows, bulls, castrates, yearlings, and calves: Differences in respect to any of these components reach no higher than 8 percent, and within each of the three groupings of our seven, the percentage differences are lower still, often null. However, slaughter percentages vary as much as 51 percent (in the case of castrates) for the seven herds, and even 19 percent (in this case, bulls) within a grouping (Table A.2).

Percentages of *calf increment* are a function of a number of possible factors and their interrelations. Fecundity itself

PRODUCTION   CAPITAL   REPRODUCTION

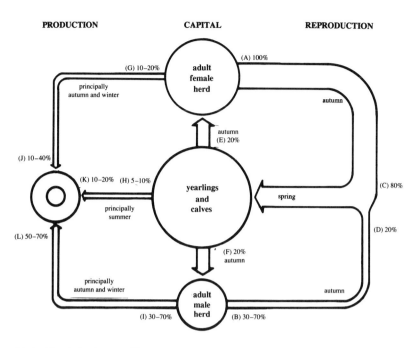

(A) % of female herd engaged in rut
(B) % of male herd engaged in rut
(C) % of females to males in rut
(D) % of males to females in rut
(E) % of yearlings to adult female herd
(F) % of yearlings to adult male herd
(G) % of female herd slaughtered
(H) % of yearlings and calves slaughtered
(I) % of male herd slaughtered
(J) % of adult female contribution to production
(K) % of yearling and calf contribution to production
(L) % of adult male contribution to production

The percentages are intended to indicate the range of "typical"; otherwise, see Tables A.6, A.7, A.9, and A.10. No adjustment has been made for losses.

The absolute sizes of adult and juvenile herds differ considerably from one case to another, but their proportionate sizes are fairly constant: Thus one circle suffices for each.

But the size of the "herd" that is slaughtered differs considerably—by as much as four times (in our sample of the seven herds). This is indicated through the use of two concentric circles—the smaller is but a quarter of the size of the larger circle.

Figure 9.1 Reproduction and production

is in part a matter of the health and weight of the cow, and these relate to circumstances on seasonal pastures: gorm fly? access to salt? relief from mosquitoes and summer heat? Theft of cows is also a factor. And besides figures telling us how many calves were born, we need an indication of how many survive beyond their first summer. Relatedly, what kinds of rodno are among the different herds? Tables A.3 and A.4 provide some of the information.

As for animal *losses* (other than slaughter) incurred in

the course of the annual cycle, one frequently hears "ten percent overall, and double that figure for calves." Our figures run between 7 and 10 percent overall and 9 to 14 percent for calves (Table A.5). Note, though, that two additional factors (so often left out) have been taken into account. First, calves lost before 15 June (or arrival at summer pastures) are not counted. As Ellon Ailu sees it, "They never were yours," that is, not until they are out of the nursery (see Chapter 6). Second, just as a proportion of the "lost" wandered out of the herd, never to return, so there are others who wander *into* the herd, un-recorded. Some of the wanderers will be slaughtered by herders in other camps as nieste-biergo (provisions). This probably befalls nanne herds—unless they are under watch the whole summer—more than njar'ga; and nanne animals more than others are prone to the debilitating scourge of the gorm fly. Yearlings especially are lost in this way. Among njar'ga herds, there will always be some animals, usually large males such as her'gi, shot and stolen by nonpastoralists. Others, this time the less experienced animals, fall prey to eagles or fall over cliff faces.

So there are ecologic patterns attached to the loss (in a diversity of ways) of the "ten percent." Excluding "hunger years" (for example, when ice prevents animals from reaching the winter lichens), owners pretty well know what their losses will be, and also when they will be: "We reckon from May to January. We don't lose deer after that" (Ellon Ailu).[2] So when they are ready for the winter slaughter, in the "peace" of the winter, owners will budget their losses then.

The proportion of male animals to females in a herd will vary according to whether the count is done before or after the winter slaughter, and the proportion of castrates to stud animals will be at its highest just before entering the rut. Accordingly, Tables A.6 to A.8 provide the following percentages (in all cases excluding yearlings and calves): (1) males to females, at the conclusion of the winter slaughter: from 24 to 50 percent, with the Gow'dojottelit figures consistently higher than those from Oar'jebelli, and the highest from a Joakkonjar'ga herd (Table A.6); (2) stud animals to females, on entering the rut: from 10 to 14 percent, except for the Iskun Biera herd, at 20 percent (Table A.6); (3) stud animals to castrates, on entering the rut: from a high of 120 percent (Oar'jebelli and Iskun Biera, with more bulls than castrates) to a low of 28 percent (Table A.6); (4) bulls to castrates by age-class, at the end of winter (castration begins with three-year-olds and is of appreciably higher occurrence on Gow'dojottelit than on Oar'jebelli; Table A.7); (5) allocation of castrates by year (reciprocal of Table A.7) and also by task, at the end of winter. In all herds the greater proportion of castrates are selected for work as draft animals, from 61 percent in a Joakkonjar'ga herd to 100 percent in a Oar'jebelli herd (Table A.8).

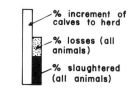

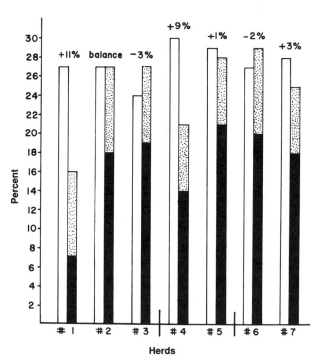

Figure 9.2 Percent gains and losses

Out of these data, detailed profiles will emerge of the different owners' slaughter practices. Winter is the principal slaughter season for several reasons: There are more castrates ready for slaughter (Gow'dojottelit practice especially), yearlings have become two-year-old males and females ready for slaughter (Oar'jebelli practice especially), and the commotion of autumn has subsided. Table A.9 provides an overview of what happens. The differences between lines (a) and (b) of the table show how the post-rut entry of yearlings into the adult herds is distributed; and the differences between lines (b) and (c) indicate the distribution of the winter slaughter.

In the case of the two Oar'jebelli owners (#6 and #7), the post-rut *adult* herd increases by 23 and 27 percent, respectively. But of these post-rut adult herd sizes, 19 and

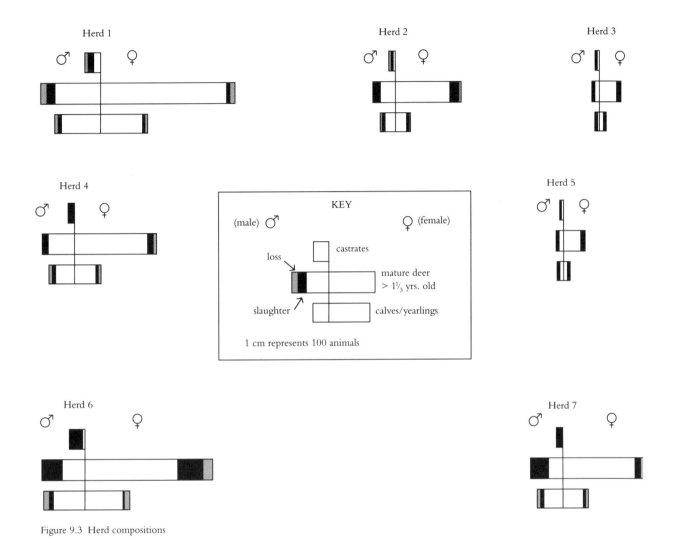

Figure 9.3 Herd compositions

16 percent, respectively, are slaughtered.[3] Iskun Biera (#1), by contrast, slaughters only 6 percent of his 22 percent increase. Others in Gow'dojottelit, with increases between 19 and 23 percent, slaughter between 11 and 15 percent. Of calves at this time of year, Iskun Biera takes 1 percent, others a few percentiles more.

Much of the information reviewed thus far is summarized in Figures 9.2 and 9.3. In the sections that now follow, I seek the *contexts* that would explain these measurements of interherd (that is, interowner) differences. Some of the differences amount to trends moving in opposite directions. Here my discussion will be anchored to the detailed slaughter or sale allocations made by each owner of the seven herds through one year.

Three Joakkonjar'ga Herds (#1, #2, #3)

Iskun Biera (#1) and Iskun Mikko (#2) are brothers, and Jorgu Biera (#3) is their first cousin (Fig. I.3). Along with other brothers, a brother-in-law, and another cousin, they make up the "Buljo crowd," who have been together for years out on the summer pasture of Joakkonjar'ga (area VII in Fig. 3.3). At other seasons they separate into two *sii'dat* (partners with a herd), whose respective compositions vary over the years. Iskun Biera is the eldest of the group at fifty-four years, Iskun Mikko two years his junior. Iskun Biera has teenage sons, and daughters in their early twenties, one of whom is married. Iskun Mikko has four unmarried sons in their early twenties, so the two men are similarly situated in terms of family development cycle. If anything, Iskun Mikko is, at the moment, the more favorably placed regarding a herding labor force (though when his sons marry, his herd will be sorely depleted). Yet Iskun Biera has more than twice the animals of this brother, who himself is the second largest owner among the Buljos. The cousin, Jorgu Biera, is forty-two years old, and the eldest of his several children is only twelve. His herd before calving numbers under three hundred animals—under half that of Iskun Mikko's; but then, he is ten years his junior.

Before anything else, it is the disproportionate herd size of Iskun Biera that begs explanation. His animals were not ill-gotten, I was told; that is, he was not a reindeer thief when he was gradually building up the herd to its present size. (The same could not have been said of the brothers' father—but that is another story—and the two elder sons were given a good start, perhaps.) Nor did Iskun Biera's wife bring a particularly large number of animals into the herd. No one pressed the factors of "luck" or exceptional "talent": Iskun Biera is certainly særra, but not notably fitmat (see Chapter 2). What was often said is that he is hanes, that is, "miserly" in its broadest sense. One does not expect favors from Iskun Biera, and you do not get much in return for looking after any of his strays. He attempts to manage without an employed hand (ræŋ'ga): "I'm his ræŋ'ga," complains his son-in-law. His domestic economy, as far as I could judge, was penny-pinching. But on the credit side, Iskun Biera is not proud or arrogant, and he is a very hard worker. He is surely canny, too.

Can such personal attributes carry the weight of the explanation we seek? I believe they do, to a great extent.

It is significant that we do not find much of a difference between Iskun Biera and the others in the composition of his and their herds, contrary to what might have been expected. The percentage of cows (pre-rut), for instance, in each of the three herds is much the same: 37 percent for Iskun Biera, 39 percent for Iskun Mikko, and

38 percent for Jorgu Biera. Or bulls: 9 percent for Iskun Biera, 8 percent for both Iskun Mikko and Jorgu Biera (Table A.9). So Iskun Biera has not used the freedom from budgetary cares that his much larger herd size could give him to change his production profile (the two Oar'jebelli herds supply examples of this). To the contrary, Iskun Biera's herd exemplifies the general pastoral ideal of slaughtering as few cows as possible, only 2 percent, compared to 20 percent for Iskun Mikko and Jorgu Biera. This amounts to 13 percent of his total slaughter (Iskun Mikko, 43 percent; Jorgu Biera, 31 percent) (Table A.10). More interestingly, he fulfills the Joakkonjar'ga value of having as many animals as possible running in the herd. He has the largest herd and, by far, the lowest slaughter percentage of all at 7 percent (Iskun Mikko, 18 percent; Jorgu Biera, 19 percent) (Table A.11).

One may wonder why Iskun Biera, slaughtering only 2 percent of his cows, does not have a higher percentage of cows than others. The answer lies in the high numbers of the other components of his herd (Table A.9), and one conclusion is that he has "too many" male animals and therefore "too few" cows.

And, we may well ask, why are cows—the *bellot,* or garden, of the herd—slaughtered at all? For the small owner it can well be a matter of need (e.g., Jorgu Biera); for others it is a touch of extravagance (e.g., Iskun Mikko); yet others show over-measured caution (e.g., Iskun Biera) (Table A.10). There are fairly uniform reasons, however, explaining *which* cows are slaughtered or sold for slaughter: They are either "old" or rodno, or, on the contrary, young animals (e.g., vuonjal) taken for their fat meat. Calves slaughtered (usually in the summer or autumn) are the injured or orphaned, or those with the much-prized white coats. These details lie behind the detailed allocations (Tables 9.1–9.3).

Iskun Biera, being miserly, is the one who "doesn't dare" *(i duost)* to slaughter a rodno—for who knows, it just might calve next year? In fact, he does take the occasional rodno, but people still talk about him like this, and the contrast, not just comparison, they draw is between him and his brother, Iskun Mikko. With more than twice the herd of his brother, Iskun Biera gives himself less income than Iskun Mikko. The pattern is repeated in

Table 9.1 Slaughter/Sale Allocations: Herd #1 (Iskun Biera)

	Domestic	Joints	On-the-hoof	Total
Summer				
Bulls	—	—	—	—
Castrates	1	—	—	1
Cows	—	—	—	—
Yearlings and calves	13	—	—	13
Total	14	—	—	14 (15%)
Autumn				
Bulls	4	—	14	18
Castrates	—	—	11	11
Cows	2	—	5	7
Yearlings and calves	4	—	—	4
Total	10	—	30	40 (42.5%)
Winter				
Bulls	—	10	10	20
Castrates	5	8	2	15
Cows	—	2	3	5
Yearlings and calves	—	—	—	—
Total	5	20	15	40 (42.5%)
Whole Year				
Bulls	4	10	24	38 (40%)
Castrates	6	8	13	27 (29%)
Cows	2	2	8	12 (13%)
Yearlings and calves	17	—	—	17 (18%)
Total	29 (31%)	20 (21%)	45 (48%)	94 (100%)

the subsistence sector of their economies: Iskun Biera slaughters fewer animals for family consumption than his brother.

Looking at castrates, the three Joakkonjar'ga herds slaughter much the same percentage (Table A.10), but because Iskun Biera has more castrates than the others, he actually slaughters more of them, so they constitute a larger percentage of his total slaughter. Perhaps the interesting comparison here is between Iskun Mikko and Jorgu Biera: The one slaughters thirteen castrates and the

other twelve, but Iskun Mikko's thirteen amount to only 13 percent of his total slaughter, whereas Jorgu Biera's twelve account for almost a quarter of his total slaughter.

It is such micro items of husbandry, repeated over the years, that build the difference in herd numbers (without corresponding changes in herd composition). Iskun Mikko, for his part, uses his herd to ensure that his family live well within the traditional style. And he looks to the day when his sons marry and have their own (modest) herds, with animals drawn from the present family

Table 9.2 Slaughter/Sale Allocations: Herd #2 (Iskun Mikko)

	Domestic	Joints	On-the-hoof	Total
Summer				
Bulls	—	—	—	—
Castrates	—	—	—	—
Cows	2	—	—	2
Yearlings and calves	15	—	—	15
Total	17	—	—	17 (17%)
Autumn				
Bulls	1	4	6	11
Castrates	—	—	8	8
Cows	5	4	11	20
Yearlings and calves	3	—	—	3
Total	9	8	25	42 (42%)
Winter				
Bulls	—	—	15	15
Castrates	—	5	—	5
Cows	6	10	5	21
Yearlings and calves	—	—	—	—
Total	6	15	20	41 (41%)
Whole Year				
Bulls	1	4	21	26 (26%)
Castrates	—	5	8	13 (13%)
Cows	13	14	16	43 (43%)
Yearlings and calves	18	—	—	18 (18%)
Total	32 (32%)	23 (23%)	45 (45%)	100 (100%)

herd—though perhaps he is not thinking enough about that. Quite dissimilar in personality from his brother, Iskun Mikko, I sometimes heard, while not particular særra, is fitmat.

Jorgu Biera is struggling, like others of the Buljo crowd. Precisely because he has such a small herd (from which he draws but a minimum income), he has to eat into it in much the same proportions that Iskun Mikko does with his herd (Iskun Mikko 18 percent, Jorgu Biera 19 percent), rather than saving like Iskun Biera (7 percent slaughter) (Table A.11). He probably could not manage

with fewer castrates: His need for draft animals is approximately the same as that of any other owner on Gow'dojottelit. He could do with fewer bulls as stud animals, letting his cows be served by others' bulls; however, his bulls must also contribute to his domestic economy (in kind and in cash) if he is not going to eat still more into his cow herd. As it is, about one-third of his total slaughter is of cows. For a man with so few animals, wherever he may turn in his herd there will be the same pressing constraints. Thus Jorgu Biera, who can least afford it, consumes a quarter of his calves and yearlings. A summa-

Table 9.3 Slaughter/Sale Allocations: Herd #3 (Jorga Biera)

	Domestic	Joints	On-the-hoof	Total
Summer				
Bulls	—	—	—	—
Castrates	—	—	—	—
Cows	1	—	—	1
Yearlings and calves	10	—	—	10
Total	11	—	—	11 (22%)
Autumn				
Bulls	2	—	4	6
Castrates	—	—	3	3
Cows	3	—	3	6
Yearlings and calves	2	—	—	2
Total	7	—	10	17 (35%)
Winter				
Bulls	—	4	—	4
Castrates	—	9	—	9
Cows	4	4	—	8
Yearlings and calves	—	—	—	—
Total	4	17	—	21 (43%)
Whole Year				
Bulls	2	4	4	10 (20%)
Castrates	—	9	3	12 (24.5%)
Cows	8	4	3	15 (31%)
Yearlings and calves	12	—	—	12 (24.5%)
Total	22 (45%)	17 (35%)	10 (20%)	49 (100%)

tion of his economy, compared with those of Iskun Biera and Iskun Mikko, is to be found in the percentages of on-the-hoof slaughter (Table A.12): 48 percent for Iskun Biera and 45 percent for Iskun Mikko, but 20 percent for Jorgu Biera—and then only in the autumn. In the winter he sells joints, sufficient to provide for his family's cash needs; his other domestic priority at that time is fat meat for the preparation of dried provisions.

Looking for some general explanation of Jorgu Biera's predicament, two things come to mind. First, his and others' are economies of families burdened with young children not old enough to contribute to the work force but whose needs draw upon herd capital. As this burden is lightened, so the family herd may grow. The other factor is altogether more complex, and tentative. It has to do with being a partner to men with herds so much larger than one's own. Most of the animals one sees are not one's own. It can very easily seem that much of the time out in the terrain is spent working for those whose animals one *does* repeatedly see. So there may be a factor of morale, perhaps draining a person of initiative and making him reluctant to commit that high degree of com-

Table 9.4 Slaughter/Sale Allocations: Herd #4 (Or'da)

	Domestic	Joints	On-the-hoof	Total
Summer				
Bulls	—	—	—	—
Castrates	—	—	—	—
Cows	—	—	2	2
Yearlings and calves	13	—	—	3
Total	13	—	2	15 (15.5%)
Autumn				
Bulls	2	—	5	7
Castrates	—	—	16	16
Cows	6	—	4	10
Yearlings and calves	3	—	—	3
Total	11	—	25	36 (37.5%)
Winter				
Bulls	—	3	6	9
Castrates	3	12	4	19
Cows	2	5	10	17
Yearlings and calves	—	—	—	—
Total	5	20	20	45 (47%)
Whole Year				
Bulls	2	3	11	16 (17%)
Castrates	3	12	20	35 (36%)
Cows	8	5	16	29 (30%)
Yearlings and calves	16	—	—	16 (17%)
Total	29 (30%)	20 (21%)	47 (49%)	96 (100%)

mitment and endurance to the very physical business of herding. In such a situation, it is likely those with the fewest animals will be hurt the most, for they have negligible margins for error.

If this is so, why do the smaller owners stay alongside one such as Iskun Biera? First of all, there are the social ties (in this case among the Buljos). Then there may be a problem of being accepted into another sii'da. Most important of all (in the present context) is the degree of symbiosis that actually pertains between the large and small owners. At least the small owner knows that as long as his animals run in the same herd as those of the large owner he derives some herd security. Seasonal pastures are assured, even herding is assured in periods of his absence, and he need not worry about being short of bulls to service his own animals. For the large owner, having partners with fewer animals means an optimal relation between the number of herders and of grazing animals. Part of the explanation of Iskun Biera's economy, then, is exactly this favorable ratio at each season. Animal numbers also add to the weight of Iskun Biera's opinions in discussions among partners.[4]

Table 9.5 Slaughter/Sale Allocations: Herd #5 (Or'da)

	Domestic	Joints	On-the-hoof	Total
Summer				
Bulls	—	—	—	—
Castrates	—	—	—	—
Cows	1	—	—	1
Yearlings and calves	10	—	—	10
Total	11	—	—	11 (18%)
Autumn				
Bulls	2	—	8	10
Castrates	—	—	3	3
Cows	3	—	6	9
Yearlings and calves	2	—	—	2
Total	7	—	17	24 (41%)
Winter				
Bulls	—	7	—	7
Castrates	—	9	—	9
Cows	4	4	—	8
Yearlings and calves	—	—	—	—
Total	4	20	—	24 (41%)
Whole Year				
Bulls	2	7	8	17 (29%)
Castrates	—	9	3	12 (20%)
Cows	8	4	6	18 (31%)
Yearlings and calves	12	—	—	12 (20%)
Total	22 (37%)	20 (34%)	17 (29%)	59 (100%)

Two Or'da Herds (#4 and #5)

In precept, at least, Or'da's pastoral production is similar to that of Joakkonjar'ga. As much is suggested by the data on the slaughter and sale of animals (Tables 9.4 and 9.5). Or'da owners, too, slaughter animals for domestic consumption and for joints (domestic consumption and for sale) and sell animals on-the-hoof. The percentage distributions show consistency between Or'da and Joakkonjar'ga. The differences follow systemically from herd size. In addition, there are individual differences of the kind between Iskun Mikko and Iskun Biera.

However, clear differences exist in pastoral practice between the two areas. At much the same time as Joakkonjar'ga became more crowded with people and animals,[5] the Danel Anti sii'da, for instance, took new space to themselves in the high terrain (or'da) behind the coast, moving there early in the summer, after calving, without first going down to the coast, as they had previously. Without fences, this means summers of hard work. The herd has to be watched to prevent its scattering in all directions under aggravation from the heat and the mosquitoes. Nonetheless, as noted in Chapter 3, some animals will be lost in the terrain, wandering far afield or expiring from exhaustion, particularly yearlings and calves (Tables A.3 and A.5). There are dividends, however. Less subjected to poachers from the coastal population, they lose fewer her'gi. By percentage, more calves are born (Table A.3). Body weights are above those of the njar'ga herds (Table A.11). There is also completer herd knowledge (Chapter 7). In balance, these factors account for the favorable economy of the Or'da owners in relation to those of Joakkonjar'ga. The higher calving percentage, for instance, allows the small Or'da owner (#5) to slaughter more animals than Jorgu Biera (#3) and still increase his herd (the total of animals lost is much the same in the two cases).

Fertility rates and body weights are in part a matter of husbandry, but they also reflect aggregated ecologic conditions of different pastures, in this case between Joakkonjar'ga and Or'da. The greater weights of slaughtered animals in the same age-class show, of course, in the kroner income generated. Whereas Joakkonjar'ga herd #2 (Iskun Mikko) receives 7,627 kroner for *sales* (joints and on-the-hoof) derived from 68 animals, Or'da herd #4 receives 8,510 kroner from 67 animals. There is a similar difference between Joakkonjar'ga #3 (Jorgu Biera) and Or'da #5: 2,497 kroner from 27 animals and 4,050 kroner from 37 animals, respectively (Tables A.11 and 9.1–9.5).

The greater pastoral efficiency of Or'da—with a smaller and better-coordinated work force than on Joakkonjar'ga—can be seen in the handling of castrates. Joakkonjar'ga and Or'da owners—all still much in the intensive management tradition (Chapter 8)—are equally committed to having an ample number of castrates in their herds, for slaughter and as draft animals. But a higher percentage of Or'da castrates are slaughtered, or sold for slaughter, than is the case with Joakkonjar'ga (Table A.10). This is explained, I think, by the Or'da owners' greater knowledge and control of their animals through the summer and autumn. Joakkonjar'ga owners, by contrast, have castrates they want to slaughter or sell but, too often, they cannot find them at the right time.

As long as Or'da owners take care not to crowd their summer pastures with animals, and as long as they exercise control (deficient as it may be) through herding rather than fences, they can expect to maintain their advantages over Joakkonjar'ga. Their relative success, however, brings its own problem: Herd #4 is expanding at 9 percent and Herd #5 at 1 percent (the difference is principally one of family life cycles). There are other herds on the or'da, too, all of which have an overall annual increment (see Fig. 9.2).

Two Oar'jebelli Herds (#6 and #7)

There *is* a change in husbandry, in precept and practice, with the two Oar'jebelli herds. The difference is greatest respecting the Joakkonjar'ga herds but present, too, respecting the Or'da herds. A dramatic gauge of this difference is in the kroner incomes derived from herds of approximately the same pre-calving size: Herd #6 yields over four times that of #1 (Iskun Biera), and #7 is far ahead of #4 (Or'da). Put most generally, between Oar'jebelli and Gow'dojottelit there is a value difference. Whereas owners on Gow'dojottelit are inclined to maximize the herd as the primary source of esteem and aesthetics, those of Oar'jebelli maximize the income derived from the herd.

From this difference there may follow another, that between constant and intermittent work commitment (Chapter 8). Along with the herd as a source of esteem and aesthetics goes a constant work commitment. A well-planned and executed intermittent work commitment, however, is capable of generating a satisfying kroner yield from the herd, and the Oar'jebelli herds are fewer and larger than those on Gow'dojottelit (Chapter 1),[6] with a higher degree of coordination of herd movements, particularly in the autumn.

Most significant of all is the way in which these factors combine. For it is the Oar'jebelli herds in our sample, not those of Gow'dojottelit, that have the greater reproductive capacity (proportion of females to males, Table A.6) *and* the higher production (Table A.11).

A closer look at Table A.7 gives an interesting twist to the husbandry contrast that I am suggesting. The two Oar'jebelli herds have more bulls than castrates, and *so does Iskun Biera* (#1)—but for quite different reasons. He wants to increase his herd on the terrain: The bulls are

Table 9.6 Slaughter/Sale Allocations: Herd #6 (Oar'jebelli)

	Domestic	Joints	On-the-hoof	Total
Summer				
Bulls	—	—	—	—
Castrates	—	—	—	—
Cows	2	—	—	2
Yearlings and calves	25	—	—	25
Total	27	—	—	27 (10%)
Autumn				
Bulls	—	—	23	23
Castrates	—	—	16	16
Cows	5	—	5	10
Yearlings and calves	—	—	—	—
Total	5	—	44	49 (17%)
Winter				
Bulls	8	—	83	91
Castrates	—	—	41	41
Cows	8	—	67	75
Yearlings and calves	—	—	—	—
Total	16	—	191	207 (73%)
Whole Year				
Bulls	8	—	106	114 (40%)
Castrates	—	—	57	57 (20%)
Cows	15	—	72	87 (31%)
Yearlings and calves	25	—	—	25 (9%)
Total	48 (17%)	—	235 (83%)	283 (100%)

studs. Furthermore, an unintended consequence of his measure of success is that he has not people enough to castrate (prior to the rut, with post-rut slaughter in view) all the deer (including four- and five-year-olds) that he otherwise would. The Oar'jebelli owners bother less about castration as a means of increasing body weight, for they concentrate their production on the sales of young males; that is, the bulk of their bulls are *not* seen as studs. The sales are on-the-hoof.

Some numbers press the point (Tables 9.6 and 9.7). Of the 114 bulls taken out of the herd by #6, 89 are varek.

The corresponding figures are even more pronounced in the case of #7: All except 3 of the 64 bulls taken are varek. And all but 8 of the 114 and 5 of the 64 are sold on-the-hoof.

There is a clear economic rationale in play here. The greatest growth of a reindeer is in its first two years. Thereafter, it grows more slowly, and each year animals are lost. So the sensible time to sell an animal is at the end of the two years. It is better to receive 105 kroner for a two-year-old than to wait another year for a possible 145 kroner for the same animal. The argument is partic-

Table 9.7 Slaughter/Sale Allocations: Herd #7 (Oar'jebelli)

	Domestic	Joints	On-the-hoof	Total
Summer				
Bulls	—	—	—	—
Castrates	—	—	—	—
Cows	1	—	—	1
Yearlings and calves	5	—	—	15
Total	16	—	—	16 (12.5%)
Autumn				
Bulls	1	—	27	28
Castrates	—	—	5	5
Cows	5	—	10	15
Yearlings and calves	—	—	—	—
Total	6	—	42	48 (37.5%)
Winter				
Bulls	4	—	32	36
Castrates	—	—	16	16
Cows	7	—	5	12
Yearlings and calves	—	—	—	—
Total	11	—	53	64 (50%)
Whole Year				
Bulls	5	—	59	64 (50%)
Castrates	—	—	21	21 (16%)
Cows	13	—	15	28 (22%)
Yearlings and calves	15	—	—	15 (12%)
Total	33 (26%)	—	95 (74%)	128 (100%)

ularly compelling for these Oar'jebelli owners on account of the heavy body weight of their two-year-olds. While this means optimal market prices, it is also the heavier young animals that are more likely to succumb from exhaustion towards the end of a hard winter, especially if they are gorm fly-ridden, as is often the case. Also, these heavy two-year-olds are especially tempting to thieves.

It is notable that the bulk of on-the-hoof sales for #6 occurs in the winter rather than the autumn. There are two reasons for this. First, logistics. Marketing animals in the autumn abounds with practical difficulties. (Even so, the *number* of animals that #6 sells out of his large herd at that time of year exceeds that of any other owner.) Second, with production centered upon the sale of male two-year-olds, uncastrated, the immediate post-rut period is clearly not the most profitable time to sell. Better to wait, letting these young males put on weight.

A percentage of two-year-old females is also selected for slaughter or sale. These are animals whose debilitated condition on account of the gorm fly raises doubts about their lasting through the winter and the subsequent spring migration. Otherwise, old cows and rodno are taken from the herd, in much the same proportions as on Gow'dojottelit (excepting Iskun Biera).

In sum, reproduction in these Oar'jebelli herds is directed to the attainment of production goals, far more than it is on Gow'dojottelit. Their on-the-hoof sales (83 percent and 74 percent) are far greater than those of Gow'dojottelit.[7]

However, while the two Oar'jebelli herds share this economic strategy, their separate ecologic circumstances make for economic differences. These are worth noticing. The summer pastures of herd #6 are njar'ga, but—in contrast to the practice on Gow'dojottelit—the cows are taken out to the njar'ga to calve. They spread across this difficult terrain at will, unattended. The male animals are not taken out there until calving is completed. This arrangement, it is argued, produces a high calving percentage and saves the young calves from having to continue on to the summer pastures after their birth. On the other hand, there is a higher than usual loss of calves to foxes, eagles, and other predators. Cows who lose their calves are counted by herders as rodno, and one of the owners reckons that by September—when he is beginning to retrieve his herd knowledge—40 percent of his cows are without calves (Table A.3), and in the majority of these cases, the cow lost her calf after birth. She is čoavčes.

But in the case of our other Oar'jebelli herd (#7), calving takes place in the manner familiar from Gow'dojottelit, that is, under watch and in separation from the male animals. After calving, the total herd is taken out to a smaller njar'ga for the first part of the summer, then through July and August the animals wander freely back to the or'da. This singular combination of njar'ga and or'da ecologies appears to pay good dividends: fewer rodno and valuable herd knowledge through calving. Around August, herd #6 joins #7 on the or'da to make one large combined herd through the autumn, with a seasonal routine that allows for good herd knowledge (Chapter 7).

Thus, in the case of #7, there is really no break in the owners' herd knowledge throughout this period—which means a constant work commitment—and this is certainly a factor in their being able to combine an 18-percent slaughter rate with a 3-percent overall growth rate. The corresponding figures for the larger herd #6 are 20 percent slaughter and *a loss* of 2 percent in overall growth rate. These last figures, however, tell of a period of readjustment following realization that the herd was "too large" for the njar'ga pasture—too large, that is, given the economic rationale behind their husbandry. Herd #7 owners also follow this rationale, and it is, perhaps, with them that the more notable adjustments may be expected. Once they have decided that they have reached optimal herd size (and I didn't find out what that might be), one can expect a near-zero growth rate. A second adjustment may be in their constant work commitment through spring, summer, and autumn. Already atypical of Oar'jebelli, it does not seem to be necessary to the production strategy that is being pursued there.

Conclusions

When composing these herds, I felt that some kind of pastoral handwriting was being revealed—or the code for deciphering an owner's value disposition. What, then, of the very different handwritings of the two large herd owners in our sample: Iskun Biera (#1) of Gow'dojottelit and #6 of Oar'jebelli?

It is as well to note, first of all, that the two have, in the main, different kinds of herd knowledge. For Iskun Biera, it pertains to reproduction and is gained at calving camps. For the Oar'jebelli owner, knowledge is relevant to production—slaughter and sale—and is needed after the rut.[8]

Now, I think the pastoral value, which Iskun Biera maximizes, leaves him quite unclear about optimal herd size. It is as though that value were something natural or organic, not one to be calculated (even though he does exercise controls, albeit minimal, on the composition of his herd). Thus he keeps biographies of his cows, and he likes *to see* his varek grow into vuobis, into godduhas, even into goassohas. It is quite different, as we know, with the Oar'jebelli herd: He is unlikely to know *how* a cow became a rodno, and varek are to be marketed. (Of course, some are saved to be stud animals, but few of these will live beyond their fourth year, unless they are castrated for work as draft animals.) With such a regime, optimal herd size *is* constantly reviewed as an economic matter.

On the other hand, Iskun Biera certainly thinks of the size of his herd in relation to those of others. He enjoys being bigger than those around him. This different notion of "optimal herd size" is consonant with the pastoral values of his life.

Whereas I believe the large Oar'jebelli owner has sound knowledge of his herd capital, I doubt whether Iskun Biera has. This paradox is attributable to the poor work routines prevailing among the Joakkonjar'ga herders for much of the year, as spelled out in the chapters of the seasons. The Oar'jebelli owner would understand such a situation to mean that the herd is "too big," but I do not think Iskun Biera sees it that way.

The on-the-hoof sales of the Oar'jebelli owner belong to a production strategy with an economy of decisions (and of time spent on them). Iskun Biera, though, spends effort and time on numerous small sales. So this owner of over a thousand animals will be seen haggling with a buyer over how much he is going to get for a joint of meat. Consonant, again, with his pastoral values, I think this suggests that his cash economy is a piecemeal matter—he seeks cash when he needs it—but it is *his* reindeer meat that he is selling, and that is worth something (I take up this point again in the next chapter).

In ideal terms, the contrast between these two owners illustrates how pastoralists, probably the world over, have to plot a course in relation to polar alternatives: either slaughter the minimum of animals—enough to look after basic needs; or keep alive the minimum—enough to ensure the reproduction of the herd.[9]

10.
Two Cultures

The place of a *market* in Saami pastoralism is a core concern of this chapter, too. Of itself, a market is not at all a foreign idea to pastoral Saami. Much depends, though, on how the deed and process of *marketing* is perceived. To that end, I now want to consider the degree to which and manner in which those ground-level differences between Joakkonjar'ga and Oar'jebelli are entangled in attendant Saami and non-Saami perceptions and ideologies. Here, I try to present a 1960s debate about the ends and means of pastoral production, and in the chapters of Part Four I follow the same debate up to the present day.

"Where's the tallow?"

One day in February, I accompany Ellon Ailu back to his winter pastures, some eight hours by reindeer and sled to the southeast of the village of Kautokeino. He has sold a dozen animals to the Kautokeino Cooperative, whose goal of raising the quality of reindeer meat as a market product he cautiously supports—cautiously, because the Cooperative's policy is to buy animals on-the-hoof, that is, alive. The Cooperative butchers the animals, grades the meat for price, keeps all (hide included)—and pays

cash. For reasons that will become clear, Ellon Ailu is reluctant to go along with this arrangement; nevertheless, he occasionally does. So as we return to the winter pastures, he has a wad of banknotes tucked away inside his heavy winter clothing, and that is all.

On cue, as we enter the cabin, the women look askance at the money and begin hectoring Ellon Ailu: "Where's the tallow? the blood? the intestinal lining? the heart? the tongue? the head? and the marrow bones?" They don't even mention the better joints of meat, and they haven't finished yet: "Where are the skins [for the clothing we all wear]? And the sinew [for the sewing of that clothing]?"

This is no isolated incident. Most of the women in the pastoral economy and a good many men, too, feel this way. The matter is spoken of in terms of Us and Them, and "they" are *daža*—the Saami word for male non-Saami (in this context, Norwegian). It is particularly the "daža" of the Cooperative who are singled out, even though most of those who work there are themselves Saami, including the manager.

The messages that the Cooperative is trying to get through to the pastoralists can be summarized thus:

Bush slaughter and skinning for winter leggings.

1. Sell your animals to us on-the-hoof, and we will best be able to dress the product for the market.
2. We have to employ a staff of butchers and packers, and a veterinary, so don't sell your animals to us just in dribs and drabs. You must help us to keep our costs down.
3. Concentrate on the sale of two-year-old males. This way you can improve your cash income and save on pasture without reducing the reproductive capacity of your herd.
4. Sell more in the late summer and autumn than has been the practice, for this is still a relatively slack season for us, and the market actually offers better prices then than in the winter.
5. Finally, sell only to us! Our financial condition is not healthy because even some of our members "shop around" (in contravention of the Cooperative bylaws).

The capacity of the Cooperative is between 150 and 200 animals a day. An annual subsidy is received from the government (20,000 kroner in 1961) to help maintain prices against seasonal market slumps. (In 1963, as part of a continuing effort to encourage autumn sales, it is announced that an extra 5 kroner will be paid for each ani-

mal sold before 10 December each year.) The Reindeer Administration in Finnmark reports:

1961: the Kautokeino Co-Operative handled 4,000 deer this year which is 500–400 more than last year. 250 were transported alive to the slaughterhouse by tractor. The [overall] economic situation is satisfactory. Begun experimenting with the market preparation of meat. . . . The lateness of autumn this year led to fewer animals being slaughtered and so there were difficulties in meeting the demands of the Christmas market.

1962: the slaughtering and handling of meat is becoming more sanitary, thus the quality is improving; regrettably, though, this is not true of all the meat that is sold and bought. . . . The modern slaughterhouse has led to a diminution in "bush" slaughter; a formidable difficulty, however, is the lack of a road network across the tundra [connecting Kautokeino and Karasjok]. . . . The Kautokeino Co-operative handled 5,970 animals—an increase of almost 2,000 over the previous year, [but still only half of all animals slaughtered].[1]

But not all official commentary is as promising. Havard Movinkel, a graduate of the Royal Norwegian Agricultural College, whose time in Kautokeino overlaps with mine and whose principal research site is the cooperative slaughterhouse, is severely critical of what he sees as the economically irrational and irresponsible practices of the

Saami pastoralists. I quote not from my conversations with him but from a research paper of his:

The marketing and treatment of reindeer meat has been characterized by casualness and disregard for all rules pertaining to proper treatment of the meat. This has resulted in the failure of reindeer meat to gain a secure position on the market which, in turn, has kept the prices relatively low. . . .

Reindeer owners have made little use of the opportunities the new slaughter houses provide for enhancing the quality of reindeer meat. It is useless to try to obtain higher prices for reindeer before this happens. . . . It is important that the reindeer owners become aware of this once and for all. . . .

Expenses for good slaughtering must be considered inevitable. It is better to pay for quality butchering than to pay for butchering that impairs quality. By having most of the herders deliver reindeer to the slaughter houses, the expenses could be minimized. Reindeer owners must be made aware that considerable government expenditure has been invested in the slaughter houses and sheds. If reindeer owners do not understand how to utilize this capital investment, then it will also be difficult to solve other problems that require government capital investment in the future.[2]

Movinkel is not alone in his view, as veterinary reports attest, nor is it lost on the Saami that this is how the daža see matters. Nils Kemi, in his late fifties and with a herd of around three hundred animals, has this to say:

On-the-hoof sales are only practical for the rich owner (say, over 500 animals and only a small family). All of us others have to take for ourselves some of the meat from each animal we slaughter (we live off that for a while) as well as selling other parts for cash. So it's a loss for us Saami to sell to the Cooperative. And they say they want us to bring more animals when we come—but, as I told you, we want meat through the winter.

Oh yes! The daža say we should slaughter to the limit of the herd, to bring to them all our two-year-old males. But what of bad years? How do we pay our debts? And what should we eat—our own bellot? And what will be left for gifts when children are baptized, when young people are married?

They also tell us that we should slaughter more in the summer and autumn, but we're too busy then, and, anyway, it's difficult then to find the animals that one would slaughter. We're too busy . . . slaughter can wait!

The Administration is well aware of at least some aspects of the current difficulties:

There are, then, these options for the pastoralist: he either brings his whole herd to the [central] slaughterhouse and, once there, separates out the animals he is selling, or brings just the selected animals—tied one to another [if there are only a few of them], or slaughters the animals himself [bush slaughter] and hopes that they will be of acceptable quality. The first two alternatives take a lot of work and time, and for this reason many [still] resort to the third option—and hope for the best. All this happens in the winter—there is [at present] no option about it—when both weight and quality are inferior to what they are in the autumn.[3]

Nevertheless, Movinkel is baffled by the poor support given to the cooperative slaughterhouse. He sees the issue in terms other than Nils Kemi's. Whereas private buyers, he argues, "keep their purchase price as low as possible and their sales price as high as possible, a co-operative returns the profit to its members."[4] That may be so, but there is another difference: Private buyers have always been willing to take parts of a carcass, the practice that the Cooperative is hoping to put a stop to. It is not just Movinkel who argues on the basis of the premises of his political economy. Nils Kemi has a political economy in his head too, and only with great difficulty will the two be reconciled.

Movinkel regrets that there is still so much uncertainty in his work of "management planning for increasing income" among the reindeer owners. For one thing, planners still have too little data to work with. He writes, "The individual reindeer owners can certainly help secure the necessary data" but acknowledges that "before this can possibly happen a total change must occur in the attitude of the pastoral Saami regarding the issue of giving information of an economic nature."[5] It is such talk of "management planning" that draws the comment (I am still citing Nils Kemi, but I hear exactly this same comment from any number of reindeer owners), "The state wants us Saami to use the large slaughterhouses, like the Cooperative, so they can exercise more economic control over us. And the next thing we know is that we have become their dependents."

Not surprisingly—for it is a view generally held by outsiders—Movinkel despairs at the apparent unwillingness or inability of the reindeer owners to "work together" and "organize themselves" so that the necessary tasks can be performed "efficiently and, first and foremost, accomplished at the correct time."[6]

For their part, the pastoralists are unimpressed by the eight-to-five clock time of the Cooperative: "Why don't they work on the weekends? Our deer don't know the difference between a Friday and a Saturday!" This is generally taken as another indication of how the nonpastoralist functionaries are not "serious" about reindeer work.

But Movinkel returns to the point that "much would be achieved if each reindeer group had its leader who could organize and distribute work among the owners."[7] Here the distance between Saami and daža, between pastoralist and nonpastoralist, is wider still. "When it comes to our animals," says a young owner with a good-sized herd already, "each of us is his own boss." This is a bedrock value, and it is arguably one with considerable adaptive merit in the circumstances of reindeer pastoralism.

There *are* foremen of pastoral districts—for such are required by law. (What the law principally has in mind is an institutional arrangement whereby compensation can be collected from a group of owners whose deer pasture illegally.) But the pastoralists themselves do not see the position as one of authority, let alone command, "for then there would only be trouble." The foreman is most likely to be chosen by his fellows for his supposed skill in Norwegian. He does not dare, or care, to exercise a fraction of the authority given him by law. There *is* authority among those pastoralists, but rather than the delegated type with the degree (however small) of hierarchy that that entails, it is better characterized as discretionary: Whenever a problem presents itself, action should be taken by whomever is there (see Chapter 7 for more on this point).

Behind the assertion that each is his own master when it comes to his animals, lie at least two others. The first is that daža do not understand reindeer, and least of all do they understand what these animals mean to Saami. The second is that the pastoralist confers a privilege on you when he allows you to buy his meat. Talking about selling animals to the Cooperative, another owner says, "When it comes to this, Johan Matte is my ræŋ'ga." Johann Matte works at the Cooperative, and in calling him his ræŋ'ga, this owner invokes the one relationship where there is hierarchy, that between an owner and his hired hand. Yet what happened that day at the Cooperative did not recognize such a relationship: "My animals were weighed without my seeing them." His anger rising, he asks those of us who are crowded around him, "What sort of practice is that?"

The prices the Cooperative offers for each quality grade are decided by the manager, though the gradings themselves are decided by the veterinarian on the basis of his inspection of each carcass. The top grade receives a x5 stamp. These animals are slaughtered in the Cooperative with a veterinarian present, looking at the bleeding of the carcass and at its organs. The cleanliness of the workplace is also a factor. Not all animals slaughtered under inspection, however, receive the higher grade stamp. Lean meat, for instance, is likely to be given the x3 stamp. Contrary to what some owners tell me they believe to be the case, the Cooperative (probably out of necessity) *does* buy meat that has been slaughtered outside, by the owners themselves, and without the presence of a veterinarian. If it is thought, on inspection, that the meat comes from a healthy animal, that it is clean and has been well handled, it will be accepted at the lower-quality grade of an x3 stamp.[8] Meat deemed to fall below the required health standards is confiscated.

Export regulations and market criteria of product attractiveness enters into the gradings. From what has already been said, it will be no surprise that owners are prone to find the gradings not in accord with their ideas of the value of their meat. Ellon Ailu, for instance, says he approves of the system in principle, and then adds: "But those who stamp the meat are usually daža, and they don't understand anything!"

Cultural Brokerage?

There is in Kautokeino an important middle ground in this confrontation. Some persons of Norwegian background were born in Kautokeino or have been there for a long time; they are fluently bilingual in Saami and have perhaps married a Saami. In several of these families, one or both of the spouses hold salaried jobs in the field of education or in municipal administration. They are in the position to be cultural gatekeepers or brokers, as well as functionaries. Most of them are concerned and well informed about the issues raised by Movinkel and Nils

Kemi, and some even make it their business to mediate in the confrontation of views—though not necessarily with much success.

For instance, they recognize the raw cultural edge to what is happening around the cooperative slaughter-house. This they wish to mute. Nonetheless, they can be counted upon to remind those in public office how, even to this day, Norwegians trivialize and underestimate the Saami way of life, especially its nomadic pastoral compo-nent. And they wish to redirect attention to what they see as the political dimensions of what could become a crisis situation.

An important person in this group on account of his close connections with the pastoralists is Gudmund Sand-vik, once a herder-owner with his wife's family, now, in his early forties, a municipal functionary. Much of what Sandvik tells me I have heard already from Movinkel: That there is serious overpasturing (particularly in the summer), and, inasmuch as this adversely affects the health and weight of the animals, it amounts to econom-ic waste; that different herds become mixed and merged into a few megaherds in the autumn, and this leaves owners without sound knowledge of their animals at a time when they would otherwise slaughter an appreciable number.

The two men also cite the same key figures: The total number of reindeer in Finnmark is about 50 percent higher than the official figure of 95,000; the total of ani-mals slaughtered each year is too little by as much as 25 percent; 62 percent of the Kautokeino owners have less than 200 animals (placing them near or below the official poverty line), while others have herds of over 1,000; and the population of Saami pastoralists in Finnmark between 1949 and 1960 increased by almost 30 percent (mainly as a function of declining infant mortality and increasing longevity).

So wherein lies the difference between the two?

Mine may be seen as a subjective evaluation, but then I believe the difference itself is, in large part, subjective in character. The important difference is how each places the Saami in his account of the difficulties facing reindeer pastoralism. Where Movinkel sees only inefficiency and incompetence, Sandvik understands the contingencies of working over open terrain with herds of animals that are not tame and are fleet of foot, and he can explain how there is, behind behavior that appears to aggravate the present problems, a meaningful cultural system (with a history of adaptive merit). The difficult part of Sandvik's message, at any rate when addressing the pastoralists themselves (at their association meetings, for instance), is that he believes some of these traditional values are no longer in the pastoralists' own best interests.

Sandvik also sees glaring inadequacies in the Norwe-gian response to the situation, inadequacies that reveal a lack of confidence in both the pastoral enterprise and the place of the Saami culture in the modern world. One ex-ample, an important one for Sandvik, must suffice: the failure to encourage reindeer owners to reinvest some of their "full corral" of animals into capital savings in the bank. The advantages of such a scheme are that it would reduce overgrazing, make room for more families, and provide security. Certainly, owners need some convinc-ing about the desirability of such a course of action, but, as some of them say to me, it probably will not be long before some of the richer owners experiment with this new "risk."

Stories circulate about small fortunes of cash and jew-elry being buried in the tundra. Here are two: The own-er (identified by name to me) of a larger herd had actual-ly deposited 47,000 kroner in a bank in Alta, then one day, because he was "afraid of the tax," withdrew the whole sum and hid it. On her deathbed, the wife of an-other wealthy pastoralist (also identified by name) re-quested that a pillow slip be placed in her coffin beside her. The pillow slip, she said, was buried under a sled on a calving grounds. It was found to contain 7,000 kroner.

These and other stories suggest that the need for a "banking" system outside the herd itself (and beyond the grasp of children who, within the conventions of antici-patory inheritance, build up their own herds with the help of capital from the parents' herd) has for a long time been present. But, I also learn, the government must dis-pel any thought that money banked, and not hidden, could be taken away from the person who deposits it. More important still, in the long term, interest rates will have to be such that the pastoralist sees for himself that they compare favorably with the growth rate of capital in the herd. Yet there is no bank in Kautokeino in 1961, even though some reindeer owners have shown the government the way to go, by themselves opening savings accounts in the post office here. Nor is it yet possible for a reindeer owner to obtain capital loans on the security of his herd.[9]

Sheriff Arvid Dahl most certainly is able to catch the attention of senior bureaucrats and politicians in Oslo[10]—and he is concerned with the problem that I gloss as the culture of production. Twice elected mayor (in addition to his government-appointed office as sheriff), he is functionally bilingual. His wife's people are Saami from Kautokeino, some of whom are reindeer owners.

I have had several conversations with Dahl, but what I bring forward here are his interventions in the debate at the annual meeting (in Kautokeino, 1963) of the national association of Saami reindeer owners and the reactions among Saami and non-Saami. A solution to the problem of overgrazing that one often hears, though rarely from the pastoralists themselves, is—as if it is simple enough—the "regulation" of numbers, both of animals and of owners. Dahl knows this is anathema for most pastoralists, and he appreciates why. Anders Oskal, a pastoralist respected for his herd management, puts one of the reasons bluntly enough: "If a Saami herder cannot have as many animals as he is able to have, he will lose interest." And as Ellon Ailu is always telling me: "All of us, then, would be the same, but we all hope to improve our situation. Every one of us wants his herd to grow—there's the motivation for our hard way of life." But if herds are allowed to increase in this fashion, will not the situation fast get out of hand? Dahl's answer is: "The total reindeer population in Finnmark is *not* too large, but there *is* an indefensible distribution. Most owners have too few animals. Yet these people are masters of their trade, and something must be done to save them from having to leave it." How is one to understand him? First, his bold assertion that there are not too many animals: Implicit in his whole approach to this question is his insistence that behind material production press the imperatives of culture. Were that not so, then being a Saami, for instance, would not be meaningful. Nonetheless, this does not answer the objection that to put no brakes on the number

of animals invites chaos. Here Dahl's insistent message to the pastoralists is that you can have more deer without there being too many *if* you slaughter more of them. He is aware this means cultural change, but he is no less aware of how Saami culture can, and in this case must, adjust as the world around it changes.

But the Saami need to be supported in making this change (rather than being coerced into it), and in this connection he addresses the meeting about two things in particular: autumn slaughter and government-sponsored credit.

Autumn slaughter has two advantages, he says: better prices than in the winter, and by extending the principal slaughter season, the Cooperative is relieved of some of its high-season pressure. The fact that he himself belongs to the Cooperative executive probably does not assist him in persuading his audience, and he is challenged on his statement that animals are heavy in the autumn and lose weight in the winter. However, he agrees that there *are* a number of practical difficulties; indeed, he makes a point of stressing them. For him, they are really logistical. For example, there should be mobile slaughterhouses with a veterinarian in attendance. Owners would then be able to receive the x5 stamp for their meat without having to take the animals into Kautokeino. He urges that such needs be brought to the attention of the government.[11]

Dahl also thinks that government-sponsored credit arrangements would help reindeer owners meet heavy expenditures in pursuing their livelihood. As matters stands, most of them run up debts with private merchants at different times of the year. This is especially the case in the spring, before leaving for the calving grounds, with repayment in the winter. Even so, by the middle of the summer families could experience a cash shortage, compelling them to slaughter animals for sale—something they would not otherwise want to do at that time of year. So apart from the personal privations of this kind of situation, Dahl deplores the way in which it can prejudice herd management decisions. I imagine that (as a firm supporter of the cooperative principle) he also deplores the way a merchant, in return for extending credit, binds the pastoralist to sell meat to him, though I also suppose that many among the pastoralists who enter into such agreements are comfortable with them. I think he also hopes that a scheme of sponsored credit *(driftskreditkasse)* may be seen by the Saami as an assurance that the government *is* serious in its oft-spoken commitment to their livelihood.[12]

"Most owners have too few animals," he said, and they have to be helped. Here Dahl is throwing his support behind a program that has been in place for a year or two but has already come under criticism. A government fund is being used to purchase animals *(livdyr)* from larger herd owners and the animals distributed—as eventual purchases on easy terms—to the needy pastoralists.[13] There is some misgiving that "Sheriff Dahl" is urging a leveling policy—that the program is, after all, a regulating ploy disguised in benevolence. A voice from the floor asks: "And what happens in bad years, when animals die on you? [All present know of years when that happened.] Regulation has already trimmed our herds, we have no reserve animals . . . What do we do then? Buy from others, you say! But who would sell?" And even among the recipients, there is some unease. They want to know more about what is expected of them in the matter of repayments.

But several owners, in no need themselves, speak approvingly of the intention behind the program: "It is our responsibility to help these people," says Ole Sara. And outside the meeting Aslak Skum talks to me about how the scheme could help to reduce jealousy and envy among the smaller owners toward the better-off and (here he is touching a basic value) how it will encourage the smaller man to catch up with the richer and also give him more reason to embrace his share of the toil of herding. It is worth noting that one owner at any rate, Eggan Anti of Or'da, who sold some animals under this program, put the money into his post office savings account.

Movinkel also speaks at the meeting. He says that as a remedial to the situation facing the reindeer industry, the program is a dangerous misconception. There *are* too many animals, and this scheme would make for still more. The necessary remedial in his view is a reduction in the number of families in the livelihood. Moreover, the price the state is paying for the animals, alive, is more than they would fetch had they been slaughtered: This,

then, is a *dis*incentive to slaughter when what is needed are incentives. All present recognize the argument (and Sandvik, for one, agrees with it), but there is no reply. It is as though Movinkel were an intruder.

Cultural Frustration

Reviewing with Ellon Ailu some of the conversations I have had with others, I am struck by the uncompromising view of this reasonable man. He knows better than most that the future of Saami reindeer pastoralism—as of any livelihood—is in large measure a matter of economic negotiation with the state (and its various agencies), yet it is the exclusive cultural factor that he stresses. Time and again he brings it all back to the differences between Saami and daža. Sandvik had told me that the problem, in his opinion, is how to direct children of the pastoralists to other walks of life. He spoke of this (along with his remarks on banking) as a need of the Saami to "reinvest." Now, Ellon Ailu does not dismiss Sandvik, or Dahl, out of hand. They may not be Saami, but they are different from the other daža. However, this talk of "reinvestment" puts Sandvik in the daža camp. Ellon Ailu is adamant. Such ideas are really incompatible with the herders' way of life, he says, and Saami children should leave school after the elementary levels. As Sandvik well knows, says Ellon Ailu, the children are not interested in more years at school.

Yet there are some moments when Ellon Ailu—sounding astonishingly like Movinkel—deplores the *ineffectiveness* of the Norwegian administration of Saami reindeer pastoralism in Finnmark. Understaffed, without responsibility for policy, the Administration amounts to little more than a policing operation, and not an impressive one. But how is this to be changed when, in Ellon Ailu's view, the nonpastoralists know nothing about reindeer and not much more about Saami pastoral society; and when the pastoralists should not bother with schooling?

It was Ellon Ailu, the reader will recall, who approved the principle of the system for grading meat, only to dismiss it in practice because most of those stamping the meat were daža. He is himself painfully aware of the dilemma he finds himself in. What particularly worries him is the daža intrusion into the market side of Saami pastoralism. Each year it becomes more evident. Plant managers, veterinarians, and other experts—people whom the pastoralists like to regard as their ræŋ'ga, are telling them about reindeer and how and when to slaughter them!

There is much frustration. I hear reindeer owners muttering about the čuor'bevuotta (incompetence) of the daža or daža-like persons who tangle with their livelihood (ironically, much as Movinkel, from his side of the cultural division, speaks of them). Should the expert with his know-how be able to demonstrate his effectiveness, things would change, of that I am sure: The Saami pastoralist is a strong pragmatist. But for the moment there is no sign of that. Instead, herders, in their dealings with the daža, seem inclined not to cultivate their own talent for compromise and not to take seriously the experts' promises and boasts (and threats), nor the regulations promulgated by the Administration.

Given the market forces behind the cultural intrusion they are experiencing, the pastoralists' resistance has a strong symbolic element to it, beyond the instrumental. And I believe that the most important emblem of all—a kind of summarizing or master symbol—is the reindeer as a staple of the domestic economy. This takes us back to where we started.

The herder's life gives men and women a strong sense of autonomy. They know they are doing what they do best and that it is something most other people cannot do, and they know that this is so because they are born to it—because they are Saami. But when they bring their animals to the cooperative slaughterhouse, there is a sense of affront to that autonomy. We saw glimpses of this as a contest in authority, but there is another side to it, too. Against their own knowledge that "we Saami get so much more from an animal when we slaughter it," there is the shock of seeing their animals "butchered like a cow": legs severed so that the tendons are cut through (thereby ruining the sinews, which the Saami use for sewing) and the blood spilled on the slaughterhouse floor instead of drained into the (cleaned) lining of the stomach.

Sometimes herders will hang around with basins in hand, on the chance that they will be allowed to collect the blood from the animals they had delivered. (Reindeer blood is mixed with flour to make a gruel for their dogs, or blood sausages will be made.) The loss of the sinews—two in each rear leg, one in each front leg, and one along the back—used for sewing their skin clothing, is even more serious: "The daža tell us it's old-fashioned to use the sinews. They say that they can offer something better [strong cotton]—but for us they are indispensable." A household uses between twenty and twenty-five sinews in the course of a year. This means that they could manage with those taken from the deer not sold to the Cooperative—but that is beside the point. And men talk about this too, not just the women.

Their reindeer meals bond families, their ræŋ'ga, and their visitors. Preparation, sometimes simple and other times elaborate, is always a serious matter. As for the cooking of the meat, it is more the responsibility of the men than of the women. The centrality of these meals in their lives tends to impart a ritualistic atmosphere also to their consumption. Something of this is caught in Johan Turi's description:

The first meal is the back, the liver, and blood sausages. . . . The second meal of reindeer is the legs, marrow bones, and head, and after that the rest of the meat is cooked just as you like. . . . The thighs and the tongue of the reindeer killed in late winter are sold, but the reindeer that are slaughtered for spring and summer food—of that, not the least little bit is sold. They are slaughtered first in the winter, . . . and for that meat they choose the fattest reindeer.[14]

There are other ways of having those first and second meals, but what is true across the culture is the love of *fat* reindeer meat, whereas that is something most non-Saami wish to avoid. As Turi says, the fattest of all is the meat salted and dried in the winter for spring and summer rations. Were this not fat, Saami explain, it would simply "dry away."

I am given a brochure printed for the Cooperative for its market in the south of Norway. The epitome of the distance between the Cooperative (and the daža they supply) and their Saami suppliers, it reads: "Reindeer meat is lean!"

Part Four
Pastoralism
by Authorization,
1979 – 1989

▲ ▲ ▲

Now that we have made our diagnosis [of the ills of the livelihood] we must be able to administer the medicine.

OLE K. SARA, CHIEF OF REINDEER ADMINISTRATION

If there is a problem of alerting pastoralists to the longer term dangers of overgrazing the land, then this is at least matched by the need of the planners to appreciate the full extent of the pastoralists' commitment to their way of life, the rationality of their rudimentary capitalist system, the strength of their morality, the meaning of their boundaries, and above all the extent to which these are aspects of a longer term adaptation. The broader the concessions that can be made to these, the greater the likelihood of success.

PAUL SPENCER, "PASTORALISTS AND THE GHOST OF CAPITALISM"

11.
The Terms
of
Authority

Max Weber has written: "Precision, speed, consistency, availability of records, continuity, possibility of secrecy, unity, rigorous coordination, and minimization of friction . . . are achieved in a strictly bureaucratized, especially in a monocratically organized, administration conducted by trained officials."[1] Supposing such is the ambition of government—in this case, the Norwegian Department of Agriculture together with the Reindeer Administration—I find in Max Gluckman the cultural qualifier that Saami pastoralists, in the main, look for. He writes: "I see the judicial process as the attempt to specify legal concepts with ethical implications according to the structure of society."[2]

Approximately, the period of time under consideration in Part Four is 1979 to 1989: the decade of unprecedented state intervention in the management of Saami reindeer pastoralism. Some see it as state "control," others as "guidance," even as "help." For some it is "unwarranted," while for others it was "overdue." The key process, I suggest, is the placing of an ethnically distinct livelihood under state license. On the one hand, this provides a pretty strong guarantee that Saami—some Saami, at the state's discretion—will be able to continue with reindeer pas-

toralism; but on the other hand, there are strong indications that it will no longer be Saami herd management that they practice.

Journeying across the seasonal pastures today, the eye, however, may not take in some of the significant structural changes wrought by the state. Evident in the administration of the livelihood, they are without a physical presence on the terrain. But there is much else that the eye *will* catch. One sees (and hears) snowmobiles or all-terrain vehicles, so one *doesn't* see her'gi drawing sleds. At the right time and place, there are naval landing craft ferrying herds to and from some njar'ga and suolo summer pastures. One notices, too, animals with colored plastic ear-tags in addition to the cut earmarks. There are fewer family camps, except in the summer, and children are away at school during critical junctures in the annual pastoral round. And more besides.

For the most part, these changes have come of their own accord, that is to say, *not* as part of the concerted state program mentioned above. I discuss them in Chapter 12 under the rubric of *modernization*. Of course the licensing or incorporation of Saami pastoralism by the state is also a force of modernization; however, its ideologic and programmatic distinctiveness warrants separate treatment under the rubric of *rationalization*. This is the word by which the state itself declares its mission regarding Saami reindeer pastoralism. Indeed, it is a shibboleth, forever recurring in public statements, all of which carry messages about a particular process of modernization.

Chapter 13 first sets forth the precepts under which such state incorporation is undertaken and documents its principal practical features. Attention then switches, in that chapter, to the difficulties of implementation encountered by the state. In part, these arise from local Saami opposition, as might be expected, to particular features of the state program; but inherent ambiguities, too, are revealed in the very precept of the state's intentions, and some of the practical measures are found to have contradictory implications.

Perhaps what I find to be the most interesting feature of this material is that the two processes, modernization and rationalization, cannot be assumed to work in tandem. Far from synchronization and interdependence between them, there is sometimes serious disjunction. Or, the state's "rational" prescriptions will somehow have to accommodate steps, taken independently by individual pastoralists or groups of them, towards "modernizing" on their own terms.

The state works for the extension of social democratic principles to Saami pastoral society: principles informed by an economic ideology of equality combined with market efficiency. But Saami pastoralists—as much as they may now differ among themselves about how best to manage the livelihood—all follow (to varying degrees) that ethic of possessive individualism mentioned in Chapter 8. Most of their moves to modernization are taken by them with that in mind.

There is another difference between the two processes, one of much aggravation among the pastoralists. In the one, there is an individual's decision to improve his pastoral standing without necessarily making changes in his value system; and in the other, there is the state's determined belief that "improvement" *depends precisely on changes in that value system.* Even in the former case, the individual usually experiences an element of compulsion in making his decision, but it is a different kind of compulsion from that in the state alternative: The individual is likely compelled by the constraints of peer competitiveness, but it is this very competitiveness the state wishes to scotch (for reasons that will be explained). In the one process, then, "control" is diffuse and indirect and at ground level: The individual is free to risk *not* modernizing. But in the other, control descends upon the pastoralists—all of them—by government fiat: They *shall* rationalize their herd management.

The principal instrument for the rationalization of Saami pastoralism is the biennial Agreement (Reindrifts-avtalen) between the state and Norges Reindriftsamers Landsforbund (NRL), or Norgga Boazosabmelaččaid Riikasærvi, the national association of Saami reindeer pastoralists, whereby considerable sums of money are allocated to the livelihood for specified objectives. All the primary resource livelihoods in Norway have had such agreements in place for some time, as an article of social democracy. The Agreement for reindeer pastoralism was drawn up as recently as 1976. Its precise budget is negotiated between the Department of Agriculture and NRL. A fact of particular significance for an understanding of what the state is trying to accomplish vis-à-vis Saami reindeer pastoralism is that the Agreement is modeled, in precept, on the one state has with agriculture.

Behind the Agreement stands the legal bulwark of the 1978 Reindeer Management Act (Reindriftsloven), whose opening paragraph states: "The objective of this Act is to ensure *socially beneficial use of the reindeer pasture resources* in such a way as provides economic and social security and protection of rights for those whose livelihood is reindeer pastoralism, and *to preserve reindeer pastoralism as an important component of Saami culture.*"[3] Therein is the seed of the ambiguity, sometimes amounting to contradiction, in the state's policy towards Saami reindeer pastoralism. If the state defines "socially beneficial use"—and it soon becomes apparent, even in reading the Act, let alone the way it is practiced, that such is the case—what is the worth of the intention "to preserve reindeer pastoralism as an important component of Saami culture"?

Among the specific directions included in this opening paragraph of the Act is "regulation of relations between the pastoralists." And in successive paragraphs the Act gives to the state the responsibility for deciding how many and which Saami may register as pastoralists, and the size of herds. The Act introduces a three-tiered administrative system for the interpretation, application, and enforcement of the regulations.

The "Norwegianness" of the thirty-five paragraphs of the Act (including the reference, in its context, to the promotion of Saami culture) go a long way towards explaining the threat of ambivalence so often hovering over relations between functionaries of the state and pastoral practitioners. In previous generations, the Norwegian state conducted its relations with the Saami pastoralists on the premise of succession and dominance of Social Darwinism, whereby the "nomadic" would yield to the "sedentary" and the pastoralist to the cultivator. Today, however, the premise being that of social democracy, there is the paradox of Tzvetan Todorov's "prejudice of equality," whereby the notion of equality overrides that of difference.[4]

I will pay particular attention to various dimensions of the often unhappy relationship between the pastoralists and outside experts in Chapter 14. As viewed by many of the Saami practitioners, these experts offer no more than desktop pastoralism. The experts themselves refer to the controlled field experiments they have undertaken. "Desktop" or not, it is, by and large, the experts that the state listens to. The state "understands" the experts. And the Saami? Many of them say, "The state misunderstands our pastoralism." Others among them, though, take the state and its experts seriously, endorsing many of their proposals.

After all, the principal plank in the rationalization program is *to reduce the size of herds while increasing the income derived from the herds.* This will be accomplished through changes in herd composition. In its details and the sanctions with which it is armed, it is a radical program; yet we know that thirty years earlier some Kautokeino herder-owners were thinking along these lines—for example, those on Oar'jebelli (Chapter 9). So we will find, across a range of issues, arguments and voices from that time continuing today. However, the measure of the failure of the state is evident in its own alarm, after ten years of its programs, over the prospect of a "commons

tragedy" overtaking reindeer pastoralism in Finnmark. In Chapter 15 I give critical attention to this notion of tragedy.

Below are short biographic notes on some of the principal persons in the chapters that follow.[5] All but one are Saami by birth—Ansgar Kosmo is Norwegian—though I use their Norwegian names in the text, except for Ellon Ailu (whose Norwegian name is Aslak Bals). Nils Thomas Utsi is from a sedentary Saami family; all of the others are from pastoralist families, and most are pastoralists by occupation. Respecting education (Norwegian) and commitment to cultural and civic responsibilities, these are lives of notable diversity and distinction.

ELLON AILU, PASTORALIST

Born 1928; active pastoralist for fifty years; executive of Kautokeino branch of NRL for twenty years and president for twelve years (1976–88); alternate representative on NRL executive since early 1970s; various NRL and municipal council committees; Area Board for West Finnmark 1979–83.

JOHAN J. EIRA, PASTORALIST

Born 1949; state Reindeer School 1975–76; NRL president 1978–82; several-time member of the Nordic Saami Council; alternate member of the National Reindeer Council 1979–83; president of the Kautokeino reindeer slaughterhouse from mid-1980s; member of Kautokeino municipal council executive committee from mid-1980s. Johan J. Eira was killed in a helicopter crash over the tundra in October 1990.

NILS ISAK EIRA, PASTORALIST

Born 1953; school A-levels 1973; B.A. University of Tromsö (Saami language, philosophy, social science) 1980; researcher at Nordic Saami Institute 1980–81; Saami Education Council 1981–82; returned to full-time pastoralism in 1982.

ANSGAR J. KOSMO, REINDEER AGRONOMIST

Born 1945; B.Sc. Norwegian Agricultural College (agroeconomics) 1970; research positions in North Nor-

way 1970–74; reindeer agronomist in the South Saami
district of Snåsa 1974–86; research leave 1980–81; project
leader for Reindeer Administration 1987– 90; senior
consultant with Reindeer Administration from 1991.

MATHIS M. SARA, PASTORALIST
Born 1939; mayor of Kautokeino 1976–77 and council
member 1972–83; member of Norwegian Saami Council
and of executive of Kautokeino branch of NRL through
the 1970s and 1980s; founding president of BES (Boazo
Ealohus Særvi, or Society of Those Who Live by the
Reindeer) in 1988; elected to Saami Parliament in 1989.

MIKKEL NILS SARA, TEACHER
Born 1953; school A-levels 1972; B.A. University of
Tromsö (Saami language, philosophy, social science)
1977; secretary of the Norwegian Cultural Council
1977–84; researcher at the Nordic Saami Institute
1985–88; reindeer pastoralism research group
(BAJOS) 1988–90; teacher at the Saami senior high
school, Kautokeino, from 1991.

OLE K. SARA, ADMINISTRATOR
Born 1936; junior high school 1953; commercial college
1954; officers' training school 1956; officer 1957–61;
Reindeer Administration 1961–67; reindeer agronomist
in Finnmark 1968–79; Labor Party, alternate parliamentary representative for Finnmark 1969–81; deputy minister (political appointment) Department of Agriculture
1973–79; Kautokeino Municipality executive committee
1967–75; Finnmark Provincial Council 1979–87; chair

of Finnmark Educational Committee 1979–83 and
1986–90; chief of the Reindeer Administration from
1979.

ODD ERLING SMUK, PASTORALIST AND ADMINISTRATOR
Born 1956; school A-levels 1975; B.Comm. College of
Business Administration and Economics, Bergen, 1981;
NRL executive 1980–82 and president 1984–92. Assis-
tant bank manager, Sparebanken, in Vadsö.

JOHAN MATHIS TURI, PASTORALIST
Born 1953; NRL executive 1982–84 and vice-president
1984–92; advisor to NRL 1992; first National Reindeer
Council 1979–83 and 1992–95; number of committees
handling relations between reindeer pastoralism and the
state; Kautokeino municipal council 1977–80 and
1981–84.

NILS THOMAS UTSI, TEACHER AND APPLIED RESEARCH
Born 1953; school A-levels 1973; teaching diploma
1976; Saami language and pedagogy courses, University
of Tromsö, 1978 and 1989; Finnmark Regional College
(data handling) 1986; primary school teacher at Lappolu-
obbal (Kautokeino) 1976–78; consultant Saami Educational Committee 1979–89; Kautokeino municipal council and chair of Cultural Committee 1984–87; National
Association of Norwegian Saami (Norske Samers Riksforbund, or Norgga Samiid Riikasærvi, NSR) communi-
cations project leader from 1989, and NSR president
from 1991.

12.
Modernization

What can you call "traditional"? . . . Even coffee came once from outside [the culture], though most people would suppose that belonged [to the traditional culture]. Older people have said to me that "before the snowmobile came," their reindeer management was traditional. For then, reindeer were also draft animals. Young people who have grown up with the snowmobile will say that *it* is part of "their" tradition. People who were grandparents during the war [World War II] have told me that milking and subsistence economy were the hallmarks of traditional management.

DAG T. ELGVIN, INTERVIEW IN *Reindriftsnytt*

A salesman who came up to Kautokeino from Alta in the spring of 1961, hoping to sell the first snowmobile, left without a sale. A few years later, virtually all the pastoral units had one or more machines. "The snowmobile took over," says one of the pastoralists, "not out of love for new technology, but it became essential for everyone the moment the first in each reindeer District bought such a machine."[1] The advantage it bestows in terms of mobility (and time saved) would quickly leave anyone who disdained to use the machine without a competitive edge. Nor should we lose from view its appeal as an artifact of modernity—to youth particularly. They find pleasure in excelling with the machine; they ignore the likely physical costs they are incurring while crouched astride these vibrating "tin-plated reindeer,"[2] perhaps for hours at a time.[3]

All of two-thirds of annual expenditures are now spent by the Kautokeino pastoralists on mechanized means—35 percent on the purchase, repair, and upkeep of snowmobiles alone.[4] In addition, there is the cost of vehicles used on snow-free terrain. The financial burden is shared within family and herding units. Much of it can be met through the combined contributions of family allowance and pension checks and, not least, specific government subsidies (all entitlements of the social democratic system). Nonetheless, the burden is considerable. Nor does the cost of the machines, any more than their use, fall evenly on all. Younger men use the snowmobiles most and are usually the least able to afford them. If they are still single, they pay the least, the two-generation (or more) family unit covering the cost. But if they are married and nurturing both a growing family and herd, the burden is heaviest—equal to fifty to sixty reindeer in the 1960s, though half as many by the 1980s.[5] Early on, mechanical inexperience added considerable costs of repair.

Beyond the monetary costs, however, are a variety of other consequences—all, to one degree or another, unanticipated at the time, or where anticipated, inadequately understood. No one really knew, for instance, what the consequences would be for herding.[6] Herders simply found themselves astride these brand-new purchases and with a job to do.

In fact, herding with snowmobiles reverses some of the earlier principles and routines. Thus a herd is now seldom led, but driven—and in quite a different way from before:

Tin-plate *her'gi* at calving ground. Photo by
Ivar Björklund, Tromsö Museum.

Mechanized caravan. Photo by Lloyd Villmo,
Reindriftsadministrasjonen.

When a man on foot [or skis] gathers reindeer, the reindeer
move before him at a "safe" distance. The gatherer may shout
or wave, but, unless the flock tries to turn in a wrong direction,
. . . the herder and his dog do not intend or need to panic the
reindeer into flight . . . Reindeer may even stop to graze briefly
while being gathered. The shout of the herder may then be
used to arouse the reindeer from this lapse into a grazing
context.

Gathering by snowmobile, however, often sends reindeer . . . into panic flights. The roar of the motor is constant,

unlike the shout of a herder, and the snowmobile is fast enough
to keep the pressure of panic on a flock, no matter how far
ahead it tries to run. The reindeer which finally becomes less
sensitive to roaring engines . . . has *not* become more tame. On
the contrary, he has often become harder to handle and demands the escalation of herding mechanization.[7]

Herding becomes more extensive and control, more than
ever before, a matter of "stopping" *(doallat)* the animals.
Thus along with the use of snowmobiles and all-terrain
vehicles (according to season), as well as field telephones,
is the increased use of portable burlap or wire-netting
fences. In short, control is moving into a passive mode.
But it is evident that techniques of mechanized herding
are constantly changing on a trial-and-error basis. Snowmobiles, skis, two- or three-wheel motorcycles, walkie-
talkies, dogs, and even lead animals are combined in different ways, and on occasion, airplanes or helicopters are
also used.

At the time of the snowmobile's introduction, most people mistakenly supposed it would result simply in different herding technique, replacing the her'gi. In fact, a
cluster of changes soon followed. The introduction of the
snowmobile did not cause them, for they were already
incipient, but it did help facilitate them and, in some cases, exaggerate their effects.

Portable separation corral of nylon netting: before movement to spring pastures. Photo by Ivar Björklund, Tromsö Museum.

Housing is a case in point. For some time before the 1960s, pastoral families had been acquiring reasonably modern dwellings, in addition to cabins and tents on the seasonal pastures. Practicality and sociability jointly dictated that such a dwelling be built in or around the tundra villages and hamlets such as Kautokeino or Masi, Hemmugiedde or Mieron. In his annual report for 1962, the reindeer administrator *(lappefogden)* notes that this development has led to a crowding of winter pastures nearest to the villages, leaving distant pastures underutilized. (He also notes approvingly that some pastoralists are taking advantage of this situation and moving their herds out to what are, for them, new pastures—the distant ones.) He concludes his note on this topic with the comment that better communication links across the tundra will make all the difference. What he had in mind was the building of the trans-tundra highway between Kautokeino and Karasjok (completed some years later).[8] Actually it was the appearance of the snowmobile rather than the completion of the one road that brought the change—and it happened quickly. The machine cuts distance as time. It also makes its own trails across the tundra. One is able to live in a permanent dwelling and still visit, in a matter of a couple of hours or less, the herd that is pasturing thirty or fifty kilometers away in any direction.

Through the years, larger and more expensive houses were built, and this gave added reason for them to be situated in a focal community, preferably Kautokeino, even though there were roads by now. The reindeer owner, no less than others, wishes to guard against depreciation of resale value of this considerable capital investment, and a

Table 12.1 Mechanization Profile: Kautokeino

Year	Units	Snowmobiles	Motorcycles	Cars	Tractors	Motorboats	Total Vehicles
1984	268	407	107	101	0	45	660
1985	266	400	116	97	7	33	653
1986	260	354	79	72	3	29	537
1987	259	434	140	124	43	51	792
1988	299	418	194	116	4	45	777
1989	294	443	192	117	26	48	826

Source: Reindriftstyret 1984–89
Note: "Unit" (driftsenhet) can be taken to mean a residential family, with about four or five persons.

house in Kautokeino will fetch a better price than the same house out on the tundra.[9]

People also moved into the local centers because the children were there for most of the year. Earlier, the schooling of children of pastoral families had been concentrated into three to four months of the winter, when, if necessary, they would be boarded at the school. But in the mid-1960s the nine-year school was introduced for all, and the children are now in school from the end of August to the end of June.[10]

Looking now at these separate changes together, one cumulative consequence above all others is apparent: loss of reindeer husbandry knowledge. Let us consider again, briefly, *who* most often work with the herds and *what* knowledge they bring to their work.

Inasmuch as access to the herds is contingent upon mechanized transport—a family may have no more than one snowmobile, seldom more than two, at the most three (Table 12.1)—the men, particularly the younger of them, are those with priority of access. By contrast, on the winter pastures in 1962, all members of a family—unmarried daughters as well as their brothers, and the senior generation, too—had their own her'gi; thus there was no idea of priority of access. A related point is that all (the youngest with parental permission) had independent mobility. Girls didn't have to beg a ride (to wherever they were going) with their brothers. In short, such mobility, while it was time intensive, was open to all. It also had a social component that can be lacking today.

Travel by her'gi added overnight stops, at others' camps, to the longer journeys—journeys that can now be completed within a few hours, providing there is no broken axle or an empty fuel tank.

And what herd knowledge do these young men, today, bring to their work? Nils Isak Eira is not alone in his concern over what he sees as a most serious breakdown of herd knowledge among the young today, but he, unlike others, writes about it. Few would quarrel with his account. Of the now bygone era of "sled reindeer," he writes:

These animals were a source of education for the child. . . . Because the children learned the different hair colour and horn structures of the various sled reindeer they also had a basis for deciding horn structure and hair differences of other reindeer, animals they occasionally saw in the herd. . . . Sled animals got their own special names, and in most cases these were related to the animals' appearance or behaviour. In these ways [and others] the sled reindeer had an educational function. It wasn't only for transport.[11]

The new school year demolished herd knowledge even more effectively than the advent of the snowmobile:

[Before], the children took part in most of the reindeer herding activities. Now, they are home only in the slackest season. . . . Earlier, it was possible to evaluate children by the same set of values that applied to grown-ups in respect to ability, or inability, in working with reindeer. After the change to the 9-year school this reference of values is no longer possible.[12]

Eira calls the change "brutal and destructive" and charges the school system with "extreme inflexibility." Family life is now geared around the school year as much as it is around the pastoral year.

In a way, then, the attenuated relation with the herd that mechanized herding brings fits with this fractured pastoral training. Similarly, the tasks of husbandry are also reduced. Milking has ceased. And with the changes in household economy towards a cash nexus,[13] *which* animal one slaughters, or saves, while still an important decision, is decidedly less so than before. (Reindeer hide and skin clothing, for instance, is being replaced by mass market purchases.) The "pensioning off" of her'gi relieves the husbander of a series of tasks (Chapter 5). The "simpler" composition of herds, with a reduced number of male animals, does not, however, make for simpler herding. Rather, the contrary is the case: the males, in various situations, could be counted on to help hold flocks together.

Mechanization, then, supports extensive herding, which now only seems viable through mechanization.[14] Little wonder that, once in place, mechanization is held to be indispensable. Nils Isak Eira recognizes as much, even as he and others deplore another apparently inevitable happening—the loss of pastoral knowledge. Nor is his position only one of romantic grief. He recognizes that extensive pastoral management, too, has grades of efficiency and competence respecting both herding and husbandry.

Does it not speak for itself that knowledge of terrain and pasture through changes in season and weather, of herd behavior and the identity (appearance, age, and sex) and habits of individual animals, are prerequisites of pastoral competence? Eira makes a special point of the need for herder-owners to be able to *communicate* such information to each other about animals which, at that moment, *are not in sight*—as is so very often the case. For this, one needs the rich technical language of Saami reindeer pastoralism, though that in itself is not enough (after all, it can be acquired through scholarly study). The skills, in Eira's own case, were acquired by socialization into the language through field experience while a child. Today, though, there is a break in just that "learning process whereby information was passed from generation

to generation." Eira ends the paper from which I am citing by saying: "Today it is too late to do anything about this, except to attempt, in the best possible way, to compensate for this loss by offering this form of knowledge as a subject in school."[15] To compensate—and to restore?

These are issues of professionalism, and not "merely" cultural in the sense of endowing a distinctive way of life. Nils Isak Eira (born in 1953: a youngster at the time of my fieldwork) sees himself not as a traditionalist but as expert practitioner, and such knowledge that he speaks of, and for, cuts across any traditionalist-modern dichotomy. I return to this issue in Chapter 14, considering the perspectives that nonpractitioner pastoral experts and the pastoralists themselves have of each other.

With its seasonal movements, reindeer pastoralism is necessarily an area-extensive enterprise. This is true even where there is a regime of intensive management. So where there are settled populations within the same area one can expect mutual reproaches (not just from the settled population) of territorial encroachment. In Finnmark, today as before, the great majority of the population is settled along the coast or on offshore islands, and each summer some 200,000 reindeer graze out there: cause enough for collision of interests.[16]

This side of the pastoral dilemma, in contrast to the constant and high-profiled attention given to the problem (and it is one) of the increases in the number of reindeer, is under-reported. More than that, it is now officially acknowledged that reindeer pastoralists have difficulty getting their interests taken properly into account at provincial and local government levels. In part, this is attributable to "ill will" towards the livelihood.[17] Here, the opposing interest is likely to be farming, which in Finnmark is itself unusually area-extensive, that is, with much outfield. Land is also appropriated, with consequent restrictions and other disadvantages for pastoralism, for military purposes, National Parks, and industrial projects.[18] A more recent phenomenon and a particular aggravation is the increased use of the inland tundra by urban dwellers as a recreational area. This recreational pattern—of hunting, fishing, berry-picking, hiking with overnight cabins—is also markedly area-extensive. It has a powerful political lobby, too. Senior officials of the provincial government of Finnmark declare that it is only by "assuring the use of the tundra for *all* sectors of the province" that one arrives at a "balanced use" of the natural resources; and "in this day and age the tundra areas of the province are, first and foremost, important as recreation areas."[19]

One notable advantage, on the other hand, comes the way of the pastoralists through the use of naval landing craft to ferry herds out to some of the farthest (njar'ga and suolo) summer pastures in the spring and back again in the autumn (Fig. 12.1). This began in 1969. In 1987, for instance, over twenty thousand animals, belonging to thirty-six families, were transported out between 22 April and 13 May.[20] For the return journey in the autumn, by which time the numbers had been swollen by a new increment of calves, half were ferried back, and half swam.[21] Among those groups availing themselves of this opportunity (its cost is a matter between the Reindeer Administration and the Department of Defense) is Ellon Ailu's. Their summer pasture is now actually outside the inclusive Kautokeino summer pastures area, on Lyngen peninsula, to the immediate southwest (earlier used by Saami from Karesuando in Sweden). Without this sea transport, it really would not be feasible to have summer pastures out there and winter pastures in the interior of the Kautokeino tundra. It means, of course, that Ellon Ailu no longer has a spring camp during which he watches over calving and afterwards makes the long journey, with the young calves, out to the summer pastures, an arrangement about whose advantages he was so convincing. Today, as the landing craft draws into the Lyngen shore, the pregnant cows run free, finding their own nurseries in the broken terrain. What matters, Ellon Ailu tells me, is that his deer are *heavier.* Certainly, there are logistic difficulties of various kinds, but he gives no emphasis to these. In 1986, they left Buolčajav'ri (Fig. 5.8) on 12 April, making their rendezvous with the navy, at Kvitberg in Kvaenangen, about two weeks later. Return in the autumn, in the middle of October, was completed in shorter time.[22]

I now want to consider the kind of issues the current wave of mechanization raises concerning the future of reindeer pastoralism in Kautokeino. First, let us look at

Embarking: Ellon Ailu's herd leaving summer pastures. Photo by Ivar Björklund, Tromsö Museum.

questions raised by the state. They appear in *Reindriftsnytt,* the quarterly publication of the Reindeer Administration. I have the feeling that they are questions only by default—official policy is in a quandary. I think there is an awareness, too, that *implementation* of any "answers" the state comes up with will be highly problematic.

The underlying question is how to interpret clause 10.3 of the 1978 Reindeer Management Act concerning "the right to use customary [*vanlige*] conveyance and transport means that are necessary for reindeer pastoralism." What does "customary" (or "ordinary") mean here? For that matter, how is "necessary" to be evaluated?

According to the assistant deputy minister (ADM) responsible for reindeer pastoralism, "customary" means (as

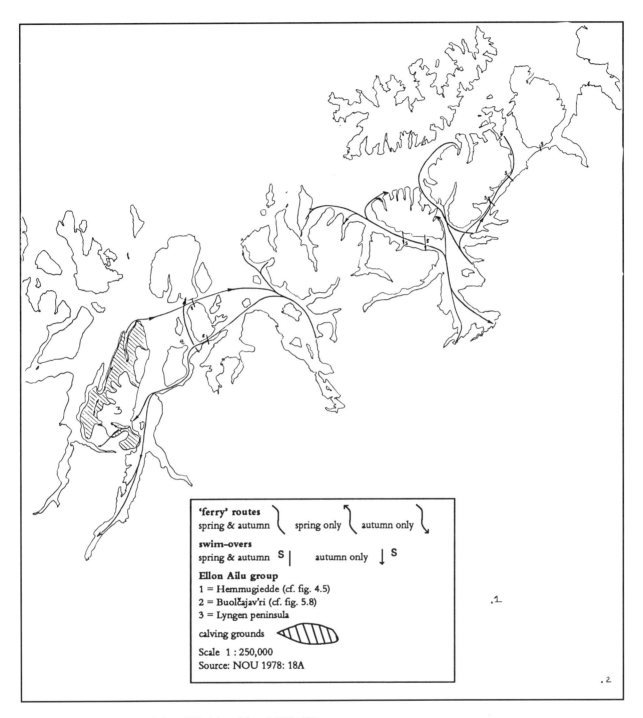

Figure 12.1 Ferry routes, Kautokeino, 1978. Adapted from NOU 1978

Trucking. Photo by Lloyd Villmo,
Reindriftsadministrasjonen.

one might expect) "traditional"—but does that mean *no* mechanization at all? Helicopters and terrain motorcycles are not considered "traditional," says the ADM, but neither are they forbidden.[23] By another reading of the regulations, however, mechanized vehicles are not allowed where there is no snow cover: in other words, snowmobiles only. Further, the state is reconsidering its policy of assisting in the purchase of snowmobiles.[24]

The ADM also says that the Saami themselves must decide what kind of pastoralism they want: "The Department will sit back and watch and take note of what transpires." Saami who read that statement must have been struck by its disingenuousness, considering the determined planning on which the state had embarked. And as one might expect, the ADM is upset to learn that some Saami are saying that they have the right to use whatever mechanized help they choose. That approach, he says, would lead to a pastoralism quite outside the understanding of the 1978 Act and the biennial Agreements.[25]

It seemed that the state wished reindeer pastoralism to be labor intensive. For the ADM, the value sought here is the solution of the employment problem; for one of

the researchers, on the other hand, it is the value of pastoral husbandry: "close contact between herder and animals."[26] Mechanization works against both these values. Regarding the first, attention is drawn to the experience of Norwegian agriculture, where mechanization led to a halving of the work force between 1949 and 1972; and so another principle sees the light of day: "Now that reindeer pastoralism has entered the market economy it will be subject to the same economic 'laws' as other livelihoods."[27] Thus the state was heard as saying, in effect, "labor intensive but with fewer practitioners than at present." As emerges in the chapters that follow, this perceived ambiguity left many a pastoralist skeptical (and cynical in not a few cases) as to just what the state did have in mind.

A rider to the above—which the ADM stresses very firmly—is that Saami, now being part of an integrated socioeconomic system, must, in their pursuit of pastoralism, take into account the interests of those other livelihoods with which they come into contact.[28] As much is said specifically in the opening clause of the 1978 Act; nonetheless, the emphasis now given to it by the ADM gave due cause for a number of Saami, in their turn, to be upset. Is mechanization in reindeer pastoralism to be contingent on agreement by the settled population?[29] Among the articles in *Reindriftsnytt* from the early 1980s, one argues that the reindeer pastoralist should be the last person to be constrained by regulations concerning use of mechanized vehicles, including helicopters. It might well be the case that mechanized pastoralism runs counter to the interests of others, but the objection is dismissed—particularly when it is simply the "recreation" of others that is in question.[30] But, counters the ADM, the Saami should never forget that it has always been to the credit of reindeer pastoralism that it did not damage the ecology. Are they, then, going to prejudice this reputation through reckless mechanization? This would be to throw away one of their strong suits politically (the other is ethnicity). And, if they did that, what arguments would there be left to put against the use of snowmobiles and all-terrain vehicles by those who come to the tundra for "recreation"?[31]

That kind of debate belonged to the early 1980s. Then, the pastoralists and the nature conservationists were in alliance against government-backed hydroelectric development schemes. In particular, common cause (including civil disobedience) was found in opposing the damming of the Alta/Kautokeino River. But for the pastoral Saami, this was an incursion into ancestral territory and invaluable pastures, whereas for the conservationists it was a rapacious act against the wilderness.

So the alliance was one of pragmatic politics without reflecting a coidentity of values.[32] By the end of the decade and well into the era of the Brundtland Commission (a government initiative), with its warnings of global ecologic irresponsibility and urgings of policies of "sustainable development," the conservationists drew nearer to government, now apparently enlightened, and away from the pastoralists, much about whose practice was seen to be an ecologic liability.

In most recent years, then, Saami pastoralists have had to defend and justify their livelihood *in natura*. That is the first point: the conservationists speak of "nature," and speak in its defense, as often as they do of ecology. That is to say, in their public rhetoric at least, they incline to representations of nature as "wilderness" rather than as an

infinite complexity of intra- and inter-species relationships that includes the human species. And when they do speak of "ecology," too often it is as a corrupt (but fashionable) synonym of nature as a value universe embedded—paradoxically—in bourgeois, intellectual, urban roots.

A notable response to the charges of pastoral irresponsibility was made at the 1989 annual meeting of NRL, beginning with a plenary address by Johan Mathis Turi:

Where do we find Europe's last wilderness? [And where can one find such areas] in which valuable use is made of them without injury to their natural foundation?

It should be easy to answer these questions. On this continent it is *only* the land of the pastoral Saami that fits the description! Nor am I exaggerating when I say that this land area would not have been so today had it not been for reindeer pastoralism.[33]

That was the rhetorical high note of the pastoralist case. As with the conservationists, the appeal was to *value,* though different from the conservationists'. Thus the "ownership" of value is an issue that places the two sides farthest apart. For the conservationists, "nature" (e.g., the Finnmark tundra) belongs to all; for the pastoralists, their relationship with what the conservationists designate as nature is not a contingent one—they "own" that relationship.

However, in the wake of a January 1989 conference with high-level government participation on "reindeer pastoralism and the natural environment,"[34] NRL and its local branches, at their annual meeting in June, gave careful consideration to the complaints, both specific and general, brought against them.

Looking at each season in turn: Winter use of snowmobiles does little or no damage to the natural environment, they conclude.[35] However, the Kautokeino branch of NRL, for instance, notes how the myriad snowmobile trails across the winter pastures makes pastoralists' work all the more difficult, for reindeer follow trails, and there will be many unintended ones. In addition, there is a call for a stop to the use of snowmobiles (not least among the nonpastoral population) during spring calving.

It is conceded that use of motorized vehicles (e.g., two- and three-wheel terrain-adapted motorcycles) dur-

ing summer and autumn when there is no snow cover
does damage ground vegetation; but that, it is argued,
cannot be avoided, and the vehicles are ordinarily not
used in excess of what is necessary. What could *reduce*
their use and thus the wear-and-tear on the ground
vegetation would be more reindeer fences, and NRL-
Kautokeino proposes that the autumn pastures of each
District be fenced in—this is very much in line with the
Administration's thinking. Ironically, it is the "erosion" of
vegetation along the line of a reindeer fence coupled
with the stress attributed to animals crowded at the fence
that is one of the principal targets of the conservationist
lobby.[36]

In general, both sides of the issue are addressed by
NRL and the local associations. On the one side, care is
taken not to trivialize the issue of environmental protection. It is recognized that individual abuse occurs among
their membership, and action is promised on a unified
regulatory plan that has already passed through the committee stage. On the other side, the claim made by Johan
Mathis Turi (above) is repeated; unlicensed as well as licensed use of the tundra by *non*pastoralists, in all seasons,
is noted as the principal source of environmental abuse;
and more say in the making of environmental regulations
is demanded.

Constructing fence on autumn pasture. Photo by Lloyd Villmo,
Reindriftsadministrasjonen.

What Johan Mathis Turi left unsaid in his address was
how pastoral technological updatedness, and opposition
to that, raises the issue of discrimination and ultimately
of hegemony. "If, the herders ask, other industries, and
especially those exploitive industries which destroy reindeer grazing land, are encouraged to mechanize for the
sake of efficiency, is it fair for the Saami to be denied
similar possibilities?"[37] The words are those of an observer of the Swedish scene, but I believe they correctly
express a general sentiment among the Finnmark pastoralists. And buried in the morass of charge and coun-
tercharge is the variable of ethnicity. Should the Saami as
Saami be allowed to be their own ecologists on the tundra that is their ancestral workplace (while it may be
someone else's wilderness)? Or should environmentalists'
reading of ecology apply regardless? Conservationists, according to Beach, reason that the ethnic argument implies returning to the pursuit of reindeer pastoralism with

"traditional" (and eco-friendly) technology, and therefore, continued use of modern technology (i.e., "nontra-
ditional" and prone to eco-abuse) disqualifies any appeal
to ethnic privilege. Either way, self-determination will be
denied, in the one case through the imposition of "traditionalism" and in the other through incorporation into a
unitary system.[38]

Returning now to the significance of mechanization for
the pastoralists themselves and its possible perils, most
important of all, I think, is an argument about *the cost attached to time*—clock time—now that reindeer pastoralism
is incorporated into the market economy. The pastoralist
nowadays cannot afford to be days late in bringing ani-

mals to a corral where the people of a field abbatoir are waiting (who will pay them for all that time?), or late bringing a herd to the naval landing craft, which has its own time schedule to follow. And—so this argument runs—without snowmobiles or all-terrain vehicles, and helicopters when necessary, there can be little assurance about *when* herds will arrive.

Now, if all that mechanization meant was that clock time is pushing itself (albeit selectively) into Saami pastoralism, there would indeed be little for them to worry about.[39] The paradox is, though, that rather than entering the *regulation* of clock time, reindeer pastoralism is entering a runaway world. It is technically possible to move herds over the terrain with a few relatively inexperienced herders *and a helicopter.*[40] So why not? And if this gives a competitive edge to whomever adopts such a practice, will not others follow, if they possibly can? It is not clear where "mechanization" will stop. But it is clear why the commitment to it has not slackened: competition (as Nils Isak Eira intimated) combined with a perception, false or otherwise, of saving on work time.

But are there no cultural barriers to limit the process? One entry in *Reindriftsnytt* explains that as the snowmobile substitutes for the her'gi and becomes part of the Saami culture, a similar process of incorporation respecting that more recent arrival, the all-terrain vehicle, is taking place: It substitutes in the summer for the snowmobile.[41] An entry the following year extends the point. A Karasjok herder-owner and his herd of four hundred animals made the spring migration of 500 kilometers by truck in six trips for a total of 3,000 kilometers in the course of three and a half days![42]

The point that I would close on is the spiraling of competition through mechanization. It is not difficult to see how this can easily, and quickly, become counterproductive. When all have snowmobiles, no one person, on that account, is ahead of another, but everyone may be worse off. The question, then, facing these pastoralists is how to break the spiraling, in a culture where competition is itself a basic value. It has been on many agendas (as a matter of fact, Ellon Ailu brought up the matter at a NRL meeting),[43] but there is still no resolution or really any resolute moves by either NRL or the state. The latter does attempt to put a break on mechanization by offering now larger subsidies to those Districts with low mechanization. However, although a majority appear to support the precept, it has had little effect.[44]

In this respect, mechanization is a story of how modernization can buck, or run contrary to, rationalization. Ansgar Kosmo, a key researcher with the Reindeer Administration, sees this clearly. Lecturing at the Royal Agricultural College, he proposed a "freeze" on mechanization at a given technical level. Short of that, he said, soaring expenditures will exclude many Saami who would otherwise be pastoralists—and he sees that as contrary to what the state has in mind.[45] But this returns us to the issue of self-determination. Touched upon briefly here, it will be of increasing relevance as our argument unfolds in the concluding chapters.

13.
Rationalization

It is essential to recognize that the Act *[reindriftsloven]* and the Agreement *[hovedavtalen]* have given reindeer pastoralism a legitimacy it has never before had.

ANSGAR J. KOSMO, "REINDRIFTSKURSET: MÅLSETTINGER OG VIRKEMIDLER I REINDRIFTSPOLITIKKEN"

Ideologies of equality . . . serve to justify inequality whenever they fail to account for cultural differences.

THOMAS HYLLAND ERIKSEN, "THE TENSION BETWEEN NATIONALISM AND ETHNICITY"

Since the 1970s, the Norwegian state, in its unprecedented involvement in the affairs of Saami reindeer pastoralism, has been guided by a sacred premise: equality within a social democratic state—"sacred," for it is on this premise that Norwegian civil society is, ideally, built. The premise has a unitary assumption. It embraces *all* citizens whether "Norwegian" or "Saami," so that the notion of cultural *difference* is accommodated, where it is, only with considerable difficulty.[1] As pointed out in Chapter 11, the problem is evident even in the opening paragraph of the 1978 Reindeer Management Act; it becomes still clearer from the account that now follows of the state's rationalization program.

The objectives of this program were clear enough, and an enormous amount of money and planners' energies have been spent on them; however, largely on account of the factor of cultural difference, the objectives had not, at the end of the first ten years, been fulfilled. Far from it: The intention was to reduce both the total number of reindeer (in Finnmark) and differences in herd size of individual owners, but in 1988 there were more animals than in 1978, and the large herds had grown larger, for

the most part. It is this paradoxical situation that the present chapter sets out to explain.

The 1978 Act and Its Predecessors

The singular character of the 1978 Act can best be appreciated through comparison, in broad strokes, with those that preceded it. In 1852 the Russians closed the Norwegian-Finnish border, along the eastern perimeter of Finnmark, for the seasonal passage of the pastoralists (it has remained closed).[2] At that time, some fifty thousand reindeer from the Norwegian side had winter pastures in Finland, and around fifteen thousand animals from the Finnish side pastured in Finnmark in the summer.[3] The considerable reduction in the total area of winter pastures (now that the border was closed) necessitated, in the view of the Norwegian state, strict(er) demarcation of boundaries of pastures, winter and summer, of herds within Finnmark. Further, there was a political, geographical factor: The Norwegian-Swedish state was concerned with the demographic defense of its northern boundaries vis-à-vis possible Russian territorial ambitions. Thus the extensive (from the coast to the borders in the interior) "Norwegian" Saami pastoralism served the state well, in this context.

First and foremost, then, a series of Acts from 1854 to the end of the century authorized the provincial authorities in Finnmark to allocate, as they saw fit, the boundaries of seasonal pastures. Also at this time, the codification of Saami reindeer pastoralism in (Norwegian) law began. Two observations from informed and influential Norwegian circles, when taken together, catch much of the sense of this early legislation. It was noted, on the one hand, that while relations between pastoralists were subjected to regulation, little attention was paid to relations between the pastoral and sedentary populations;[4] and on the other, that what went into the Acts was "in the main, in accordance with the Saami pastoralists' own ideas of what was proper practice."[5] In both respects, this would change.

Social Darwinism increased apace as the century drew to a close, and pertinently, it was an instrument of nationalism. Geopolitics became geocultural politics, and programs of "Norwegianization" were conceived.[6] Thus in 1904—the year before Norway became an independent nation-state (breaking away from its post-Napoleonic union with Sweden)—the complaint was made that it was misleading to have the laws pertaining to reindeer pastoralism called "Lapp Laws [Acts]" (lappeloverne, or lov om lapperne); for the rights contained therein addressed the livelihood, not the rights of the Saami themselves.[7]

The Social Darwinism of the day saw reindeer nomadism (the preferred designation over "pastoralism") as "an historical survival" whose "natural" demise—because "the weak must give away to the strong"—was only a matter of time. It would be tolerated as long as it did not become a hindrance to the expansion and development of agriculture. The Norwegian presumption is made clear: Entitlement to pursue reindeer pastoralism in any given area is given by law—it is a gift of the state—and, accordingly, is subject to changes in the law.[8]

Such was the prevailing ideology behind the 1933 Act. A consequence was an asymmetry in the distribution of rights and responsibilities. Rights (with compensation for their infringement) were, for the most part, enjoyed by the sedentary farming population, and responsibilities (legal liabilities) were left, for the most part, with the pastoralists.[9] The nomadic pastoralists were now less of a geopolitical asset in the national scheme of things and, instead, more of a hindrance to the effort to colonize the north from the south. In addition, antipathy between pastoral Saami and the (relatively) large coastal population of Saami was growing apace, principally as a consequence of the "Norwegianization" programs.[10]

In fact, the 1933 Act, for all the empowerment it gave to the authorities, was rarely enacted at all strenuously. The Act spoke of compulsory counts of herds every five years. This did not happen. It spoke of maximum herd sizes per District and per individual, but these were not invoked. Two explanations, quite different from each other but interrelated in practice, suggest themselves. One is that the Administration was hopelessly understaffed and underfinanced with one lappefogden and the nucleus of a staff for the whole of Finnmark. All that could really be achieved was the paperwork (e.g., registration of reindeer ownership marks) and a superficial overview of the seasonal round of pastoralism (e.g., seeing that in the autumn herds were on the autumn pastures, which they often weren't). The other explanation rests upon the symbolism of law, whereby the importance or authority of a law is found less in the actual regulations it imposes than in the comfort it offers that our interests are being safeguarded.[11] In the case before us, the interests are, first of all, those of the nonpastoralists in the area—and an appearance of pastoral order in accordance with the accepted precepts may prove sufficient. At the same time, the pastoralists' own interests are cared for through the inactivation of clauses of control present in the law. As part of this pattern, pastures are collected administratively into Districts, each of which has to elect a foreman (this is still the case: see Chapter 14). In the 1960s this person was less likely to be chosen on account of his (only men were elected) pastoral reputation or prominence among his fellows as for his proficiency in Norwegian and (just as important) "discretion" when dealing with the Administration. The administrative system, then, was externalized, as far as possible, by the pastoralists.

Where this structure of make-belief breaks down, of course, is in the courts, where the one party charges the other with irresponsible neglect (e.g., farmers claiming trespass against pastoralists) or worse (e.g., suits brought by one pastoralist against another).[12]

My fieldwork was done while the 1933 Act was still on the books, and the annual lappefogden reports from that time usually confirm the kind of situation I have suggested. Typically, the 1961 report is embroidered around the assurance that "relations between the pastoralists are good." But then, unexpectedly, in 1962 the tone changes, the mask dropped: "Relations between the pastoralists are *seemingly* good." And this explanation follows:

But their subjective approach to their common problems, a frequent lack of cooperative will and of understanding for each others' problems—these are the problems of reindeer pastoralism today.

Such subjectivity is not something that has come about recently, nor the failure of a will to cooperate with each other. But the need for cooperation is so much greater these days. . . . [Instead], each wishes to make his own decisions and no one will defer to another.[13]

The entries for these two years—I surmise—were not written by the same person. In 1961 the report was written by the lappefogden, but in 1962 by the *reindrifts-ekretaer* (an official in the lappefogden's office) in the Finnmark office, who in a few years was to be one of the architects of the 1978 Act and thereafter the first chief of the Reindeer Administration. The 1962 entry concludes by remarking how for centuries little changed in reindeer pastoralism,[14] but that now, on account of unprecedented change and development in the world at large, Saami reindeer pastoralism *must* change, too. Attention is drawn to the claim that over the previous ten years the number of pastoralists had increased by 30 percent without a comparable increase in the number of animals. The inescapable suggestion is that without radical remedial action, future immiserization among the majority of pastoralists is likely.

Some years down the road much about this 1962 annual report—with regard to tone as much as substance—would be echoed in departmental government documents. Thus a 1974–75 policy memorandum (requested by the minister of agriculture of his officials) states that the future of reindeer pastoralism depends on *structural*

change and that the present Act (1933) provides no mandate in that respect. On the one hand, there are too many pastoralists striving to maintain a livelihood with too few animals—that is to say, most have too few; and on the other, the bearing capacity of pastures is being seriously overextended on account of the number of pastoral units. So there are both too few and too many animals. The memorandum focuses on the need for viable schemes to persuade older pastoralists to retire and some of the younger to change livelihoods.[15] The same problem is addressed in a 1976–77 document (preparing the ground for the parliamentary passage of the 1978 Act) but with a more radical solution in mind: It is necessary for the state to be able "to limit or regulate entry into the [pastoral] livelihood."[16] The case for structural change is also broadened to include the three-tiered authority structure that is now in place and which, along with other changes, will be discussed throughout this chapter.

The climate of change over these years—itself changing, as I think the author of the 1962 lappefogden report well knew—also needs to be noted before proceeding further. Putting ethnicity aside, reindeer pastoralism becomes increasingly regarded as one primary resource in the national economy among several. Thus it is included in a system in which "change" means "development" and whose principal conduit is a *statism* (state bureaucracies) morally connected to the premises of social democracy. These premises are themselves contractual in nature. The state, on behalf of society as a whole, offers monetary and other support to primary resource livelihoods on the understanding that the *rationality* and *efficiency* of production is ensured. At the same time, the state is also concerned that the pursuit of production goals, in each case, happens without prejudice to other livelihoods. Furthermore, as the state is concerned with the welfare of all and—as far as possible—with the equality of all, so mobility of labor (even retraining of persons into other livelihoods) can be a justifiable means to this end. An inevitable adjunct to the system is the use of *experts* (as opposed to practitioners) to advise the state on the limits of possibility within a livelihood and on alternatives of strategy. It is in this context that government planning on behalf of reindeer pastoralism (even though it is a symbolically charged Saami niche) should be understood:

[Reindeer pastoralism] lags behind in development, and the committee believes it is important that the livelihood be helped to catch up [with contemporary developments]. To this end, technical knowledge and especially new thinking are necessary, leading to changes in traditional practices whose roots go back 1,000 years.[17]

The quality of the intention is notable; but exactly on account of its inclusive and nondiscriminatory embrace, such a scheme carries within itself the stuff of controversy from embedded cultural positions. It is one thing to promote a quality-of-life program in economic terms, but quite another to recognize quality-of-life as having also to do with ethnic self-identity. The separate challenges facing the state and the pastoralists—which they have yet to show they are not failing in—is the bringing together of these two kinds of "quality."

Meanwhile, the 1978 Act sanctioned the restructuring that had been urged: The "help" was set in motion.[18] And yet, in the view of many, the 1978 Act brought little "comfort" (Arnold), or comfort at too high a price. Among the sedentary population, non-Saami and Saami alike—what comfort in seeing "help" being lavished on the still-persisting "nomadic" and emphatically "ethnic" way of life?[19] And among the pastoral Saami—what comfort in the realization that the price of the "help" is to be tutelage?[20] Pastoral rights remained those of usufruct.[21] Parliament declared that it was *not* taking a position on the question of Saami land rights.[22]

Three clauses of the Act, in particular, were the source of pastoralist consternation. The first of these concerned the appointment of persons to Area Boards *(områdestyrene)*. The idea of an Area Board as an authoritative body overseeing a number of Districts was itself accepted without difficulty. As the state said: "The present arrangement with District foremen is insufficient: they have too little authority and are without the [necessary] support of an administrative apparatus."[23] The Area Boards, each responsible for a number of Districts and answerable to the national board, became the middle tier in a new three-tier authority structure. Pastoral alarm and indignation arose over the ruling of the Act that the members would be *appointed by the provincial governor* (clause 7) and not elected by the pastoralists of each area.

Considerable authority was invested in the Area Boards to ensure compliance with the intent of the Act and, most important, with decisions and instructions promulgated by the state from time to time.

Many specifics (the application of "rules") were left to the judgment of the particular Area Board; notably, decisions as to the maximum number of animals per District. These led into decisions on viable maximum numbers of animals per pastoralist and the viable maximum of pastoralists in particular Districts. Thus clause 4 of the Act reads: "To begin in reindeer pastoralism as a livelihood requires the agreement of the Area Board." So the state, through its area appointees, controls entry into what had always been open to Saami as a right. The reasons for controlled entry, of course, follow directly from the premises (above) of social democratic statism. Hence the disapproval of the 1933 Act, whereby Saami "have an unconditional right to pursue reindeer pastoralism without regard to the sufficiency of the natural resources and whether there is place enough for them."[24]

The third clause, to which many of the pastoralists took the strongest exception, concerned the ownership of reindeer marks. As noted in Chapter 2, the significance of the complex lexicon of these earmarks and their individual ownership goes far beyond their being a means of recognizing animals: Giving a child its own reindeer earmark helps to commit that child to the pastoral livelihood. Of itself, this is cause for concern among those charged with the program of rationalization. In addition, the state sees a confusion in the multiplication of earmark patterns and looks forward to some rational regulation (Chapter 14); but no move is made in that direction, at this time, out of recognition of the high sensitivity of "tradition" in this matter. The state does, however, make ownership of a reindeer mark dependent on entry into the livelihood, and that entry is now controlled. Furthermore, the children of a registered pastoralist do not qualify for reindeer marks—and this *is* a radical break with a precious "tradition."[25]

For the pastoralists, the intention and implications of those bleak clauses of the Act itself were not difficult to unlock; but the same could not be said of the spirals of propositions, hypotheses, and calculations that preceded the Act and followed, seemingly forever, in its wake. For the 1978 Act followed the modern format of leaving (as far as possible) the interpretation and even enhancement of each clause to subsequent written instructions and regulations promulgated by the government department in question; and the department takes recourse to a battery of "experts." Little wonder that those whose livelihood is being addressed express frustrated incomprehension from time to time: "When one reads the scholarly experts' debates about reindeer pastoralism, it is all made to sound so complicated that one really can't understand what the problem is."[26] But what is arcane to them is taken as a familiar-enough exercise by the civil servants and experts versed, as they are, in their respective disciplines. After all, they, or their predecessors, had put together Jordloven (the Agricultural Act), and they negotiate the Agreements with the farmers and their rival national associations. So dealing with reindeer pastoralists should simply be a matter of applying knowledge, insight, and technique learned in one domain (with *its* animals and practitioners) to another. The Royal Agricultural College itself has become an important training and research center for reindeer pastoralism.

Such quite dissimilar experiences of the two parties—the experts and the pastoralists—pitting theory and controlled experiment against everyday practice and *its* theory, should leave us unsurprised by the difficulties the implementation of the rationalization program ran into. There is another factor, too. It looked as though it would be an uneven contest, with the experts, backed by the sanctions of the state, producing uncontrovertible evidence and reasoning for their claims and proposals. Indeed, for the first time it seemed that the state had the monopoly of authority in these matters, whereas, when dealing with agriculture or fisheries, these industries had their own battery of legal and technical experts as well as powerful parliamentary lobbies.[27] In the event, however, much about the practice of reindeer pastoralism (in the terrain, not at experimental field stations) proved arcane to the experts.

After a while, though, one could not truthfully speak of *the* Saami position regarding the 1978 Act. For some, a minority, it became something close to an ideological protocol, not a document of tutelage. And for all—whatever interpretation given to it—it became an economic

resource exploited with increasing effectiveness. These developments will be amply demonstrated.

Let me return, for a moment, to the state's point of view. Whereas the 1933 Act (work on it began in 1919) accepted reindeer pastoralism on sufferance—as being there "for the time being," the 1978 Act recognized that it was here to stay, and therefore socioeconomic integration into the national system had to occur. This proves to be an ambitious task of codification of (often new) rules of behavior, of (often new) rewards and penalties. Much really comes down to who "owns" the (new) rules, rewards, and penalties.[28] In whose hands are they (politics)? Whose precepts are in play (knowledge)? In this chapter and the next I will attempt to show that throughout the ten years under review, these questions of "ownership," for all parties, including opposing factions among the Saami pastoralists, are *the* issue—the disputed prize.[29]

Calculations and Means

I begin with an appreciation of the difficulties facing the planners, before going over to their specific calculations.

The key proposition that the state wishes to see realized is that of *more people living better off fewer animals.* For this to begin to take effect, two things must start to happen at about the same time: More animals must be slaughtered, and animals' weights must rise. If numbers are reduced without a perceptible increase in animal weights quickly following, whatever pastoral confidence there had been in the scheme is likely to evaporate and be replaced by mistrust.

Compulsory slaughter of his animals is about the last thing a pastoralist wishes to suffer, and the situation in question is all the more critical on account of the two-pronged campaign that is required: The *total* number of animals of an area, say West Finnmark, must be cut back to a number that accords with its calculated bearing capacity; and the sizes of individual owners' herds have to be regulated, and the larger herds reduced, to allow for the optimal number of herds within the inclusive bearing capacity of the area. There are likely to be severe problems with both the determination of correct numbers and their implementation in respect to both requirements. For, as I will argue, one is not dealing with an exact science for the calculation of bearing capacity. Nor can it be assumed that there is but one set of criteria for determining the optimal sizes of individual herds.

The first question, then, that the planners need to answer is, how many animals are there at present in West Finnmark? Given the status of the annual returns (Chapter 8), any estimate is immediately open to challenge. The next question is, how many fewer animals should there be? How this is answered is crucial to all of the herd owners and may raise a storm of defiant protests (among other things it influences decisions concerning allowable differences in herd size).

This last is a question that cannot be answered by referring to a concept of "natural bearing capacity," for the pastoral adaptation overtakes the natural when the reproductive and life spans of the animals are determined for them (see Chapter 1). Furthermore, as the practice of pastoralism itself differs, so there will be differences regarding what is an acceptable bearing capacity.

This is not to say that animal weights do not vary with the number of animals pasturing in a given area. They likely do.[30] It is a factor that falls especially to the state biologists to argue—often in the face of pastoral opposition. Thus newspapers may be used to justify the good sense of the reasoning in proposing reductions in animal numbers, for example: that the meat yield (seven hundred tons) from 105,000 animals on the pastures of West Finnmark would be equaled by that from 70,000. Therefore (the argument ran), one can safely reduce the number of animals by 35,000, and there would be advantages in doing so.[31]

In fact, any answer to the question of carrying capacity will be multifactorial, with interrelated *socioeconomic* determinations, and there will therefore be a range of theoretical answers from which to choose. The important determinations include: the target income for a pastoralist; the target number of pastoralists; and the target optimal weight of animals.

It is through the priorities attached to each of these factors that the *desired* carrying capacity is determined.[32] So a review of a proposed "moderate reduction" of reindeer in Finnmark to 160,000 reasons thus: "Given 160,000 reindeer, and an increase in productivity of from 8.7 to 10 kilograms [per animal], the number of licensed units will have to be reduced from just over 500 today to 400 if the average recompense for labour and capital is to increase to about 100,000 Norwegian kroner [per annum, per unit]."[33] Here *two* "carrying capacities" are determined: of animals in relation to weight, and of owners in relation to monetary reward. Regarding the first, the review prefaces its remark about a "moderate reduction" with the observation that "it is impossible to establish with certainty what the maximum number of reindeer should be." As for the second determination, it is clearly one that prioritizes monetary income per unit even at the cost of reducing the number of pastoral units by one fifth, notwithstanding repeated government promises that rationalization programs would not entail a reduction in the number of pastoralists.

The notion of desired carrying capacity, then, carries suppositions of *efficiency* operating within agreed socioeconomic, ecologic, and cultural parameters; and this efficiency is expressed and quantified as "pastoral-labor years" *(årsverk)*, a concept taken from agronomics. On the premise that reindeer pastoralism should be kept at a labor-intensive level and offer a reasonable monetary income to all who participate, a pastoral-labor year is set at 250 animals.[34] Thus, for a District, its total of pastoral-labor years is arrived at by dividing its total number of animals by 250. Overly simplistic as it may be when applied to reindeer pastoralism, and with margins of error that are not really calculable, the state needs such a concept if it is to "measure" efficiency—and to stimulate and reward efficiency.

The principal stimulus and reward of this concept are its *operating grants*. In the first years (beginning in the late 1970s) these were given to Districts (Distrikttilskudd) and to individuals (Drifttilskudd) separately (the changes that were to come are looked at in the next section). In the case of a District, the size of the operating grant was a function of its number of pastoral-labor years. This is unlikely to be the same as the number of pastoralists belonging to the District. Operating grants to individuals, on the other hand, were (and are) tied to slaughter quotas under veterinary supervision, and these quotas are progressively scaled: The larger a herd, the larger the per-

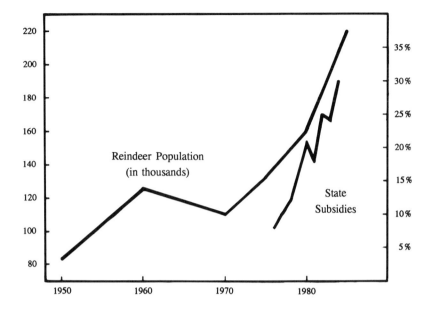

Figure 13.1 Saami reindeer pastoralism in Norway, 1950–1985: growth of reindeer population and growth of subsidies as percentage of the total income of the livelihood. From NRL 1987a, 1:18, 26

centage of animals that have to be slaughtered to qualify for the grant. The required slaughter percentages vary from 22 percent to 56 percent.[35]

Another stimulus and reward from this time has been the calf slaughter subsidy with the intention "to stimulate a rational use of pastures, to reduce losses, to stimulate a better selection of breeding animals, to even out differences in losses between Districts, and finally, to improve the income of the individual owner."[36]

The third plank in the state's reward system aimed at stabilization is a guaranteed minimum price (with a built-in state subsidy) for the sale of reindeer meat, together with centralized marketing.

Such intrusive programs raise the question whether the state should use monetary incentives to forward structural changes where it is known, or believed, that the changes by themselves would be disapproved and unwelcome by those targeted. The District foremen were actually asked this question, and the answers were very divided.[37] What was not asked, however, is whether acceptance of these gifts from the state morally obliges the recipients to use them in the way intended by the state. Judged by the pastoralists' behavior, the answer would be no. This is particularly interesting in view of the apparently widespread acceptance that the disbursement of such gifts usually serves the state's ends, and even though such is patently *not* the case with the state's gifts to the pastoralists.[38]

What Went Wrong?

By 1987, it was quite apparent what had gone wrong with the state's rationalization program. The chief of the Reindeer Administration put it thus: "To simplify a little, we can say that the economic improvements which the Reindeer Agreements brought have, in large part, been used not on consumption but on investments in more reindeer."[39] Worse still, the tendency is especially noticeable among the larger owners: In 1976 only 7 percent of herding units *(driftsenhetene)* had more than 500 animals, but by 1985 this had climbed to 25 percent.[40] In short, at the end of the first ten years of the state programs, a *smaller* percentage of animals were being slaughtered. True, "production" (i.e., animals slaughtered) increased by nearly 50 percent over the ten years, from 38,000 to 70,000 animals, but the herd increase was much greater and should—if only to stabilize numbers at the 1976 level—have meant the slaughter of 97,000 animals.[41]

The principal reason for this state of affairs is that the

pastoralists (especially those in Finnmark) used the state grants and subsidies in the livelihood to support their monetary needs, thus *reducing* the need to slaughter. The only subsidy or grant that was conditional upon a slaughter percentage being fulfilled was the personal operating grant, and that amounted to but a small fraction of the total disbursements from the wide-ranging register of state programs.[42] Thus the total number of reindeer and total amount of state subsidization, expressed as a percentage of the livelihood's total income, climbed *together* (Fig. 13.1).

That the state failed to foresee this would happen speaks to the distance separating it from the practicing pastoralists (who build up herds to be inherited by their children). The pastoralists understand the presuppositions of the state well enough to be able to balk them; but the state appears not to understand the pastoralists' presuppositions, or, more likely, it drastically underestimates their seriousness. Meanwhile, one notes an irony. The state, quite beyond its intention, enables the opening paragraph of the 1978 Act (Chapter 11) to be enacted to the pastoralists' advantage on their own terms: for the time being.

The Administration was particularly perplexed over the admitted failure of the calf slaughter subsidy.[43] There appear to be two general factors at play here. The first is how the two values, cash increment and herd increment, weigh against each other. The different outcomes correlate quite closely with differences in the size of herd: Among owners with less than 100 animals, 50 percent slaughtered some calves, whereas all of 85 percent of owners with herds of between 250 and 350 animals availed themselves of the program. The largest herd owners of all showed very little interest.[44] I take this as indicating that the program presented the owners of the smallest herds with the hardest choice of all. They were in dire need of cash at the same time as they wished to build up their herds, but to do that they could not afford the extra income if it meant surrendering some of their already too-few calves. The 50:50 split on the decision mirrors their dilemma. The decision was not nearly as difficult to make for the owners whose herds were well established. They could cull their calves without prejudicing the future growth of their herds; and, topped up

with the subsidy, the cash value of the sales became an important increment to their household economy, reducing their need to slaughter cows. As for the largest herd owners, the subsidy is no temptation. Indeed, calf slaughter—beyond household needs (e.g., clothing) and excepting the weakest of the calves—runs counter to the husbandry practice that produced the large herds.

The second general factor is the way in which the state taxes the pastoralists. The structuring of this state program—of taxation—compromises the calf slaughter subsidy program. At one period, taxable income was related, using different formulae, to the size of the herd. This being so, owners were likely to under-report appreciably their herd sizes. However, this also meant that the number of animals an owner slaughtered had to be comparable to the under-reported size of his herd, lest suspicion be aroused in official quarters. Nils Isak Eira, himself a pastoralist, draws out the consequence of this situation:

Let us imagine an owner who for tax purposes declared that he had a herd of 250 animals [but] in reality had 500. . . . This means he can only slaughter 70 animals, in keeping with the size of his "official" herd. In reality, he could have slaughtered 150 animals. . . . So what does he do? He really has no choice, he has to get as much money as he can from the slaughter of the 70. *So he slaughters the heaviest animals.*[45]

Eira believed this to be common enough practice also when it came to selecting calves for slaughter. The irony is palpable twice over. First, *fewer* calves slaughtered, and second, the *heavier* (and healthier), whereas the program was intended to cull the lighter (and weaker).

Then the taxation principle was changed. Taxes were not computed from the size of the herd but from animals sold or consumed. However, as another part of the rationalization program, mandatory slaughter percentages *are* related to the size of the herd—so the Eira scenario holds here, too. Thus it was that the calf slaughter subsidy program *contributed* to the current increase in overall animals numbers, and the Administration is left arguing that the contribution was "only" 5 percent (of an overall increase of 70 percent over the ten years).[46]

The state's marketing and guaranteed minimum price policy has continually been in trouble—for a variety of reasons. Some of these reasons relate to external market factors, and others, once again, to pastoralists' own responses. Already in the 1960s, the state saw its first responsibility as the securing of a guaranteed minimum price for reindeer meat (such was already in place for other meats). This would be secured through a state subsidized contract with a marketing board, to which was attached a guarantee of delivery-and-acceptance of a set tonnage of meat.[47] To facilitate this overall scheme, the state generously financed a few regional slaughterhouses (in West Finnmark, it is the Kautokeino Cooperative).[48] These purchase from the pastoralists and deliver to the central marketing board. Thus the state solution lay in centralization, but among many of the pastoralists this has been seen as visiting the bane of "monopolization" on them.[49]

The centralization has its pitfalls even for the state, but these are of a logistical kind: persisting difficulties in bringing in customers while the autumn herds are still far from Kautokeino, even though autumn slaughter makes such good sense; working at over-capacity—with its ensuing delays—when the herds are in the winter pastures; and having to lay off employees through the slack summer season. Many herd owners are deterred by these logistic tangles, but a far more important factor (persisting from 1962) is the sense of the state pushing them into a no-choice situation. A common response is, in fact, to exercise a choice of one's own determining: Still today, many of the reindeer sold in Finnmark (some say most of them) are sold privately.[50]

To guarantee a minimum price does not amount to control over the market; in the first years, reindeer meat made a strong market showing, relative to other meats, but suffered a severe downturn after 1975—a contributing factor being the increase in production (along with the still greater increase in total reindeer population). From the point of view of the state, quite clearly, the market plan was folding back on itself. More interesting, though, is how herd owners responded to the market swings, and here we return to some familiar turns in pastoral logic. For many, a strong market price reduces the need to slaughter. Weak market prices certainly constrain some to sell more to meet cash commitments and debts, but all, their household economy permitting, will see it

as a time to save their herds—selling no more than one or two animals at a time, which may mean more frequent recourse to private sales.

Putting to one side such market variables, the following scenario, in conclusion, suggests the unspoken transaction into which the pastoralist drags the state with its gift of a price subsidy: "Two reindeer owners with herds of 200 and 600 animals, respectively, of which they slaughter 30% . . . will increase their income by 20,000 and 60,600 kroner, respectively, as a consequence of a price subsidy."[51] In consequence: "Both of the owners are in a stronger position to *reduce* their slaughter percentage, thereby *enlarging* their herds. Furthermore, the subsidy has a marked social implication whereby the owner of the larger herd gains added advantage over the other: next time he can 'save' 40 more cows than can the owner of the smaller herd."[52]

Internal Review

I close this chapter with a look at what amounted to an internal review in 1986–87—jointly authorized by the Department of Agriculture and NRL—of the state programs since 1978.[53] A volume of papers emerged.[54]

One of these papers pressed the point that it was necessary to wean the pastoralists away from their individual self-insurance to a sense of collective insurance.[55] Here the state had failed—thus far. Similarly, another of the papers urges that the goal of the state should be to help the pastoralists to switch from investing in a large herd to finding the insurance they need in the biennial Agreements that NRL makes with the state on their behalf.[56]

It became clear to both the Administration and NRL that there was a gaping hole in the state strategy: the mandatory slaughter percentage. Intended as a key to the whole rationalization policy—in return for which the state offered its gifts—in fact, its application was notably lax regarding the personal operating grants, and not even a condition of eligibility for the other programs. In a proposal originating with NRL, a greater proportion of the subsidy programs, *including the personal operating grants,* would henceforth be paid to the Districts. Once satisfied that all conditions of eligibility were met—most important among these was the mandatory slaughter percentage of each herd owner, but they also included a "work plan and budget" and an official count of the herd—the District would pass on the money to the individual herd owner. Thus the hole would be plugged. And more than that, a correct procedure of insurance and sense of collectivity would be ensured. For the individual herd owner was drawn into the Agreement with the state, and he who does not live up to its conditions will be acting "illegally" and cut off from any support.[57]

Decisions of the review committee are presented as the will of the majority: "One should not reward those who do things in ways other than the majority wish," Ole K. Sara (chief of the Administration) tells a meeting of District foremen.[58] At the same time as the review committee empowers the Districts, it *obligates* them to exercise—in form and substance—the authority delegated to them. The Area Boards are the watchdogs over the Districts.[59]

The review committee insisted on another necessary correction. The work force must be regularized with a set number of work days for *every* person. The Districts set the number—perhaps 210 days, perhaps 250. This will also ensure that labor is rewarded (per diem calculations) on the basis of equal effort, the implication being that owners of larger herds have, up to now, unfairly used the labor of the others.[60]

However, this still leaves the correct distribution of wealth (i.e., herd-size differentials) undecided. Undecided in practice, that is, for in principle it has been enshrined since 1978. It is the intention neither of the Act nor the Agreement that anyone has a herd larger than needed for a comfortable standard of living, says one report used by the committee.[61] Addressing the District foremen, Ole K. Sara puts a political slant to it all. Parliament, he says, has been much concerned these last years over *who* benefits the most from state support. The question being asked is whether this support is helping to reduce income differences. He makes a "common property" argument, too: An important reason for controlling differences in herd sizes is that the pastures belong to all equally.[62] He even plays with the thought that "if the total number of reindeer in Finnmark were redistributed equally, then each of the 466 production units would have 386 animals."[63] But he knows that absolute equality

of herd size is not attainable, perhaps not desirable. Nonetheless, he says, the committee finds the present distribution of herd wealth unacceptable.[64]

However, the statistical data with which the committee reaches its conclusion deals either with "units" without any information about their social composition, or with individuals grouped in age-classes.[65] Such data, bereft of social coordinates, hide the processes that generate the distributive patterns—processes which account for what the committee finds unacceptable and which the pastoral community may be clinging to as essential to the passage of generations through the livelihood. Given that most of the units are strongly kin-based, absence of information about the stages in the domestic life cycle of each of them is the most glaring omission. For example, a unit of four persons may be composed of two siblings and their spouses with young children; *or* four unmarried siblings; *or* parents with two of their adult unmarried children; *or* two couples—old or young, with or without children, who are only distantly related or even unrelated; and so on. Though each adds up to the same number of individuals, these units are not comparable—particularly with respect to the processes of the distribution of wealth—until account is taken of the stage each has reached in its family development cycle or of alliances made.

This explanation of the fact that what is important to the pastoralists is unimportant to the state brings us back to their respective notions of insurance, with linkages to different collectivities. It is not enough to see pastoral insurance as linked to a large herd, but also—and perhaps more importantly—to the passage and redistribution of the herd to the next generation. We should think of parents as the custodians of their *own* family herd, and each family will be at a different stage of its domestic cycle. The state, on the other hand, sees itself in quite a different custodian role, one in which it is responsible for *all* the pastoral units—that is, of those units it has licensed. Furthermore, through application of the same industrial management calculations that project standard pasture carrying capacities, standard reindeer weights, a standard work load, standard productivity levels, and a standard pastoral income, these units, as well, are projected as uniform—as a category, not as social groups with many differences between them.

What, then, did this internal review of state policies produce? It was acknowledged, on the one hand, that the pastoralists had managed to turn some of the more important of the policy measures to unintended ends; and on the other, that adjustments would have to be made to ensure that the policies had their intended effect. At the end of the day, "planners" and "pastoralists" (with some pastoralists now in the company of the planners) re-mained far apart. Planners continued to look askance at pastoral *society* as blighted by asocial individualism; and persisting among the pastoralists was the sense that the collective insurance the state wished to offer them would deliver them into an unaccustomed status of dependence (hedged with uncertainties). The chapter that now follows attempts to understand the apprehension and disso-nance—along with some defiance and internecine con-flict—this situation aroused among a number of the Saami pastoralists.

14.
Contrary Perception, Unsettling Consequences

What do they [the politicians, bureaucrats, and experts] understand of
our problems?

ANNE K. EIRA, PASTORALIST

Well, if it is more important to quarrel [among yourselves]—please yourselves!

KRISTIAN G. LINDMAN, OFFICER MANAGER,
REINDEER ADMINISTRATION

Where, one may ask, are the Saami in all this planning and programming, setting of production targets and ideal herd sizes? There is a great deal of discussion behind the making of each biennial Agreement between the state and NRL. Proposals are drawn up, some dismissed, others accepted. Perhaps with modifications, funds are voted, and for *that,* the Agreement has to go before Parliament. The place of the practitioner in all this—except for the few of an inner cabinet of NRL—is marginal at best. There is too much to consider and too little time. Besides, there is the feeling that so much has been decided beforehand—so what's the point? It seems to be the kind of situation where the one party (the state with NRL) may well believe that they *do* consult and *do* ask for inputs, and the other party (the local associations and the rank and file) nonetheless perceive themselves as outside the process.

The previous chapter showed the state guided by social democratic ideals in the making of its policy regarding reindeer pastoralism. I think it is also the case that measures pressed by the state for inclusion in the biennial Agreements are influenced by its perceptions of Saami society and its reindeer management. Likewise, Saami re-

actions to what the state proposes, or sets out to implement, can be accountable, in appreciable measure, to their perceptions of the state. This chapter, then, tries to take account of the likely political effects of the perceptions each party has of the other.

The view that the state has of *Saami* pastoralism is very much a unitary one; the same cannot be said, however, of the pastoralists' perceptions of the state and its policy affecting them. I will begin with the crucial but changing role of NRL in such interplay between state and pastoralists, and end as the decade under review (1978–89) ended, climactically, with the compulsory count undertaken by the Administration of the reindeer herds of Finnmark.

NRL between the State and the Pastoralists

NRL was unhappy with the Reindeer Management Act of April 1978, and in May, a joint press release with Norske Samers Riksforbund, or Norgga Samiid Riikasærvi (NSR), the national association of Norwegian Saami, included, among other criticisms, the following:

"It is disappointing that Parliament, in 1978, set aside fundamental Saami interests. The Saami associations, however, will continue to endeavor to get the Norwegian state to recognize and honor Saami concepts of law and tradition."[1] And at NRL's annual general meetings of 1978 and 1979, similar declarations of principle were proclaimed:

Reindeer pastoralism . . . must develop along traditional lines and be based on Saami premises. . . . In the planning of the use of pastures, therefore, there must be no encroachment on Saami rights and usufruct practices. Saami themselves must be included in decisions concerning the use of the Saami areas, in the development of reindeer pastoralism and, as well, of the other livelihoods [within those areas].[2]

Already, though, the large state subsidies were flowing, and NRL, as it bargained with the state to ensure a sustained flow, came to share many of its positions. At first, this was, one supposes, a pragmatic political move, but over time a common conviction over policy became evident. There must be a reduction in the number of animals, recruitment of herders must be controlled, differences of wealth must be reduced—in sum, a policy which *questions* the appropriateness of "Saami premises" in today's world. First signs of the shift were apparent already by the 1981 general meeting. And it was there, too, that the tendency began among the rank and file of identifying NRL with selling out to the state planners, without giving NRL due credit for the economic benefits that its state partnership brought. *Was* NRL merely doing the state's bidding?

In fact, NRL did register objections from time to time. In 1979–80 and again in 1985–86, for instance, it complained that in the three tiers of authority and decision-making, introduced by the Act, Saami representation and engagement was short-changed. Corrections followed.[3] Similarly, the NRL proposal that operating grants be distributed through the Districts was well received (Chapter 13). Again in 1986, there was an attempt to correct the impression that the association believes there are too many reindeer in Finnmark: "NRL's point of view is not precisely that, rather it wishes to see an increase in production."[4] This was in an official memorandum, directed "up," but it was not seen by most of the membership.

After 1986, I think, little difference remains between what NRL sees and what the state sees. Both insist there is a crisis situation. There are "too many" deer and, it is sometimes added, "too many" people. NRL agrees with the diagnosis and urges application of the medicine. Beyond reductions in numbers, there are suggestions (thus far not acted upon) of a reordering of customary (Saami) pasture rights in Finnmark. The crisis has another dimension, too. Economically, Saami reindeer pastoralism now lives off the state; expenditures outrun income. But it helps NRL little that its leadership condemns such a state of affairs,[5] for the expenditures have become so large exactly on account of the state subsidies NRL had worked hard for on behalf of the pastoralists. Besides, critics within the association had been saying for years: "The state is buying us off with the subsidies; meanwhile we are losing pasture areas."[6] It seemed that the state was bent on turning Saami-born pastoralists into employees of a Norwegian-directed stock-rearing enterprise.

Pasture Control, Pastoral Research

If NRL, to some, looks likes the creature of the state, the principal instrument of state policy is the Reindeer Administration, with its central offices in Alta. There are outspoken supporters of both the Administration and its mandate, but these are a small minority among the pastoralists; another minority are outspoken in their hostility. The divisive issue is "Norwegianness." Supporters will affirm Ansgar Kosmo in his conviction that the Act and the Agreement gave reindeer pastoralism its legitimacy. For the dissenters, it is a cruel irony: The Act and parts of the Agreement are at the root of what *ails* Saami reindeer pastoralism today. Control has been taken away from the Saami. Those who vocalize their dissent are in no way marginal figures, and, I suggest, much of what they say is felt (if left publicly unexpressed) by the majority: "As far as I can make out, there are 14 Norwegians and 5 Saami working in the Administration. None of them with the exception of the Head, and possibly one other, have practical knowledge of reindeer pastoralism. They are people with agronomist training."[7] That was in 1981, and in 1991, from a discussion of problems the Saami pastoral groups are prone to today:

Strategic work decisions [taken by the herder-owners] are of greater consequence for the resolution of these problems than ever are demands that the size of herds be reduced. . . . [However, a good part of the problem is] the controlling authority of Norwegians and for Norwegians. This has a clear consequence: reindeer pastoralism is still a culturally anchored livelihood, and one can well expect opposition and mistrust when it comes to involving Norwegians in the resolution of [our own] internal problems.[8]

With the wresting of control from the Saami, there has been a failure to understand the kind of adaptive planning this pastoralism requires. A number of individual statements attempt to return attention to this. Here is one of them:

Supposing that for two years in a row one had the same weather at the same points in time, the same number of animals and the same herd composition, and the same number of herder-owners with the same age distribution and the same level of competence, in such a case one could expect approximately the same sequence in the reindeer management in the two years. But two such identical years never occur of course. The notion is purely hypothetical, presented simply to emphasize that unforeseen change is a law which necessarily sets its stamp on reindeer pastoralism and its pastoralists.[9]

The author is Mikkel Nils Sara of the Saami Institute in Kautokeino. His didactic tone is not accidental. The statement was formulated in a NRL seminar (to which I return) and is intended to be heard by those Norwegians who have administrative or research responsibilities for reindeer pastoralism. I do not believe much attention was paid to it. Instead, Saami capabilities, insight, and praxis have been ignored or, at best, underestimated rather than heralded or, at the least, acknowledged. I am left supposing that this is part of a process of "legitimating" the seizure of control from the practitioners.[10] The pastoral Saami are reinvented as a people among whom "there has traditionally been little interest in systematizing existing knowledge or incorporating new knowledge." Indeed, "The individual reindeer owner hardly notices the negative consequences of an increase in the number of his own animals." Furthermore, these pastoralists would have been better off had reputation among them rested on pastoral competence and not simply on the size of a herd. Such statements are frequent. These particular ones

are from the Norsk Institutt for By- og Regionforskning (NIBR) report commissioned by the Administration.[11] Little wonder that it is asked: "Why has the State commissioned NIBR to do research? They are probably experts in agricultural problems, but when it comes to reindeer pastoralism, the experts are the Saami who are active herders-owners. And why is no notice being taken of the recent research report Mikkel Nils Sara did for the Saami Institute?"[12]

Saami pastoral social organization, and the ethnicity factor, were to be excluded from consideration, the NIBR team says. Yet they sometimes stray in that direction, enough to misinform their readers on the dynamics of herding partnerships, especially between large and small owners.[13] It is a case of naïveté born of outsider deduction. Regrettably, even one such as the well-versed Ansgar Kosmo sometimes reinvents Saami pastoral society without checks and balances (see Chapter 7) that place limits on the individual's freedom of action. In a paper coauthored with a biologist, it is acknowledged that such constraints did exist before, but the rhetoric declares the "traditional" dead—so it is a situation calling for radical socioeconomic "engineering."[14] In this same paper, "ethnic group" is mentioned in association with the problem of how far individuals should be allowed to burden the common property pastures. Certainly that is something which has to be addressed. One might have supposed the reference to ethnic group signaled that resolution of this matter rests with them and not with outsiders. But such seems not to be the intention. Instead of signifying a measure of group autonomy and a recognition of "doing things differently," ethnicity indicates the necessity for outside control.[15]

How different from the position we saw taken by Nils Isak Eira (in Chapter 12)! He does not declare the "traditional" dead but recognizes it as being seriously mauled. For him, the task is one of winning back some of what has been lost ("I have written this paper in the hopes of starting discussion regarding this type of knowledge").[16] Kosmo, on the other hand, sees his task as that of building on the foundation of the Act and the Agreement. It is a foundation that gives reindeer pastoralism legitimacy within the framework of social democracy, and clause 4 of the Act, regulating access to the livelihood, is a linchpin clause, meant to ensure against dire economic and ecologic consequences of overrecruitment. But for Eira and others it is these very same legislative instruments—for all the economic benefits that they bring—that have done serious injury of a sociostructural kind. Clause 4 is seen as destroying "this culture's authentic form of internal self-recruitment."[17] A further consequence is that it undermines the very structure of checks and balances and sanctions that outside commentators believe to be missing in Saami pastoral society. The clause effectively means that in order to have a herd of one's own today, a license has to be granted. It is not always easy to come by one, and this can have serious, unwelcome consequences. Here is the bitter testimony of Kirsten Berit Gaup:

In a family of four sons, say, perhaps two are granted licenses but the other two aren't. This can cause deep frustration and envy among the youth. . . . On the other hand, parents and grandparents, who are not particularly active, may have licenses while the younger [members of the family] don't. Sometimes the younger ones could wish the older ones dead so that they could take over their licenses. [In these circumstances], the young have no respect for the old. Earlier, the old people were at the center of things, their experience was valued.[18]

The Administration is constantly advised to alter the distribution of herd capital in favor of the young. But (as we saw) the effect of some of the programs has been to advantage the larger herd owner over the smaller; and, for the most part, two-generational units are looked at askance.[19]

On other fronts, much of the outside research must, for the pastoralists, look like so-many rediscoveries of the wheel. For instance, it is heralded that research "has shown how changes in herd composition can significantly increase production" and demonstrated correlations between the weight of the mother and the health of the calf—as if the pastoralists didn't know![20] (The real issue is whether the "Iskun Bieras" of the tundra today wish to increase production.)

Interesting processes are at play here. First, indigenous knowledge systems are being reproduced by the outside experts. Then, so that the research findings can be applied, they are put into a cultural format amenable to the outsiders. An outstanding example is the proposal to attach color- and numeral-coded plastic ear-tags to the

reindeer. There are two purposes in mind. One is to eliminate the "confusion" the Administration says it finds in the elaborate indigenous system of earmarking by cuts (see Chapter 2) and, we may now add, to eliminate the barrier of incomprehensibility of that system to an outsider. The other purpose is to display information about each individual animal, such as its age and sex, which, it is supposed, the modern pastoralist, unlike his forbears, cannot carry in his or her head—or wishes not to.[21]

It is no surprise that the system copies one already in use for cattle, sheep, goats, and pigs.[22] Many Saami scorn the idea as fit for dažaboazodoallot, "Norwegian reindeer management."[23] Once officially adopted, the coded information would be entered into a computer data bank, including the name and District of the owner. This means that "they"—all manner of outsiders—would read this basic husbandry knowledge of each individual herder-owner without ever having to go near a herd. Strong reservations were expressed at the general annual meeting of NRL in 1982: Such a scheme must not be allowed to replace the traditional system of earmarking.[24] In 1984, the Department of Agriculture affirmed the mandatory retention of the traditional system but allowed ear-tags as an optional addition.[25]

For the moment, then, there are alternative systems. Culturally formatted "reproduction" of knowledge has not led to the *replacement* of a system. But I suppose that is likely to happen. The change (a global one) is from storing information experientially or analogically to digital storage. One likely consequence will be what happened when the her'gi was replaced by the snowmobile:[26] reduction of husbandry experience and therefore (ironically) *loss* of husbandry knowledge. There will be other consequences, too: increase in public knowledge about pastoral capital, and thus increased effectiveness in state control over that capital.

How Are Twenty Thousand Animals "Lost" Annually?

An outsider, charged by the state to reform Saami pastoralism, who *does* try to understand the "traditional" system wanders into strange terrain. The *system* of an anarchic society—that is, without any coordinating and binding authority over all of the constituent units (Chapter 7)—likely baffles him or her. In particular, he will almost certainly condemn the practice of reindeer rustling, seeing it as ethically unacceptable, with no place in a well-planned enterprise, and failing to see it as an institutionalized (anarchic) source of sanction among herder-owners. The relevance of this in the present context is how the outsider, advising the state, handles the issue of "missing" animals—over twenty thousand of them annually in Kautokeino alone, by the end of the 1980s!

Venturing into what is hidden behind the epithet "missing," we are also led to ask, what makes an "outsider"? Among Saami, daža (literally, non-Saami male) is the common synonym for outsider. But even those who are Saami by birth and upbringing can, in certain situations, be daža. Thus it was that I found Saami who worked for the cooperative slaughterhouse scorned as daža on occasion (Chapter 10). In the present case of "missing" animals, while there are three statements to report, all by Saami, there are only two positions, one of which, I suggest, is as firmly "outsider" as its author is firmly Saami by formal ascriptive criteria (at the time, he was actually president of NRL).

The astonishing number of reindeer reported lost or missing by the pastoralists themselves was made newsworthy through the 1986 headline, "*Reindeer Valued at 33 Million Kroner Become Food for Crows*."[27] Interviewed by the newspaper on the cause of losses of such magnitude, the NRL president, Odd Erling Smuk, himself a reindeer owner from East Finnmark, said: "The principal reason is that too few animals are slaughtered, the herds are too large for the pastures, and [so] we have weaker animals. . . . It is especially hard on the calves, they are too weak. Most of the lost animals are calves and older cows that should have been slaughtered long ago."[28]

From Johan Ingvald Hætta, in the Kautokeino office of the Reindeer Administration, there followed a quite different explanation: "Most of the lost deer have been stolen. . . . This is no secret either: everybody knows."[29] In other words, it has little to do with the poor health of the animals. Thus, Hætta points the matter in another direction, though he does not offer any explanation for the behavior that he pinpoints. Both Smuk and the head of

the Reindeer Administration, Ole K. Sara, were evasive when asked by the newspaper to comment on Hætta's statement.

Sometime later, however, a young Kautokeino Saami, in an article in *Reindriftsnytt* concerning pastoral social controls, had no such inhibitions. Reindeer theft *is* widespread, says Nils Thomas Utsi, and proceeds to offer an explanation.[30] It is very much in accord with the logic of our model from Chapter 7. Herder-owners, grouped in seasonal sii'da, are pressed to defend their pastures from encroachments by neighboring sii'da. Accordingly, at the same time as they try to make sure that their pastures are filled (by increasing the size of their herds), they attempt to reduce any threat of expansion into their pastures by neighboring groups. This double objective can be achieved by taking animals that come their way.

In the separation of these accounts (Smuk vs. Hætta and Utsi) from each other, it is as though the one does not see the other. I suspect this often happens between outsider knowledge and practitioner knowledge.[31] In the present case, Smuk comes forward not as a practitioner but as the principal officeholder in an organization committed to the state's program of reform of Saami pastoralism and to the state's reasons for it. He is at one with Ole K. Sara: The diagnosis has been made; now the medicine will be administered.[32] That same diagnosis explains the scandal—for that is how he saw it—of the missing animals: overpasturing. Smuk also accepts the suggestion of the newspaper headline: The animals are gone, a total economic write-off, food for the crows. This is also part of the scandal, with its own angst. The situation is, he says, "a burden vis-à-vis the authorities, both national and local, and it is a burden on society as a whole. We wish to be taken seriously in this livelihood, and we are dependent on having a good reputation, especially when it comes to our continual negotiations with the state."[33] And the answer? "The reindeer Districts must be given more authority" so that the required controls on numbers can be enforced.

But returning now to Hætta's explanation for the missing animals, the occurrence of and reasons for reindeer rustling are widely known through the Districts, and the authority to report *illegal* behavior is already there. This must lead us to ask, do all the pastoralists see the rustling as a problem? Such is by no means the case, I am sure. But among those who do, do they all see it as the same problem? Again, no. I make clear my reasons presently. First, though, a brief review of numerical records concerning "missing" animals over the last decades will be helpful.

The story that broke around the "33 million kroner . . . food for crows" headline in 1986 shocked the public—those Saami managed to "lose" all those animals![34]—even as there was a "what-else-can-you-expect?" undercurrent. Pastoralism was having a consistently bad press, with stories of irresponsible overgrazing beckoning ecologic catastrophe. An enormous number of animals were "lost," yet from the pastoralists' perspective and experience there was nothing extraordinary about it. This is immediately seen when the losses, over a number of years, are computed as percentages of the total herds (Table 14.1).

What of the earlier period, the time of my fieldwork? For some reason or another, the reports of the reindeer office in Kautokeino give no figures for animals missing or lost. However, the formula passed to me was "expect 10-percent losses overall, and double that for calves," and the figures in the budgets of Chapter 9 run between 7 and 10 percent for overall losses, 9 to 14 percent for calves (Table A.5). If we accept these numbers, more or less, then losses by 1977 had risen appreciably but thereafter remained level on a percentage basis.

There are a couple of factors to be taken into account here. First, the reports from the Kautokeino office for 1977 and 1978 list "unknown cause" in the case of 69.8 and 48.5 percent, respectively, of all losses. It is reasonable to suppose that the "unknown cause," in the majority of cases, was, in fact, appropriation by a competitor.[35] Second, calf losses in the 1980s amounted to nearly *half of the total losses,* and 20 percent or more of the number of calves born.[36]

Put together, these factors suggest a stepping-up in the appropriation of motherless calves (ædnihis miessi), along with a persisting significant number (say, ten thousand) adult animals. Together, the animals provide important increments of herd growth and cash income. The risk is minimal when incorporating an unmarked calf into one's herd; with adult animals it is safer to slaughter them and sell the meat on the unofficial (and uncontrolled) market.

Table 14.1 Annual Losses of Animals as a Percentage of Total Herd

1977	14.3
1978	12.5
1979–83	no data
1984	9.1
1985	13.4
1986	13.8
1987–88	no data
1989	15.5

Sources: Lappefogden i Vest-Finnmark 1977–78; Reindriftstyret 1984–89

However, some ædnihis miessi will be sold to that market, and some of the adult animals will have their earmarks altered and be incorporated into the herd of their new owner. Ironically, some of the calves, duly earmarked, will be sold through the official channels and the state subsidy for calf-slaughter collected! The overall effect of "missing" animals on the state program for increasing calf-slaughter is, however, probably negative. As Hætta points out, herder-owners take into account this percentage loss when making decisions about their herd compositions: "They keep more calves than they would were that risk of losing them not present."[37] Also, there are those (among the pastoralists themselves) who express concern over a possible detrimental effect to the quality of stock. Ordinarily, an owner is likely to select the *weakest* of his animals, including calves, for slaughter, but this will not be the case with "missing" animals, where the intention on the unofficial market is to sell "the best meat at the cheapest price," thereby speeding up all such transactions.[38]

Overall, the situation may be seen as a consequence of the interplay between three current key issues. One is *crowding:* increases in numbers of animals,[39] herds, and pastoralists. This exacerbates difficulties of herd control and surveillance (making undetected rustling all the more feasible), and gives due cause for the territorial motivation of reindeer rustling of which Utsi speaks. Another is the difficulties young pastoralists face today in *getting started* with a herd and thereby increasing their chances of becoming a registered pastoralist. The third factor is the pressures a *monetary economy* places on individuals for a ready supply of cash. The younger age groups are particularly susceptible to material enticements but have meager material means. Illicit appropriation of animals and transactions on the unofficial market beckon. In Chapter 4, I spoke of a tournament ethos in the competition, among the young, over ædnihis miessi. Obviously, this metaphor of *play* is less appropriate today. The imperatives of *need* are too strong.

The social implications of what I have been politely calling "illicit appropriation" of animals are considerable, and the individual situations of pastoralists determine their views on the matter. I believe few, even among those who echo the official dismay, would deny that the constant threat of losing animals to others is a spur to conscientious herding in these days of otherwise lax control, or that its actual occurrence may, in given circumstances, provide a necessary sanction (Chapter 7). Of course there are those who gain and those who gain the most, and those who lose and those who lose the most. There are no statistics on this particular kind of loss, but one supposes that those with the larger herds lose more than others, and those who lose the most are (like Iskun Biera in his time) the large herd owners with too little help at certain seasons. These are traditional equations. A new likelihood is that rustling by the young, whether for their own herd or for ready cash, is recognized by parents as well as by the young themselves as a way of acquiring what they *should* have and what they *need*. It is recognized, too, that some of today's needs have to do with the surrounding, nonpastoral world.

All in all, the ten thousand or so animals reported "missing" each year from the Kautokeino herds through "causes unknown" amount to a significant redistribution through the informal economic system.[40] Such a redistribution also implies an adjustment to relations of power between pastoralists—old and young, large and small owners. The animals do more than "feed the crows."[41]

Reading the Pastoral Landscape

Another domain of Saami/practitioner-outsider/expert differences is the evaluation of pastures, particularly in respect to the damage that encroachments can wreak. Thus

in March 1986 at Jukkasjav'ri, in Swedish Lapland, a small group of Norwegian and Swedish Saami pastoralists sat down together to explore ways of getting across their approach to the relevant non-Saami, such as pasture consultants employed by the state:

We ourselves usually have a pretty good idea what damage and inconvenience an encroachment will bring. What we don't understand is why the others don't understand. And when we don't know what we should say so that the others can understand, we find we are left answering questions which the others put to us. . . . The reason for this seminar is that we should get onto the offensive in this matter.[42]

Consultant and practitioner appear to use different kinds of data, as is so often the case. An anthropology colleague puts the difference in these terms:

While the consultant with his technical training (Agricultural College) is primarily interested in *averages* based on studies of vegetation in selected areas, the Saami, in addition to their own observations of the vegetation, closely observe the health of the animals. Their behavior is also recorded: whether they pasture quietly, alongside each other, or whether they are in constant competition, chasing each other away.[43]

Saami practitioners and the expert consultants each dispute the competence of the other; but the feeling of difference, at any rate as far as the Saami are concerned, runs deeper than that. To evaluate pasture one has to understand the constraints of pastoralism, and this means, among other things, being able to read the pastoral landscapes. They see this as practitioner knowledge.

For Mikkel Nils Sara, the conceptual key for the reading of a landscape is what he calls "the principle of alternatives." Just as davas (movement "out" in the spring) is the alternative to luksa (movement "in" during the autumn), and the one needs the other, so each season's landscape should contain alternatives. These will be prized by the pastoralist. Some examples are: *vaggi* and *rašša* (valley and high, stony terrain), *duoddar* and *vuobme* (open tundra and sheltered terrain), and *giellas* and *leahti* (high ridges and low ridges). Sara, at the seminar, set forth his principle of alternatives thus:

To make the best use of a reindeer pasture area it is necessary to "balance," in one's mind, the alternatives inherent in the landscape. Over a longer period of time, no one of them is of greater importance than any other. If, for example, in summer pastures, valued for its landscape alternatives, the authorities give permission for the construction of cabins in an area of vaggi, one consequence will be that not only a portion of vaggi is lost but access to its alternative, rašša, too. Moreover, outside intrusion of this kind into the summer pastures is likely to have a chain effect way beyond the areas allocated to cabins, even all the way to the winter pastures.[44]

Reasonable, and even elementary, as this might seem, it was a lesson that the state, as far as the Saami were concerned, had yet to learn, or to practice at any rate. On hand was evidence from the much-publicized 1978 parliamentary debate over the proposal to dam the Alta/Kautokeino River. There, in apparent ignorance of the kind of pastoral knowledge that Mikkel Nils Sara was now talking about and in flagrant disregard of Saami sensibilities, it was said: "As far as reindeer pastoralism is concerned, the only loss would be the flooding of some pastures. Their value approximates to food for 21 reindeer for 115 days."[45] This was all the more astounding, and shocking, in view of a 1974 report, officially commissioned and jointly authored by two Saami pastoralists and one pasture consultant, where it was stated that the proposed flooding "is likely to be a much more important matter for reindeer pastoralism, in the spring, than what is suggested by speaking simply of direct loss of so many acres of pasture—the loss of any spring pasture there will have repercussions for the whole of the pastoral ecologic year in the area."[46]

In general terms, the state, embracing an outsider view, was guilty of failing to acknowledge that the pastoralism of Kautokeino—of many thousands of animals and several hundred persons—necessarily composed a spatially extensive system of considerable ecologic and logistic complexity. The government lived to rue the day it spoke of "21 reindeer for 115 days." Time and again in public debate through the media this was held up as a measure of how uninformed or misinformed or simply uncaring it is. Government may open the purse strings for reindeer pastoralism, but, its critics say, it keeps its mind firmly closed concerning Saami pastoral principles. Bit by bit—and with each bit there are likely chain reactions—the state allows the pastures to be reduced, in extent or in value or both, by incursions.[47]

Mikkel Nils Sara continues:

The more landscape types one has—that is, alternatives with which to meet different situations—the more secure reindeer pastoralism will be over a longer period of time. Contrariwise, in a uniform landscape without alternatives, one is left helpless when faced with natural changes [within a season, between years].

This principle of landscape alternatives is still important even when the natural conditions in an area have not changed over a number of years. If, for example, reindeer for the past four years have had no need to use the high barren part of the landscape, where stone lichen [Parmelia centrifuga] is just about the only vegetation, in the fifth year this very same area may be of decisive importance.[48]

But encroachments continue bit by bit, subverting the principle of landscape alternatives.

What Do the District Foremen Think?

On the last day of the 1987 meeting of the district foremen,[49] the delegates (who had been listening to prepared presentations for most of the first two days) were asked to consider the following questions: What is an optimal number of deer in your District? How should herd composition and work organization be altered so that optimal production can be achieved? Does the projected optimal production suggest that there is a possibility for increasing the number of herder-owner participants?[50]

These are, of course, the central questions with which the Administration and its commissioned experts had been wrestling: and probably already answered. At all events, they were now brought down for the consideration of the pastoralists, who, nevertheless, were told by a key NRL figure, one of the two pastoralists on the government committee, Johan Mathis Thuri of Kautokeino, that there were "too many reindeer" (evident from "the low weights and poor quality of slaughtered animals in particular Districts"), and there are "many too many herder-owners" (evidently true because there were "far too many who are in the process of building up their herd").[51]

It was Ellon Ailu, in the first instance, who responded on behalf of the Kautokeino owners:

We are unable to answer the question, what is the optimal number of reindeer for Kautokeino. [However], we are largely in agreement that there are too many animals on the winter pastures . . . perhaps as much as 10–15,000 too many. . . . We have also discussed whether it would not be sensible to divide up the autumn pastures—at present, they are common to all. . . . Perhaps that would make for a more "rational" use of the pasture?[52]

The NRL president (Odd Erling Smuk) wanted to know whether the Kautokeino people had any firm ideas about how to control the total number of their animals—to keep the total constant. He also asked if they had any thoughts on the economists' suggestions of the payment of a fee for the licensed use of pasture. And what about dividing up the winter pastures? Ellon Ailu avoided answering these questions;[53] instead, he stressed that an important way of raising production is by improving the facilities for autumn slaughter, and that means "stimulating" the prices offered for animals slaughtered in the field.

A delegate from Karasjok agreed with Ellon Ailu that it is very difficult to set a figure for the maximum number of animals. However, he said, the Administration's figure of 48,000 for East Finnmark was not acceptable because it would mean that some herder-owners would have to close down. The figure should be more like 60,000 animals. Smuk again put his questions about licensing and the division of pastures. The Karasjok delegate said he didn't know. But concerning optimal herd composition, he said it should be "like it is in Karasjok," and as production increased, so could the number of herder-owners.[54]

A delegate from farther east in Finnmark (Polmak/ Varanger) coupled the question about optimal number of animals to that of income for individual herder-owners. The present situation was far from satisfactory, he said; dependence on the state subsidies was no answer; they had to free themselves from that. He believed there was no place for more herder-owners in his area, but nor could the present number of animals be reduced. As for herd composition: "We have 5 different pasture areas and 5 different herd compositions."[55]

In the previous year, a questionnaire had been sent out to the District foremen. Designed by Ansgar Kosmo, it drew replies from fifty-three of the seventy-five foremen of the Saami reindeer districts across the country.[56] Some of the questions (of which there were twenty-one), to-

gether with the answers, raise a number of considerations of interest to us:

Question 6: Does everybody in a District put in the same work effort? Overall, just under half replied positively. However, the size of the District (number of herder-owners) is revealed as an important variable. In the case of small Districts, the positive replies amounted to 60 percent and fell to 33 percent in the large Districts.

Question 7: What should be the principle for the division of labor, the same for everybody or according to the animals each person owns? Overall, the first alternative drew 50 percent of the responses and the second alternative 35 percent (15 percent "don't know"). Again, the number of herder-owners in a District appears as a determinant of the distribution of responses between the options. Where there are many, the opinion for taking into account differential herd sizes grows stronger. But for the Kautokeino Districts the percentage distribution between the two options is pretty much reversed. This divergence (other examples follow) seems to reflect the crowded situation and shared seasonal pastures there.

In general, though, our interpretations of the responses would be securer, and probably gain in subtlety, if we knew more about what kind of persons are chosen today by Districts as their foremen and what the Districts expect of them. In the 1960s, Districts were really a formality—a Norwegian requirement, satisfying a sense of order on paper. Foremen were usually those with the better Norwegian (Chapter 13). Certainly, there has been significant change here. For one thing, sound abilities in speaking and writing Norwegian are now the norm. Most significantly, Districts are now seen by the pastoralists as an indispensable conduit of state benefits; and as far as the Administration is concerned, the District foremen are in place to see that the many promulgated regulations are fulfilled. As it is, one is left to make guesses about the kind or kinds of persons who are foremen today. There are likely to be differences between Districts as well.[57]

One structural feature, however, accrues to the office independent of its holder: its ideal "in-betweenness." The District foreman is placed in-between his own people and the Administration and in-between differences arising between members of his District. But no sooner do we posit this structural feature, as an ideal, than we have to recognize that, in actuality, few foremen will be symmetrically placed between the different sii'da and different (and overlapping) kin groups within his or her District.

In responding in writing, and in the safe knowledge that responses will be codified, foremen are afforded the luxury, denied them in the real exercise of their office, of *not* having to face both ways simultaneously—face the Administration and face their copastoralists. So responses to some of the questions (e.g., numbers 6 and 7) may reflect a foreman's *own* problems only.

The questionnaire, of course, raised some of the issues exercising the internal review committee from the previous chapter, and this gives special cause for wondering how the responses were read. I believe the chances of unwarranted conclusions were high. This is principally because the questionnaire presented abstract options bereft of context and all equally weighted. The answers were within the range of the already-given options, not within the range of possible options in the mind of a respondent—and the two, we know, may well be very different. The options that are presented may thus be regarded as *licensing* answers, even directing respondents to particular answers. Consider the following examples.

Question 3: What should be done to correct the growing discrepancy between increases in expenditures over increases in income (for the livelihood as a whole)? Respondents were to choose between three given options. That of reducing the number of herder-owners was rejected by a large majority. The alternative options were "reduce expenditures" (29 percent) or "raise incomes" (60 percent).

In rejecting the option of reducing the number of practitioners, are the foremen saying that to have as many practitioners as possible is a pastoral value? There are reasons, relating to pastoral competition, why this might not be so. Or, have the foremen selected the politically expedient answer, which, at the same time, puts the problem back in the lap of the state?

Kosmo reads the little interest (11 percent) given to the option of reducing the number of herder-owners as evidence that the District foremen "do not want any structural change to the livelihood."[58] But asked, as they were, to choose between the three options in the abstract, it would surely have been remarkable had the ma-

jority of responses *not* been in favor of "raising incomes." On the evidence of that question and its answers, there is very little that one can say, one way or another, about dispositions to structural change.

Question 13: Does one's own District slaughter too few? A solid 56 percent said no (13 percent "don't know"). But the second part of the question is, do other Districts slaughter too little? Here the "no" falls to 18 percent (a significant 40 percent "don't know"). These figures are for all the Districts. Selecting out Kautokeino, we find a slide in the percentages: The 56 percent is reduced to 45 percent, and the 18 percent to 14 percent.

Question 14: Do problems arise on account of *other* Districts having too many reindeer? Overall, 70 percent of the respondents recognize such problems. Among the Kautokeino Districts, the situation is, apparently, much more aggravated: A full 95 percent declare there are problems, most of them "large" rather than "small."

In view of the persistence with which the state claims that there are "too many" reindeer and "too few" slaughtered, questions 13 and 14 are potentially interesting. Here we see the large majority of foremen not in-between but championing the interests of their own Districts. However, the real questions for the pastoralists are (and there will be a range of differences in their answers, among themselves and particularly vis-à-vis the blanket assertion of the state in this matter): "too many" and "too few" *for whom and from what point of view?*

In sum: Options stifle answers. What little the responses tell us about Saami perceptions of their problems may be misleading; they tell us somewhat more about Saami (albeit the foremens') perceptions of how the state thinks. The questions, on the other hand, are quite indicative of what the state perceives to be the problems of Saami pastoralism, and the responses are made within that framework.

In the place of respondents' contexts, we have the state's presuppositions. Thus, if the responses to questions 13 and 14 are read in the same manner as the questions are asked—that is, without context, but with presupposition—then the state may well feel it is dealing with a people who are intractable and who cling, among themselves, to a Hobbesian worldview. The ethnographic evidence, however, makes this quite implausible: This is a pastoral society notable for pragmatism and the place giv-en to contingent thinking, and thus for its adaptive skills. But it is anarchic, in the technical sense of being without institutions of overarching authority and having a mini-mum of routinized procedures. Conversely, those are im-portant attributes of Norwegian society, and Norwegian bureaucracy expects the Saami pastoralists to abide by the values *it* attaches to authority and routines, rather than by their own notions of them.

In consequence, the Saami-Norwegian interface, con-cerning pastoralism, is a rather uncommunicative one. There is a weight of directives but little bilateral negotia-tion beyond the circle of the NRL executive and state functionaries. One supposes the Norwegian-run admin-istration, beginning at the very highest level, suffers more than its share of frustration. There is a culturally distinc-tive defiance on the part of the pastoralists: Witness the way they managed, through the first ten years, to manip-ulate the biennial Agreements to their own ends. But there is little argument. This was so even at the confer-ence for the District foremen. On the first day, Ole K. Sara complained that, on his travels, he hears little debate among herder-owners about the important questions fac-ing the livelihood. And during the three days, criticism of NRL/state policies was muted on the whole. The for-mal presentations, crammed with statistics and graphs, were probably a powerful dissuasion. Actually, dissent, within NRL and against the Administration, had been brewing for some time, and when it came to the fore, battlelines hardened.

Emergence of Dissent and the Enforced Count

Boazo Ealahus Særvi (BES) emerged in March 1987, a few months before the NRL conference, as a rival orga-nization to NRL. In literal translation, BES is "the Soci-ety of Those Who Live by the Reindeer." It is no acci-dent that it is known by the acronym of its Saami name, for that itself distinguishes it from NRL (a Norwegian acronym).[59] Mathis M. Sara, a founding member and the first president of BES, was at the NRL conference. Odd Erling Smuk, NRL president, lost no time in delivering a challenge: "We hope that Mathis M. Sara will frequent

the rostrum during these days so that we may all hear the arguments of his organization." Sara, however, did not oblige—not until the closing session. He represented, he said, a District at the conference, not BES. Smuk found such evasiveness typical of BES, which he characterized as an organization bent on the destruction of all the work of NRL through the years.[60]

Behind the differences between NRL and BES are contrastive worldviews, reminding us that among Saami pastoralists today there is cultural division, even within Finnmark. At its source is the relationship Saami pastoral-ism has entered into with the state, leaving individual pastoralists to make their peace, or otherwise, with this new force of munificent assimilation.

Much of this division is encapsulated in the contrast between the personalities and biographies of Smuk and Sara. Smuk, the younger of the two (born 1956), is from a pastoral family in the far east of Finnmark, Varanger. He left for a while to go to a business school in the south of the country with the intent of applying the lessons he learned there to reindeer management—and his presi-dency of NRL provided him with a platform to that end. For Sara, born in 1939 and practicing his pastoralism in the heart of the crowded Kautokeino ranges—on Gow'dojottelit—Smuk was undermining *Saami* pastoral-ism (inevitably, dubbed "traditional") with alien ideas about profit.

But if Sara played the traditionalist to Smuk's mod-ernist, that did not mean he was a stranger to institution-al organization. He believes that Saami pastoralists must be organized and well represented. His energies in this regard have been recognized: as a substitute on NRL's national committee, a president of the Kautokeino branch, and also mayor of Kautokeino for a period. Once a believer in NRL, he now opposed the direction Smuk and his colleagues were taking the national association.

But of course the point I wish to make is grounded in factors beyond the more surface phenomena of personal-ity. We arrive at the same point by comparing some of the official statistics over the reindeer management in the Districts of these two men and some of their near kin: Varanger in East Finnmark and Spalca in West Finnmark (Kautokeino), respectively. Spalca has twice as many herder-owners, but three thousand fewer deer (almost

Table 14.2 Production Profiles (averages 1985–89)

	Spalca	Joakkonjar'ga	Favran	West Finnmark	East Finnmark	Varanger
Full-time pastoralists	89	60	75	1,185	604	41
Pastoral Units	20	16	19	282	216	15
Reindeer	7,200	5,184	9,032	104,460	83,420	10,200
Animals per full-time pastoralist	81	86	120	90	148	225
Herd composition:						
% cows				63	63	
% calves				31	28	
% males				6	9	
% lost animals	23	19	18	19	15	12
% slaughter	30	30	35	29	32	48
% calves among slaughtered	29	32	31	26	36	61
Weights (kg) of slaughtered						
adults	27	28	26	28	29	32
calves	17	17	17	16	17	19

Source: Reindriftstyret 1985–89

one-third). That such a ratio is possible in Varanger reflects the fact that reindeer pastoralism there is seen as an alternative among several viable livelihoods. Consequently there is a flow of persons—more than ever is the case with the Gow'dojottelit people—from pastoral families into other livelihoods. This is all the more possible on account of the relatively more urban or semiurban regional environment around Varanger. Having arrived at such a herder-owner:herd ratio, other things follow: Herding units are fewer (by about a third), and the degree to which pastures are shared is also less. Also, the percentage of "lost" animals is smaller, and the percentage of animals slaughtered greater and their weights heavier than those from Spalca.

These data are presented in Table 14.2 along with the same data from two other Kautokeino districts—Joakkonjar'ga and Favran[61]—as well as a comparison between West Finnmark (all of the Kautokeino districts)

and East Finnmark (including Karasjok, with strong affinities to Kautokeino pastoralism, in addition to Polmak and Varanger). East Finnmark scores consistently stronger than West Finnmark, and Varanger is well above the East Finnmark average. Within West Finnmark, Spalca is close to typical.

Let us now consider the linkage between Saami pastoral ideals, which many see in the Spalca type of reindeer management; the political voice of Mathis M. Sara (against that of Odd Erling Smuk); and third, the emergence of BES as a cultural movement in opposition to NRL. It is necessary to return to the promulgation of the 1978 Act.

At first, NRL had registered its objections to the clause in the Act severing the transmission of rights from parent to child (clause 4), but subsequently the association accepted it as a necessary premise of the overdue restructuring. Now, a decade later, Odd Erling Smuk even goes so far as to declare at a public meeting of a Norwegian political party (Senterparti) that a form of Norwegian *odelsrett*, inheritance of an estate by the eldest, should replace the Saami tradition of multiple and anticipatory inheritance (by all the children, even while their parents live). This, along with suggestions at the foremen's conference favoring the licensing of pastures, gave a clear indication, to all who cared to notice, of the direction Smuk had in mind for the livelihood.[62]

For some time there had been growing concern among NRL members, writes Inger Anna Gaup, over the introduction of "Norwegian" procedures:[63] One had to speak from a podium, and do so in a well-developed "meeting language" that included foreign words even when using Saami; one had to prepare well what one was going to say before one said it; and of course one had to get one's name onto the list of speakers. Most speakers addressed, and supported, in effect, the state's agenda of issues. And there were usually proportionately few speakers from Inner Finnmark (Kautokeino and Karasjok). The influence of the South Saami (a minority of members) was disproportionate.[64] Consequently, as NRL gained credibility in its relations with the state, it was losing credibility among members, and many withdrew from active support and payment of dues, particularly in Kautokeino and Karasjok.[65]

The inaugural meeting of BES, in March 1987, was held without a secretariat, and, for Gaup, the impression was one of organizational inexperience; and yet at the first annual meeting, in July of that year, there were three hundred members, all from Kautokeino and Karasjok—more than NRL had had for a long time.[66] But even as BES gathered a physical and vocal presence, with an agenda of basic issues, NRL denied any loss of membership to BES;[67] and the state—for whom the issues raised by BES were settled long previously, in paragraphs of the Act and the subsequent texts of the biennial Agreements—paid no attention to BES's claim to its right of being a negotiating partner, along with NRL, to the Agreements.[68]

As NRL spokesmen[69] made their budgetary analyses, bemoaned a looming situation of "self-liquidation" for reindeer pastoralism, and berated fellow pastoralists for bringing this state of affairs upon themselves through their misguided practices, so others—of the BES persuasion—placed the blame with the state "whose support policies are fast turning us into wards of the social welfare department."[70]

And yet, probably few BES supporters were prepared to urge the scrapping of the whole system of state subsidies: Among District foremen at all events, eighteen out of twenty-one in Kautokeino and ten out of ten in Karasjok answered the "positive" option put to them by Kosmo as the first question in his questionnaire: Have the state subsidies had "positive" effect? But the price of this state support, the unescapable logic runs, is acceptance of other parts of the state agenda as well. BES's possibility for maneuver therefore seems constricted.

Where BES argues from greater strength is in respect to the Districts. NRL complains of BES's negativism, even though NRL is urging the Administration to grant greater authority to the Districts. BES wants that, too, but argues that before the Districts can be effective much of the mushrooming bureaucratic culture that has been imposed on them has to be severed. It was on this point that Sara, in the closing session of the District foremen's conference, formulated his criticism of the partnership between the Administration and NRL, rebutting the diagnosis that much of the ill-functioning of the Districts is attributable to bickering and indecisiveness among the pastoralists themselves.[71] Perhaps more to the point, though, are the difficulties on account of the imperatives—often mutually contradictory—of separate systems: Saami and Norwegian. That there might be such difficulties and that most of the pastoralists cope passingly well in the circumstances is sometimes lost sight of by persons who "administer" from outside: to wit, the patronizing disparagement of the second epigraph at the head of this chapter.

At the dawn of 1988, the Administration announced that a compulsory count would be taken of all herds in Finnmark. The count was to be conducted by the Administration, superseding the annual returns that Districts themselves are required to deliver to the Administration. It was to be completed between 15 February and 25 March on the winter pastures.[72]

The count failed and was deemed "valueless":[73] Only

65 percent of owners took part, and Ole K. Sara recognized that, apart from practical difficulties, "tradition and culture" kept others from having their herds counted.[74] But there was no weakening of the Administration's will. To the contrary, pressure on recalcitrant owners was stepped up: The count *would* happen the following winter. Those who had thought of refusing again were reminded that such a course of (in)action was "illegal" and would be punished accordingly. If necessary, counts would be undertaken by force. Thus BES was presented with a *cause célèbre*.

In preparation for the 1989 winter campaign, the Administration head, Ole K. Sara, and the chair of the national board to which he reported (Reindriftsstyret, in Oslo), visited Kautokeino and Karasjok early in October: "Those of you who continue to resist the animal count will be met with stronger measures. The official count *will* be completed this winter," the head of the Board told a gathering of pastoralists in Kautokeino.[75] He added that because there are more animals than ever on the tundra, the slaughter quotas will be increased[76] in the case of Districts whose total count (as recorded by the Districts) is still above the allotted maximum. He thought this a mild and reasonable decision in view of Parliament's demand that herds be reduced.[77]

That same day in Kautokeino, a protest meeting of herder-owners (with a reported attendance of 130) issued a statement that included the following points:

1. Any compulsory count conducted by the Administration amounts to an "attack" *[overgrep]* against Saami reindeer pastoralism.[78]

2. It is also contrary to Parliament's intention in view of their having struck the Saami Rights Commission,[79] and the whole exercise should therefore be set aside until the Commission makes known its findings concerning land rights.

3. Both associations (BES as well as NRL) should take part in the annual budgetary negotiations with the state, not just NRL.[80]

A District foreman openly declared that he would continue to refuse to allow his animals to be counted by the state. Here one must note that the majority public opinion in Finnmark was, and is, biased against reindeer pastoralism and its practitioners, and newspapers were pleased to feed the public tidbits; for example, that this particular District, by its own count, actually had twice as many animals as it should have.[81]

In responding to outraged herd owners, Ole K. Sara would ask: "If they believe our figures are wrong and their own are correct—what do they have to lose from an official count?"[82] But numerical correctness was not the issue for those opposing the count; it was that they believed the state wished to make its own count to justify immediate reductions of herd size (reductions set by the outsider experts, moreover). The issue, for both sides, was clearly that of *control*. In his comments to the media, Odd Erling Smuk was less than diplomatic: "Behind the opposition to the compulsory count is a vulgar-liberal philosophy by which everyone will do what they want, when they want and where they want."[83]

But if evidence was needed that the Administration (with the NRL executive) had more on their hands than a protest from the fringe, the Area Board for West Finnmark (the body above the Districts in the three-tiered authority structure) supplied it, voting three to two against the compulsory count. The intention of the Administration to proceed with the count was regarded, by this slim majority of the Board, as loss of confidence in their District foremen. The proposer of the motion suggested that the state was pursuing a program of "Norwegianization" reminiscent of earlier policy along the coast. The Area Board believed there was room for well over 105,000 animals in West Finnmark—earlier, it had set the figure at 90,000. The Area Board also sent a message to the Kautokeino Municipal Council, requesting special measures be taken to improve the local employment situation. A "balance" will never be obtained in the pastoral sector, it said, until other jobs are available.[84]

BES took the offensive at the beginning of 1989. Mathis M. Sara:

We are not against the compulsory count that is under way. But we are afraid of its consequences. Namely, compulsory slaughter of animals that would leave many owners with herds too small to live off. . . . It can well be so, as the authorities maintain, that there are too many reindeer in certain Districts but, if so, that is the fault of the clumsy regulations and not of the owners. . . . We are the largest and most representative organization within Saami reindeer pastoralism. . . . [Whereas] we are taken seriously locally and have the support of local politicians and also places on the Area Boards, the central authorities never ask us for our advice and refuse to recognize us as an organization.[85]

And Anna Logje Gaup:

With my knowledge of practical reindeer pastoralism (which is my occupation) I am upset by the slanted information given out by the authorities and the way they have broadcast suspicions about us [concerning our opposition to the compulsory animal count]. . . . What we have tried to point out is that, perhaps, the measures proposed by the state are inappropriate. . . . We who draw our livelihood from reindeer pastoralism are anxious lest the kilogram price [for meat] falls at the same time as the number of animals is reduced.[86]

BES drew into their campaign the widespread dissatisfaction regarding the sale and turnover of reindeer meat. This was a concern of longstanding, even from the days of my fieldwork (see Chapters 8 and 10); however, the ground had shifted somewhat since that earlier time. Then, how carcasses were butchered (the "surrendering" of one's animals to the Cooperative, which was run on daža principles) was of principal concern; now, the source of aggravation was perceived as the flawed principle of monopoly outlet (based on an economy of scale argument) together with its lagging logistics.

Mathis M. Sara again:

The principal reasons that BES is against the monopoly are the lower prices that it means, as well as transport problems and generally poorer service to customers.[87]

And Anders Somby, Jr.:

We are already losing 4–5 kroner per kilogram on account of there being no [buyers'] competition.[88]

And Anne K. Eira:

What would the Norwegians say if we Saami decided that there should be only one fish-buyer in Finnmark? . . . [As it is] we are out there working without any income for we can't slaughter the necessary number of animals. . . . What has to happen is

that other slaughterhouses in Finnmark be given the same advantage as [the Cooperative in Kautokeino].[89]

Later that month, however, came a broadside from the minister of agriculture herself, reported in the newspaper under the banner headline "Reindeer Pastoralism Ought to Put Its House in Order." As before, the warning was issued that those individuals who defied regulations would be sanctioned; at a minimum they would disqualify themselves from receiving any subsidies. But the minister also spoke of the possibility that "society" would lose confidence in reindeer pastoralism, and if that happened, it would be extremely difficult for the government to work together with the pastoralists' representatives (that is, NRL). "Society," she said, gives reindeer pastoralism significant economic support and, in return, expects the livelihood to contribute to the making of secure employment and sound values at the local level.[90]

The speech was given in Alta, a few weeks before the second attempt at a reindeer count was due to begin. The minister would also have been aware that some figures summarizing the economic performance of reindeer pastoralism over the past year had been released to the press earlier in the month. These figures showed a gross income of 88 million kroner (an improvement on the previous year), giving a net income of 30 million kroner (also an improvement); however, state subsidies amounted to 38 million kroner. The *Finnmark Dagblad* ran the headline: "Reindeer Pastoralism in Great Difficulties." A senior bureaucrat's comment on the state subsidies was that NRL had been very successful in its requests for state support; but, he added, the problem remained the same: an "explosion" in costs and too few animals slaughtered.[91] Although a debit account (in this case of 8 million kroner) is a recurring feature in Norway's other primary industries,[92] it provided the minister with a stick to wave at recalcitrant pastoralists just at that moment when "stick" rather than "carrot" was called for.

There was an ecologic stick, too. The occasion of the minister's speech in Alta was a two-day conference, "Reindeer Pastoralism and the Natural Environment."[93] Over the last few years there had emerged a national understanding that marine resources were in deep trouble, particularly in North Norway. Finnmark's inshore fisheries, for example, were virtually closed because there were no fish. Whatever its probable causes, this crisis situation raised ecologic awareness, and "overfishing" became an issue of popular concern, causing bewilderment, anxiety, and anger.

For the Reindeer Administration, grappling with the problem of "too many" deer on the tundra, as defined for them by politicians and researchers, the marine crisis helped to call attention to the crisis (as they believed it to be) threatening the tundra. By metaphorical projection, "overfishing" easily slid into "overpasturing." Thus when speaking to the press about the failure of the 1988 count, Ole K. Sara himself commented: "I'm afraid that the ocean resource crisis may be followed by a resource crisis on land."[94] Items had already appeared in the newspapers about the ecologic threat reindeer pastoralism—or just reindeer[95]—posed to the tundra. Aside from overgrazing, there was concern over the ecologic damage that mechanized pastoralism may do to the tundra environment. Given the self-definition by the pastoralists of the "naturalness" of their livelihood, and the general acceptance of that view up to then, such talk was all the more injurious (see Chapter 12). The current of ecologic awareness seemed to be running *against* the Saami.

It was sufficient for the minister's purposes to remind the gathering that "government and parliament and the pastoralists themselves have a collective responsibility towards the environment; it is a responsibility that extends beyond present needs to those of coming generations."[96] There were sharper words and plain accusation in the opening plenary address from a biologist: The pastoralists are using a commons, and controls must be put upon them. (Oblivious to the question of Saami land rights, currently under research, the speaker declared that "the Finnmark tundra is not an exception"—it is a commons.)[97] Among the Saami who attended the conference and were interviewed by *Reindriftsnytt,* pained rebuttals were made to the charge that reindeer pastoralism is now a serious "polluter" of the tundra environment.[98]

The following month, after a four-hour-long debate, the Kautokeino Municipal Council declared itself in disagreement with the Reindeer Administration over reduction of the number of animals. However—as one of the councillors put it—"opinions on the matter were as

spread as a reindeer flock that has taken flight."[99]

As a gauge of the breadth of opinion, Ellon Ailu is on the one side, and a one-time mayor of Kautokeino on the other. The ex-mayor, Klemet O. Hætta, a prominent figure at both levels of politics, local and provincial, believes the state should listen more carefully to the reindeer owners (betraying himself as an outsider of sorts, he seems to assume that they will be of one voice). He is afraid herds may be reduced in size without leading to an increase in the weights of the animals. He believes one should find out how many animals there are *before* deciding on slaughter percentages: "I haven't met a single herder/owner who is against the count itself, but what upsets them is the state's apparent loss of confidence in the District foremen and its insistence on a count *after* decisions about slaughter percentages have already been taken."[100]

The mayor makes an important point; but concern among pastoralists themselves (how many of them, it is not possible to say) over the continued increase in the total number of animals, while total pasture areas remain constant or diminish, must not be lost from view. In 1986, the Kautokeino branch of NRL (with Ellon Ailu in the chair) had noted the continued increase in the number of animals and urged a policy of overall zero-growth and special measures "to motivate" owners, where necessary, to increased slaughter percentages. And in a 1989 interview, on the occasion of his retirement from elected office, after fourteen years service, Ellon Ailu, now aged sixty, said that there are too many deer on the tundra:[101] It was difficult to find fresh winter pastures, and animals' weights had fallen since 1981. He believed that the compulsory count should be seen in connection with the support that the state gives to the livelihood. As for BES, "It seems that they don't want any kind of control from the state: but if we don't accept control, there'll be no subsidies."[102]

To agree with the state on this question of numbers does not necessarily mean, however, that one wants state control. That is not at all what twenty-year-old Lars Johan Sara, of Kautokeino, has in mind when, speaking as though on behalf of his age group, he says: "We would rather have a small and good [quality] herd. It is easier to herd and husband. Management is also cheaper, one

Table 14.3 West Finnmark (Kautokeino), 1960–1989 and 1991: Full-time Pastoralists, Reindeer Population, and Annual Slaughter

| Year | Pastoralists (registered full-time) | Reindeer (nearest thousand; herd before calving) | Slaughter | |
			Animals	Weight (kg)
1960		47,000		
1965		55,000		
1969		38,000		
1970		41,000		
1971		42,000		
1972		53,000		
1973		52,000		
1974		45,000		
1975		48,000		
1976		52,000		
1984	1,060	82,000	23,000	388,000
1985	1,058	95,000	24,000	571,000
1986	1,097	103,000	26,000	617,000
1987	1,150	105,000	28,000	643,000
1988	1,173	105,000	26,000	666,000
1989	1,356	112,000	47,000	1,000,000
1991	1,400	91,000	26,000	608,000

Sources: For 1965–76, NOU 1978:236; for 1984–89 and 1991, Reindriftstyret 1984–89 and 1991.

doesn't need to hire help. . . . [We] are concerned with the slaughter weight of the animals and the health of the cows so that they are able to give birth to strong calves."[103] His mind is set on managing his own affairs, although it is a pastoralism nearer Ansgar Kosmo's prescription than, perhaps, his father's. But this wish for "a small herd" by a young man who has yet to secure his pastoral reputation is made under pressure: not from the state but the heightened pastoral competition.

The supervised count was completed in April 1989 with returns from slightly over 90 percent of all herds. The discrepancy between this supervised count and the figures (from 1987–88) submitted by the Districts was a good deal smaller than one had been led to expect—10

percent overall, and for West Finnmark (Kautokeino), only 6 percent.[104]

Table 14.3 reviews official figures for full-time pastoralists, reindeer, and the annual slaughter of animals over the last thirty years in West Finnmark. Bearing in mind that some of these figures are no more than estimates, there are still some interesting features about them. First, there is the clear difference between the figures for the reindeer population before and after the early 1980s: The returns for the earlier period were perhaps too little by half.[105] There are two principal reasons for the change: alteration in the taxation system, and the stricter enforcement and control of animal counts (Chapters 8 and 13). Second, the reindeer population fell dramatically in 1969, the direct result of execrable pasture conditions in the spring of 1968. Significantly, the stock steadily recovered its numbers in the years that followed. And third, the equally dramatic increase in slaughter during 1989 is attributable to the compulsory count and limits imposed on herd sizes. Two years later, the reduction in animal numbers is noticeable; however, the number of full-time pastoralists continues to climb.

Attempting to relate these figures to the intentions of the state, we must be clear as to the criterion by which maximum numbers are decided. In fact, there are contending criteria at play. One had understood that the state's criterion was the biological/ecological carrying capacity as computed by the outsider experts. However, what we can call the political carrying capacity now appeared in the calculations (the criterion of cultural ecology was still omitted): Whereas experts affixed the carrying capacity for the Kautokeino ranges at 60,000 animals,

the Administration in Alta edged it up to 70,000, and the National Board (Reindriftsstyret) raised it still further—to 90,000, an increase of 33 percent over the experts' figure.[106] And as noticed earlier, the Area Board of West Finnmark (Kautokeino) had moved their original figure of 90,000 up to 105,000.

I think the point is that there is no one truth in this question. While the experts' assessments may be "objective," they are, in the final analysis, inadequate on account of their knowing disregard of "soft," or social and political variables; and politically sensitive assessments are at risk on account of their tampering with the experts' measurements. Can a release from this problem be expected by turning to the pastoral practitioners themselves? This is possibly the most important question of all—I return to it in the final chapter.

15.
Tragedy of the Commons or Pastoral Tragedy?

Freedom in a commons brings ruin to all.

G. HARDIN, "THE TRAGEDY OF THE COMMONS"

One can recast Hardin's statement as a question: If a commons has in practice become an open access resource, what historical factors have brought this about?

PAULINE E. PETERS, "EMBEDDED SYSTEMS AND ROOTED MODELS: THE GRAZING LANDS OF BOTSWANA AND THE COMMONS."

Over a decade after the Reindeer Management Act, the talk of crisis has not subsided—far from it. It remains rooted in a mistrust of Saami pastoral practice; indeed, the voice of Havard Movinkel, from the early 1960s (Chapter 10), is still heard. Today, however, the specter of the "Tragedy of the Commons" (hereafter simply "the Tragedy")[1] makes for a fierce and ideologically tinted argument. For some, Saami pastoral practice is bringing down the Tragedy. This is seen as a fact. For others, it is but a hypothesis and, furthermore, one that is ecologically and culturally flawed. An alternative view, emerging from the kind of data presented in the preceding chapters, is that the condition on which some would put the Tragedy label speaks to, more than anything else, the malfunctioning of relations between the state and the pastoralists.

As applied to pastoralism,[2] the Hardinian commons theory has this to say: "The rational herdsman concludes that the only sensible course for him to pursue is to add another animal to his herd. And another, and another . . ." And so, by the cumulative process of such "rational" action, "each man is locked into a system that compels him to increase his herd without limit—in a world that is limited."[3] But this "[when] freedom becomes tragic"[4] view of the commons fallaciously assumes that "because people are engaged in common-property activity, they are involved in a tragedy of the commons."[5] This cardinal error arises through conflating "common" or "free" or "open" property and property that is "communal" or "in-common" to a designated group or livelihood.[6] Other invalid assumptions are that "private property protects resources from abuse and waste, and common property does not," and that overcapitalization or overinvestment is diagnostically linked with the Tragedy. As to the first of these two propositions, it is not supported in the cross-cultural literature;[7] but belief in it, nonetheless, tends "to restrict solutions to the commons dilemma to the intervention of external authority on the one hand and privatization on the other."[8] Regarding the second proposition, Patricia Marchak has argued that there is no such diagnostic link: Overcapitalization happens in forestry, where the forests are subject to "contractual property rights"; it happened in the automobile industry in the 1970s, "and automobile manufacturing is certainly not common property."[9]

A study of considerable relevance to our concerns, conducted in Botswana among cattle pastoralists, stands Hardinian explanation on its head.[10] Herds were growing at a rate that promised to outstrip the carrying capacity of the ranges. The proposed government remedy was based on the explicit assumption that unless livestock owners are tied down to specific grazing areas, "no one has an incentive to control grazing."[11] In other words, it was supposed that if left to themselves "individuals will act in their own self-interest but to their ultimate disadvantage."[12]

But what the anthropologist found among the pastoralists was not an asocial individualistic ethic (the Hardinian premise) but complex and indeterminate relations between competing groups, which, in their competition with each other, are aware of the multiple strands of their interdependence. Prior to government intrusion, the world of the Botswana pastoralists was one of overlapping rights and constraints to pastures, both in space and time. The closely reasoned conclusion from the Botswana research was that the current crisis originated with the state's allocation of exclusive pastures and not with the pastoralists' ethic and their social organization.[13]

As with Botswana pastoralism, so with that of the Saami. It has been socially constructed around pastures that are in-common, not free; and among themselves there has been a system, relatively complex in its flexibility and permutations, of exclusive usufruct to specific pastures at specific times of the year. Therefore it has not been a matter of Hardin's "everybody's right is nobody's right." However, the intervention of the state between the pastoralists, and its allowing *non*-pastoralists to use the tundra (with certain restrictions) as common property of open access,[14] has seriously compromised the ecologic and social logic on which reindeer pastoralism is premised.

I elaborate this point further on. Respecting the Hardinian theory of Tragedy, what it points to is that the theory itself rests upon the fulfilment of certain assumptions: open access to the resource in question; selfish exploiters bent on maximizing short-term profit regardless of possible long-term effects; exploitation exceeding sustainable yield. This means that we should not start with the idea of a Tragedy but with an inspection of the circumstances preceding any such idea, and then turn our

attention to how the assumptions necessary for its fulfilment (or belief in it) are created.[15]

Respecting the present case, the preceding chapters provided much of the data on which the answer rests—and include a measure of my own interpretation. Summarized, the answer probably lies in the conflation of three factors: rhetoric justifying the bioeconomic engineering of the experts and providing bureaucrats and politicians with the moral high ground; unintended and unexpected runaway implications of the state's rationalization programs; and the pastoralists' own runaway mechanization of their livelihood with consequent inattention to husbandry and erosion of its knowledge.

The present chapter is devoted, in the main, to the positions taken by other social scientists on the Tragedy debate respecting Saami pastoralism. First, though, further clarification of the nature of nomadic pastoral capital is necessary.

Globally, nomadic pastoral capital has probably been characterized by its few conversions: Animal capital has tended to remain in the herds.[16] Its value has been in *self-reproduction*—still more animals—and in so doing, it has given the owners a high measure of *self-realization*. Thus pastoralists have "used" their capital in a singularly restricted way, for what otherwise usually distinguishes capital is its "liquidity, or ease of conversion into goods and services of another kind."[17] This historical portrait is founded in circumstances in which there was little or no control by a central state; room for pastoral expansion into areas of marginal population density; and limited access to markets for pastoral products and limited motivation to convert animal capital, via cash, into alternative investments. Conversion from the pastoral/nomadic way of life to another was exceptional and usually the result of failure. Of course there were differences in the valences of the factors, but they invariably combined to imprint on the pastoralist an ever-present possibility of loss of a herd, leaving him and his family in a far more hapless condition than a farmer who suffers a crop failure; and the need to live close to the herd, moving with it through the year. In sum, on-the-hoof capital has had intrinsic value, for the pastoralist, far outweighing its commodity value.

Thus, in an earlier essay, I portrayed pastoralists as

"rudimentary capitalists"—capitalists on account of their perceived ecologic (and hence cultural) imperative to expand their herds, and rudimentary ones on account of the few conversions they make with their capital. I saw a "modal parsimony" among them: "The successful pastoralist hoards (and gloats) rather than hosts."[18] Iskun Biera, then, far from being aberrant, was, instead, an archetypical nomadic pastoralist in his handling of animals as capital. And, we may well notice in passing, his economic philosophy distinguished itself both from the Robinson Crusoe model, where a strong work ethic combined with parsimony leads, triumphantly, to economic diversification (helped with the gift of a Man Friday); and from Marshall D. Sahlins's model of hunters and gatherers as "the original affluent society," where limited material aspirations allow for a life rich in leisure and ceremony.[19] In terms of a comparison with classical "peasant", economy, pastoral economy is not—or was not—Chayanovian. Peasants work their resources with income targets in mind; that is, they have limited aspirations. Pastoralists have always aspired to increase their herds.[20]

But in Scandinavia the first two of the historic circumstances are dismantled today. The state assumes responsibility and control; nonpastoral encroachment replaces pastoral expansion. Market conversion of on-the-hoof capital, however, is a patchwork despite the firm intentions, and various devices, of the state. The patchwork is already evident in our budgets from the 1960s: Compare herds #6 and #7 of Oar'jebelli (where some of the preconditions for a Robinson Crusoe-like pastoral economy appear) with the others (Chapter 9). And it is evident today in the bold contrast, within Finnmark, between the Varanger and Spalca herds (Chapter 14). Still, few persons change from the pastoral life to another. Young pastoralists are aware that the world outside is "Norwegian," and not only that, Finnmark is burdened with a growing unemployment rate.

The current situation is therefore open to separate and different interpretations. For planners, the salient feature is that grazing, perhaps for the first time, is "a limiting factor," and this calls for radical changes in the organization of Saami reindeer pastoralism.[21] But for many (I suspect the great majority) of the pastoralists, the "historic" fear of losing one's herd is *still* present; indeed, aspects of

government policy tend to be read, by many, as justifying this fear (Chapter 13). Advocates of radical change say that only by means of government policy will Saami pastoralism survive. The skeptics, on the other hand, are left worrying over two questions: Is Saami reindeer pastoralism becoming a thing of the past, replaced by Norwegian pastoralism with Saami herder-owners? It is certainly easily mistaken for such. And will this "new" pastoralism of outsider design, backed by government fiat, have viability? The answer will not be known for a while.

Social anthropologists are found on each side of this divide and, in consequence, there are opposing positions among them regarding the Tragedy hypothesis. Tim Ingold, a British anthropologist, has put a name to the key process of radical change that he believes to be essential: *stock-rearing*.[22] He distinguishes it from "pastoralism": "Whereas pastoralism recommends a man to slaughter only the minimum of deer needed to maintain his family, stock-rearing requires him to leave alive only the minimum needed to maintain his herd."[23] Stock-rearing "assumes the existence of a full developed market structure as well as the acceptance of commercial values."[24] It also minimizes husbandry requirements, and, in consequence, will be associated with a radical diminution in the pastoral stock of knowledge—for much of that will have become redundant. It therefore weakens the "way of life" aspect of reindeer pastoralism with its many cultural habits and values. Truly, stock-rearing (to which the Varanger herds tend) soon becomes something other than pastoralism. Correlates are enfenced, exclusive, private or rented pastures (advocated, by some, at the 1987 NRL conference: Chapter 14), and cooperatively owned stud animals.[25]

Ingold's field experience was in Finland, where there is a system of "associational management" among reindeer herder-owners (the *paliskunta*).[26] Extending the paliskunta idea, he associates stock-rearing with cooperative or collective and "rational" management, "in which all [herding and] husbandry decisions would be taken jointly in accordance with production goals and a defined pasture and selection policy."[27] Replacing the present system, which "tends to pit reindeer men against each other," he sees it as securing the future of reindeer pastoralists (come stock-breeders). But he concedes "it would be futile to suggest that such a system could successfully or even meaningfully be imposed on an entirely contrary set of values. Any move towards collectivization would presently be unacceptable ... where the fierce economic individualism of traditional pastoralism is still prevalent."[28]

From all the evidence, the Norwegian state would like the Saami pastoralist to become a stock-breeder. Another term of Ingold, "predatory pastoralism," catches the entropic associations to which the state is prone when considering Saami pastoralism on the Finnmark tundra today.[29] Indeed, Ingold's radical program—unencumbered, as it is, by political constraints such as the state faces—sometimes runs ahead of state proposals. In the late 1970s, for example, he spoke of "the handing down of now obsolete tradition from father to son" that should be replaced by state-financed professional training courses (in Finland).[30] The Norwegian state still would not dare to declare the "from father to son" tradition obsolete—clause 4 of the 1978 Act notwithstanding. On the other hand, there is now a fully fledged Reindeer Management School in Kautokeino.[31]

Ingold's notion of stock-rearing implies a fundamental restructuring of Saami reindeer pastoralism such as was discussed in Chapter 13 under the rubric of *rationalization*. Far-reaching criticism of such a program—both of its ontology and its practice—has come from Hugh Beach, an American anthropologist working among the Saami pastoralists in Sweden. He writes: "It is vital to seek clarity in the question of *to whom* the rational-herding policy is rational. ... Different answers are given. (1) It is in the community's or the nation's best interests, (2) it is to raise the living standard of the herders or (3) it is to help to preserve Saami culture."[32] In fact, explanation for what the state is doing is to be found in each of these alternatives, and serious contradictions ensue. Much of the reason for such a state of affairs, following Beach, stems from the divorce of rationalization "as an abstract principle from the object or cause behind it."[33] It is also well to have in mind the general tendency to relate *modernization* and *progress* "to a world view rooted in concepts of universalism and bureaucratic and administrative rationalism," especially as relating to economic be-

havior.[34] This can be much to the prejudice of minority cultures, and in Beach's view of the Swedish case, "The State barrels ahead with its rationalization programme to increase the efficiency of the reindeer industry seemingly in oblivion of its cultural implications."[35]

After World War II, Saami reindeer pastoralism in Sweden was faced with accelerating problems on two fronts. On the one hand, the Saami have been "caught between a continually rising subsistence minimum of reindeer and a continually reduced grazing capacity due to the combined encroachments of the timber, tourist, mining and hydro-electric power industries." And on the other hand, there is a race between the cost of living and the price of reindeer meat in which the former increases faster than the latter.[36]

It is against this background that the Swedish state's rationalization program came into being, its principles enshrined in the current Herding Act of 1971 (nearly a decade ahead of similar legislation in Norway). The herding livelihood had to be improved, giving it a living standard in line with that of a Swedish industrial worker and *fewer* practitioners.[37] Consonant with the guiding premise that social democratic principles should be applied to the Saami pastoralist as to any other citizen (Chapter 13), the state would "protect" the Saami from "unequal opportunity" through, for example, the notion of "illegalized or unacceptable poverty," even though this "means the decimation of the already low herding population." At the same time, then, as the state declares such a policy necessary for the preservation of Saami culture, it deals a "deadly blow" to it.[38]

Such redirecting and restructuring of Saami reindeer pastoralism in Sweden has largely proved a failure. Government reports commonly put the blame on the "traditionalism" of the Saami herders (Ole K. Sara sometimes says much the same concerning his problems with the Kautokeino pastoralists). But there is more to the explanation than "traditionalism." There are differences between Swedish and Saami in precepts. First of all, the state (as in Norway) drew much of its inspiration for "rationalizing" reindeer pastoralism from what had been accomplished in the agricultural sector; and failure is explained through such a comparison as well: "The demands attached to agricultural support, for profitability in a business perspective, should in principle be applied to the herding business. . . . Herding has not been able to make the best of gains from rationalization to the same extent as has, for example, agriculture."[39] Swedish Saami themselves, rather like their fellow pastoralists in Norway, refer to the state's program of rationalized husbandry as "the pig farm ideal."[40]

Second (and more important in the long term), pastoralists and the state disagree over which is more desirable: "a large [pastoral] population with a low average income or a smaller population with a higher living standard?"[41] Following Beach, the answer is that "as the Saamis continually point out, a living standard in line with that of a Swedish industrial worker is less important to them than a life in the north within the traditional herding livelihood."[42] An outcome in moral terms is that "the herding culture, which the State has sworn to protect at the cost of restricting the economic initiative of the herders, is now supposedly to blame for not changing fast enough."[43]

For Georg Henriksen, a Norwegian anthropologist with field experience among pastoral Saami of Helgeland in Nordland province (North Norway), a serious implication of the state rationalization program is the double-bind situation in which it places the pastoralists, particularly the District foremen. For as the situation now stands (late 1980s), their behavior and their decisions are attributable to two mutually incompatible, even antagonistic, normative and legal systems: the Norwegian and the Saami. As already noticed (Chapter 11), the opening paragraph of the Reindeer Management Act (1978) mixes the unitary premises of a social democratic society and the particularistic premises of an ethnic minority, and Henriksen, in the field, observed how this produces recurring situations of ambiguity and contradiction, especially for those pastoralists burdened with responsibility for the execution of the administration's behests. Thus, respecting the Saami sii'da (sij'ten in Helgeland Saami), or herding unit, the Norwegian-controlled Administration both recognizes it as the crucible of Saami pastoral organization and makes it the instrument of state policy.[44] While the state holds up as a fundamental principle that the Saami themselves must make decisions, it systemati-

cally takes away from them decision-making responsibilities.[45] From the viewpoint of the state, its responsibility is to delegate and distribute its authority; thus it is the Saami District foremen who exercise authority, stresses the state. However, the 1978 Act obliges these foremen to enforce the policies of the state. In practice, then, they are caught between Saami tradition and Norwegian fiat. The issues of concern are those discussed in the previous chapters.[46]

Henriksen details how the Helgeland Saami pastoralists (like those of Kautokeino to the north) are upset at Norwegian intrusion into matters which, they believe, should be left to them to resolve. That they are not, is, in part, a consequence of Norwegian perceptions of the inadequacy of Saami social organization and, in part, a persisting legacy of Social Darwinism respecting nomadism: And Saami know this. On the first count, there is Norwegian dependence on "the typical," "the average," and hence on routinized action and response. On the second, reindeer pastoralism is still viewed as standing in the way of agriculture and industry. From seeing Norwegian stereotyping of Saami people and reindeer pastoralism, Henriksen finds stereotyped Norwegian behavior revealed.[47]

In structural terms, "the meeting between Saami and Norwegian society," he says, "is one between a non-centralized society and a centralized state system," with the consequence that "Saami society is systematically hindered from developing [to meet changing circumstances] its own institutions and control mechanisms"—mechanisms that the state, for the most part, is blind to.[48] Again, the field observations from Helgeland are consonant with those from Kautokeino.

And, too, there are despairing Saami voices—that can still just be heard—speaking about "identity," "self-image," and the knowledge that comes from experience. A man who on account of his age had been removed from the register of his pastoral District wrote to the authorities:

I have never had any other livelihood than reindeer management. For the whole of my life I have belonged to my District. . . . I feel that the whole of my identity is bound up with my reindeer District. . . . I feel it to be a wholly unreasonable and unacceptable attack on my person and my self-image that, with a stroke of the pen, I am taken off the register and thereby

. . . lose my rights, which I have inherited from my father and his parents in accordance with Saami customary law. . . .[49] [I also want you to know] that my old father, after he could no longer work in the mountains, was of invaluable help to us on account of his long experience. . . . Precious knowledge about climate, plant and animal life, gathered through years of direct experience, is an invaluable capital which old persons possess, and it is both their right and obligation to pass on such knowledge to the generations who follow.[50]

Returning now to the Finnmark tundra, principal issues of the commons controversy are brought to the fore in the respective positions of Ivar Björklund and Ottar Brox.[51] Björklund, an anthropologist with considerable field experience among the pastoralists, is concerned with the falsity of "an underlying assumption in the literature that pastoralism [embodies] the very conditions under which the 'tragedy of the commons' is likely to occur."[52] The argument runs, he says, that because pasture is a "free" resource, overgrazing inevitably follows, with calamitous consequences. Such, indeed, is close to the position taken by Brox, who adopts the economic modeling of H. Scott Gordon, with its key notion of "sustainable resource rent."[53]

Björklund, for his part, believes that overgrazing on the Finnmark tundra has been much exaggerated by biologists and administrators. He asserts that there is little historical evidence of overgrazing. Natural catastrophes that periodically decimate the herds have nothing to do with (over)grazing. For example, animals are unable to reach the lichen on account of "icing": hence the marked drop in numbers in the reindeer censuses of 1875, 1935, and 1969 (see Fig. 13.1). Animals are lost but not the lichen beds. Therefore the rebuilding of herds is feasible at a rate that would not be possible had there been overgrazing.[54]

His principal response to the "free" resource and overgrazing argument, however, is that the "carrying capacity" of pastures is *mediated* by the pastoralist through continual seasonal adjustment of herd sizes on given pastures.[55] A prerequisite of being able to "mediate" is that the pastoralists themselves are left to make the decisions. Such, through the centuries, has been the case. But now, under government authority, strong measures are being taken to reduce this autonomy.

Björklund is polemical. He seriously questions the validity—and possibly even the relevance—of some of the quantitative data (on pastures' bearing capacity, weights of animals, the Finnmark reindeer population curve over recent years) that are used—uncritically, he suggests—by the state. He recognizes that grazing is now a limiting factor, but asks how one arrived at such a situation. Regrettably, his opponents, especially those working with the economic models of Gordon and Hardin, discount his insightful accounts of Saami pastoralism as—until quite recently—a responsible and viable ecologic system. Instead, equations are brought into play that are acultural (seen as a virtue) and presented, therefore, as "objective" and "rational." Thus Brox writes as though the indigenous system of herding and husbandry (inasmuch as he gives it a thought) is, for all essential purposes, a thing of the past, which it is certainly not, either ecologically or culturally. He is not only convinced that there is overgrazing in serious proportions but believes (misguidedly, in my view) that Saami pastoral society fails on account of the prevalence of zero-sum competition. If this is allowed to continue, we may expect the worse, he says. The only hope for stabilization and long-term viability is Norwegian moderating (cf. "mediating") regulations.[56]

But let us run through this part of the Broxian argument without any assumption of the Tragedy outcome. The very competition that he sees as beckoning the Tragedy is, I suggest, rather more likely to hinder, even obstruct, an owner from continually expanding his herd—should his competitors find his behavior overly aggressive and threatening to their own interests. Likewise, the "inequality" to which the few megaherds (say, those of over one thousand animals) are said to bear witness also puts various controls on the rich owners. Examples abound, but let one suffice: Iskun Biera with his megaherd and Jorgu Biera with his two hundred animals were, we know, often together. Neither could have managed alone. It simply is not an unmediated zero-sum game—not in the 1960s, nor in the 1980s—but rather one in which quite often (not always) informal controls are effectively at play—including reindeer rustling (Chapter 14). Brox's characterization of the situation shows that he sees only what he understands to be the putative *price* (ecologic irresponsibility: a runaway world) of this competition, and is blind to its *benefits* (social control exercised by competitors).[57]

Underlying his argument is the belief that the lichen beds and grasses (like the biomass on which the fish in the sea feed, indeed the fish themselves) are "free" resources.[58] However, to characterize unqualifiedly the lichen beds as "free" (which in a formal economic sense they are) is to neglect the element of husbandry of the pastures, as well as of the animals, such as has been described in earlier chapters and belongs to my Model 1 (Fig. 7.2) and to Björklund's notion of mediation. Overgrazing—of course it occurs—is a *failure* of that husbandry, not a natural or inevitable consequence of competitive Saami reindeer pastoralism.

While it is true that critical attention to the Tragedy phenomenon (or phenomena) "forces us to keep aggregate consequences of individual adaptations and careers constantly in mind,"[59] it matters a great deal whether or not we grant to the individuals whose livelihood is in question an understanding of "aggregate consequences." It is this issue, perhaps more than anything else, that separates the positions just reviewed.

The one position, looking at the recent past of Saami pastoralism, notes an elaborate system of checks and balances that is likely to protect the livelihood from dire "aggregate consequences," but notes, too, that where necessary the pastoralists are mindful of such. Pastoral mediation is a key notion in this scenario.

The other position, in its concern over the immediate present and future, dismisses evidence from the recent past as irrelevant, and announces that dire "aggregate consequences" are imminent and plain for all to see—*and* that the problem is all the more critical on account of the pastoralists' unmindfulness of it. An absurd proposition it may seem to be, yet it is close to what some commentators hold to be so.

What I think happens is something rather different, though just as dangerous. It is that a serious implication of the intervention by the state in relations between the pastoralists has a "decentering of reality" effect, with acceptance that "the preponderant reality is elsewhere"

than among one's fellows.[60] Increasingly, that reality is in individuals' relations with the state, and this likely engenders that asocial, self-interested personality on the basis of which the Tragedy is predicted. In this case, too, mediation is necessary: this time between the state and the pastoralists, and it is failing.

At the heart of the position for which I am arguing, then, are two closely related matters. First is the notion of pastoral mediation as quintessentially *relational*—enveloping persons, animals, and landscapes, and continually negotiated. It therefore carries with it a view of property different from that found in the Hardinian scheme: "[Property] is not mere possession, it ultimately rests in some moral consensus about the relationships between people and between people and things [and animals]. Property is a right socially constructed."[61]

This means we must not allow our understanding of pastoral ecology to be subverted by a view of pasture as "boundaried space" containing "non-problematic energy resources" reducible to "a finite number of tokens for measurement,"[62] or by rough-and-ready translations into the argument from the fisheries crisis.[63] Nor should faith be lost in the relevancy of Saami values for the sake of economic determinism and the ideological programs of the state.

Second, really a corollary of the above, is the conviction that even when approached as an economic enterprise, the praxis of reindeer pastoralism is embedded culturally and socially.[64] The costs of disregarding the embeddedness factor (and in worse-case scenarios, terminating it by legislation) can be enormous even in economic terms. However, to say values and understandings are embedded is not to mean they do not respond to changes in the total environment; but such changes have to emerge through *trust* between the pastoralists and between them and the state. Trust, too, is relational in nature—each party has to demonstrate it to the other. As earlier chapters have shown, the situation is not a happy one at the moment, and this prejudices the passage of knowledge: "People," writes a sociologist of science, "do not simply not understand science when they are seen to disregard it; they do not recognize it, or identify with it, morally speaking."[65]

16.
The Prejudice
of Equality

If it is incontestable that the prejudice of superiority is an obstacle in the road
to knowledge, we must also admit that the prejudice of equality is a still greater
one, for it consists in identifying the other purely and simply with one's own
"ego ideal" (or with oneself).

TZVETAN TODOROV,
The Conquest of America: The Question of the Other

I believe a diachrony of changing arrangements of herd management is to be found in the data presented in this book. It is this that I want to convey first, and proceed thence to Todorov's ironic paradox.

The account of herd management from my fieldwork in the early 1960s was written with the model of "commensurate proportions" in mind (Model 1 of Chapter 7, reproduced here in Fig. 16.1). While it may not have been achieved too often, all owners strove towards it. Increases in herd size were to be expected on account of the pronounced tendency to attach value to the self-reproductive capacity of pastoral capital, and the model foresaw commensurate increases in personnel through the recruitment of children and—most critically—in pasture through expansion (although this was already beginning to become a limiting factor). A hallmark of such herd management was the responsibility it gave to the head of a family herd for just about all decisions.

Such a model, however, becomes obsolescent in a situation where, as herds continue to increase, pasture either remains constant or actually diminishes. Such was soon to be the situation in Finnmark (Model 2 of Fig. 16.1). Intrusion of nonpastoral interests, both private and pub-

lic, reduced the expanse of seasonal pastures or diminished their pastoral utility even as state subsidies to pastoral family economies inadvertently stimulated herd sizes. Further damage was done to the model of commensurate proportions through weakening of the indigenous system of checks and balances when the state began to assume responsibility for various pastoral decisions.

In response to a deteriorating situation (readily read by some as beckoning a tragedy of the commons) the state took control over decisions affecting two of the three factors of production: herds and personnel (i.e., herder-owners). Respecting pastures, traditional usufruct rights continued to be exercised. This development is represented by the clipped Model 3 of Fig. 16.1. Even in the marketing of their animals, once a prerogative they held dearly to themselves (Chapters 8 and 10), herd owners find that the state has a decisive say. With such erosion of the pastoralists' responsibilities, "irresponsibility" in the form of asocial individualism likely follows.

Such is the dismal situation at the time of writing, but I wish to hypothesize a future development. In Model 4 (Fig. 16.1) the incommensurable values of Model 2 are corrected, and pastoral responsibility, taken away in Mod-

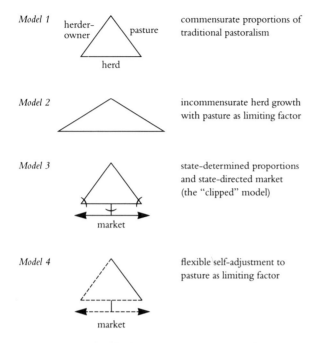

Figure 16.1 Models of herd management. In variations of Model 2 there may be an incommensurate increase of herder-owners or both herds and herder-owners

el 3, is returned. The key is to make the values attached to pastoral capital and to the marketing of animals *mutually* supportive.[1] At the moment they are too often in opposition to each other. There is a need here for flexibility from the side of the state. For instance, it would help were a pastoralist able to bank money from marketing animals and be taxed on it only when it is withdrawn from the account: "Simply put, the deer could be slaughtered according to ecological factors but utilized according to herder needs."[2]

Model 4 presumes, however, the resolution of several problems by the pastoralists. One is the organization of extensive herding with its periodic work commitment (Chapter 7). There is the risk of breakdowns, both in the coordination of work teams and in herd knowledge, so that pastoral production deteriorates to a catch-as-catch-can. This is what I felt when writing those journal entries from the autumn of 1962. But there is another side to it. The large separation corrals with their multiple pens were making the herders learn new techniques and routines, and learning they were. Differences in herd

management between Oar'jebelli and Gow'dojottelit, at that time, also spoke of capacity for change and adaptation and strategic planning. It was a capacity that flowed from pastoralists who were their own managers. There was little state tutelage or control.

Model 4 also leaves crucial decisions about optimal numbers to be resolved—of animals in relation to pastures, for example. Responsible pastoral praxis will return, I believe, with decisive weight being given to the input of groups of practicing pastoralists (perhaps at the District level) regarding such an issue.

In the situation as it is at present there are those who urge the placing of controls to dampen pastoral competition. Model 4 would *draw* upon pastoral competition. In the past, the competition has assured the ecologic and cultural health of the pastoral enterprise; and in the future that I envisage—with value attached to both pastoral capital and the marketing of animals—the importance of competition will be no less.

Is there, then, a release for the state from the problems it faces by leaving it to the pastoral practitioners themselves to find the solutions? The answers flow from the presuppositions. A government presupposition is that the tenets of social democracy must prevail, and for that to happen there must be an administrative ability and authority such that the pastoralists do not possess. Alongside that goes the presupposition (with currency beyond government circles) that, left alone, Saami pastoralism will bring the tragedy of the commons down upon itself and upon others who also use the tundra (Chapter 15).

There are Saami who agree with that, but there is, as we have seen, a strong countervailing presupposition among them, too. Fundamental to it is, first, that the pastoralists themselves identify the problems for which a solution is needed—they will not always be the same problems that are of concern to the state; second, that having identified pastoral problems in their current situation, pastoralists will be able to evolve the appropriate institutional ability and authority with which to address them. Something different from both "traditional" Saami pastoralism and pastoralism by state fiat would emerge.

However, the political reality is, of course, that the likelihood of the problem-solving being left to the pastoralists themselves is infinitesimal, whereas the continuation of the state as *formal* problem-solver is a firm likelihood. This being so, it is appropriate to return to a brief review of the prevailing relationship between state and pastoralists.

The first feature that comes to notice is the degree of abstraction with which the state (and its consultants) discuss (and plan for) its pastoral clients. It is a "they" that is written about. Perhaps planners are not aware of this, but many Saami are. Mutual cultural misapprehension is sown. I think this helps to explain why many positions adopted by the planners are ignored, whereas in other circumstances they would evoke understanding from the target audience. There is much to the observation that "the real boundary that exists is not around the scheme, but between planners and planned."[3]

Thus when the expert-fueled Reindeer Administration says of something, a herd size, for instance, "That may be all right for the individual, but not for the livelihood as a whole," herder-owners may well ask themselves, "What is really being said? What does the Administration *really* have in mind?" And the planners, puzzled and shocked by the Saami system, make their own pastoralist models *for* the Saami. A research team commissioned jointly by the Ministry of Agriculture and NRL took as its "purpose . . . to reduce the resource-destructive, cost-intensive and conflict-generating competition." Accordingly, it was proposed that "no distinction will be made between 'my' reindeer and 'your' reindeer."[4] From the culturally indigenous perspective, this is tabula rasa "planning" with a vengeance. But there is, of course, a political ideal behind it all.

As shown in Chapter 13, the state defines public morality, and the practice of reindeer pastoralism is to be no exception. Indeed, far from being privileged as an exception, the pastoralists are seen as presenting special problems. They are *on the move;* they lay claim to *so much space;* they appear to *lack social cohesion* and would *defy regulation.* At the root of the problem, as the state sees it, is the free-for-all competition between herding groups (whose compositions and combinations are liable to change seasonally) over "shared" pastures. This situation lends itself to unbridled expansion of herds for some (it is thought), impoverishment for others. So together with

an ecological crisis from overgrazing (as it is seen to be), there is an equally pressing social problem. Hence the Reindeer Management Act (1978). In addition to regulating access to the livelihood, the Act, with its subsequent additions, is directed to the realization of the state's political philosophical code in which the notion of equal well-being is central.

Here it should be stressed that a bedrock commitment of the state is to play fair by the pastoralists, albeit according to Norwegian norms; and a natural corollary is the state's concern to see that the pastoralists, too, play fair by those norms. But this leads straight into Todorov's "prejudice of equality" syndrome, with the state imposing upon the pastoralists its understanding of utility and reward, predicated on a universalistic notion of the rational: Like it or not, the state finds itself assuming the superordinate authority of a *patron.*[5] Thus the 1978 Reindeer Management Act is spoken of (without irony) as giving the livelihood "a legitimacy it has never before had."[6] This patron-client relationship between state and pastoralist is also characterized by an asymmetry concerning the knowledge each has of the other. Paradoxically perhaps (but a logical outcome of the structure of the relationship between them), here it is the state, not the pastoralist, who is the more unknowing of the other.[7]

But to turn the issue around: The state may well ask (as has Beach, arguing from the other side of the case), what, then, constitutes an ethical minority policy? "Should cultural self-determination gain precedence over individual well-being, or should the ideal of the socialistic welfare state be prior to those of cultural pluralism?"[8]

In a formal way, the state acknowledges Saami ethnicity. In practice, though, I think the state views the Saami *as Norwegians,* but lacking in organizational skills, all the same. The question then becomes one of how much discretion over the affairs of their livelihood should these pastoralists, as practitioners, be allowed? Quick reference to other primary livelihoods in Norway, such as fishing and farming, suggests that the answer is, to a notable extent, a political one: *Those* practitioners have powerful political lobbies. Seen from the Saami point of view, an essential part of the problem is one of *minority* politics. The pastoral Saami have no political lobby comparable to that of the other primary livelihoods. It is particularly in this political context that they are hampered by their acephalous tradition.

The pastoralists' deaf ear to what the state decrees or experts advise is a legacy of minority politics as well. Jon Aarseth Melöy et al., for instance, warn that "moves to increase guidance over the reindeer management will awake opposition . . . on account of the unclear relationship between the Saami as a minority people and the state as their guardian, together with the historical experiences of this relationship."[9]

For the state, on the other hand, the imperatives have been those of intervention, and by 1988, faced with pastoral defiance, the kid gloves were off. From the state's point of view, the question was not, "Is intervention justifiable?" but, "How, even with the pastoralists' (and not the state's) own situation in mind, can there *not* be intervention?" The state is swayed by the evidence that "they"—the pastoralists—want to modernize; therefore, surely, they realize that their "traditional values" may be seriously inadequate in their contemporary circumstances? "Objectively," the state sees pastoral defiance as a minor feature of relations with the state when weighed against the dependence on the state.

The state, however, has not attained its own objectives. For one thing, it accelerated what it had intended to halt. A principal objective has been the reduction of the size of herds, and yet the majority of the subsidies had no slaughter quotas attached to them. With the extra money coming in from the subsidies, families had *less* reason to slaughter. Another principal objective has been to strengthen cohesion and trust among the pastoralists, but reducing the decision-making authority of the sii'da—subordinating it to the District, and the District, in its turn, to the Area Committee—undermined these qualities.

In this connection, one may bear in mind Ivar Björklund's general stricture that many of the problems (even in the view of a number of administrators as well as the practitioners) besetting reindeer pastoralism today arise out of state intervention. The state sees a runaway system on the tundra. Some of the measures taken by the state helped to induce it, but the state, nevertheless, diagnoses it as a condition rooted in Saami pastoralism. Yet before state intervention, the Saami system, with its own checks and balances, was not a runaway one.

In its repetitive chant—"too many animals"—the state

has been irresponsible in its cultural clumsiness and insensitivity. The sophistication of the pastoralists' own methods of evaluating pastures was lost on the state; instead, mechanistic kilogram-per-hectare formulae were employed (Chapter 14). Worse still, the state chose to attribute motives to the Saami (without any ethnographic fieldwork) about why they have "too many." This was crudely done, repeatedly falling back on the asocial individualism of G. Hardin (Chapter 15): An owner has to have as many animals as possible on account of zero-sum relations with all other owners. But most owners (at the time of my fieldwork and later) were parents and as such were custodians for the next generation, and the family herd was actually dispersed in their lifetime through anticipatory inheritance (Chapter 1, note 10). Owners were accorded respect, perhaps most of all, on account of the quality of their husbandry, in which herd *composition* is as significant as herd size (Chapter 2): These are social motivations.[10]

Still today, the pastoralists (but not the state) also have in mind the situational context concerning what "too many" means in any particular case. An owner losing animals to others may recognize that he has "too many" to handle. He may seek to employ a hired hand until his children begin to reach the age when they can help with the herding. And when that time comes, there will *not* be "too many" animals—perhaps "too few." Or, "too many" may mean "too little" pasture, and the owner looks for access to other pastures at certain seasons. Much used to depend on the relations he had with other owners. Today, however, there may be no other pastures with a place for him. This is the limiting factor to which the pastoralist must now adapt.

Or one who has "too few" animals may well find it worthwhile to echo the general statement of the state that there are "too many" for the bearing capacity of the tundra. His own chances will be improved by some overall reduction, he hopes. But with the fulfillment of such an expectation, he is likely to change his opinion about *what* is, and *who* has, "too many." By no means all of the Kautokeino pastoralists opposed the compulsory count, and reasoning along these lines, I suggest, helps explain why. It also suggests that those who supported the state in this issue were not necessarily endorsing the principle espoused by the state, but their own.

In each of these scenarios (which I believe are "true" to the pastoral culture) the pastoralist is his own strategist. He takes responsibility for his own decisions. The state will take this away from him. It does so, in its own estimation, for the best of possible reasons: "to reach higher incomes with fewer animals [thus] making room for as many as possible pastoralists." This could mean, however, that "the individual pastoralist cannot vary the size of his herd according to his own wishes."[11] Nor is this the only price the pastoralist would have to pay: It is the state who makes that decision of principle, not the pastoralist. From everything that has been said in this book about the pastoral sense of self, we know that this is a very high price indeed.

Many, perhaps most, of the Kautokeino pastoralists did not believe the message that the present number of owners will not be reduced along with the total number of animals.[12] That smaller herds (with improved productivity) allow for *more* herder-owners, was the message that the state wished to get across (Chapter 13). But with regulated entry (by license) into the livelihood already introduced, the message that pastoralists were more inclined to hear was: "too many animals and too many people."

There is a still more interesting twist to this matter. The state assumes that "as many as possible" pastoralists is itself a pastoral value. My understanding is that this, too, is highly situational. Granted that fellow-pastoralists are competitors, then why would one want "as many as possible?" On the other hand, with pastoralism being pressed to the wall by other interests and the pastoral Saami being but a minority within a minority, there are good reasons for wanting "as many as possible"—as long as they do not crowd one's own pastures. Further: What is supposed by the state to be a Saami value but, in actuality, is only so in a qualified way, *is*—provided the controls of "rational" herd management are in place—arguably a benefit (if an unintended one) for the state. It is so on two counts: It looks as though the state is responsive to Saami ethnicity, and it helps assuage the growing unemployment problem in Finnmark.

My verdict on the "patron" relationship that the state exercises over Saami pastoralists is regrettably negative. First, it is *misguided*. Notable here are the subsidy policy and the misreading of pastoral strategy; the plight of the basic

herding unit at the bottom of a three-tier authority structure, making the retrieval of the earlier sense of responsibility all the more difficult; and attempts to reinvent reindeer pastoral praxis through applying agronomic expertise, as though reindeer pastoralism can be managed in conditions similar to those of "the controlled environments of the barnyard."[13]

Second, it is *morally questionable*. What business has the state determining that certain ideas of prestige (as far as the state understands them) among the pastoralists are outmoded and should be squashed?[14] Likewise, what business is it of the state's to determine what *should* be the principle for the distribution of wealth among the pastoralists? And if the answer to both is because the pastoralism takes place on Norwegian soil and the pastoralists are Norwegian citizens, what, then, does the state really mean when it talks of Saami rights of self-determination? Or, if it is because the pastoralists receive heavy subsidies from the state, is it, then, morally correct for the state to offer bribes in this manner, to get people to do what many of them would otherwise oppose? And is it morally *in*correct for pastoralists to take the bribes but not heed the state's will?

Third, it is *legally questionable*. In regulating Saami pastoralism on the tundra and, at the same time, recognizing it as a citizens' commons (with due regulation), the state acts outside notions of Saami land rights that may be applicable (or become so) both in international and Norwegian law.[15]

In sum, it is both *overexclusive* and *overdetermined* in its authority and ideology—other parties with a warrant to be heard are marginalized (not only BES as a rival to NRL, but also, most notably, the Saami Parliament).[16] It assumes (vis-à-vis the pastoralists) "a monopolistic right to sort out the 'fitting' from the 'unfitting,' the 'worthy' from the 'unworthy' categories, and to spell out the conditions under which passage from the second to the first may take place."[17]

At the same time, though, the state shoulders the strong *inclusive* responsibility of linking together all the citizens of Norway within the social democratic embrace, where *all* are "worthy"—and equally so. Thus the state is always on the edge of a double-bind situation in respect to the two constituencies: Saami pastoralists, Norwegian citizenry. A number of things the state gives to the pastoralists are not necessarily supportive of pastoral management, least of all of the kind of management the state seeks; but the state cannot (by the premises of social democracy) withhold from one group of its citizens benefits that the Norwegian public at large expects and enjoys.[18] Nor, vis-à-vis the non-Saami populations of Finnmark, can the state place the tundra off limits to them, even though it likely means that historical Saami rights are being chiseled away in the process.[19]

The state is left in a no-win situation.

Meanwhile, the future of Saami reindeer pastoralism remains deeply mired in unresolved questions. The authors of one report write: "The most important thing about the cultural goals of reindeer pastoral planning is not first and foremost to protect individual cultural traits, but to arrange conditions so that as many Saami as possible can continue with reindeer pastoralism *in a manner that they themselves consider to be Saami.*"[20] Together, these authors are equally familiar with theoretical models of pastoralism and its practice on the ground and, furthermore, demonstrate an intuitive appreciation of individual pastoralists and differences between them—this, as I have said, is unusual. And their recommendation sounds seductively simple; but of course it is not. Too much has happened over recent decades for there to be a consensus on what it is to be a Saami pastoralist and how the pastoralism should be conducted.

I have been conditioned to think of the earlier generation, who were active herder-owners in the 1960s; but some herder-owners today, astride their snowmobiles,

may well be thinking about eventual ownership of a helicopter. Sitting on a sled harnessed to a reindeer, as their parents did, may be laughable to them. *That's* not a part of being Saami, not for them.[21] But among the variously accented identities and aspirations that have since emerged, who is *the* Saami today? Is it Odd Erling Smuk, head of NRL through the critical years of the late 1980s, with a business school diploma as well as a herd of reindeer, and for whom BES represents vulgar liberalism? Or is it the BES leadership?

Let us suppose that the state hands over the whole package (along with the annual grants) labeled "the pastoral problem" to the Saami Parliament (in Norwegian, Sametinget; in Saami, Samediggi; see note 16). Remembering that the pastoral Saami are but a minority within the Saami national minority, how would Saami parliamentarians resolve matters? How would they define "traditional Saami pastoralism?" Would they restore the autonomy of the sii'da? Would they limit herd sizes? What policy would they adopt towards mechanization? It is most unlikely that they would reach uniform opinions and mutually consistent criteria in tackling such conundrums.[22] Conversely, how would the pastoralists themselves react to a Saami Parliament so empowered?[23] For the moment, however, the state is not contemplating handing such responsibilities to the Saami Parliament. Instead, a new round of proposals to advance its "rationalization" program is being prepared for presentation to the Norwegian Parliament—leaving the Saami Parliament very much out on the sidelines.[24]

Appendix 1.
Rangifer tarandus

Saami pastoralists introduced me to *Rangifer tarandus,* and whatever I learned about the animal during my fieldwork came to me through that pastoral filter. In writing this book I saw it as important not to mix in subsequent knowledge gained from reading about *Rangifer tarandus.* However, with the writing done, it seems sensible to review briefly my readings of field studies of *Rangifer tarandus* by biologists and ethologists. The studies (with the fewest exceptions) are of the animal in the wild.

Rangifer tarandus are indigenous to northern Europe and Asia, where they are called reindeer, and to northern North America, where they are called caribou.[1] Both form large groups loosely called herds, which inhabit tundra, taiga, and coniferous forests. Their ancestors were hunted in the wild; today caribou and some reindeer are still hunted.[2]

Morphological and behavioral differences between Old World and New World stocks are slight,[3] probably less than differences between stocks of forest and tundra. Forest animals are larger, less gregarious, and individually more wary than tundra animals, living mainly in the forest, with short seasonal migrations. Tundra animals live mostly on open ground, making long migrations across the tundra. Tundra stocks have lent themselves more readily to pastoralism.

Wild reindeer and caribou form gatherings that may number in the thousands. These are sometimes called herds, a name used also for much smaller groups of a few dozen closely interacting animals. Alaska has thirteen designated caribou herds, of which the largest, the "Arctic herd," was estimated in 1964 at between 250,000 and 300,000 animals and ranged over 360,000 square kilometers (140,000 square miles). Among the smallest, the "Delta" herd numbered only 5,000, with a range of 7,680 square kilometers (3,000 square miles).[4] T. Skogland's Norwegian studies encompass sixteen geographically denoted herds ranging from a few hundred animals to one numbering 19,000.[5] Several papers in the *Proceedings of the First International Reindeer and Caribou Symposium* use herd in this sense, to denote a large, geographically defined group. Yet terms like "herd behavior" generally imply intimate reactions that are known to exist within much smaller units, which may or may not be important in groups of several thousand.

Physical Characteristics

Reindeer are mobile animals of impressive strength and stamina. They can, for example, keep up a trot at forty kilometers per hour over rough ground and escape at speeds of up to seventy or eighty kilometers per hour.[6] Mobility and shyness make them elusive, though they move and rest in predictable diurnal rhythms:

Reindeer activity is characterized by a more or less regular alternation between periods of activity and rest. Typically, after a few hours of grazing and moving, the animals lie down to ruminate and rest for a similar period. This rhythm holds true for individual animals, groups and herds of all sizes. Reindeer in a herd of hundreds or even thousands show a marked tendency to synchronize their activity, so that within a quarter-hour a herd may have switched from all grazing and moving to all lying.[7]

Most tellingly, shyness in reindeer is balanced by curiosity. People can locate and approach their groups even in the most difficult terrain and indeed are often approached by the animals. Natural herds are loose social groupings, sometimes crowded closely together, at other times dispersed. The groups tend to be smaller in high latitudes, except when predators are prominent.[8] Rudimentary leader-follower relationships and dominion within a herd change seasonably, notably with the growth and shedding of antlers.

Sexual dimorphism is marked among reindeer and associated with polygamy. Males are typically larger than females, heavier (weighing up to 100 kilograms), and with more formidable antlers. Males lose weight considerably during the rut, in which they may die as a consequence of their exertions. Costs of reproduction among females increase with the number of pregnancies[9] and are particularly severe when food is limited. A female must reach a critical weight to conceive but probably maximizes her fitness by using her available energy more on fetal growth and lactation than on body growth.[10] Essentially, males put a premium on developing large size to be successful breeders, while female success appears in nursing rather than growth.[11]

Some cows breed in their second year, but most in their third, when they weigh between sixty and seventy-five kilograms; thereafter they conceive each year. Twins are very rare. Bulls may exceed sixty kilograms in their second year but are unlikely to be successfully competitive breeders until their fourth or fifth year. Individuals may live for twenty years, but mortality increases sharply after about the age of ten, principally because cheek-teeth become worn, and the animals can no longer feed efficiently.

The reindeer's speed comes from its long and powerful legs. In evolution the species has developed the longest, swiftest limb form possible.[12] Large, dish-shaped cloven hooves provide a solid footing over rough terrain and low weight-loading on snow and ice. Reindeer are excellent swimmers.[13] In the water their hooves act as paddles, and the air-filled hairs of their coats provide buoyancy. The coat also provides excellent insulation. With few sweat glands, reindeer suffer in hot weather despite their summer molt. In summer they avoid heat and swarms of flying insects in high-altitude pastures with snow patches, even wandering on glaciers to keep cool.

Diet

Reindeer diet changes markedly with the seasons. During the long winter months of perpetual snow cover the staple is a carbohydrate-rich lichen, the so-called reindeer moss (Cladonia spp.). As snow recedes in spring the animals enrich their diet by searching out the emergent grasses and plants. During summer they graze protein-rich green plants and grasses, then with the decay of the plant biomass in the autumn they look for the bases of grasses and sedge plants that remain green longest. In autumn they seek out fungi, especially mushrooms, which reproduce efficiently in the season of falling temperature and shortening daylight hours and have a higher fat and protein content than other plants of the autumn twilight.

Reindeer growth is based on summer diet; winter is nutritionally little more than a survival period. Skogland makes the general point that there is a well-defined period of plant growth in northern temperate and arctic regions: The more extreme the climate, the shorter the season of growth and the higher the nutrient concentration in growing plant tissue. Such important life processes as growth, reproduction, fattening, and lactation are all closely linked to the protein-enriched diet, which ungulates synthesize from green plant tissue.[14] Good diet remains available into early winter as snow cover refrigerates and preserves some of the summer grasses, berries, and other plants. Lichens are a staple diet. Heather and even brushwood, as well as willow and birch leaves, are supplementary winter food resources.

Foraging Behavior

Growth of grass is stimulated by cropping, little injury being caused by the normal traffic of hoofed animals over the vegetation. Lichens are more susceptible to damage, especially in summer, when they are dry and brittle. Reindeer or caribou stampeded by man or biting insects may damage their forage seriously for the future. They seem reluctant to browse bruised lichens, and regeneration of lichen beds can take up to thirty years.

More serious still may be the sealing off in winter of lichen beds by a barrier of snow and ice. Weather conditions that bring this about are quite common: a thaw turning snow into slush, which is frozen and buried under new snow. Reindeer hooves are well suited to digging in snow and breaking crusted snow and thin layers of ice. However, unless they can escape to ice-free pastures, many animals lose weight and die. Weather conditions in autumn can predetermine the animals' access to the lichens, which are their main winter resource.

Reindeer feed delicately, picking their food with their mouths rather than tearing at it, snatching a little here and there. They select, for example, clumps of soft lichen between dry heather and leave few traces of where they have fed. They nibble as they move, small groups perhaps collecting in spots of particular food interest, only to disperse shortly afterwards. Loose social grouping thus accords with their feeding pattern, which is well adapted for existence on subarctic vegetation. Concerning their nomadism, A. E. Speiss writes: "The distance covered by each major movement is a direct function of the distance between ecological zones and between habitats that are best for the herd at different times of the year. . . . Long-distance migratory behaviour seems to raise the carrying capacity of the area over what it would be with only localized movement."[15]

On the move, reindeer tend to follow contours, using

ridgelines, the lowest passes, and the most gentle slopes. They follow trails, tending to take almost the exact path of animals that preceded them, even where the terrain is seemingly featureless.[16] For about half their annual cycle they walk, wade, and feed through snow. In W. O. Pruitt, Jr.'s, study of barren-ground caribou in snow, the animals favored soft, light snow less than fifty to sixty centimeters thick. Hard surface snow hinders feeding, as does snow that has been disturbed by reindeer digging ("cratering") for buried lichens.[17] According to F. Skuncke:

They paw their way down through the snow where mostly isolated podetia are taken with the muzzle while others are kicked up onto the surface of the snow. The digging continues one or a few metres in one direction or another, depending on the nature of the surface of the ground, but the first obstacle that is encountered causes the digging to begin at a new place. If the ground is undulating, it is dug in an uphill direction, and the digging tracks become long and have the form of 20 to 30 cm wide "paths" that are often rather regular. If the reindeer try to graze within the same area more than once during the same winter, they cannot normally continue from the edge of a feeding hole made before, as such edges soon become hard.[18]

This practice accounts for much of the animals' daily movement in winter. Tolerance of hard snow increases as winter progresses; then in spring, snow develops a sun crust, and the animals move towards softer and lighter snow. The thaw that follows also causes the animals to move, and about this time the spring migration begins.

There are three points of particular importance here. First, the animals are drawn together by changes in the snow cover. This is particularly so in spring, when snow conditions determine the timing, speed, and route of the migration. Second, a winter range can safely support many fewer animals than may be suggested by studies of available vegetation because cratering and other snow conditions limit the vegetation available. Third, there is a continual shrinking of accessible food as winter wears on, and competition develops between individuals for the waning resource.

Among barren-ground caribou, bulls show a higher threshold of sensitivity to snow hardness, density, and thickness than cows and young, effectively segregating them from each other.[19] Skogland noted that mature bulls, having rutted in early winter, are the first to shed their antlers in November and December. Without antlers they lose rank. Young bulls shed their antlers and leave the females later.[20] J. Henshaw found that pregnant cows, which retain antlers in winter, use them to gain access to feeding sites in deep snow.[21] Sven Skjenneberg and Lars Slagsvold noted that yearlings, though often pushed away from craters, could use their limited size and small antlers to benefit from the smaller craters.[22] Skogland reported that in winter foraging groups of mixed sex and age, animals with the largest antlers preferred smaller groups, avoiding conflict with matched opponents; smaller animals preferred larger groups, in which there was considerable peer competition.[23]

Such interesting differences persist in the spring. Cows make an early start from the winter pastures to the calving grounds. After calving, while both sexes look for green grasses and plants, the bulls press on with their migration to summer pastures, whereas the cows and calves seek shelter, protection, and rest. Through summer, males roam more widely and in smaller groups than cows, calves, and yearlings.[24]

Antipredator Strategies

Reindeer evolved alongside wolves. Susceptibility to predation has been of major account in the evolution of their morphology and behavior. As risk-averting foragers they run or bunch together. When individuals attempt to outrun predators, whether they succeed depends on such factors as their physical condition and the nature of the ground surface. For example, wolves may be marginally at an advantage on soft snow.[25] A group of grazing reindeer usually bunch into a tight herd when alarmed.

Herds are most vulnerable to predators during the weeks following the birth of calves. A sequence of antipredator strategies accords with the physical development of the calves. Before giving birth the mother finds a semiconcealed spot in terrain of broken relief, close to early-season plant growth but a little distance from other cows, many of which will be calving at the same time.[26] Y. Espmark noted that seclusion at parturition is more marked among forest reindeer.[27] The newborn, small and cryptically colored, lie concealed in the presence of intruders but soon become mobile. Both wild and pastoral

calves gain their feet within half an hour of birth and suckle about an hour later.[28] Skogland argues that low environmental productivity prohibits long hiding out. Though the calves are born as hiders, they must move very soon after birth.[29]

During their first few days the calves remain alone with their mothers, gaining in bodily competence, learning the maternal signals, and forming strong mother-offspring bonds.[30] Pruitt recorded that neonate barren-ground reindeer sleep and rest for periods of fifteen minutes to one hour.[31] Suckling usually lasts only about ten to twenty seconds. After suckling the calf frequently stands while the doe licks its anal region or face, then the doe moves off to graze a few meters away, usually remaining within 100 meters. Soon after the birth the mother sheds her antlers and joins a nursery group of cows and calves, feeding, resting, and searching out good forage. The wild reindeer herd of Hardangervidda (Norway), for example, moves from the high to the lower alpine zone, where melting snow exposes rich vegetation.[32]

Nursery groups stay together through the summer, joined by yearlings and cows without young. They depend for protection against predators on a "swamping" strategy made possible by the close synchrony of births, when thousands of mothers and calves move together for weeks across open terrain. Predators eliminate individuals that breed late or are out of synchrony. The growing calf during this time learns to socialize with its peer group, recognize hierarchies within the herd, and follow signals both of its mother and of other animals. Mortality among the calves may be high. Exhausted calves fall easy prey to wolves, which follow the herds. On the Canadian tundra, blizzards in mid-June may cause many calves to die of cold within a few hours of birth, or become irretrievably separated from their mother and starve.[33] During warm summer days in June and July swarms of flying insects, notably mosquitoes, warble flies, and nostril flies invoke both bunching and stampeding among reindeer. Stampeding animals may injure themselves and trample underfoot vegetation, which will then remain unused for food. More effectively they bunch in shallow water, on snow, or on exposed, windy ridges. According to P. G. Ion: "Movements towards and away from snow were observed as an immediate response to fluctuation in insect activity. For example, sudden rain squalls temporarily suppress insect flight and animals move off snow to graze under reduced levels of harassment."[34]

Bunching offers less surface area for insects to land on. Reindeer at the edge of a group are less protected than those in the center. Warble flies and nostril flies concentrate their attacks on the outer ring, and the more senior herd members in the center escape their attacks. Competition for the center may cause the group to spin around its own axis. If driven by hunger to leave their snow patch while insects are biting, the reindeer fan out and forage quickly, moving against the wind and clumping again if harassment becomes intolerable.[35] Insect harassment is debilitating and may contribute seriously to loss of condition.[36] By the time of the onset of the severest insect attacks, the calves are about six weeks old and strong enough to join the cows in evasive action.

Breeding Synchrony

Over a period of eight years Skogland recorded a variation of only five to six days in the mean annual calving date of a wild reindeer herd in Norway; 90 percent of the calves were born within a seven-day period in May. In his words, "Natural selection has directed timing of birth to coincide with the seasonally most favourable period, thereby optimizing neonate survival." For reindeer and caribou alike the most favorable period offers little margin for error. The calves are born as the snow cover begins to retreat and the vegetation emerges. "A short burst of plant growth produces a seasonal wave of green tissue which passes unevenly over the landscape following the regression of snow-cover. . . . Births occur two to three weeks prior to the mean dates of the major release from snow-cover."[37]

Parturition is early, and birth weights are among the lowest for all ungulates. Thus the short summer is "optimized for nursing and neonatal growth." Growth of tundra plants peaks after forty to fifty days, but because the difference in time of release from snow cover between different plant communities can be up to a month, the actual season of early plant growth lasts up to seventy days. By the time the calves are weaned at three to four weeks, new plant growth is plentiful.[38] As Skuncke puts it:

The snow [influences] pasture conditions by its gradually melting away, thus causing the plants to grow up little by little so that during the entire summer reindeer have access to the much-sought after tender stages or parts of the pasture plants. This tender, new vegetation has a higher nutritional value (including a higher percentage of digestible protein) than the fully grown stages.[39]

In Skogland's view the animals demonstrate "a deliberate behavioral tracking of the wave of plant production," throughout the summer selecting habitat types with the highest concentrations of green plant biomass.[40] After the peak of plant production has been reached, so the pace of postnatal development of calves and recovery of nursing cows slackens markedly. By their seventieth day female wild reindeer calves have completed 85 percent of skeletal growth, and duration of suckling has fallen 70 percent. Calves born late in the season depend longer on milk and prejudice the mothers' chances of full recovery by the end of the season.[41]

Synchrony of births requires a short mating period. Estrus lasts between twelve and twenty-four hours and recurs at intervals of eleven to twenty days. Up to ten cycles are possible each season.[42] However, Skogland found that most mating occurred within one week.[43] Mature cows gather in harem groups under the control of a senior bull. Rival bulls display aggressively, and the cows reject the sexual attentions of younger bulls. Dominance among males is principally a function of physical size and maturity, in which antlers are probably the most important signals. The bulls' antlers, larger than those of the cows, are sometimes weapons of earnest conflict; more often they are instruments of ritualized threat and courtship displays. It has been plausibly suggested that gestures expressed through antlers in either sex are an important code in the iconographic language of this species.[44]

Harems and Polygamy

Senior bulls maintain their harems by chasing away other bulls trying to intrude, and prevent the cows from scattering too widely. If cows leave the congregated herd the bull immediately runs after them and brings them back into the herd.[45] Harem bulls are only occasionally drawn into serious physical combat with other bulls, and then only with peers in age and size. Constant vigilance and threat display suffice to keep younger bulls at bay, at least until the rut is far advanced. Among pastoral herds in Scandinavia harems vary from a dozen up to eighty cows, of whom a quarter may be in heat at any one time.[46] A senior bull that is displaced by a rival imprints his authority over other bulls and his attraction over other cows elsewhere in the terrain. Maintenance of a harem depends primarily on the sheer physical stamina of the bull. Exertions in attending to cows and repelling competitors leave little time for grazing and rest. His rut ends in a state of exhaustion, and it is then that younger bulls capitalize on their chances, mating with cows that are still in heat.

Without this social arrangement at the rut, mating and parturition would not be synchronized. Later in summer, when the reindeer range far in their search for the last green vegetation of the year, matings would become catch-as-catch-can. Synchrony would become impaired, and more cows would mate with young bulls not yet in their prime, whose abilities to survive had not been fully tested.[47]

There are two other points of interpretation to which I would draw attention. During the rut the harem moves within a large area, and distances between neighboring groups remain fairly constant.[48] The bull is the harem marker. His antlers, profile, rutting postures, displays, sounds, and especially his strong odor (notably from ritual urinating over the lower part of his hind legs) identify the group and distinguish it from others. Though apparently male-dominated, the cows play an active role by remaining together. Indeed it can be argued that the females, rather than being herded by the males, group voluntarily for mutual protection at parturition and allow a single male to join the group. The reproductive efficiency of polygamy may rest in the exclusion of unnecessary males from optimal feeding grounds.[49] Espmark noted that in roaming during the rut "the oldest cows, one at a time, take the lead while the bull follows and by his herding influences the direction of the wanderings in an indirect way."[50] Thus the cows find the patches of rich vegetation, and the bulls keep the cows together. Cows also play an active part in mate selection by not accepting younger bulls readily while the harem bull is still active.

This keeps them off long enough for the harem bull to chase them away.

For each cow the rut ends as soon as she is fertilized. Thereafter, unencumbered by males, she is free to find the best possible nutrition. In the ensuing winter she carries antlers long after the bulls have lost theirs and so can stand her ground when feeding in the snow.

Dominance and Leadership

Among *Rangifer* species, dominance and leadership are distinct qualities describing different kinds of social relationships within a herd. *Dominance* arises from physiological status, marked by the possession of antlers. It shifts according to season, antlered bulls having their own hierarchy and being dominant over cows in autumn, and cows achieving their own hierarchy and being dominant over antlerless bulls in the winter. Senior bulls shed their antlers earlier than their juniors; yearling and sterile cows shed toward the end of winter; pregnant cows and calves (see later discussion) retain theirs throughout the winter. *Leadership* is associated with security. Most instances of leadership are occasioned by alarm. When alarmed, reindeer seek protection in the herd, bunching tightly together and often revolving in a circle without breaking ranks. H. G. Cumming regards the individual caribou on the open plain, running to seek shelter in the herd, as analogous to the white-tailed deer running from open field to woodlot. Reindeer separated from the herd by dogs or people put all their effort into rejoining it. Those on the periphery push to gain the greater protection of the center, and there is a constant changing of places.[51]

N. P. Naumov and L. M. Baskin label this flight to the herd the "protective reflex." If the threat is not perceived to abate, the herd is likely to run, following any animal that breaks away. They interpret this as a process whereby the "protective reflex" is outweighed or overtaken by an active "defensive reflex."[52] They and B. R. Thomson consider the leaders in this situation the more sensitive and more nervous animals. I suggest they are also among the more alert and experienced. Naumov and Baskin say that age and sex have little to do with it: The animals may be calves, yearlings, or fully adult. Particularly nervous are wild reindeer that temporarily join a pastoral herd.[53] Thomson records cows, especially when accompanied by calves, as frequent leaders. These animals clearly have the most need to be alert to danger.[54]

The difference between nervous and experienced response to alarm is easily observed in the field. Young and nervous animals usually run into wind and uphill, disregarding the position of the source of alarm. Experienced animals are more likely to note the position and if appropriate lead downwind to avoid it.[55]

Leadership is seen also where there is no alarm. Cows aged five or six years take the lead where experience may be important. They are commonly found leading herds, for example, along established trails between pastures. Here the "leadership" of an individual is probably less significant than the tendency of the herd to follow. The leader becomes an "action model" for the other animals.[56] The experience of this kind of leader becomes the "common property" of the group.[57] Natural selection will favor those that follow. The loner that wanders off on its own is more likely to encounter a predator. Among those that lead from experience, there is no evidence of competition for the role. Leadership passes readily from one animal to another and, unlike dominance, is not won and lost by agonistic behavior.

Both dominance and leadership may appear at any season. During the rut harem bulls dramatically exhibit dominance, while the herded cows quietly lead each other with the bull or bulls following. Thomson notes that in all-male groups outside the rut, only males that have shed antlers assume the role of leader; males that have yet to shed show dominance at feeding and lying sites, but no interest in leadership. Indeed in such groups in winter pastures a dominant animal may force another into continuing its leadership. Senior cows on winter pastures show dominance over access to craters and leadership in finding foraging areas with optimal snow cover conditions.[58]

Social Signals

The premier signal of dominance is possession of a head of antlers. In the winter, little display on the part of the antlered females is necessary for them to dominate at the craters. As Skogland observed:

Confrontations involving antler fights, leg kicks or rushes at the crater holder were the least frequent acts, followed by antler threats. The most commonly observed act was a direct approach, often from a distance of 20-30 m., towards a crater holder, upon which the holder abandoned the crater. [This behavior] increased significantly as winter progressed.[59]

In autumn, when male domination is directed towards the monopolization of females, male demonstration signals include antler rushes at other males, bush-trashing (i.e., beating bushes with the antlers), and muzzling and pawing the ground.[60] A common alarm signal is a "prolonged urination stance, a high-stepping gait with tail up and an alarm bark."[61] The signal of leadership seems to be simply being out in front: The movement of the leader leads others to move, whose movement leads yet others. This happens through chain reaction, which looks like imitation yet is governed by reflexive, not deliberated response.[62] Naumov and Baskin describe the process vividly as an unexpected shock passing through the flock, much as a jolt from a locomotive is transmitted from carriage to carriage.[63] The animals do what they see being done:

When the leader, who may be ten to fifteen metres in advance of the herd, starts trotting so the herd behind trots; when the leader stops so the herd stops behind; when the leader walks the herd walks; and so on. The direct visual control of activity between leader and followers continues until the leader returns to normal activity, such as grazing or lying, and is re-integrated into the herd.[64]

Olfactory signals may also be involved, according to Thomson: In response to a trail scent from the interdigital glands of the deer ahead, animals behind the leader dip their muzzles to the track, assessing and copying the same activity even when the animals ahead are out of sight.

Sensory signals that facilitate social organization are evident from the earliest moments in a calf's life. Following birth, mother and calf stay in continuous close proximity long enough to allow mutual recognition based on olfaction. When the mother starts grazing, the calf is not always able to follow closely. Its grunts or bleats prompt the mother to join the calf and to smell, lick, and nurse it. Repeated reunions with subsequent care provide mutual rewards, which reinforce and accelerate learning.[65] Body contact occurs between animals only during the maturing relationship between mother and calf, and during mating.

Cows that have lost their calves, or are barren, will attempt to attract the newborn calves of others. A mother with her new calf maintains "a sort of moving, defended territory."[66] Should they find themselves separated after they have joined the herd, calf and mother each remember where they were last together and return to that place to await the other.

Visual signs are used among adults in a foraging group. For example, dominance is established by antler size and shape, and most ritualized threats are visual. Grazing in sight of other animals may induce an imitative response;[67] the sight of a nursing calf may release the stimulus for a strange calf to try sucking.[68] Alarm postures are entirely visual.

At distances beyond the group, visual recognition of signals is less certain. Sounds are little used except during the rut: Only smells are available to reinforce the distant signals that are indistinctly seen or heard. A reindeer can pick out distant movements and (especially with such common predators as wolves and men) discern a telltale visual pattern. If uncertain it is likely to postpone flight and move downwind of what it sees, so catching its smell.[69] Sense of smell is also used directly to follow a leader that has passed out of sight.

Social Organization in Herds

In view of our interest in reindeer pastoralism, where discrete herds of animals are maintained through human control, it is appropriate to review the question of what constitutes a natural herd of reindeer. In the foraging and reproductive groups we have examined, order exists because each animal maintains its position in relation to the others, at distances determined by its food and reproductive requirements according to sex and age, and enforced through signals of dominance. Each animal has a place in the group according to a "definite dominance hierarchy, with the result that the outcome of almost any confrontation could be predicted according to this relationship."[70]

In winter, for example, confrontations are mainly about the use of craters. Following Skogland, a crater is "a territory which the holder must be able to defend if the energy exerted in digging it is not to be wasted."[71] The first line of defense is energy-conserving signals of dominance, and the antlerless males do not waste energy in competing with the cows. As an Alaskan reindeer herder put it: "In the rut the bulls are male, but the cows are male in the winter."[72] Calves do not attempt confrontations with larger animals, but antlered calves in their first winter use the antlers in confrontation with each other and may even nudge an adult male out of the way.[73] The calves' ability to fend for themselves is important since it enhances the viability of gravid mothers and hence of the population as a whole.[74] Only among young animals are group rules offended. Yearlings may try to attach themselves to mothers (not necessarily their own) with new calves, even showing aggression toward the calves when signals fail, the mothers rebuffing them by physical force and driving them away, especially during the early post-calving period.[75]

These hierarchically informed groups live in a definable pattern of social interactions, with no constancy of group composition. The herds can still be "temporary, tenuous associations of individuals."[76] Such structure ensures that any animal that joins the group takes its dominance-determined place within it.

It is not clear whether reindeer are aware of each other as individuals, independent of their awareness of categories of sex and age. Espmark's conclusion that "the ability of individual recognition in socially living animals is an important basis for the maintenance of the social organization" may apply to a small group of animals in the confines of a research station but is almost certainly an overstatement for larger groups.[77] Herd aggregations can be maintained on the category distinctions of age and sex, and little more than that is likely to be possible when animals are in large groups.[78]

F. L. Miller et al. wrote of "the supposition . . . that one of the primary functions of post-calving migratory movements among caribou . . . is socialization by creating a favourable situation for regrouping of previous social groups with minimal social strife."[79] It would be helpful to know whether individual reindeer select each other's company and whether groups exclude individuals that wish to join them. Miller implies that this is so: "The core of the wintertime cow-juvenile band is formed by a matriarchal bloodline, supplemented from time to time by neighbouring caribou as and when the group accepts them."[80] Otherwise, instances of selection and rejection relate to categories of sex and age rather than individual animals: the antagonistic bulls in the rut; the protective nursing cow; and, most interestingly, the dispersal (but not forcible ejection) of male calves from their natal groups, which effectively prevents incestuous breeding.[81]

A herd, then, is a small group that is interacting for the time being, and no more or less than that. Within a herd there may very well be coteries of animals, like intimates in a crowd, that keep each other company through the seasons: for example, the "matriarchical bloodline" that Miller mentions, and which the Saami confirm.

Conclusions

Three principal features in the social organization of a reindeer herd have been identified: synchrony, dominance, and leadership. The first two are dramatically demonstrated in the rut and at calving—the climactic occasions in the annual cycle. But we see also all the principles of social organization activated in the everyday occasions of flight, bunching, and dispersal again into loosely separated foraging groups, and in peaceful movement across the terrain. Continuously through the year, they set the pulse beat of a herd, wild or pastoral.

We see this social organization as a system of signals and responses, and an important step toward understanding it is taken with the separation between relations of dominance and leadership and their respective signals. The transition from wild to pastoral herds happened within the framework of this social organization. It endures, in the main, in pastoral herds today.

Appendix 2.
Composing Herds
(Tables A.1 –A.12)

Table A.1. The Seven Herds (herd size before calving)

Gow'dojottelit		Oar'jebelli
3 njar'ga	*2 nanne*	*1 nanne and 1 njar'ga*
(group A, Fig. 7.1)	(group A/B, Fig. 7.1)	(group B, Fig. 7.1)
#1 1,000	#4 500	#6 1,000
#2 400	#5 200	#7 500
#3 200		

Table A.2. Herd Variances

(a) Variances in herd composition as % of total herd, before calving.

	Across the 7 herds	*Within the herd groupings*		
		#1–3	#4–5	#6–7
Cows	7	2	2	5
Bulls	2	1	0	0
Castrates	8	6	3	0
Yearlings	8	3	0	5
Calves	6	3	1	0

(b) Variances in slaughter of herd components, end of winter

	Across the 7 herds	*Within the herd groupings*		
		#1–3	#4–5	#6–7
Cows	14	14	5	6
Bulls	39	19	17	6
Castrates	51	17	15	5
Yearlings	—	—	—	—
Calves	10	8	6	1

Table A.3. Reproduction: Calf Survival Percentages

Cow Herd	Date				
	15/5	15/6	31/8	31/12	1/5
#1	80	74	?	67	64
#2	76	69	?	58	56
#3	70	65	?	53	51
#4	88	84	?	73	71
#5	95	88	?	75	72
#6	?	?	60	58	53
#7	75	70	65	64	59

Note: ? = owner without sufficient knowledge

Table A.4. Reproduction: Percentages and Kinds of Rodno

Cow Herd	Mother and Calf	Sæiva-Rodno	Čoavčes
#1	74	20	6
#2	69	24	7
#3	65	30	5
#4	84	12	4
#5	88	5	7
#6	(60)	(10)	(30)
#7	70	15	15

Note: ( ) = owner has uncertain knowledge

Table A.5. Losses through twelve months (1 April to 1 April)

Herd	% of Herd	% of Calves	% of Yearlings	% of Cows	% of Males
#1	9	9	2	7	23
#2	9	9	4	5	21
#3	8	9	6	3	18
#4	7	10	3	5	9
#5	7	10	5	5	10
#6	10	14	7	10	5
#7	7	10	4	5	13

Table A.6. Percentages of Male Animals

Herd	Males to Females (at end of winter)	Studs to Females (entering rut)	Studs to Castrates (entering rut)
#1	40	20	102
#2	38	12	43
#3	50	11	28
#4	34	10	42
#5	43	14	46
#6	24	13	120
#7	25	14	112

Note: Yearlings and calves excluded

Table A.7. Percentages of Bulls (at end of winter)

Herd	% of All Males			>4-yrs. as % of All Bulls
	2 yrs.	3 yrs.	>4 yrs.	
#1	100	59	26	12
#2	100	41	24	18
#3	100	23	10	9
#4	100	50	47	30
#5	100	57	24	18
#6	100	81	42	28
#7	100	100	62	66

Note: Yearlings and calves excluded

Table A.8. Percentages of Castrates (at end of winter)

Herd	% of All Males			>4 yrs as % of All Castrates	% as Draft Animals
	2 yrs	3 yrs	>4 yrs		
#1	0	41	74	64	69
#2	0	59	76	71	86
#3	0	77	90	64	61
#4	0	50	53	77	96
#5	0	43	76	68	79
#6	0	19	58	85	70
#7	0	0	38	100	100

Note: Yearlings and calves excluded

Table A.9. Changing Herd Percentages

	% of Cows	% of Bulls	% of Castrates	% of Yearlings	% of Calves	Total
#1(a)	37	9	5	22	27	100
(b)	48	18	7	–	27	100
(c)	47	15	5	–	26	93
#2(a)	39	8	6	20	27	100
(b)	48	17	8	–	27	100
(c)	40	12	6	–	24	82
#3(a)	38	8	11	19	24	100
(b)	47	14	15	–	24	100
(c)	41	10	10	–	21	82
#4(a)	35	8	4	23	30	100
(b)	47	15	8	–	30	100
(c)	43	13	3	–	27	86
#5(a)	33	8	7	23	29	100
(b)	45	16	10	–	29	100
(c)	38	10	6	–	25	79
#6(a)	40	7	3	22	28	100
(b)	51	14	7	–	28	100
(c)	44	6	3	–	26	79
#7(a)	35	7	3	27	28	100
(b)	48	19	5	–	28	100
(c)	44	10	2	–	26	82

Note: (a) pre-rut; (b) post-rut; (c) after winter slaughter

Table A.10. Production: Slaughter Percentages

Herd	As % of Herd Component	As % of Total Herd (post-rut)	As % of Total Slaughter for the Year
	Bulls		
#1	30	3	40
#2	57	5	26
#3	45	4	20
#4	27	2	17
#5	77	6	29
#6	(75)	7	36
#7	(70)	10	50
	Castrates		
#1	37	2	29
#2	37	7	13
#3	43	16	24
#4	(75)	5	36
#5	63	4	20
#6	(75)	4	20
#7	(70)	3	16
	Cows		
#1	2	1	13
#2	20	8	43
#3	20	6	31
#4	12	4	30
#5	19	6	31
#6	16	6	35
#7	11	4	22
	Yearlings and Calves		
#1	3	1	18
#2	7	3	18
#3	10	5	24
#4	4	2	17
#5	8	4	20
#6	4	2	9
#7	4	2	12

Note: ( ) = uncertain figure

Table A.11. Production: Income in Kroner

	Slaughter %	Annual Kroner	Kroner:Animal Ratio	% Growth
#1	7	6,885	5	11
#2	18	7,627	14	1
#3	19	2,497	9	(−3)
#4	14	8,510	12	9
#5	21	4,050	14	1
#6	20	30,515	20	(−2)
#7	18	11,415	19	3

Note: Kroner incomes are based on the following median slaughter weights of adult animals at 5 kroner per kilogram:

	Weights (kg)		
	Maximum-Minimum	Median	Kroner
#1–3	41–19	27	135
#4–5	44–22	30	150
#6–7	43–21	29 and 21	145 and 105

Figures are approximate. Slaughter weights are probably on the low side, but this is balanced, in part, by the price per kilogram usually being something less than a full 5 kroner. Joints are calculated as half of slaughter weights. The figures for herds #6 and #7 take into account the large number of varek sold (at 21 kg and 105 kroner).

Table A.12. Production: Modes of Slaughter and Sale (%)

Herd	Domestic	Joints	On-the-hoof
#1	31	21	48
#2	32	23	45
#3	45	35	20
#4	30	21	49
#5	37	34	29
#6	17	0	83
#7	26	0	74

Notes

Preface

1. "Lapp" carries negative connotations. The people's own name for themselves is, in nominative singular, *sabmi;* in accusative and genitive singular, *sami;* and in nominative plural, *samit.* Following Anderson (1978b:179), I use Saami "for both singular and plural, individual and society, culture and language, noun and adjective." The "aa" in this English-language rendering is phonetically appropriate, avoiding the sounds of "Sam" and "same."

2. Nevertheless, there is a problem: While able to disregard changes that I know have happened subsequently to this reindeer pastoralism, I am less able to account for changes or developments in my thinking about what I recorded years before. However, I have taken care not to mix information gleaned from my readings of biologists and other scholars (see Notes and Appendix 1) with what the Saami told me about their pastoralism. Also, where I am uncertain about the source of an entry I find in my journal (for instance, "the deer seem to dig more with right foot than left"), I either omit it or note the uncertainty.

Introduction

1. There are these authoritative sources on Kautokeino: Smith 1938 (in Norwegian, with German summary) is a history from the sixteenth century to the early twentieth century; the author was the pastor in Kautokeino between 1910 and 1922. Steen 1956 and 1963 (in Norwegian) are archival studies of Kautokeino and Masi; the author worked with Norges Finnemisjonsselskap. Anderson 1978a (in English) is an exhaustive account of resource management (and other matters); the author did anthropological fieldwork in Kautokeino over a five-year period (1972–77).

2. Thirty thousand is an (unchanging) official estimate; however, all such figures are no more than rough indicators (see Aubert 1978). In the 1960s, language (as an "objective" criterion) was the decisive marker deciding who is a Saami for census purposes. Today, though, weight is given to the "subjective" criterion: "I consider myself a Saami" or "I am not a Saami" (Hætta 1992:10).

3. Of course, the Norwegians are making inroads into the niche, through administration, sport fishing and hunting, mining, NATO, and hydroelectric schemes. Since the 1960s, these incursions have assumed symbolic significance in Saami ethnopolitics (Paine 1982, 1984, 1985).

4. For an ethnohistorical account of the Alta area, see Björklund 1985.

5. Grimsby and Hull trawlers on their way to and from the fishing grounds in the Barents Sea would steam—under pilot—inside the islands off the North Norwegian coast, perhaps refueling or provisioning at Tromsö and taking on

or dropping off the pilot at Lödingen, in the Lofotens, and Honningsvåg, at the North Cape. Courtesy of the trawler skippers, I thus hitched my way out to the field or back to Oxford on several occasions.

6. See Eidheim 1971 [1966]:25–37.

7. Paine 1957 and 1965.

8. Towards the close of World War II, the retreating Germans carried out a scorched-earth policy throughout Finnmark. A few inhabitants, but just about all of the reindeer Saami population, hid in the terrain. The majority were evacuated to the south. So the 1950s were a time of rebuilding.

9. I also had two other teachers: Jacob Börretzen of the then Finnemisjonen (his master stroke was to melt down the several hundred turgid pages of the classic Konrad Nielsen grammar to an assailable thirty odd); and Thor Frette, the pioneer in Norway of Saami radio (his childhood was in Karasjok) and subsequently lecturer in the Department of Finno-Ugric, University of Oslo.

10. In the following chapters, that spring migration concludes the sequence of seasons.

11. Research results were published in Paine 1982, 1987, and 1989. Contamination from the Chernobyl fallout affected the South Saami area. Pastures in Finnmark were untouched at that time.

Chapter 1. The Pastoral Logic

1. Vorren and Manker 1962 is the standard ethnographic overview of Saami culture in English. Odner 1985 is an archaeologist's discussion of ethnic processes in northern Fenno-Scandia. Among Saami authors writing about reindeer pastoralism are the 1910 classic, Turi 1931 (English translation); Skum 1955 (in Swedish); and Ruong 1956. Vorren 1951 (in Norwegian) is a description of Saami reindeer pastoralism from the 1940s in South Varanger, in Finnmark; and Vorren 1962 (in Norwegian) is a cartographic description of the seasonal migration routes of the Saami of Finnmark from 1952 to 1957. Several anthropologists have published monographs from Saami pastoral communities (with more emphasis, in most cases, on social relations than on pastoral ecology and economy): Whitaker 1955, Pehrson 1964 [1957], Pelto 1962, Ingold 1976, Svensson 1976, Anderson 1978a, and Beach 1981.

2. Also, of the different species in the deer family (Cervidae) only the reindeer *(Rangifer tarandus)* has been included in nomadic pastoralism (Vorren 1951:17).

3. For more on these matters, see Ingold 1980.

4. On "milk" or "milch" and "carnivorous" pastoralism in general among the Saami, see Beach 1981, Ingold 1980, Hultblad 1969. Falkenberg (1986:7–29) gives a key description (from the South Saami) of the change from primarily milk production to primarily meat production.

5. Skjenneberg and Slagsvold 1968:50–124. See also Appendix 1, this volume.

6. And "seasonal changes in the climates of *Rangifer* are extreme in comparison to those of all other *cervidae*" (Henshaw 1968:225).

7. Consider, for instance, the Nuer pattern in the Sudan, in contrast to that of the Basseri in Iran (Evans-Pritchard 1940; Barth 1961).

8. However, the Reindeer Management Act of 1978 has since restricted this practice (see Part Four).

9. Unlike other pastoral economies, with the tundra reindeer there has been a direct transition from hunting to pastoralism, with little taming. Ingold (1980:85, cf. 141) suggests this accounts for its "apparent 'wildness,' both morphological and behavioral."

10. As with most pastoral nomadic societies, these Saami practice anticipatory inheritance. Thus, family herd capital is redistributed as each child marries.

11. This is entirely a matter of emphasis, for all nomadic pastoralism is a movement between pastures and, hence, "transhumant."

12. For other discussions of some of these points see Beach 1981, Dyson-Hudson 1972, Ingold 1980, Salzman 1967, and Whitaker 1955.

13. Supposing the pastoral animals escape illness and all predators, and are not slaughtered, they may, according to Vorren (1951:23), live as long as twenty years, even twenty-five in the case of cows.

14. Salzman 1986 is a collection of papers on the theme of territoriality among cattle, camel, and sheep, as well as among reindeer nomadic pastoralists. See also Nelson 1973.

15. A separate matter are Saami (aboriginal) land claims. See Thuen 1980, with an extensive bibliography.

16. Officially, summer pastures are open between 1 May and 30 September, and winter pastures (area 31) between 1 October and 31 May. A few herds (e.g., those from Stjernöy, numbers VIII and IX in Figure 4.2) are allowed to winter in area 30, designated as autumn pasture. Most Gow'dojottelit herds also calve in area 30. A few families from Kautokeino have herds on the island of Söröy, but because these remain out there all the year round (their herd management is characterized as "stationary"), no account is taken of them here.

17. Most of all, perhaps, the state wishes to regulate and limit numbers of both reindeer and pastoralists. At the time of

which I write, this had not yet come about (but see Part Four).

18. For an account of how international boundaries have affected pastoral movement, see Elbo 1952.

19. For Gow'dojottelit, the 1962 figures are 84 percent for married men and 65 percent for married women (the difference reflects the greater engagement of men in herding). For a fuller account, see Paine 1970a.

20. Saami kin and affinal relations are on a thoroughgoing bilateral/cognatic basis, so that near "siblinghood" reaches to cousins and siblings' spouses. For the classical statement, see Pehrson 1964 [1957].

21. External incursions (see note 3, Introduction) are another matter. For a case study see Björklund and Brantenberg 1981; Paine 1982.

22. Lappefogden i Finnmark 1961:8.

23. Lappefogden i Finnmark 1962:12.

Chapter 2. Herding and Husbandry

1. The word for reindeer herd is ællo (cf. ællem, life; and ællet, to live), literally "what one lives on" (Ruong 1967:44).

2. However, there is evidence from elsewhere and from another time of greater intervention. Among the Saami of Jukkasjav'ri (Sweden) before World War II, for example, it was said, "[We] keep the strain of our animals pure by castrating any strange bull [that wanders into the herd]" (Ruong 1937), and there is a similar report from South Varanger (Vorren 1951). Actually, this may have been a general practice where herds were kept effectively separated from one another, as was common also in Kautokeino before World War II. On the other hand, perhaps planned breeding of livestock should only be expected in the context of a market economy (Ingold 1980:84); and in the increasing market orientation of herd production in Kautokeino already in the early 1960s (see later chapters), some Saami shared that view even while largely frustrated in their efforts to implement it.

3. This was no longer the case after the Reindeer Law of 1978. For a Saami glossary with English translations of sadjek, see Anderson 1978a:94–97.

4. Of these, several hundred belonged to sedentary Saami, with a few animals in the care of pastoralists.

5. Lappefogden i Finnmark 1961:9 and 1962:14.

6. There is, of course, a flow in the other direction too: A husbandry measure such as earmarking is of assistance in herding; similarly, allocation of gaskek (essentially a husbandry decision) as draft animals facilitates the work of herders.

7. Ingold (1980:116–18) notes in some detail "the striking continuity on the technological level between [reindeer] hunting and pastoralism."

8. For the importance of taming in the evolution of viable reindeer pastoralism, see Ingold 1980. Milking of reindeer (a practice by 1992 all but disappeared among the northern Saami) also requires a degree of tameness. On the earlier importance of "milch pastoralism" among reindeer breeders see, besides Ingold, Beach 1981 and Hultblad 1968.

9. Ruong (1968:294) noted an association between tameness and herd cohesion among Saami herds in Sweden. However, he interpreted this as accentuating "herd instinct"; I think the proper general proposition must be, as tameness increases, herd instinct goes into operational decline. In known cases of extreme tameness, among some Tungus herds and the Cairngorm herd in Scotland (Shirokogoroff 1929:35; Utsi, personal communication), individual animals are even given names to which they respond on call.

10. Beach 1981:41.

11. Espmark 1971b:75. For background to this point, see Appendix 1.

12. At the heart of the matter there is even the problem of how to recognize this awareness among reindeer, even where we suppose it should be present. How, for instance, does one interpret the fact that a person may wander into a pastoral herd and kill an animal (noiselessly, with a knife), then and there, without causing any apparent disturbance to its fellows? Does it mean an absence of individual awareness of each other? Or is it evidence of awareness being manifested in indifference? The question remains an open one for me.

13. Thomson 1975:471.

14. Miller et al. 1975:62.

15. Reimers (1972) has data concerning factors (herding stress and insufficient nutrition being the principal ones) associated with loss of weight by pastoral reindeer in South Norway and comparisons with the weights of wild reindeer in that region.

16. Skuncke 1969:44.

17. Nick Tylor, personal communication.

18. Thomson 1975:468. See the discussion of Rangifer "leadership" in Appendix 1.

Chapter 3. Summer Growth

1. Information from Nick Tylor, a biologist.

2. Ibid.

3. See Skjenneberg and Slagsvold 1968:125–64.

4. See Eidheim 1971 [1966]:25–37; Paine 1957:249–51.

Chapter 4. Autumn Commotion

1. However, multiple-pen corrals were in use earlier elsewhere in Norway, Finland, and Sweden.
2. See Vorren 1944; Ingold 1980:56–57.
3. See Figure I.3 for the relationships of the principal actors.
4. These men had all used areas V or VII in past years. This year the unusual arrangement of putting their combined male herd on V and the remainder of their animals on VII was made opportunistically.
5. See Appendix 1.
6. Information from Nick Tylor, a biologist.

Chapter 5. The Dark and the Peace

1. Castrates shed their antlers later than bulls; exactly when varies. See Chapter 2.
2. At Christmas, people are usually too busy to leave the herds for long.
3. In 1951, on a Nuor'tabelli autumn migration, we spent seven and a half days on a separation without corral.
4. In some Saami areas remote from Finnmark the her'gi is approached from the right—the point is, however, that this, too, is a consistent rule learned by both the animal and its handlers.
5. Iskun Biera, with a herd of over one thousand animals, has around seventy castrates to choose from—7 percent of the herd; Jorgu Biera, with fewer than three hundred animals, has no more than about twenty castrates—yet this amounts to about twice the (post-rut) herd percentage of Iskun Biera.
6. The explanation lies in the ecology of the pastoral seasons (see Chapter 3). Spring (calving) herds are usually smaller than winter herds.
7. These issues will be explored in *Saami Camps: Politics of Reindeer Wealth,* in preparation.

Chapter 6. Spring Calves

1. These journal excerpts are based on notes kept by Inger-Anna Gunnare Paine.

Chapter 7. Patterns and Process

1. There are exceptions. In one case on Nuor'tabelli, for instance, calving happens short of the summer pastures yet a good distance from—and davelli of—the male herd (Fig. 6.2).
2. Regarding castration, see Chapter 2; on slaughter, Chapters 8 and 9.

3. See Paine 1970b for a fuller account.
4. The model is discussed again in Chapter 16, with new inputs.
5. On the social organization of the reindeer, see Appendix 1.
6. Again, I draw upon Paine 1970b.
7. These and kindred issues will be explored and documented more fully in *Saami Camps,* in preparation.

Chapter 8. Value Shift

1. Nils Nilsson Skum (1872–1951) spent his life in Swedish Lappland, but, like Johan Turi (1931), he was a Kautokeino Saami by parentage (Skum 1938).
2. I take the term from Macpherson 1962.
3. All outer clothing is of reindeer skin.
4. On intensive and extensive herd management, see Hultblad 1936; Skum 1955; Whitaker 1955; Ruong 1956; Paine 1972; Ingold 1976; and Beach 1981.
5. Reindeer sinews are used for sewing reindeer skin clothing.
6. A situation similar to the one I have described pertains among the Skolt Saami of Finland: "The decision as to whether or not to slaughter comes to depend not on the quality, age and sex of the deer, but on whether it happens to be found" (Ingold 1976:43). This contrasts dramatically with earlier accounts of intensive herd management with herding and husbandry closely synchronized (Utsi 1948; Beach 1981:88ff.).
7. For animals of one year and over, 130 kroner; for calves, 65 kroner.
8. Movinkel 1968 [1962]:347, table 18.
9. Anyone in Finnmark can read in the newspapers the amount of taxes a person paid in the previous year. The presence of a few Saami pastoralists each year among the highest taxpayers in the province unfailingly evoked comment, and this put something of a brake on any popular perception of "those reindeer Saami" as tax dodgers.
10. However, it is really only the tax authorities who would wish (or have the authority) to compare figures, and there are institutional safeguards. The county might wish to make a check, but permission of the head of the provincial tax office is required; and so, in practice, it is, I think, an uncommon occurrence.

Chapter 9. Composing Herds

1. Compositional difficulties with two "herds" from Nuor'tabelli led me to abandon them.
2. The important exception, on the Oar'jebelli range particularly (see below), is the loss of emaciated (gorm-fly-rid-

den) calves and yearlings towards the end of winter.

3. In the case of herd #6: cows 7 percent, bulls 8 percent, and castrates 4 percent (total 19 percent); and herd #7: cows 4 percent, bulls 9 percent, and castrates 3 percent (total 16 percent; Table A.9). Table A.10 summarizes the distribution of slaughter by herd category among the seven owners.

4. Similarly, we saw how at the autumn separations in the multiple corrals, Iskun Biera, as the person with the largest herd, had proportionately the least work (see the discussion of vuoððo, Chapter 4).

5. Besides the Buljo crowd, there have always been some others.

6. The historical process behind this situation will be treated in *Saami Camps*, in preparation.

7. Table A.12 summarizes the distribution of the different modes of slaughter among the seven owners.

8. Ideally one should have both of these two kinds of herd knowledge, and in our sample it is the owners of herds #4, #5, and #7 who approach nearest to this ideal.

9. This ideal type formulation is Ingold's (1980:239). It is a powerful heuristic. Ingold, however, uses it to make the distinction between "pastoralism" and "ranching." In the context of my Kautokeino data, I am unhappy with such a separation, preferring to let "ranching" denote one particular pastoral strategy, that is, the "Oar'jebelli" kind. (Incidentally, among Kautokeino pastoralists in the 1960s there were *metaphorical* references to the allegedly uncontrolled pastoralism over at Karasjok as "ranching" and the "wild west." The animals were so "wild" that guns sometimes replaced lassos.)

Chapter 10. Two Cultures

1. Lappefogden i Finnmark 1961:4–5; Lappefogden i Finnmark 1962:7.
2. Movinkel 1968 [1962]:272–76.
3. Lappefogden i Finnmark 1962:7.
4. Movinkel 1968 [1962]:273.
5. Ibid., 276.
6. Ibid.
7. Ibid.
8. The Reindeer Administration in Finnmark mentions in its annual reports for 1961 and 1962 that the stamping of "bush"-slaughtered meat *is* satisfactory (i.e., permitted) except that those responsible are without the reindeer marks' protocol. So there could be a trade in stolen carcasses. It hopes to correct this in the near future (Lappefogden i Finnmark 1961:5–6; Lappefogden i Finnmark 1962:9).
9. This did not happen until 1968, and then not through

private banks (Statens Landbruksbank only).

10. He had come to Kautokeino (after studying law) as a young police officer before the war, and during the war (still in Kautokeino) he was a key figure in the Norwegian underground intelligence. Thus, the seeds of the legend that grew up around the man were sown. He was awarded the Order of St. Olav and, in 1956, was appointed to the Royal Commission on the Saami Question (Komiteen til å Utrede Samespörsmål).

11. Compare the comments of the Reindeer Administration cited earlier in this chapter.

12. Dahl's efforts on their behalf in this matter were often remarked upon, as was also the reluctance of the government. The scheme was introduced a few years later.

13. Note is taken in the annual reports of the Reindeer Administration in Finnmark of progress, or otherwise, with the scheme: "No money voted this year. But many of the pastoralists require such help—if they are to remain in the livelihood" (Lappefogden i Finnmark 1961:7). Again in 1962, no money is voted, but it is understood that there will be a vote of money next year. The report includes the following update since the program's inception: "Between 1953/55, 50 families [in Finnmark] received 2725 animals. These were added to their stock of 4199, making a total of 6924 in 1955. Six years later the total was 9071, an increase of 2147 or 31%. 30 of the families have increased their herds, 7 have remained the same size, 5 have left pastoralism, and in 16 cases the herds have decreased. Overall, these results must be considered as positive" (Lappefodgen i Finnmark 1962:7).

14. Turi 1931:70–71. Johan Turi began life as a herder in Kautokeino, later moving to North Sweden.

Chapter 11. The Terms of Authority

1. Weber 1969:153.
2. Gluckman 1969:170.
3. Storting 1978, emphases added. The inclusion of "and protection of rights" came in with the final version approved by Parliament. It was not in the draft prepared by the Ministry of Agriculture (Landbruksdepartementet 1976–77).
4. Todorov 1984:165.
5. Odd Mathis Hætta provided the information for these notes (Nov. 1992).

Chapter 12. Modernization

1. Eira 1984:56. It appears to be a similar story across northern Fenno-Scandia. Over the border from Kautokeino, in

Utsjoki, Finland, four reindeer Saami purchased machines in late 1962, and "within four years . . . the traditional reindeer sled [with her'gi] was abandoned in favor of the snowmobile" (Muller-Wille and Pelto 1971:14). See Pelto 1987 for detailed account from among the Skolt Saami of Finland; cf. Ingold 1975. And on North Sweden, see Beach 1981; cf. Whitaker 1978:172.

2. Ingold 1975.

3. NIBR 1990:165.

4. NIBR 1990:41.

5. Eira 1984:56.

6. Thus a 1966 report on Saami reindeer pastoralism expected that the introduction of snowmobiles would make herding easier and more efficient (Landbruksdepartementet 1966:19).

7. Beach 1981:436–37.

8. Lappefogden i Finnmark 1962:5.

9. Eira 1984:57.

10. Ibid., 56.

11. Ibid., 57.

12. Ibid., 58.

13. I do not have the data for a household budget—more on household economy in the next chapter.

14. As to the introduction of mechanization, I think it would be incorrect to say that it followed as a consequence of the trend, already evident, towards "extensive" herding (argued for Finnish Lapland in Ingold 1975 and 1978).

15. Eira 1984:61.

16. Full treatment of this multidimensional problem is still lacking; see the bibliography in Thuen 1980. Storting 1978 addresses, in legal terms, issues of rights, culpability, and redress of concerned parties.

17. *Reindriftsnytt* 1986 (3): 20–22; see also 1979 (4): 24–25; 1980 (1): 8; and 1984 (1): 31.

18. For a case study see Björklund and Brantenberg 1981; Paine 1982.

19. Cited in Paine 1982:77, 80.

20. The official schedule, in 1992, for ferrying Kautokeino herds out to their spring pastures lists no less than sixty-eight ferries running to a clockwork timetable to serve several locations each day over a period of three weeks, each side of Easter.

21. *Reindriftsnytt* 1987 (2): 14–15.

22. My field notes.

23. *Reindriftsnytt* 1981 (4/5): 3.

24. *Reindriftsnytt* 1981 (1): 30–31.

25. *Reindriftsnytt* 1981 (4/5): 3–4.

26. *Reindriftsnytt* 1981 (4/5): 4 and 1981 (1): 30.

27. *Reindriftsnytt* 1987 (4): 21.

28. *Reindriftsnytt* 1981 (4/5): 4.

29. *Reindriftsnytt* 1982 (1): 4–5.

30. This was in 1982. And in 1987 NRL found it necessary to warn that it would contest in the courts any ruling that disallowed terrain motorcycles.

31. *Reindriftsnytt* 1981 (4/5): 4; and 1987 (4): 20.

32. I deal with these issues in Paine 1982 and 1985.

33. Turi 1989:1.

34. *Reindriftsnytt* 1989 (1): 22–25 (see Chapter 14).

35. My source for this and the following two paragraphs is NRL 1989.

36. For a comparable account from Sweden, see Beach 1992.

37. Beach 1992:11.

38. Beach 1992:12, 14. His own position is quite clear: "Regulations protective of the environment must be formulated and assessed with an awareness of the needs of threatened ethnic groups dependent on that environment" (Beach 1992:14–15).

39. In the early 1960s, most herders wore catalogue-ordered wristwatches, but we very often did not know what day of the week it was, and—as the story of the seasons made very clear—we often kept others waiting and were ourselves kept waiting, days at a time.

40. *Reindriftsnytt* 1987 (4): 21.

41. Ibid., 19.

42. *Reindriftsnytt* 1988 (2): 15. The investment in the truck with its specially designed interior was of the order of 220,000 Norwegian kroner (over $20,000 U.S.).

43. *Reindriftsnytt* 1982 (2): 29.

44. Kosmo 1987e:179, 196–99; Kosmo 1987h:270.

45. Kosmo 1986a [1983]:48.

Chapter 13. Rationalization

1. Whereas advocates of the state's position stress that Saami have obtained "equality" *(likhet)* with Norwegians, Saami advocates fear that this will eventually ensure the demise of Saami culture. What must be achieved, they argue, is not "equality" but recognition of "equal worth" *(likeverd)*.

2. In 1809 Sweden surrendered Finland to Russia, and in 1814 Norway was separated from Denmark and united with Sweden. Concerning the implications of national frontiers for Saami reindeer pastoralism, see Elbo 1952.

3. Landbruksdepartementet 1932:2.

4. Ibid., 5.

5. Solem 1933:183. Solem was a district judge in Finnmark (Tana) for many years and later a preeminent figure in Norwegian jurisprudence. His book *Lappiske Rettsstudier* is a classic.

6. For more detailed treatment see Paine 1984, which I also draw upon here.

7. Landbruksdepartementet 1922:35–36. For commentary see Arnesen 1980 and Tönnesen 1977.

8. Landbruksdepartementet 1922:42–43.

9. A farmer was allowed to shoot a reindeer that wandered into his hay meadow; a pastoralist was not allowed to shoot a dog that was worrying his animals (he should report the incident to the authorities). The conflict-ridden situation was aggravated by the markedly "extensive" nature of northern agriculture, often with more "outfield" than "field."

10. In 1875, the population of Finnmark totaled 24,075 persons, of which 9,807 were entered on the census returns as "Norwegian"; by 1930 the population had advanced to 53,308, of which 35,895 were "Norwegian" (state censuses, cited in Paine 1957:71).

11. Arnold 1969.

12. I deal with this in *Saami Camps*, in preparation.

13. Lappefogden i Finnmark 1961:8 (emphasis added); Lappefogden i Finnmark 1962:13, 16–17.

14. This is not strictly accurate at all.

15. Landbruksdepartementet 1974–75:4–5, 13–14. The retirement program has been spurned (early retirement at sixty-two—instead of sixty-seven—was calculated to produce a reduction of forty-eight thousand animals), and young men (fewer women) stand in a queue to enter the livelihood (NRL 1987c, 1:24, 2:34; Kosmo 1987c:93.

16. Landbruksdepartementet 1976–77:2.

17. Landbruksdepartementet 1976–77:6; Saami reindeer pastoralism is a tradition of a few hundred years (Chapter 1).

18. In monetary terms, the negotiated Agreements (Chapter 11) amount to many millions of kroner annually—as they do (with still more millions) in the case of each of the other primary resource industries. The first Agreement was actually drawn up in 1976, thus preceding the Reindeer Management Act.

19. See the twenty-eight printed pages of negative comments, at both local and national levels, from the other primary resource industries, and from local and provincial government (Landbruksdepartementet 1976–77:11–39).

20. In deep cynicism clothed in bitter irony, the president of the Saami reindeer owners' national association (see Chapter 14)—he watched the passage of the 1978 Act from Parliament's visitors' gallery—remarked: "It's too bad for reindeer pastoralism that it isn't the Norwegians who are the pastoralists!"

21. Arnesen 1980.

22. Storting 1977–78:6. This matter, though now more of an issue (see NOU 1984), has still not been resolved.

23. Landbruksdepartementet 1976–77:6.

24. Ibid., 48.

25. Ibid., 59, and clause 17 of the 1978 Act. Clause 18 of the 1933 Act allows a reindeer owner's spouse and children, irrespective of their age, their own marks—although in the case of Finnmark, there is provision for the province to deny family members their separate marks (as far as I know, this never happened).

26. *Reindriftsnytt* 1991 (1): 4–5.

27. Ottar Brox, personal communication.

28. Following Gusfield (1981:10–15), ownership of such entities is a matter of interplay between "knowledge" and "politics."

29. It is important to know that persons and committees working for the state were also sorely divided at times on questions of cardinal importance. Whereas the existence of the 1978 Act sowed seeds of dissension among the pastoralists after the event, the battles among the state functionaries occurred over the *making* of the Act. A committee struck in 1960 delivered a report in 1966 (Landbruksdepartementet 1966), which, on the key issues just discussed (viz., clauses 4, 7, and 17 of the 1978 Act), was prepared to trust the pastoralists with the prize.

30. And there is, of course, an ultimate "natural" limit to the numbers of animals any pasture can sustain, and when it is surpassed the animals die—from starvation and disease. There are also occasions when natural disasters (not ones that may look "natural" but are in fact induced by pastoral practice) overtake the best-husbanded herd—for example, the icing of winter pastures (Chapter 5).

31. *Nordlys,* 19 Jan. 1988. See also Kosmo and Lenvik 1987; Riseth 1988:5–9.

32. It seemed necessary to spell this out since "natural bearing capacity" has on occasion been used in determinations, and, moreover, the state has allowed (encouraged?) the public to think in such terms—even as the state, from the outset, recognized a responsibility to arrive at a socioeconomic determination of carrying capacity.

33. NIBR 1990:xxix. NIBR (Norsk Institutt for By- og Regionforskning) is an Oslo-based research institute commissioned in this instance by the state and the Saami pastoralists' national association (NRL). For alternative "models" of carrying capacities, see Kosmo 1988:39–42.

34. NRL 1987a, 3:33. In Sweden it is set at 350 animals (Beach 1983:13).

35. Kosmo 1987f:218. They vary not only between individual owners but also between Districts—njar'ga Districts being set at a higher percentage than the others. Such a program of course raises a number of pragmatic issues, aside from the principle of the scheme, and one of these is whether the slaughter percentage should be calculated on the basis of the *number* of carcasses or their *weight*. The former calculation favors those with a high percentage of calf slaughter but penalizes those who, of preference, still select older animals (Kosmo 1987e:205).

36. Kosmo 1987d:110.

37. Of the respondents, 32 percent said no, 28 percent "didn't know," and 40 percent answered it was correct for the state to put down rules—but some said that the rules had to be "for the good of" the livelihood. Those were the countrywide responses. In West Finnmark, however, the "no" was appreciably higher, at 45 percent (Kosmo 1987h:288–89). Other questions that were asked, together with the validity of the questionnaire, are discussed in Chapter 14.

38. Kosmo 1987e:205.

39. Ole K. Sara in NRL 1987a, 1:19.

40. NRL 1987a, 1:22.

41. Sara 1987a:40; see also NRL 1987a, 1:16–20.

42. I call attention just to those programs having direct bearing on the regulation of herd sizes. For an overview of all the programs, see NIBR 1990.

43. Sara 1987b:31ff.; Kosmo 1987d passim.

44. Sara 1987b:47.

45. Eira 1981:8 (emphasis added).

46. Sara 1987a:41. And beyond this matter of calf slaughter, it must also be noted that a tax structure based on the number of animals slaughtered runs directly in the face of a state policy to increase—and dramatically so—slaughter percentages.

47. In the early years, contracts were made with Nord-Norges Salgslag (the marketing board for North Norway) and subsequently with Kjøtt og Flesk Sentralen, the national meat marketing board. See NOU 1977:8.

48. It later became Reinprodukter A/L. For controversy over its management and bankruptcy, and the rebuilding of a modern slaughterhouse in Karasjok, see NRL 1987c, 1–3.

49. Evident in the 1960s (Chapter 10), this sentiment later became politicized (Chapter 14).

50. NIBR 1990:83.

51. Included under price subsidy are "indirect" supportive measures (such as transportation costs) put in place by the state so that the whole amounts to a subsidy of around 12 kroner per kilogram as per 1983–84 (Kosmo and Lenvik 1987:46).

52. Kosmo and Lenvik 1987:46 (emphasis added).

53. The chief of the Reindeer Administration (Ole K. Sara) and the head of the Reindeer Division at the Department of Agriculture represented the state, and two pastoralists— one from Kautokeino (Johan Mathis Turi), the other a South Saami—represented NRL. Ansgar Kosmo and a pasture consultant were enlisted for research assignments.

54. Protokoll 1-Utvalget 1987a, 1987b.

55. Kosmo 1987b:91.

56. Melöy et al. 1987 [1985]:63.

57. NRL 1985; Sara 1987a; Kosmo 1987e, 1987f.

58. Sara 1987c:33.

59. A District that allows any of its members to evade the regulations will itself be cut off from support until the irregularity is rectified.

60. Sara 1987c:33; cf. Kosmo 1987h and discussion in Chapter 14.

61. Melöy et al. 1987 [1985]:61. Estimates are offered.

62. Sara 1987c:33.

63. Ibid., 30.

64. Ibid., 33.

65. Thus two-thirds of the reindeer in West Finnmark are owned by one-third of the pastoral units (Kosmo 1987g:257); and 34 percent of the pastoralists are under thirty-five years and own 22 percent of the total animals, 43 percent are between thirty-five and fifty-four years and own 54 percent, and 23 percent are fifty-five years and over and own 24 percent between them (NIBR 1990:107).

Chapter 14. Contrary Perceptions, Unsettling Consequences

1. NRL 1977–78:12.

2. *Reindriftsnytt* 1979 (4): 16. And again, the executive, in 1981, avers the primacy of "customary rules and premisses" (NRL 1981).

3. NRL 1979–80:15; NRL 1985–86:14.

4. Turi 1987a [1986]:19.

5. *Reindriftsnytt* 1987 (3): 40–41; NRL 1987a, 1:50, 52.

6. *Reindriftsnytt* 1981 (3): 19.

7. Hans Tömmervik, with eleven years as an active pastoralist, studying biology at the University of Tromsö at the time of this statement, was later appointed secretary of NRL (Tömmervik 1981:20).

8. Nils Thomas Utsi (1991:4–5). At NRL meetings through the 1980s the matter of culture conflict would be raised from the floor.

9. Sara 1986b:62. I have found similar statements by Johan Mathis Turi, Kautokeino pastoralist and an influential figure in NRL (Turi 1986), and in a memorandum from Saami pastoralists in Nordland Province (Norway) addressed to the provincial reindeer administration (Henriksen 1986:40–41). I am sure there are others. The contrast with the belief of reindeer administrators in "person work years" and their experts' calculations thereon is stark (Chapter 13).

10. And the pastoralists, in such a situation, need to exert their own sense of legitimacy. Fieldwork among a South Saami group, dependent on outside know-how to get their reindeer pastoralism back on its feet following the contamination of pastures from radioactive fallout from Chernobyl, put this issue under a strong light. Clearly, it

was difficult for them to live with the idea that scientists know more than they do about reindeer and about how to go about correcting the pastoral situation. So, in accepting the experts, they began, at the same time, energetically to defend themselves from them. For example, they rearranged arrangements suggested by experts, thereby exhibiting (to themselves) knowledge beyond the experts' knowledge and reestablishing themselves as practitioners (Paine 1989).

11. NIBR 1990:xxvi, 35, 59.
12. Mathis M. Sara in *Finnmark Dagblad*, 6 Jan. 1989.
13. E.g., NIBR 1990:31, 45.
14. Kosmo and Lenvik 1987:45.
15. Ibid., 43.
16. Eira 1984:61.
17. Eira 1979:1.
18. Gaup 1988. Kirsten Berit Gaup is a Karasjok pastoral Saami.
19. An exception here is Melöy et al. (1987 [1985]:58–59), which took an unqualified favorable view of the traditional two-generational units.
20. NIBR 1990:35, 62. Cf. Lenvik 1988.
21. *Reindriftsnytt* 1980 (1): 20–23.
22. Ibid., 20.
23. *Reindriftsnytt* 1987 (4): 19.
24. *Reindriftsnytt* 1982 (2): 7.
25. *Reindriftsnytt* 1984 (2/3): 12. In the Administration's report for 1989 (Reindriftsstyret 1984–89) there is a note about work on a national system for marking all domesticated/ tamed animals *(husdyr)* with plastic ear-tags that could be read electronically (p. 22).
26. And it is worth noting that the pastoral practitioners themselves were instrumental in effecting this substitution.
27. *Nordlys* (a Tromsö newspaper), 22 Nov. 1986.
28. Ibid.
29. *Nordlys*, 20 Feb. 1987.
30. Utsi 1991:3–7.
31. See discussion in Paine 1989.
32. NRL 1987a, 2:33.
33. *Nordlys*, 23 Feb. 1987.
34. The 33 million kroner spoke to the estimated loss for all Saami pastoralism in Norway—35,000 animals; the Kautokeino share was 20,000 animals.
35. The assumption is strengthened in the light of the inclusive percentage distribution of all the different causes provided by the 1978 report. It is also interesting to note, in view of Smuk's view of the cause of losses, that "sickness" accounted for a mere 3.6 percent of reported losses and "undernourishment" for even less—a paltry 2.9 percent.
36. Reindriftsstyret 1983–84 to 1986–87.
37. *Nordlys*, 20 Feb. 1987.

38. Utsi 1991:6. This is another case of the larger (stronger) calves being selected for slaughter. See Chapter 13.
39. Thus in 1977 the 14.3 percent animals "missing" amounted to 8,000, but by 1989 the 15.5 percent amounted to 26,000.
40. This includes 90 percent of the meat sold on the informal market, Hætta reckons (*Nordlys*, 20 Feb. 1987). The informal market is estimated as handling one-third of all meat sold, or 450 tons (Finnmark) and 600 tons (countrywide): NIBR 1990:83.
41. Beyond the public statements of Hætta and Utsi, there has been a noteworthy—but understandable—silence on the topic or "problem" of "missing" animals. It does not appear in the annual reports of the NRL, nor was it on the agenda, or raised from the floor, of the 1987 NRL-sponsored conference for District foremen (see below). The question of compensation, if any, for lost deer has always been seen as problematic by the state, and its policy here has not been consistent.
42. NRL 1986:1 (transcript of a seminar jointly sponsored by NRL and its Swedish counterpart).
43. Henriksen (1986:12, emphasis added), from field research in Nordland Province of Norway.
44. Sara 1986b:64–65.
45. Storting 1978–79:1293. See the discussion in the previous chapter concerning the inapplicability to pastoralism of a concept of "natural carrying capacity"—of which this statement is an example.
46. Baer et al. 1974:32.
47. For a strong account, see Björklund and Brantenberg 1981 (or in English, Paine 1982).
48. Sara 1986b:65.
49. Tillitsmannskonferanse om Reindriftsavtalen; see Chapter 13.
50. NRL 1987a, 3:7.
51. NRL 1987a, 1:54–55.
52. NRL 1987a, 3:11. For problems that occurred in autumn pastures (and continue today), see Chapter 4.
53. At the time of my fieldwork, however, he—along with all others with whom I spoke about it—was adamantly against any allocation of specific winter pastures to specific herds: See Chapter 5 for the reasoning. On this subject, I would be surprised had opinions today changed much from what they were.
54. NRL 1987a, 3:13–15.
55. Ibid., 16–17.
56. Kosmo 1987h:265–93.
57. And unlike the situation in the 1960s, there are now a few women in this office.
58. Kosmo 1987h:271.
59. Of course this organization has a Saami name (Norgga

Boazosabmelaččaid Riikasærvi), but "NRL" is the common(er) reference.

60. NRL 1987a, 1:7; 2:50, 53.

61. Of Gow'dojottelit and Oar'jebelli, respectively: Compare the 1962 herds of Chapter 9.

62. *Finnmark Dagblad,* 25 Jan. 1989.

63. Gaup is from Kautokeino. My references are to a student paper she wrote while at the University of Tromsö (I. Gaup 1988).

64. I. Gaup 1988:14.

65. Ibid., 15–16.

66. Ibid., 13, 17.

67. "Our membership has increased since the founding of BES. . . . It is impossible for BES to have that many members in Kautokeino and Karasjok, as they claim" (NRL 1987b:3).

68. Precedent for BES's claim is found in the representation, at the bargaining table with the state, of Norwegian farming interests by two (rival) national associations.

69. Odd Erling Smuk (Smuk 1987) and Johan Mathis Turi (Turi 1987b).

70. NRL 1987a, 3:16.

71. Ibid., 50.

72. It is worth noting that the 1933 Act (clause 9) mandated the provincial governor to undertake compulsory counts every fifth year. The intention of the 1978 Act is much the same, but clause 8 places the responsibility with the District committees and provides them with the authority to enforce counts on defiant herd owners.

73. *Finnmark Dagblad,* 22 Sept. 1988.

74. *Finnmark Dagblad,* 16 Aug. 1988. But in an interview with *Reindriftsnytt* (1988 [3]: 33), he dismissed such a view. Saami "culture and tradition" has always been concerned with "facts," he said.

75. *Nordlys,* 11 Oct. 1988.

76. From 27 percent and 33 percent, according to the grading system (Chapter 13), to 37 percent and 43 percent.

77. *Nordlys,* 11 Oct. 1988.

78. But see NRL 1987a, 3:16.

79. The commission, Samerettsutvalget, was appointed in 1980 in the aftermath of the confrontations over the damming of the Alta/Kautokeino River (NOU 1984).

80. *Nordlys,* 11 Oct. 1988.

81. Ibid.

82. Ibid.

83. Ibid.

84. *Finnmark Dagblad,* 29 Oct. 1988, and *Sagat,* 29 Oct. 1988.

85. *Finnmark Dagblad,* 5 Jan. 1989.

86. *Finnmark Dagblad,* 6 Jan. 1989.

87. *Finnmark Dagblad,* 5 Jan. 1989.

88. Ibid.

89. Ibid. Eira is from Karasjok and a member of the Area Board for East Finnmark. State policy and difficulties were discussed in Chapter 13.

90. *Nordlys,* 19 Jan. 1989.

91. *Finnmark Dagblad,* 9 Jan. 1989.

92. Trond Thuen, personal communication; see Brox 1989.

93. The conference was sponsored jointly by NRL, the Reindeer Administration, and the provinces of Finnmark and Troms. It drew an attendance of some 250 people, of whom 150 were invited (*Reindriftsnytt* 1988 [3]: 29; 1989 [1]: 22–25).

94. *Finnmark Dagblad,* 16 Aug. 1988.

95. "Reindeer are the greatest 'milieu threat' to nature in Finnmark today, some people say. We believe they may be right" (*Finnmark Dagblad,* 12 Jan. 1988).

96. *Nordlys,* 19 Jan. 1989.

97. Professor Nils Chr. Stenseth, as reported in *Finnmark Dagblad,* 18 Jan. 1989.

98. *Reindriftsnytt* 1989 (1): 23–25.

99. *Finnmark Dagblad,* 11 Feb. 1989.

100. *Sagat,* Jan. 1989.

101. Even so, as he said at the District foremen's conference, it is not clear what the threshold figure is, or should be.

102. *Finnmark Dagblad,* 21 Mar. 1989.

103. *Finnmark Dagblad,* 22 Sept. 1988.

104. NIBR 1990:91.

105. Björklund 1986:5–6.

106. NIBR 1990:92.

Chapter 15. Tragedy of the Commons or Pastoral Tragedy?

1. The phrase was coined by Hardin (1968); preceding it was the key theoretical notion of "sustainable resource rent" (Gordon 1954).

2. The application is in itself unusual: Most of the commons debate has been waged over the fisheries.

3. Hardin 1968:1244.

4. McCay and Acheson 1987:4.

5. Ibid., 7.

6. Marchak 1987:4–5.

7. McCay and Acheson 1987:9; Marchak (1989:2) also notes that the Tragedy may be "caused by privatization of common property rather than the reverse" (see Botswana case study, below).

8. McCay and Acheson 1987:7.

9. Marchak 1987:28–29.

10. Peters 1987.

11. Ibid., 172; the citation is from a government document.

12. Ibid., 175; the "prisoner's dilemma" formulation.

13. Ibid., 179ff.

14. See "the tragedy of incursion" (McCay and Acheson 1987:29).
15. This methodological procedure is elegantly stated in Maurstad's short paper (1992).
16. I risk this generalization even though the issue has still not been fully studied (Spooner 1971; Dyson-Hudson 1972). Aside from reindeer pastoralism (Leeds 1965, Ingold 1980), see Dahl and Hjort 1976, Boonzajer Flaes 1981, Spencer 1984, as well as the kind of exception to the generalization documented in Barth (1961:101–11).
17. Firth 1964:20. More recently, the very notion of animals as pastoralists' capital has been questioned (Ingold 1980:228 ff.).
18. Paine 1971:167–70; the contrast was with hunters.
19. Brox 1989:18–20; Sahlins 1968.
20. This has been identified as "a universal positive value for all herding peoples" (Aschmann 1965:267).
21. NIBR 1990:xxvi.
22. Ingold 1976, 1978; "ranching" in Ingold 1980.
23. Ingold 1976:89 (cf. Ingold 1978:121 and Ingold 1980:239).
24. Ingold 1978:121.
25. Ibid., 122.
26. Ingold 1976:22.
27. Ingold 1978:122.
28. Ibid., 122–23.
29. Ibid., 104. Actually he intends "predatory pastoralism" to convey a condition out of which emerges ranching (Ingold 1980:235)—hence also "proto-ranching" (Ingold 1980:260).
30. Ingold 1978:127.
31. As reported in *Reindriftsnytt* 1988 (2): 20–21; and 1988 (3): 16–21, the school is accomplishing much, but as late as 1986–87 the Administration was being criticized by the Kautokeino branch of NRL for delays and deficiencies with the school (Kautokeino Flyttsamelag 1986–87:7).
32. Beach 1981:287.
33. Ibid., 347.
34. Simic 1991:21, 27.
35. Beach 1983:16.
36. Ibid., 15.
37. Beach 1981:353; Beach 1983:13, 16.
38. Beach 1981:353; Beach 1983:16. Today there are only about nine hundred active herders in all of Sweden, whereas one hundred years ago there were over five thousand.
39. From government reports (1971) cited by Beach (1981:287, 288).
40. Beach 1981:338; cf. text at note 23, Chapter 14.
41. Beach 1981:356.
42. Beach 1983:13. Even so, low incomes do force herders to leave the livelihood. Thus the pastoralists see the necessity for improvements in income; statutory reduction of the number of pastoralists is, however, a price they are unwilling to pay (cf. Beach 1981:295–96). The political reality of the situation is, nonetheless, that "the point of balance between the ideals of a decent living standard and cultural preservation is decided . . . by the income the State fixes as desirable for herders and the means by which it tries to ensure the herders this minimum income" (Beach 1983: 13). The authorities have recommended that this minimum be set at 50,000 Swedish crowns, requiring a herd of at least 350 animals, but only a minority of the active pastoralists has a herd of this size or larger (Beach 1983:16).
43. Beach 1983:12.
44. Henriksen 1986:9.
45. Ibid., 55–56. In the process, Saami customary law and customary rights are set aside: The state sees itself as the only depository of law (Henriksen 1986:64–65; Arnesen 1980).
46. See also Björklund 1986:10–16 and Henriksen 1986 (chapter 5).
47. Henriksen 1986, especially chapter 4.
48. Ibid., 1986:33–35.
49. See note 45, above.
50. Henriksen 1986:51. Compare the statement by Kirsten Berit Gaup in Chapter 14 for an account of changes in intergenerational relations attendant upon programs of rationalization.
51. Brox 1989, 1990; Björklund 1986, 1988a, 1988b, 1990, n.d.a, n.d.b.
52. Björklund 1990:76.
53. Brox (who received his early training at the Royal Agricultural College, like Movinkel before him and Kosmo today) has models in mind drawn from the study of other primary-resource industries such as agriculture and the fisheries.
54. Björklund 1990:79.
55. Ibid., 80. Compare the description and analysis in Part Two of this book.
56. Henriksen, critical of such a position, interprets it as follows: "Without state control, herders will continue in uncompromising competition with each other, with the weakest having to leave the livelihood. . . . In other words, the state [as it sees itself] is necessary to ensure the security of the weakest, optimal use of pastures, and to avert the tragedy of the commons" (1986:34).
57. Brox 1990:231.
58. And quite unaccountable is the statement that "like fishing, reindeer pastoralism is fundamentally a matter of *harvesting,* and not production" (Brox 1989:163).
59. Brox 1990:234.

60. Fernandez 1987:286.
61. Marchak 1989:2.
62. For example, hectares of pasture containing so-many tons of nutrient for so-many animals consuming so-many kilograms per units of time for so-many days (Beach et al. 1991:87). Compare Mikkel Nils Sara's statement about reading pastoral landscapes (text at note 44, Chapter 14). Note may well be taken, too, of the emphasis in Milton Freeman's essay from field studies among Inuit hunters: "*Behavioural* knowledge of the species was the critical basis of Inuit knowledge, contrasted with an inexact quantitative perspective held by the game management service" (1985:273).
63. Most notably, Brox has transported such into the argument (see chapter 6 of Brox 1989); I attend to this side of his argument in Paine 1993. Even the Reindeer Administration, as already noted, has been tempted, notably at press conferences, to allusions to the crisis in the fisheries.
64. Again, Freeman (see note 62, above) on the comparable situation of the Inuit: "[In view of] recent technological changes increasing hunters' harvesting abilities, and the growth of human population, it is not unreasonable to question whether these traditional systems are still capable of operating effectively under new circumstances. . . . But in seeking answers to these questions, it is important to realize the complexity of the problem being addressed. . . . It is not simply a question of economics (i.e., having enough material and food coming in) but . . . involves emotional and psychological, as well as physical/material needs and satisfactions, and that ensures reinforced attachment to a worthwhile past, as well as to an uncertain present and future" (Freeman 1985:276).
65. Wynne 1992:282.

Chapter 16. The Prejudice of Equality

1. In Figure 16.1, this is expressed by the broken lines, indicating choice, initiative, and flexibility.
2. Beach 1992:13.
3. Spencer (1984:72), writing of East African pastoralism.
4. NIBR 1990:xxviii–xxix.
5. The decisive diacritical of a patron, in my use of the term, is that "only values of the patron's choosing are circulated" in a patron-client relationship (Paine 1988:15).
6. Kosmo 1986a:35.
7. This appears to remain true even when the state *does* try to learn what pastoralists think about current issues. See the discussion in Chapter 14 of the questionnaire to the District foremen.
8. Beach 1983:9.

9. Melöy et al. 1987 [1985]:68.
10. A fuller account will be given in *Saami Camps,* in preparation.
11. NIBR 1990:67.
12. And the skepticism has been proven well founded, though official statements carefully speak simply of "reduced recruiteering" (e.g., Storting 1991–92:14).
13. Beach 1990:290.
14. At the same time, the conservationist lobby (Chapter 12) declares that Saami pastoralists should *keep* (or be kept) to their traditional technological means.
15. See the ILO Convention no. 169 concerning aboriginal rights as well as the ongoing work of the Saami Rights Commission (NOU 1984; Eidheim et al. 1985; Paine 1991; Storting 1991–92). For historical and legal reviews, see Tönnesen 1977 and the essay collection in Thuen 1980.
16. Located in Karasjok, the Parliament was opened by the Norwegian king in October 1989. For the time being it is principally an advisory body to the Norwegian Parliament and state. See Brantenberg 1991; Hætta 1992; Thuen 1992.
17. Bauman (1991:158) is actually describing the pretensions of the modern state (though not in its emergent postmodern form), but I cite the passage for the way it catches an essence of the state's dealings with the pastoralists.
18. Besides the issue of subsidies discussed in Chapter 13, there are those presented in Chapter 12: housing, schooling, mechanization. The question here is not whether pastoralists should enjoy modern housing and schooling and avail themselves of mechanization, but the design and management of these amenities in optimal accord with the context of pastoralism.
19. The issue of Saami land rights opens a Pandora's box. I have been speaking of the rights of the Saami pastoralists, but what of nonpastoral Saami of the tundra villages? And among the coastal population (with interest in the tundra), who is and who is not a Saami? And what of competing historical Norwegian rights? The Saami Rights Commission, struck in the fall of 1980, has yet to report on the matter of land rights (see NOU 1984). All the while, life goes on, new interest groups (regarding the use of the tundra, for example) enter the play, and pragmatic political and administrative decisions have to be made.
20. Melöy et al. 1987:68; emphasis added.
21. But let us not forget, from the time when it *was* part of being Saami, how the putting of sled and animals together involved sequences of husbandry tasks.
22. Perhaps this gives pause when judging the Norwegian Parliament. Besides doing the bidding of its own will in these matters, it is also in a predicament regarding the

moral (if not also legal) claims of cultural pluralism. See Eidheim et al. 1985.

23. As of the date of this writing (1992), NRL (still led by Odd Erling Smuk) have boycotted the Saami Parliament in protest against the failure to reserve any parliamentary seats for the pastoral Saami. BES, by contrast, are represented in the Parliament by its leader, Mathis Mathisen Sara.

24. Notwithstanding some general statements to the contrary (e.g., Storting 1991–92:9).

Appendix 1. Rangifer tarandus

Appendix 1 is excerpted, with minor changes, from the author's article, "Reindeer and Caribou, *Rangifer tarandus,* in the Wild and under Pastoralism," *Polar Record* 24, no. 148 (1988), published by the Scott Polar Research Institute, University of Cambridge.

1. Banfield 1961:103.
2. Burch 1972:339–68.
3. Thomson 1980:545.
4. Speiss 1979:55–56; and see Burch 1972:359–60.
5. Skogland 1985.
6. Burch 1972:345.
7. Gaare et al. 1975:207.
8. Skogland 1985:10–11.
9. Nick Tylor, personal communication.
10. Skogland 1986:54.
11. Ibid., 15.
12. Ibid., 21.
13. Burch 1972:345.
14. Skogland 1985:11.
15. Speiss 1979:64.
16. LeResche and Linderman 1975:58.
17. Pruitt 1959:165–69.
18. Skuncke 1969:31.
19. Pruitt 1960:22.
20. Skogland 1986:53.
21. Henshaw 1968:223.
22. Skjenneberg and Slagsvold 1968:97.
23. Skogland 1986:96.
24. Pruitt 1960:29–30; Speiss 1979:40–66.
25. Pruitt 1960:30.
26. Skogland 1986:44.
27. Espmark 1971b:48.
28. Pruitt 1960:27; Skogland 1986:83.
29. Skogland 1985:13.
30. Ibid., 12; and see below.
31. Pruitt 1960:31.
32. Skogland 1985, 1986.

33. Kelsall 1963:6–7.
34. Ion 1986:135.
35. Skogland 1986:42, 72.
36. Ion 1986:114.
37. Skogland 1986:17, 77.
38. Skogland 1986:77.
39. Skuncke 1969:12–13.
40. Skogland 1985:9.
41. Skogland 1986:77.
42. Skjenneberg and Slagsvold 1968:38.
43. Skogland 1986:65.
44. Bubenik 1975:436.
45. Espmark 1964a:159.
46. Skuncke 1973:38.
47. Skogland 1985, 1986.
48. Espmark 1964a:160.
49. Bernard Stonehouse, personal communication.
50. Espmark 1964a:160.
51. Cumming 1975:492; Naumov and Baskin 1969:2; Skogland 1986:72.
52. Naumov and Baskin 1969:2.
53. Ibid., 4, 9.
54. Thomson 1975:462 and table 3.
55. Naumov and Baskin 1969:12.
56. Naumov and Baskin 1969:11; Thomson 1975:463.
57. Thomson 1975:468.
58. Ibid., 466, 469.
59. Skogland 1986:35.
60. Ibid.
61. Thomson 1975:468.
62. Scott 1956:215.
63. Naumov and Baskin 1969:11.
64. Thomson 1975:463.
65. Espmark 1971a:300.
66. Pruitt 1960:33.
67. Pruitt 1960:5.
68. Espmark 1971b:55.
69. Speiss 1979:36–37.
70. Espmark 1971b:74.
71. Skogland 1986:35.
72. Cited by Henshaw (1968:225).
73. Henshaw 1968:224 (citing various observers).
74. Ibid., 225.
75. Espmark 1971b:73.
76. Lent 1965, cited by Valkenburg et al. (1983:125).
77. Espmark 1971a:295.
78. Tim Caro, personal communication.
79. Miller et al. 1975:435.
80. Miller 1974:62–63.
81. Skogland 1986:19, 87.

Saami Words
in Text

A

aidna-valdo : strongest male reindeer at rutting time

aldo : fully grown female reindeer; hence aldo manus : nursery area on calving ground

al'go-rat'ke : the first phase in a reindeer separation by hand

B

baggjel-rašša-jottet : migration route over high stony ground

baha : bad (especially of behavior)

bellot : "garden" of a herd, i.e., female animals

bieð'ganit : to scatter; bunched rather than single-file (of reindeer)

biegga : wind; hence biegga mielde : following wind, and doares biegga : side wind

biergo : meat; hence gaupe-bier'go : reindeer joints for sale; see nieste

biew'la : snow-free terrain

boaris : old (e.g., boaris aldo; Boaris Mikkel)

boazo (pl. boccu) **:** reindeer; see nieste

Č

čabbat : handsome (reindeer earmark); pretty (girl)

čak'ča : autumn

čak'ča-dal've : wintery end of autumn

čalloher'gi : lightly castrated, strong draft animal

čiel'ga-ællo : the "clean" resulting in unmixed herd at conclusion of a herd separation

čoar've : antler; hence čoar've-dakkat : "making antlers" (their growth through the winter)

čoavčes : cow who lost her calf ("became calfless")

čoawje : stomach; hence čoawjek : pregnant cows, and čoawjek-ællo : female herd at calving time

čokki : of a reindeer herd that is tightly herded

čora : a small collection of reindeer, part of a larger herd

čorastad'det : working with a čora to collect a herd

čuojal : reindeer bell with high timbre

čuojatæbme : reindeer bell with low cracked sound

čuol'de-rat'ke : middle phase of a reindeer separation (see rat'ket)

čuor'be : incompetent; čuor'bevuotta : incompetence

čæp'pe : competent, clever (of persons)

čærbmak : yearling (either sex); hence čærbmak-ædne : cow followed by her yearling, and čærbmak-aldo, a yearling cow that has given birth

čæw'lai : proud, haughty (of persons)

D

dal've : winter

davas : spring movement "out" (also compass point north); hence davelli : "to the outer side"

daža : non-Saami male, in common usage as "[male] Norwegian"; hence dažaboazodoallot : "Norwegian reindeer husbandry"

dietto : knowledge

dii'hme : person who has difficulty in identifying individual reindeer and their earmarks

doallat : to hold, as in to hold reindeer in check, or to pursue the pastoral livelihood

doldi : much trampled and cropped winter pasture (see fieskes)

dowdat : to know

duoddar : open tundra

duos'tat : to dare, as in i duost (do not dare)

F

fastes : ugly reindeer earmark (and of other things)

fieskes : trampled winter pasture

fitmat : person talented in identifying individual reindeer and especially their earmarks

G

gabba : white reindeer calf (much prized)

gaskek : castrated reindeer (from the verb "to bite")

giðða : spring; hence giðða-dal've : towards spring (April), and giðða-gæsse : the spring of summer

giellas : high ridge

gil'ka : reindeer bell with a high tinkle

gip'poragad or **gip'porag-ai'ge:** concluding phase of the rut; hence gipragat : its activity

goatte : family tent

godduhas : four-year-old male reindeer (senior bull)

goassohas : five-year-old male reindeer (senior bull)

gow'do : middle; hence Gow'dojottelit : "middle movement" of Kautokeino reindeer range

guoðohit : to let reindeer pasture under supervision; to herd

guoibme : herding partner

guos'sek : visitors (to reindeer herd or camp), strangers

gæi'dno : path followed by herders, reindeer trail

gæsse : summer

gæssek : late-born calves (towards the summer)

gæs'sit : to drag (e.g., by hand or lasso) a reindeer when separating a herd

H

haga : woman who is fitmat

hanes : miserly

her'gi : draft reindeer (castrate); hence her'gi dievva : tethering place for her'gi

hil'bat : wild, unmanageable, shy (of reindeer); hence hil'bat ai'ge : time of year when reindeer are difficult to manage

hæppat : shameful behavior

I

ised : male head of family herd, sometimes of a combined herd of several families; owner of animals

J

jallas : stupid, e.g., of yearlings: jallas čærbmak

jav'ri : lake

joga-rai'ge : riverbed; in winter, the frozen river course

jogastat : a dram (drink)

jokka : river

jottet : to move (e.g., a seasonal migration)

jæg'ge : marsh; hence jæg'ge-rai'ge : path across a marsh

L

laidestit : getting reindeer to follow by using a lead reindeer (with bell and halter); hence laidestæggje : the herder who leads the led animal

lavvo : herders' tent

leahti : low ridge

liv-ai'ge : rest period of reindeer

logjes : tame, quiet (of draft reindeer); hence logjes-her'gi

luksa : autumn movement "in" (also compass point south)

luondo : nature, character (humans, animals)

luovas : male reindeer herd (bulls and castrates); hence luovas-ællo

M

mar'kan : six-year-old male reindeer (senior bull)

miessi : reindeer calf (both sexes); hence miessi-čoawjek : a calf pregnant after the rut of its first autumn; miessi-aldo, a female that calves in her second spring; ædnihis miessi, a calf without its mother

muotta : snow (extensive technical vocabulary)

mærralaččat : people who live by the sea

N

nalli : breed; of reindeer, progeny in female line

nammalappen : seven-year-old (or older) male reindeer; literally "lost name" (senior bull)

nammoaive : reindeer with velvet on antlers

nanne : inland, out of sight of the coast (of herds and camps)

nieste : provisions; hence nieste-biergo : provisions of dried meat; nieste-boccu : reindeer slaughtered for domestic consumption; giðða-nieste : spring provisions of dried reindeer meat

njar'ga : peninsula

njiŋŋalas : female reindeer

nul'po : male reindeer that has shed its antlers or had them removed; hence nul'po-aldo : female reindeer that has shed its antlers

nuor'ta : east; hence Nuor'tabelli : "eastern half" of Kautokeino reindeer range

O

oai'vi : head of body; hence oaive-olbmai : leader, "headman"; also a hill shaped like a head

oar'je : west; hence Oar'jebelli : "western half" of Kautokeino reindeer range

or'da : above treeline

R

rafes : peace, peaceful; hence rafes-ai'ge : the peaceful time of winter

rag-ai'ge : time of the rut; hence raggat saggje : rutting place

raide : baggage caravan of draft reindeer

raidulaš : person in charge of a caravan

rakki-her'gi : a bull that was lightly castrated and partakes in the rut

rat'ket : to separate a herd

rašša : alpine, stone-strewn terrain

roappe : reindeer bell whose sound does not carry far: usually placed on animals who hold to the rear of a herd

roawda : physical edge or side of a herd in the terrain

rodno : female reindeer that failed to calf or lost calf; see čoavčes, sparro-rodno, stainak, suoppa-rodno, sæiva-rodno, šadda-rodno, rotsun

rotsun : see sparro-rodno

ruov'dicuono : frozen or "iron" snow surface

ruw'ga : the plaintive call of a calf or its mother when separated from each other

ruw'galit : reindeer stray from herd, typically in single file (snow cover)

ræŋ'ga : employed herding hand (usually boys or young men)

S

sæiva-rodno : see stainak

sabmi : Saami (see note 1 of the Preface)

šadda-rodno : reindeer that "became calfless"

sadjek : "words" (singular sadne), the notches cut in various combinations to make a reindeer's ownership earmark

sarak-čora : some younger males chasing cows that are still in usterus towards end of the rut (cf. gip'poragad)

sarves : collective word for senior bulls in a herd

sii'da : basic herding and unit (the animals and their herders); hence sii'da guoibme, herding partner

skabma : darkness; hence skabma-ai'ge, dark time of the year, and skabma-dal've, the dark(est) part of winter

spailek : castrate in training to become draft animal (her'gi)

sparro-rodno : two reindeer—mother and daughter—that have both lost their calves and now keep together

stainak : a three-year-old (or older) reindeer that still has to calve

suoi'dne : sedgegrass, used to line mocassins

suoitce : an area of terrain that is ecologically varied as pasture

suoppa-rodno : reindeer that rejects her newborn in favor of her yearling

suolo : island

særra : man who is fitmat

sær've : collection; hence sær've-gar'de : fence at entrance of separation corral; sær've-ællo : the mixed herd that has to be separated

særvi : an organization with membership

V

vaggi : valley, often with a river

vaiban : tired

varadat : using high places in terrain to find animals

varek : two-year-old male reindeer (junior bull)

varri : hill

verdi : partner in a reciprocal relationship of services between pastoralist and nonpastoralist

vierro boccu : stray animals (reindeer)

vuobis : three-year-old male reinder (junior bull)

vuobme : gentle valley (cf. vaggi) with sheltered scrub vegetation, perhaps wooded

vuoððo : animals that are left after each phase of a separation

vuojanæggje, or **vuojetæggje** : one who drives herd from behind

vuojat : to drive a herd of reindeer

vuole : below; hence vuole-rašša-jottet : "to move below the alpine route"

vuonjal : two-year-old female reindeer (not fully adult); hence vuonjal-aldo : a cow that calved in her second year

vuorbmanak : long entrance arms to separation corral

væitalis : reindeer that wander unherded, or open-range herding; hence væitallitit : herded towards end of day, otherwise unherded

værkeguoðohit : night-herding up to midnight

Æ

ædne : mother; hence ædnihis miessi : motherless calf; and
 ædne-čuovvo-ragge : a reindeer cow followed by her calf and
 her yearling and perhaps its calf

ællo : herd (from ællem, life, and ællet, to live); hence allemin
 vuovdet : meat sold on the hoof (live animal); ælahus :
 livelihood

Bibliography

Anderson, Myrdene. 1978a. *Saami Ethnoecology: Resource Management in Norwegian Lapland.* 3 vols. Ann Arbor, Mich.: University Microfilms International.

———. 1978b. "Mobility and Bilingualism in North Norway." *Ethnos* 3/4:178–92.

Arnesen, A. G. 1980. "Reindriftsamenes Rettslige Stilling i Norge." In *Samene: Urbefolkning og Minoritet,* ed. Trond Thuen. Oslo: Universitetsforlaget.

Arnold, Thurman W. 1969. "Law as Symbolism." In *Sociology of Law,* ed. Vilhelm Aubert. Harmondsworth, England: Penguin Books.

Aschmann, Homer. 1965. "Comments on the Symposium 'Man, Culture, and Animals.' " In *Man, Culture, and Animals,* ed. Anthony Leeds and Andrew P. Vayda. Washington, D.C.: American Association for the Advancement of Science.

Aubert, Vilhelm. 1978. *Den Samiske Befolkningen i Nord-Norge.* Oslo: Statistisk Sentralbyrå, nr. 107.

Baer, A., O. K. Hætta, and L. Villmo. 1974. "Skader og Ulemper for Reindriften ved en Eventuell Regulering og Utbygging av Altaelva, Joat'kajavrit med Overföring av Tverrelva, samt Jiesjav'ri." Stencil.

Banfield, A. W. F. 1961. "A Revision of the Reindeer and Caribou, *Genus Rangifer.*" *National Museum of Canada Bulletin* 177. Biological Series 66. Ottawa.

Barth, Fredrik. 1961. *Nomads of South Persia.* Oslo: Oslo University Press.

Bauman, Zygmunt. 1991. "Modernity and Ambivalence." In *Global Culture,* ed. Mike Featherstone. London: SAGE Publication.

Beach, Hugh. 1981. *Reindeer-Herd Management in Transition: The Case of Tuorpon Saameby in Northern Sweden.* Acta Universitatis Upsaliensis. Stockholm: Almqvist & Wiksell.

———. 1983. "A Swedish Dilemma: Saami Rights and the Welfare State." *Production Pastorale et Societé* (Spring): 9–17.

———. 1990. "Comparative Systems of Reindeer Herding." In *The World of Pastoralism: Herding Systems in Comparative Perspective,* ed. John G. Galaty and Douglas L. Johnson. New York and London: Guilford Press; London: Belhaven Press.

———. 1992. "Filtering Mosquitoes and Swallowing Reindeer: The Politics of Ethnicity and Environmentalism in Northern Sweden." In *Environmental Arguments and Subsistence Producers,* ed. G. Dahl. Stockholm Studies in Social Anthropology. Stockholm: University of Stockholm.

Beach, Hugh, Myrdene Anderson, and Pekka Aikio. 1991. "Dynamics of Saami Territoriality within the Nation-States of Norway, Sweden and Finland." In *Mobility and Territoriality: Social and Spatial Boundaries among Foragers, Fishers, Pastoralists and Peripatetics,* ed. Michael Casimir and Aparna Rao. New York: Berg Publishers.

Björklund, Ivar. 1985. *Fjordfolket i Kvænangen. Fra Samisk Samfunn til Norsk Utkant 1550–1980.* Tromsö: Universitetsforlaget.

———. 1986. "Guovdajohtin: Noen Förelopige Observasjoner." Photocopy.

233

————. 1988a. "Reindrift og Ressursforvaltning på Finn-marksvidda." In *Glött*. Trömso: Trömso Museum.

————. 1988b. "For Mye Rein i Finnmark?" *Finnmarksdagblad* 29 (Dec.).

————. 1990. "Sami Reindeer Pastoralism as an Indigenous Resource Management System in Northern Norway: A Contribution to the Common Property Debate." *Development and Change* 21:75–86.

————. n.d.a. "Konsekvensanalyse av Samisk Reindrift som Ökonomisk Tilpasning." Photocopy.

————. n.d.b. "Guovdageaidnu 1980s." Photocopy.

Björklund, Ivar, and Terje Brantenberg. 1981. *Samisk Rein-drift—Norske Inngrep*. Oslo: Universitetsforlaget.

Boonzajer Flaes, Robert M. 1981. "Surplus Creation and Surplus Circulation in Pastoral Nomadism." In *Contemporary Nomadic and Pastoral Peoples: Asia and the North,* ed. Vinson H. Sutlive et al. Williamsburg, Va.: College of William & Mary, Department of Anthropology.

Brantenberg, Terje. 1991. "Norway: Constructing Indigenous Self-Government in a Nation State." In *The Challenge of Northern Regions,* ed. Peter Jull and Sally Roberts. Darwin: Australian National University.

Brox, Ottar. 1989. *Kan Bygdenæringene Bli Lönnsomme?* Oslo: Glydendal Norsk Forlag.

————. 1990. "The Common Property Theory: Epistemological Status and Analytical Utility." *Human Organization* 49 (3): 227–35.

Bubenik, A. B. 1975. *Significance of Antlers in the Social Life of Barren-Ground Caribou*. University of Alaska Special Report 1, Biological Papers. Fairbanks.

Burch, E. S., Jr. 1972. "The Caribou—Wild Reindeer as a Human Resource." *American Antiquity* 37:339–68.

Cumming, H. G. 1975. "Clumping Behaviour and Predation with Special Reference to Caribou." In *Proceedings of the First International Reindeer/Caribou Symposium,* ed. J. R. Luick, P. C. Lent, D. R. Klein, and R. G. White. Fairbanks: University of Alaska.

Dahl, Gudrun, and Anders Hjort. 1976. *Having Herds: Pastoral Herd Growth and Household Economy*. Stockholm Studies in Social Anthropology 2. Stockholm: University of Stockholm.

Dyson-Hudson, Neville. 1972. "The Study of Nomads." In *Perspectives on Nomadism,* ed. William Irons and Neville Dyson-Hudon. Leiden: E. J. Brill.

Eidheim, Harald. 1971 [1966]. "Lappish Guest Relationships under Conditions of Cultural Change." In *Aspects of the Lappish Minority Situation*. Oslo: Universitetsforlaget.

Eidheim, Harald, Georg Henriksen, Per Mathiesen, and Trond Thuen. 1985. "Samenes Rettsstilling: Likeverd, Velferd, og Rettferdighet." *Nytt Norsk Tidsskrift* 2:68–85.

Eira, Nils Isak. 1979. "A Critical Evaluation of the New Reindeer Management Law in Norway." Abstract of presentation to the Second International Reindeer/Caribou Symposium.

————. 1981. "Om Reindriftsavtalen." Seminar presentation to Sami Nuorras. Jokkmokk. Photocopy.

————. 1984. "Saami Reindeer Terminology." *Dieðut* 1:55–61.

————. 1986. "Snötermer." NRL 1986:12–17.

————. 1987. "Scenarium: Reindrift mot år 2000." NRL 1987a, 2:32–36.

Elbo, J. G. 1952. "Lapp Reindeer Movements across the Frontiers of Northern Scandinavia." *Polar Record* 6:348–58.

Elgvin, Dag T. 1991. "Hovedoppgave om Sör-Samisk Reindrift." *Reindriftsnytt* 1:26–27.

Eriksen, Thomas Hylland. 1990. "The Tension between Nationalism and Ethnicity." Working Paper no. 5. Oslo: Department of Social Anthropology, University of Oslo.

Espmark, Y. 1964a. "Rutting Behaviour in Reindeer *(Rangifer tarandus L.)*." *Animal Behaviour* 12 (1): 159–63.

————. 1964b. "Studies in Dominance-Subordination Relationship in a Group of Semi-Domesticated Reindeer *(Rangifer tarandus L.)*." *Animal Behaviour* 12:420–26.

————. 1971a. "Individual Recognition by Voice in Reindeer Mother-Young Relationship: Field Observation and Playback Experiments." *Behaviour* 40:295–301.

————. 1971b. "Mother-Young Relationship and Ontogeny of Behaviour in Reindeer *(Rangifer tarandus L.)*." *Z. Tierpsychol* 20:42–81.

Evans-Pritchard, E. E. 1940. *The Nuer*. Oxford: Clarendon Press.

Falkenberg, Johs. 1986. "Fra Nomadisme til Fast Bosetning blant Samene i Röros-traktene (1890 årene-1940 årene)." *Sæmien Sijte, Årbok* 2:7–28.

Fernandez, J. W. 1987. "The Call to the Commons: Decline and Recommitment in Asturias, Spain." In *The Question of the Commons,* ed. Bonnie J. McKay and James M. Acheson. Tucson: University of Arizona Press.

Firth, Raymond. 1964. "A Viewpoint from Economic Anthropology." In *Capital, Saving and Credit in Peasant Societies,* ed. Raymond Firth and B. S. Yamey. London: George Allen & Unwin.

Freeman, Milton M. R. 1985. "Appeal to Tradition: Different Perspectives on Arctic Wildlife Management." In *Native Power: The Quest for Autonomy and Nationhood of Indigenous Peoples,* ed. Jens Brösted, Jens Dahl, et al. Oslo: Universitetsforlaget.

Gaare, E., B. R. Thomson, and O. Kjös-Hansen. 1975. "Reindeer Activity on Hardangervidda." In *Fenoscandian Tundra Ecosystems, Part 2,* ed. F. E. Wiegolaski. Vol. 17 of *Ecological Studies, Analysis and Synthesis*. New York: Springer-Verlag.

Gaup, Inger Anna. 1988. "Dannelsen av Boaza Ealahus Særvi (BES)." Universitetet i Tromsö. Photocopy.

Gaup, Kirsten Berit. 1988. "Å Vaere Flyttsame." *Haugesunds Avis,* 25 Jan.

Gluckman, Max. 1969. "The Judicial Process among the Barotse of Northern Rhodesia." In *Sociology of Law,* ed. Aubert Vilhelm. Harmondsworth, England: Penguin Books.

Gordon, H. Scott. 1954. "The Economic Theory of a Common Property Resource: The Fishery." *Journal of Political Economy* 62:124–42.

Gusfield, Joseph R. 1981. *The Culture of Public Problems.* Chicago: University of Chicago Press.

Hætta, Odd Mathis. 1992. *Sametinget i Navn og Tall.* Karasjok: Sametinget.

Hansen, Sigurd Winther. 1960. "The Climate." In *Norway North of 65,* ed. Örnulv Vorren. Tromsö: Tromsö Museums Skrifter.

Hardin, G. 1968. "The Tragedy of the Commons." *Science* 162:1243–47.

Henriksen, Georg. 1986. "Statlig Kontroll og Samisk Reaksjon: En Rapport fra Helgeland." Sosialantropologisk Institutt, Universitetet i Bergen. Photocopy.

Henshaw, J. 1968. "A Theory for the Occurrence of Antlers in Females of the Genus *Rangifer.*" *Deer* 1:222–26.

Hultblad, Filip. 1936. *Flyttlapparna i Gällivarre Socken.* Uppsala: Geographica.

———. 1968. *Övergång från Nomadism till Agrar Bosättning i Jokkmokks Socken.* Stockholm: Nordiska Museet.

Ingold, Tim. 1975. "The Tin-Plate Reindeer: Further Thoughts on the Snowmobile in Lapland." Presented to Society for Applied Anthropology. Photocopy.

———. 1976. *The Skolt Lapps Today.* Cambridge: Cambridge University Press.

———. 1978. "The Rationalization of Reindeer Management among Finnish Lapps." *Development and Change* 1:103–32.

———. 1980. *Hunters, Pastoralists and Ranchers.* Cambridge: Cambridge University Press.

Ion, P. G. 1986. "The Snowpatch as Relief Habitat for Woodland Caribou (*Rangifer tarandus* Caribou Gmelin) at MacMillan Pass, N.W.T." M.Sc. diss., University of Alberta.

Kautokeino Flyttsamelag. 1986–87. Årsmelding. Photocopy.

Kelsall, J. P. 1963. "Barren-Ground Caribou and Their Management." *Canadian Audubon Magazine,* Nov.–Dec., 2–7.

———. 1968. *The Caribou.* Ottawa: Queen's Printer.

Kosmo, Ansgar J. 1986a [1983]. "Reindriftskurset: Målsettinger og Virkemidler i Reindriftspolitikken." Lectures at Norges Landbrukshögskole. Photocopy.

———. 1986b. "Hvor Går Sör-Samisk Reindrift?" In Sæmien Sijte, Årbok 2:166–70. Snåsa: Sörsamiske Samlinger.

———. 1987a. "Reindriftspolitiske Mål." In Protokoll 1-Utvalget, Vedlegg 11.

———. 1987b. "Dokumentasjonsbehov ved en Omlegging av Reindriftsavtalens Virkemidler." In Protokoll 1-Utvalget, Vedlegg 12.

———. 1987c. "Etablering av Reindrift." In Protokoll 1-Utvalget, Vedlegg 13.

———. 1987d. "Kalveslakttilskuddet som Virkemiddel i Reindriftspolitikken." In Protokoll 1-Utvalget, Vedlegg 16.

———. 1987e. "Distriktstilskuddet." In Protokoll 1-Utvalget, Vedlegg 17.

———. 1987f. "Drifttilskudd." In Protokoll 1-Utvalget, Vedlegg 18.

———. 1987g. "Eierstruktur i Vest-Finnmark Reinbeiteområde." In Protokoll 1-Utvalget, Vedlegg 26.

———. 1987h. "Spörreundersökelse med Distriktsformenn i Samisk Tamreinområde 1986." In Protokoll 1-Utvalget, Vedlegg 28.

———. 1988. "Muligheter i Reindriftspolitikken." *Reindriftsnytt* 2:39–42.

Kosmo, Ansgar J., and Dag Lenvik. 1987. "Ressurstilpasningen i Reindriften." In Protokoll 1-Utvalget, Vedlegg 7.

Landbruksdepartementet. 1922. *Utkast til Lov om Reindriften. Utarbeidet av Riksadvokat Kjerschow.* Oslo.

———. 1932. *Om Utferdigelse av en Lov om Reindriften.* Ot. prp. nr. 28. Oslo.

———. 1966. *Innstilling fra Reindriftslovkomiteen.* Oslo.

———. 1974–75. *Om en Aksjonsplan for de Sentrale Samiske Bosettingsområder.* St. medl. nr. 13. Oslo.

———. 1976–77. *Om lov om Reindrift.* Ot. prp. nr. 9. Oslo.

Lappefogden i Finnmark. 1961. Beretning. Photocopy.

———. 1962. Beretning. Photocopy.

Lappefogden i Vest-Finnmark. 1978. Årsmelding. Photocopy.

Leeds, Anthony. 1965. "Reindeer Herding and Chukchi Social Institutions." In *Man, Culture, and Animals,* ed. Anthony Leeds and Andrew P. Vayda. Washington, D.C.: American Association for the Advancement of Science.

Lent, P. C. 1965. "Rutting Behaviour in a Barren-Ground Caribou Population." *Animal Behaviour* 13:259–64.

Lenvik, Dag. 1988. *Utvalgsstrategi i Reinflokken.* Alta: Reindrifts-administrasjonen.

LeResche, R., and S. Linderman. 1975. "Caribou Trail System in Northeastern Alaska." *Arctic* 28:54–61.

Macpherson, C. B. 1962. *The Political Theory of Possessive Individualism.* Oxford: Oxford University Press.

Marchak, Patricia. 1987. "Introduction." In *Uncommon Property: The Fishing and Fish Producing Industries in British Columbia,* ed. Patricia Marchak, Neil Guppy, and John McMullan. Toronto: Methuen.

———. 1989. "Property: Common and Otherwise." Regional Conference, University of British Columbia. Photocopy.

Maurstad, Anita. 1992. "Closing the Commons—Opening the 'Tragedy': Regulating North-Norwegian Small-scale Fishing." Third Common Property Conference, Washington, D.C. Photocopy.

McCay, Bonnie J., and James M. Acheson. 1987. "Human Ecology of the Commons." In *The Question of the Commons: The Culture and Ecology of Communal Resources.* Tucson: University of Arizona Press.

Melöy, Jon Aarseth, Ole Mathis Eira, and Jan Åge Riseth. 1987 [1985]. "Tiltak for Tilpassing av Reinbestanden: Reindriftsavtalen 1984–1985." In Protokoll 1-Utvalget, Vedlegg 8.

Miller, F. 1974. *Biology of the Kiminuriak Population of Barren-Ground Caribou.* Part 2. Canadian Wildlife Service Report Series 31. Ottawa.

Miller, F. L., A. C. Vithayasai, and R. McClure. 1975. "Distribution, Movements, and Socialization of Barren-Ground Caribou Radio-Tracked on their Calving and Postcalving Area." In *Proceedings of the First International Reindeer/Caribou Symposium,* ed. J. R. Luick, P. C. Lent, D. R. Klein, and R. G. White. Fairbanks: University of Alaska.

Movinkel, H. 1968 [1962]. "Ökonomiske Forhold i Reindrift." In *Reindriften og Dens Naturgrunnlag,* by Sven Skjenneberg and Lars Slagsvold. Oslo: Universitetsforlaget.

Muller-Wille, Ludger, and Pertti J. Pelto. 1971. "Technological Change and Its Impact in Arctic Regions: Lapps Introduce Snowmobiles into Reindeer Herding." *Polarforschung* 1/2:142–48.

Naumov, N. P., and L. M. Baskin. 1969. "Lederskap i Reinflokker som Gruppeadopsjon." *Zhurnal Oshchei Biologii* 30:147–56.

Nelson, Cynthia, ed. 1973. *The Desert and the Sown: Nomads in the Wider Society.* Berkeley, Calif.: Institute of International Studies, University of California.

Nielsen, Konrad. 1932–38. *Lappisk Ordbok-Lapp Dictionary.* Vols. 1–3. Oslo: Instituttet for Sammenlignende Kulturforskning.

Nielsen, Konrad, and Asbjörn Nesheim. 1956–62. *Lappisk Ordbok-Lapp Dictionary.* Vols. 4 and 5. Oslo: Instituttet for Sammenlignende Kulturforskning.

NOU (Norges Offentlige Utredninger). 1977. *Reinslaktingen i Finnmark.* NOU 8. Oslo: Universitetsforlaget.

———. 1978. *Finnmarksvidda: Natur-Kultur.* NOU 18A. Oslo: Universitetsforlaget.

———. 1984. *Om Samenes Rettstilling.* NOU 19, nr. 18. Oslo: Universitetsforlaget.

NIBR (Norsk Institutt for By- og Regionforskning. 1990. *Mot et Baerekraftig Samfunn i Indre Finnmark. Del I: Problemanalyse.* Oslo.

NRL (Norsk Reindriftsamers Landsforbund). 1977–78. Årsmelding. Photocopy.

———. 1979–80. Årsmelding. Photocopy.

———. 1981. Landsmöteutskrifter. Photocopy.

———. 1985. "NRL's Krav til Reindriftsavtalen for 1986–87." In Protokoll 1-Utvalget, Vedlegg 3.

———. 1985–86. Årsmelding. Photocopy.

———. 1986. "Seminara Boazobargu Giella Čohkkiras." Photocopy.

———. 1987a. "Tillitsmannskonferanse om Reindriftsavtalen." 3 vols. Photocopy.

———. 1987b. "NRL's Informasjon." Photocopy.

———. 1987c. "NRL's Informasjon: Extranummer." 3 vols. Photocopy.

———. 1989. "Natur og Miljövern i Reindriftsområdene." Photocopy.

Odner, Knut. 1985. "Saamis (Lapps), Finns and Scandinavians in History and Prehistory." *Norwegian Archaeological Review* 18 (1–2): 1–35.

Paine, Robert. 1957. *Coast Lapp Society I: A Study of Neighbourhood.* Tromsö: Universitetsforlaget.

———. 1965. *Coast Lapp Society II: A Study of Economic Development and Social Values.* Tromsö: Universitetsforlaget.

———. 1970a. "Boundary Maintenance among Lappish Reindeer Nomads." Presented at the 68th Annual Meeting of the American Anthropological Association. Typescript.

———. 1970b. "Lappish Decisions, Partnerships, Information Management, and Sanctions—a Nomadic Pastoral Adaptation." *Ethnology* 9 (1): 52–67.

———. 1971. "Animals as Capital: Comparisons among Northern Nomadic Herders and Hunters." *Anthropological Quarterly* 44:7–172.

———. 1972. "The Herd Management of Lapp Reindeer Pastoralists." In *Perspectives on Nomadism,* ed. William Irons and Neville Dyson-Hudson. Leiden: Brill.

———. 1978. "Spring Herd—Kautokeino 1961." *Ethnos* 3–4:122–45.

———. 1982. *Dam a River, Damn a People?* Copenhagen: IWGIA.

———. 1984. "Norwegians and Saami: Nation-State and Fourth World." In *Minorities and Mother Country Imagery,* ed. Gerald Gold. St. John's: Institute of Social and Economic Research, Memorial University.

———. 1985. "Ethnodrama and the Fourth World: The Saami Action Group in Norway, 1979–1981." In *Indigenous Peoples and the Nation-State,* ed. Noel Dyck. St. John's: Institute of Social and Economic Research, Memorial University.

———. 1987. "Accidents, Ideologies and Routines." *Anthropology Today* 3 (4): 7–10.

———. 1988 [1971]. *Patrons and Brokers in the East Arctic.* St. John's: Institute of Social and Economic Research, Memorial University.

———. 1989. "Making the Invisible 'Visible': Coming to Terms with 'Chernobyl' and Its Experts, a Saami Illustration." *International Journal of Moral and Social Studies* 4 (2): 139–62.

———. 1991. "The Claim of Aboriginality: Saami in Norway." In *The Ecology of Choice and Symbol: Essays in Honour of Fredrik Barth,* ed. Reidar Grönhaug, Gunnar Haaland, and Georg Henriksen. Bergen: Alma Mater Forlag.

———. 1993. "Social Construction of the 'Tragedy of the Commons' and Saami Reindeer Pastoralism." *Acta Borealia* 9:2.

Pehrson, Robert N. 1964 [1957]. *The Bilateral Network of Social Relations in Könkäma Lapp District.* Oslo: Norsk Folke-museum (Samiske Samlinger).

Pelto, Pertti J. 1962. *Individualism in Skolt Lapp Society.* Kansatieteellinen Arkisto 16. Helsinki.

———. 1987. *The Snowmobile Revolution: Technology and Social Change in the Arctic.* Prospect Heights, Ill.: Waveland Press.

Peters, Pauline E. 1987. "Embedded Systems and Rooted Models: The Grazing Lands of Botswana and the Commons." In *The Question of the Commons,* ed. Bonnie J. McKay and James M. Acheson. Tucson: University of Arizona Press.

Protokoll 1-Utvalget. 1987a. *Instilling.* Alta: Reindriftsadministrasjonen.

———. 1987b. *Vedlegg.* Alta: Reindriftsadministrasjonen.

Pruitt, W. O., Jr. 1959. "Snow as a Factor in the Winter Ecology of the Barren-Ground Caribou *(Rangifer arcticus).*" *Arctic* 12:158–79.

———. 1960. "Behaviour of the Barren-Ground Caribou." *Biological Papers of the University of Alaska* 3:1–43.

Reimers, E. 1972. "Growth in Domestic and Wild Reindeer in Norway." *Journal of Wildlife Management* 36 (2): 612–19.

Reimers, E., D. R. Klein, and R. Sorumgard. 1983. "Calving Time, Growth Rate, and Body Size of Norwegian Reindeer on Different Ranges." *Arctic and Alpine Research* 15 (1): 107–18.

Reindriftsadministrasjonen 1979–91. *Reindriftsnytt.* Alta.

Reindriftsstyret. 1983–91. *Melding om Reindrift.* Alta.

Riseth, Jan Åge. 1988. "Reintall og Beiteressurser." *Reindrifts-nytt* 3:5–9.

Ruong, Israel. 1937. *Fjällapparna i Jukkasjärvi Socken.* Geographica 3. Uppsala.

———. 1956. "Types of Settlement and Types of Husbandry among Lapps in Northern Sweden." *Studia Ethnographica Upsaliensia* 11:105–32.

———. 1967. *The Lapps in Sweden.* Stockholm: Swedish Institute for Cultural Relations with Foreign Countries.

———. 1968. "Different Factors of Reindeer-Breeding." *Inter-Nord* 10:293–97.

Sahlins, Marshall D. 1968. "Notes on the Original Affluent Society." In *Man the Hunter,* ed. Richard B. Lee and Irven DeVore. Chicago: Aldine Publishing.

Salzman, Phillip C. 1967. "Political Organization among Nomadic Peoples." *Proceedings of the American Philosophical Society* 111:115–31.

———, ed. 1986. *Control and Alienation of Territory among Nomadic Peoples.* Special issue of *Nomadic Peoples* 20. Montreal: Commission on Nomadic Peoples, International Union of Anthropological and Ethnological Sciences.

Sara, Mikkel Nils. 1986a. "Landskapstypene." NRL 1986:20–21.

———. 1986b. "Samiske Landskapstermer: Reindriftens Arealutnytting." NRL 1986:62–65.

Sara, Ole K. 1987a. "Noen Tanker omkring Reindriftspolitikken." Protokoll 1-Utvalget, Vedlegg 6.

———. 1987b. "Om Reindriftsavtalen-Reindriftspolitikk." NRL's Tillitsmannskonferanse I, Tromsö. Photocopy.

———. 1987c. "Innlegg." NRL's Tillitsmannskonferanse III. Tromsö. Photocopy.

———. 1988. "Ole K. Sara om Reintelling." Interview. *Reindriftsnytt* 3:32–35.

Scott, J. P. 1956. "The Analysis of Social Organization in Animals." *Ecology* 37:213–21.

Shirokogoroff, S. M. 1929. *Social Organization of the Northern Tungus.* Shanghai: Commercial Press.

Simic, Andrei. 1991. "Obstacles to the Development of a Yugoslav National Consciousness: Ethnic Identity and Folk Culture in the Balkans." *Journal of Mediterranean Studies* 1 (1): 18–36.

Skjenneberg, Sven. 1965. *Rein og Reindrift.* Lesjaskog: A.s. Fjell-Nytt.

Skjenneberg, Sven, and Lars Slagsvold. 1968 [1962]. *Reindriften og Dens Naturgrunnlag.* Oslo: Universitetsforlaget.

———. 1979. *Reindeer Husbandry and Its Ecological Principles.* English trans. of 1968 [1962]. Juneau, Ala.: Bureau of Indian Affairs.

Skogland, T. 1985. "Life History Characteristics of Wild Reindeer *(Rangifer tarandus L.)* in Relation to Their Food Resources: Ecological Effects and Behavioral Adaptations." In *Meddelelser fra Norsk Viltforskning* 3, Serie 14. Trondheim.

———. 1986. "Comparative Social Organization of Wild Reindeer in Relation to Food, Predator Avoidance and Mates." Manuscript.

Skum, Nils Nilsson. 1938. *Same Sita—Lappbyn.* Stockholm: Nordiska Museet.

———. 1955. *Valla Renar.* Uppsala: Almqvist & Wiksell.

Skuncke, F. 1969. "Reindeer Ecology and Management in Sweden." *Biological Papers of the University of Alaska* 8:1–82.

———. 1973. *Renen i Urtid och Nutid.* Stockholm: Norstedt.

Smith, P. L. 1938. *Kautokeino og Kautokeino-Lappene.* Oslo: Instituttet for Sammenlingnende Kulturforskning.

Smuk, Odd Erling. 1987. "Reindrifta Bli Lönnsom!" *Reindrifts-nytt* 3:40–41.

Solem, Erik. 1933. *Lappiske Rettsstudier.* Oslo: Institutt for Sammenlignende Kukturforskning.

Speiss, A. E. 1979. *Reindeer and Caribou Hunters: An Archaeological Study.* New York: Academic Press.

Spencer, Paul. 1984. "Pastoralists and the Ghost of Capitalism." *Production Pastorale et Societé* 15:61–76.

Spooner, Brian. 1971. "Towards a Generative Model of No-madism." *Anthropological Quarterly* 44:198–210.

Steen, Adolf. 1956. *Kautokeinostudier.* Oslo: Norsk Folke-museum.

———. 1963. *Masi—En Samebygd.* Oslo: Norsk Folke-museum.

Storting. 1977–78. *Innstilling fra Landbrukskomiteen om Lov om Reindrift.* Innst. O. nr. 37. Oslo: Stortinget.

———. 1978. *Vedtak til Lov om Reindrift.* Oslo: Stortinget.

———. 1978–79. *Forhandlinger.* Oslo: Stortinget.

———. 1979–80. *Om Regjeringens Arbeid med Gjennomføringen av Stortingets Vedtak om Utbygging av Alta Vassdraget.* Stortingsmelding, nr. 61. Oslo: Stortinget.

———. 1991–92. *En Baerekraftig Reindrift.* Stortingsmelding, nr. 28. Oslo: Stortinget.

Svensson, Tom G. 1976. *Ethnicity and Mobilization in Saami Politics.* Stockholm Studies in Social Anthropology 4. Stock-holm: University of Stockholm.

Thomson, B. R. 1975. "Leadership in Wild Reindeer in Nor-way." In *Proceedings of the First International Reindeer/Caribou Symposium,* ed. J. R. Luick, P. C. Lent, D. R. Klein, and R. G. White. Fairbanks: University of Alaska.

———. 1980. "Behaviour Differences between Reindeer and Caribou *(Rangifer tarandus L.)."* In *Proceedings of the Second International Reindeer/Caribou Symposium,* ed. Eigel Reimers, Eldar Gaare, and Sven Skjenneberg. Trondheim: Directoratet for Vilt og Ferskvannsfisk.

Thuen, Trond. 1992. "Quest for Equality: Norway and the Sami Challenge." University of Tromsö. Typescript.

———, ed. 1980. *Samene—Urbefolkning og Minoritet.* Oslo: Universitetsforlaget.

Todorov, Tzvetan. 1984. *The Conquest of America: The Question of the Other.* New York: Harper & Row.

Turi, Johan. 1931. *Turi's Book of Lappland.* London: Jonathan Cape.

Turi, Johan Mathis. 1986. "Årsykluser." NRL 1986:27–34.

———. 1987a [1986]. "Notat til Protokoll 1-gruppen." In Protokoll 1-Utvalget, Vedlegg 4.

———. 1987b. "Inlegg." NRL's Tillitsmannskonferanse I. Tromsö. Photocopy.

———. 1989. "Innledning: Natur og Miljövern i Reindrifts-områdene." NRL 1989.

Tömmervik, Hans. 1981. "Over-og-ut for Reindrifta!" Inter-view. *Reindriftsnytt* 2:19–21.

Tönnesen, Sverre. 1977. "Om Retten til Jorden i Finnmark." In *Samenes og Sameområdenes Rettslige Stilling Historisk Belyst,* ed. Knut Bergsland. Oslo: Instituttet for Sammenlignende Forskning.

Törresdal, Ivar. 1982. "Konflikter mellom Jordbruk og Rein-drift." *Reindriftsnytt* 1:29–30.

Utsi, Mikkel. 1948. "The Reindeer-Breeding Methods of the Northern Lapps." *Man* 48:97–101.

Utsi, Nils Thomas. 1991. "Problemer i Reindrift: 'Knivstukket på Vidda.' " *Reindriftsnytt* 1:3–7.

Valkenburg, P., J. L. Davis, and R. D. Boertje. 1983. "Social Organization and Seasonal Range Fidelity of Alaska's West-ern Arctic Caribou—Preliminary Findings." *Acta Zoologica Fennica* 175:125–26.

Vorren, Örnulv. 1944. *Dyregraver og Reinjerder i Varanger.* Nord-norske Samlinger 6, nr. 2. Oslo.

———. 1951. *Reindrift og Nomadisme i Varangertraktene.* Tromsö Museums Årshefter, nr. 12. Tromsö.

———. 1962. *Finnmark Samenes Nomadisme.* 2 vols. Oslo: Uni-versitetsforlaget.

Vorren, Örnulv, and Ernst Manker. 1962. *Lapp Life and Cus-toms.* Oslo: Oslo University Press; London: Oxford Universi-ty Press.

Weber, Max. 1969. "Rational and Irrational Administration of Justice." In *Sociology of Law,* ed. Aubert Vilhelm. Har-mondsworth, England: Penguin Books.

Whitaker, Ian. 1955. *Social Relations in a Nomadic Lappish Com-munity.* Oslo: Norsk Folkemuseum (Samiske Samlinger).

———. 1978. "Some Changes in Lainiovuoma Sami Reindeer Management." *Ethnos* 43 (3–4): 163–77.

Wynne, Brian. 1992. "Misunderstood Misunderstanding: Social Identities and Public Uptake of Science." *Public Understanding of Science* 1 (3): 281–304.

Newspapers

Finnmark Dagblad
Nordlys
Sagat

Index

239